MW01129041

Worship in the Presence of God

A collection of essays
on the nature, elements, and
historic views and practice of worship

Edited by

Frank J. Smith

and

David C. Lachman

Reformation Media and Press
Fellsmere, Florida
2006

"The Second Commandment . . .", by William Young, originally appeared in Christian Opinion magazine and was reprinted in *The Biblical Doctrine of Worship*, ed. by Edward A. Robson, *et. al.* (Pittsburgh: Pa.: The Reformed Presbyterian Church of North America, 1974).

"John Knox and the Reformation of Worship in the Scottish Reformation", by Kevin Reed, is an expanded version of the "Introductory Essay" in *True & False Worship* by John Knox (Dallas, Texas: Presbyterian Heritage Publications, ©1988), and is reprinted by kind permission.

ISBN 0-9773442-2-3

First edition. Originally published 1992 by Greenville Presbyterian Theological Seminary Press, Greenville, South Carolina.

Second printing, 2006. Published by Reformation Media and Press, Fellsmere, Florida.

Dedication
This book is dedicated to the glory of God
and in memory of those
faithful saints through the ages
who have been willing
to sacrifice their all
for the cause of purity in worship.

Acknowledgment
The editors gratefully acknowledge
the labors of
Dr. Morton H. Smith
in helping to put this book together.
Without his graciousness,
patience, and diligence,
it would not have been possible.

TABLE OF CONTENTS

SECTION II. THE ELEMENTS OF WORSHIP

SECTION III. HISTORIC VIEWS AND PRACTICE OF WORSHIP

APPENDICES

INDICES

PART I

WHAT IS WORSHIP?

1 - WHAT IS WORSHIP?

Frank J. Smith

"Worship" is a word which has received much attention in Christian circles lately. The burden of this essay is to advance the thesis that worship means this: coming into God's special presence, listening to Him, and responding to Him in commanded acts of faith and love.

People often speak of worship, but do they really know what that term means? Indeed, they know what they do when they gather together for worship, and some are even aware that others have different practices, but few have any clear notion of what actually constitutes a 'special service' of worship.

One of the more popular concepts today is that all of life is worship. Often this thought is connected with the notion that in the New Covenant, somewhat in contrast with the Old, there is a broadening of the concept of worship. Advocates of this viewpoint illustrate it with such Scripture passages as Zechariah 14, where even the bells on the horses will be inscribed, "HOLY TO THE LORD," in the day of the Messiah. Paul wrote that we are to present our bodies as living sacrifices, holy, acceptable to God, which is our "reasonable service." He also wrote that whatever we do, we are to do it for God's glory. Another passage which has been used is John 4, where Jesus told the woman at the well that neither this mountain nor Jerusalem would be the only appropriate place for true worship; He was thereby laying the groundwork for the truth that not only is the (now world-wide) church the dwelling-place for God, but also that individual believers are temples of the Holy Spirit.

All of this merely highlights that which the Reformers taught: that all of life is dedicated to the service of God and that all believers are priests before Him. Both of these notions are contrary to Romanism, which retained much of the Old Covenant sacrificial system.

But this is not to say that there are no distinctions to be made. Yes, we are to brush our teeth, drive our cars, shoot our basketballs, balance our checkbooks, wash our dishes, enjoy our music, and so forth, all for God's glory and honor. All these things may be regarded as being done, in a general way, in the service of God. When done in a God-pleasing way, they are done in accordance with the right standard (God's Word--the only infallible rule of faith and practice), the right motive (love for God), and the right goal (the glory of God). However, the distinction between general service (those things which are performed in life in general) and specific worship (those things which are done in God's 'special presence,' which in a very direct and immediate way bring glory to Him) does indeed remain today. Worship is *special*.

The fact that there may be a broadening of New Covenant worship does not in the least preclude either the fact that all life in the Old Covenant was to be lived for the glory of God, or that there is a continuing distinction today. For example, John wrote that the new aeon is characterized by grace and truth, while the law came by Moses. But John 1:17 may not be used either to show that grace and truth were not present in the Mosaic economy, or that there is no law today. Rather, the verse demonstrates the emphasis which Scripture places upon the gracious character of Christ's kingdom. Paul's Spirit-law contrast in II Corinthians 3 is of the same variety. Also, Ezekiel prophesied of the time when the law of God would no longer be written on tablets of stone, but on the fleshy hearts of His people. This truth may not be used, however, to show that God's law is not found written in Scripture, nor to demonstrate that God's Old Covenant people did not have the Holy Spirit--surely man's total depravity required God's work in order for men to have circumcised hearts (Joel 2). Rather, Ezekiel was pointing to the day when God's people would enjoy the fullness of the Holy Spirit, Who was poured out by the Lord and His Christ upon the Church at Pentecost.

The distinction between general service and specific worship can be illustrated by the fact of God's special presence. The Biblical position respecting the Lord's Supper, for example, is that of Christ's special spiritual presence. This special presence can be seen in a negative fashion in I Corinthians 11, where unworthy partaking of the Lord's Supper could be fatal.

Such a negative result, which would come from sin and disobedience, would make otherwise good things into means of curse. But when received in faith, the sacraments--baptism and the Lord's Supper--are indeed means of grace and blessing. Among other things, a blessing is invoking God's beneficence by means of His presence. In the book of Numbers, one can see the blessing (and assurance thereof) which accompanied the glory-cloud. The reason why the sacraments, and the preaching of the Word, and prayer, are means of grace is because of God's special presence. They are sometimes means of curse for the same reason. One can think also in this connection of II Corinthians 2, where preaching has two effects: that of being a savour of life unto life and a savour of death unto death. Old Testament passages abound which demonstrate that religious rites were not acceptable to God because of the people's lives--lives which showed that there was no true circumcision of heart.

The Lord Jesus Christ spoke of His being specially present among two or three gathered together in His Name (Mt. 18). His occasion for speaking that, however, is in the context of ecclesiastical discipline, and shows its serious nature. But, the very fact that He is so present for effecting discipline would appear to bear upon worship, by means of an argument from the lesser to the greater (worship being of a higher order than discipline). I Corinthians 5 is a related passage, in which Paul says that Jesus is present in His power when the Church gathers to pronounce judgment.

The special presence of the heavenly court may also be adduced in support of this argument. Although one may argue that the presence of heavenly Jerusalem in Hebrews 12 relates to all of a Christian's walk in this life, yet it seems that the reason why women are to have their heads covered in worship is because of the special presence of the royal court (I Cor. 11).

The lines between general service and specific worship, general and special revelation, and six days and the Sabbath, are not the same, but they do seem to run in a parallel fashion. This can be seen when one considers God's special presence not only in specific worship, but also in special revelation (Christ and Scripture), and on the Sabbath Day. In this regard, it is important to note that neither the Second nor the Fourth

Commandment would make any sense today if there is no such thing as specific worship.

A specialness of God's presence perhaps is not too foreign an idea when one thinks of common parlance regarding prayer. We often pray, "As we come into Thy presence, ..." We do not thereby deny God's omnipresence. We are thereby merely affirming that there is a fellowship with God in prayer which is special, and which is somehow different from our other actions.

The difference may be illustrated by the following: in a kingdom which is an absolute monarchy, all things are to be done in accord with the wishes of the sovereign. However, there is a great deal more latitude in regard to that which a peasant does in the fields than that which he does when he is invited into the royal court. Out in the field, there may be an awareness of the king's ubiquitous reign, but in the court, the implicit recognition turns into an explicit one, as the subject bows before the throne. There is a difference in fellowship as well. When invited to eat at the king's table, the peasant enjoys the king's presence more than when he eats at home.

This specialness is the difference between having a conversation about a person, and actually talking with that person. Christians often enjoy fellowship with each other talking about the Lord and about what great things He has done for them. Specific worship, however, is having direct fellowship with God (as well as with each other), by listening to Him speak words of comfort and exhortation, and by talking to Him in loving response. What a great blessing it is when one is allowed not just to talk about someone beloved, but is indeed afforded an opportunity for personal fellowship. This is especially true with regard to communion and fellowship with God.

The fact that worship is special is highlighted by the article entitled, "The Fear of the Lord in Worship."

Worship is special. It is also dialogical. We do not wish to imply, through the use of the term dialogical, equality between God and man. Rather, the point of using this word is to emphasize that worship is a two-way street: God speaks, and His people respond. The public assembly is a covenantal gathering, a time and place for God to meet directly with His people. He lays down the law, and they are to bless Him in return.

This importance of listening to God may be perceived from the terminology of Scripture: "Hear, O Israel, the Lord our God is one Lord." Eccelsiastes 5:1-2 tells of the importance of listening in God's presence in contrast to sacrificing and speaking. The sign of Jonah given to the evil generation in Jesus' day was that of preaching. The Second Commandment demonstrates the importance of hearing rather than seeing. No one can see God and live; this truth, repeatedly emphasized by prophetic utterances, further illustrates the point.

Two articles in this section deal with the dialogical nature of worship. One looks at it from the Old Testament and one from the New Testament perspective.

Worship is special and it is dialogical in nature. It is also prescribed. The fact of being in God's special presence means that not only are general principles to be observed, but the very elements of service have been written out beforehand.

Imagine a hillbilly war-hero, a man who led his troops victoriously in battle, who is going to be honored by his men after their return from the war.[1] His fellow officers, however, are from Evanston, Illinois; Berkeley, California; and Short Hills, New Jersey; and they don't exactly understand their leader's tastes. As they prepare a great banquet in his honor, they think of how he enjoys listening to music, and eating, and drinking. So, they have the best chamber orchestra, caviar, and champagne that money can buy, all prepared for him and his wife whom they have in flown in from Kentucky. What's wrong with this? Well, yes, he enjoys music, but he'd much prefer stomping his feet to the sounds of a banjo, a guitar, and a fiddle. Yes, he enjoys eating, but what's this stuff called caviar? It's black-eyed peas, grits, cornbread, and venison or squirrel meat which are his pleasure. Yes, he enjoys drinking, but champagne? His speciality is "Mountain Dew" (and we don't, of course, mean the product from Pepsi-

[1]This author would like to thank David Kiester, minister in the Orthodox Presbyterian Church, for suggesting this illustration.

Cola[2]). The obvious point is that, if they had really wanted to honor their hero, they would have found out about those things which pleased him and provided those for him, rather than trying to please him their own way. Similarly, if we truly want to please the Mighty Warrior who has effected our salvation, we will find out which things delight Him, and perform those things for Him. Just as it is not simply the fact of a banquet, but also the content which is important, so it is not just the fact of worship which is important. The content--the elements which comprise worship--is important as well.

The historic Reformed position teaches that content is paramount. The great concern for the centrality of the Word of God lends itself quite properly to an evangelistic zeal and enthusiasm for personal piety. But in today's individualistic milieu, one must understand that Reformed theology also speaks of "means of grace," and of sacraments (not just ordinances), and of the importance of having the forms which Scripture itself requires.

The parts of worship have often been called elements of worship. 'Element' is almost metaphoric, invoking images of scientific reality. What we are contending for is the truth that whether speaking of a chemical element or an element of worship, the term 'element' signifies that which is fundamental, foundational, irreducible--in chemical terms, you can't boil it down any farther.

When we argue for the necessity of 'forms,' we are not saying that the forms exist independently of the elements or that the forms must be preserved for their own sakes. We are, however, maintaining that an element comes as a package deal; that it generally has form, purpose, and content; and that we cannot divorce these constitutive aspects from one another and still have the element. It is significant that the main mark of the Church has form as well as content: it is the *preaching* of the Word, and not just the Word itself.

This Reformed doctrine is known historically as the 'regulative principle of worship.' It teaches that with regard to worship whatever is

---

[2]"Mountain Dew" and "Pepsi-Cola" are trademarks of Pepsi-Cola Company.

commanded in Scripture is required, and that whatever is not commanded is forbidden.

The regulative principle of worship means that what we *do* in worship has been prescribed. There is a dynamic to worship, and it is our practices (parts, elements) that are God-ordained.

One must therefore carefully note that using such phrases as 'applying the regulative principle' can be misleading. Undoubtedly there is and must be application of this principle. But the principle does not mean that we should take various principles of Scripture, put them together, and come up with our own combinations of liturgical practices. On the contrary--we follow the inductivism of the great perpetuator of Protestant natural theology, Francis Lord Bacon, whether we are discovering the elements of chemistry by studying nature, or the elements of worship by studying Scripture.

This prescribed nature of worship is looked at more closely in the chapter on "The Second Commandment."

At this point someone might object to all of this argumentation, and might say, "But what about Christian liberty? Aren't we free in Christ? Why are we bound to do only that which Scripture requires? That sure sounds legalistic to me!"

To this, the proper reply is to note that the idea of Christian liberty is a key concept to a strict view of worship. Liberty is always liberty under law. In the Church, Christ is the "sole law-giver in Zion," the only Head and King of His people. To go beyond the laws which the Lord Jesus has instituted is really to bind men and their consciences with human traditions, rules, and regulations. The proper questions and comments with regard to Christian liberty in the Church are these: "What is your warrant for doing this? By what authority do you require this or that action? You must show positive warrant for doing this in the Church, or you may not institute it. To require God's precious flock to submit to human authority apart from divine command is the essence of legalism." To posit that Christian liberty allows just about anything a group desires to be done in worship is to argue for the tyranny of the majority, or the tyranny of the oligarchy. The fact of the universality of the Bride of Christ, and Christ's kingship over her, means that no one may impose human innovations upon her or her worship. Yes, we are free in Christ, and that is precisely why man-made inventions may not be placed on us. Christian liberty is freedom under the law of Christ, and that is why arbitrary rules and man's legislation are forbidden--not only because God does not require this or that action, but also because they impose upon one's Christian liberty.

However, there is liberty in regard to the circumstances of worship. They are to be determined by a wise discerning of that which is best in any given situation. One must remember that a circumstance is not anything which anybody wants to consider as a circumstance. George Gillespie, the 17th century Scottish theologian, wrote in his *English Popish Ceremonies* that for a circumstance to be imposed upon the Church it must meet three criteria: (1). it must be something which is truly circumstantial--that is, it must not have any liturgical significance; (2). it must be something which could not have been prescribed by the Bible (such as the language of worship, or the time or place of service); (3). it must be something which, when imposed, will not wound tender consciences.[3]

In this regard, note that historic Reformed worship is the most universal worship--by its adherence to only those elements found in Scripture. Those who take the Bible seriously should be attracted to this type of worship. Worship in non-Reformed churches is shaped with either undue reference to Old Testament worship or by considerations altogether extraneous to Scripture.

Some of these issues with regard to freedom in worship are discussed more fully in the chapter on "Christian Liberty and Worship."

One of the more important things to realize is that worship is worship of *God*, whether public, family, or private. So, the final essay in this section is on family worship.

One must always remember that there is mystery in our relationship with God, and His transcendence is perhaps best understood during worship. And when we come into His special presence to kneel before our Maker, and

---

[3] George Gillespie, *A Dispute Against the English-Popish Ceremonies, Obtruded upon the Church of Scotland. . . .* (1637).

we, with the eyes of faith, behold His shekinah glory, we know that He is God and there is none else beside Him. A seminary professor once said, "I was really tempted to announce that the topic for the next time would be 'The Incomprehensibility of God,' and then either not show up for the lecture, or engage in an hour of silent meditation."

Why do we have so much trouble in our private worship, in keeping our minds and hearts fixed on God as we pray and read His Word and sing His praise and meditate on Him? Because of the dullness of our hearts, which cannot bear to see God's glory (even as the people in Moses' day made him cover his face). Why do we not have a sense of awe, and grandeur, and majesty in our worship; why do we interrupt our times of worship by dwelling on ourselves by means of announcements and other such things? For the same reason--we simply cannot bear the glory of God.

Oh, that we might be stirred up to praise God, to worship Him! Oh, that we might know what a blessing (though a humbling one) it is to be in His presence! Oh, that the Church of Jesus might know that she dare not bring whatever she pleases before the Sovereign King, but that He Who dwells in light inaccesible is a jealous God Who wants to be worshipped His way!

Oh, that we might all be humbled by the grace of Him Who calls us into His light, simply because He loves us! May we not be arrogant or proud before Him or each other, especially as we consider the great truths of Scripture regarding worship. Rather, may we acknowledge Him Who enables us to worship Him in spirit and truth.

2 - THE FEAR OF THE LORD IN WORSHIP

Herman Hanko

Congregational worship is the highest expression of God's covenant of grace with His people. It is this truth of the covenant which determines that the fear of the Lord ought to control completely worship services of the Church.

That congregational worship is covenantal is evident if we consider the fact that the covenant of grace is essentially a bond of friendship and fellowship between God and His people in Christ in which God is the God of His people and they are His children, His sons and daughters. All Scripture emphasizes this truth--a truth already expressed to Abraham the father of all believers within the covenant: "And I will establish my covenant between me and thee and thy seed after thee in their generations for an everlasting covenant, to be a God unto thee, and to thy seed after thee" (Gen. 17:7).

God is the God of His people in all their life; but when God's people come together in worship, this blessed reality comes to its highest expression. Jesus Himself reminds us of this when He says: "Where two or three are gathered together in my name, there am I in the midst of them," an expression which refers to Christ dwelling in fellowship with His people (Mt. 18:20). Paul expresses this same truth without specifically mentioning the covenant when he writes to the Corinthians:

> "And what agreement hath the temple of God with idols? for ye are the temple of the living God; as God hath said, I will dwell in them, and walk in them; and I will be their God, and they shall be my people. Wherefore come out from among them, and be ye separate, saith the Lord, and touch not the unclean thing; and I will receive you, and will be a Father unto you, and ye shall be my sons and daughters, saith the Lord Almighty" (II Cor. 6:16-18).

This is covenantal language throughout. God's promise is here described in almost identical language with the description of the covenant made to Abraham: God will be the God of His people, and they will be His people, His sons and daughters. That this refers, at least indirectly, also to worship is evident from the fact that the people of God are called God's temple, an expression which refers back to the meeting place of the congregation of Israel in the Old Testament. This obvious reference, therefore, to the Old Testament temple where Israel met to worship connects this unmistakably to the idea of the covenantal aspect of worship.

All the elements of the covenant are present in the worship service. Because the covenant is a bond of friendship and fellowship, a crucial element in such fellowship is "conversation." Two who have fellowship together speak to one another. They cannot have fellowship without such conversation. Whether we speak of the fellowship of husband and wife, of parents and children, of friends in their mutual relationships, or of saints within the one household of faith, the communion they share is a communion of conversation. So true is this that even those who lack the power of speech must learn to communicate with others in order to share in fellowship with their fellow men. A deaf-mute learns to speak sign language. Without it he is cut off from any fellowship with those about him.

Such conversation is important because fellowship implies that two share with one another their lives. They speak to one another of their hopes and plans, of their sorrows and fears, of their longings and aspirations. They seek advice and counsel from those with whom they share their lives. They seek comfort and encouragement to support them in the distresses and troubles of life. They willingly offer sympathy and aid to those who need someone to help bear the burdens of life. All this takes place through conversation.

But this is also true of the worship service. There too a holy conversation takes place between God and His people. At the center of worship is the preaching of the Word of the gospel. The Word of the gospel is God's promise to His people, the good news of everlasting salvation in Christ. God gives to His people the assurance that His promise will be fulfilled in them. Two ideas stand on the foreground here. In the first place, through the gospel God speaks to His people. He tells them of all the secrets of His will and purpose which He has determined to do, not only in their salvation, but in all that takes place in the world. This is why the Psalmist, in Psalm 25:14, can say: "The secret of the Lord is with them that fear him, and He will show them his covenant." God tells us of Himself, of His great glory--the glory of His infinite perfections, but also of His mercy and grace and love. He tells us of all that He is in Himself in His own infinite being, sharing with us these precious secrets. He tells us of all His counsel and will which encompass all that happens in heaven and on earth, and will happen in the new heavens and the new earth when Christ shall come again. Great and marvelous secrets He shares with His covenant people.

But, in the second place, the whole Scripture makes clear that the promise which is proclaimed in the gospel and which is part of God's secret which He shares with us, also forms an essential part of the covenant. The Scriptures almost make the promise of God synonymous with the preaching of the gospel. It is for this reason that the covenant is even called in the New Testament Scriptures, a testament. The reference is very obviously to a will which contains the promise of an inheritance. This is why we read in Hebrews 9:15-17:

> "And for this cause he is the mediator of the new testament, that by means of death, for the redemption of the transgressions that were under the first testament, they which are called might receive the promise of eternal inheritance. For where a testament is, there must also be of necessity the death of the testator. For a testament is of force after men are dead: otherwise it is of no strength at all while the testator liveth."

We may conclude, therefore, that God speaks of the promise of His covenant within the worship services when the gospel is proclaimed.

But while it is true that God speaks to His people through the preaching of the Word and through other elements of the worship in which the minister speaks in God's name, God's people also speak to God. They speak to Him in the songs they sing in which they pour out their souls in expressing the deepest thoughts, desires, and emotions of their hearts. God's people speak to God when they lift up their hearts in prayer to God to bring their needs and the needs of God's Church to the throne of grace. It is in this way that a conversation which stands at the very heart of covenant fellowship takes place in the worship service. God and His people are talking together.

Yet we must be clear on the nature of this conversation. If we are to understand that worship must be characterized by awe and fear, we must also understand that this holy conversation is always initiated by God. And it is initiated by God in such a way that our part of the conversation is always the fruit of God's part. Never can it be any different. God is sovereign in all the work of salvation. He is sovereign also in His covenant. He establishes His covenant and He maintains it by His grace. The realization and continuation of the covenant are never dependent upon what we do. Though we are called to walk as God's covenant people and though our part of the covenant is to respond to God, never must this be interpreted in any other way than that God speaks first, and we respond. God speaks first because His speech is sovereign, efficacious, creative, renewing, powerful and irresistible. His speech effects our response; and our response is the fruit of His powerful Word. This is very clearly the idea in Psalm 27:8: "When thou saidst, Seek ye my face; my heart said unto thee, Thy face, Lord, will I seek." Never are we able to say, "Thy face, Lord, will I seek," unless God first says to us, creatively and powerfully: "Seek ye my face."

Although, therefore, the conversation between God and His people is truly conversation, we must not construe this as two equals speaking together; two neighbors chatting over the backyard fence; two friends talking earnestly on a walk through the woods; or two saints discussing last night's sermon. It is not even the conversation of husband and wife or of parents and children. God is God! We are and always remain creatures.

There are two aspects to this which we must consider. In the first place, Scripture makes clear that the vast chasm which yawns between the Creator and the creature is infinitely wide. "Behold, the nations are as a drop of a bucket, and are counted as the small dust of the balance: behold, he taketh up the isles as a very little thing" (Is. 40:15). Isaiah does not say: the nations are a drop in the bucket. If one has a drop in a bucket he has something, though not very much. But all the nations are as a drop of a bucket. They are all, taken in their entirety, equal to a drop which hangs on the bottom lip of a bucket, a drop which no one notices and which soon falls into the dust. All nations are no more than that! What then is one little man? After all, before Him even the angels cover their faces with their wings and cry all the day, "Holy, holy, holy is the Lord God Almighty" (Is. 6:3).

The second aspect is that we are not only infinitely small specks of dust in comparison with God, but we are also sinners. We are dreadful sinners, born in sin and depravity, unable to do any good. We are slaves of sin, dead in trespasses and sins--to use the words of Scripture in Ephesians 2:1. We daily increase the mountain of our sins and guilt until it becomes as high as the sky. The Psalmist sings: "Iniquities prevail against me" (Ps. 65:3). There is nothing in us which makes us fit for covenant fellowship with God. We are, apart from His grace, His enemies who fight against Him, attempt to drive Him from His throne, and take into our own bloody hands the power of the creation. We daily, by our sins, forfeit all right to covenant fellowship with Him and bring upon us only His just wrath and everlasting displeasure. Our natures are corrupt, and God can dwell in fellowship only with one who is holy as He is. We cannot even will to do the good; our wills are always bound in the service of sin. That God nevertheless is pleased to dwell with us is the great wonder of His everlasting mercy and love in Jesus Christ our Saviour. No saint can be in God's presence and experience the riches of communion with God without being overwhelmingly conscious of his unworthiness and the great depths of the mercy and grace of God.

These important components determine the character of this holy conversation which takes place between God and His people.

That this important element is missing in much of what goes under the name of worship in our day is to be condemned in the strongest possible language. Anything in the worship services which detracts from the holiness of God is to be abhorred. And yet, this is constantly being done by means of all kinds of liturgical innovations. In some instances the worship services become so informal that one would think he were at an informal social gathering in which people chat about the everyday affairs of life. No sense of reverence and awe pervades the assembly. In other instances, the minister opens the worship service with a cheery remark of some kind: "Hello, God"; or, "Hi, folks"; or "How is everybody this morning?" Through such opening statements, the congregation is not even led consciously into the presence of God; much less are the people inspired with a sense of the reverence which is becoming to those who enter God's presence.

Prayers and sermons follow the same pattern. God is blasphemously referred to as "Our brother in the sky" or some such familiar title which brings God down to the level of us sinful mortals and destroys the sanctity and holiness of Him whose ways are from everlasting and who makes the heavens His throne and the earth His footstool.

The Second Commandment, especially in distinction from the First Commandment, tells us how God must be worshipped. We are not in a position to decide how we ought to worship God any more than a subject of the queen of England is in a position to decide how he or she will enter the queen's presence. God alone must tell us how He is to be worshipped. We are bound, absolutely, to the principles which God Himself sets forth in Scripture. When we refuse to follow the Scriptures' instructions on this point, we break the Second Commandment, create a graven image, and bring down on us and our children the terrible judgment of God. God is jealous (so this commandment teaches us) of His honor and glory, and He will surely visit the iniquities of the fathers upon the children unto the third and fourth generation of them that hate Him. It is preposterous and the height of arrogant presumption to think that we, less than specks of dust, are going to determine how God is to be worshipped.

When we inquire from the Scriptures concerning how God would have us worship Him, one central feature stands out above all others. We are to worship Him with fear. What does Scripture mean when it speaks of fear? In his book, *Principles of Conduct*, John Murray begins his chapter on the fear of God with the startling statement: "The fear of God is the soul of godliness."[1] He considers it to be the central feature of all Christian ethics, from which the whole of the Christian life arises. If this is true, then surely the fear of God is also the one distinctive feature of worship.

The idea of the fear of God is so all-pervasive in Scripture that one can quote almost where he will to demonstrate how important Scripture considers this attribute to be. In Job 1:8 God pronounces His own verdict on His servant Job with words spoken as a challenge to Satan: "Hast thou considered my servant Job, that there is none like him in the earth, a perfect and an upright man, one that feareth God, and escheweth evil?" In Ecclesiastes, a book which we may consider Solomon's own confession of the sins of his reign, he speaks of what is the conclusion of the whole matter: "Fear God, and keep his commandments; for this is the whole duty of man" (12:13). Again and again God's people are described in Scripture as those who fear the Lord. And indeed, Scripture repeatedly reminds us that the life of faith which the saints lived arose out of the fear of God which ruled in their hearts. It may even come as somewhat of a surprise that our Lord Himself is described as possessing the Spirit of fear: "And the spirit of the Lord shall rest upon him, the spirit of wisdom and understanding, the spirit of counsel and might, the spirit of knowledge and of the fear of the Lord" (Is. 11:2). And the author of the epistle to the Hebrews tells us concerning Christ: "Who in the days of his flesh, when he had offered up prayers and supplications with strong crying and tears unto him that was able to save him from death, and was heard in that he feared; though he were a Son, yet learned he obedience by the things which he suffered" (5:7, 8). If it was true

---

[1] John Murray, *Principles of Conduct* (Grand Rapids: Eerdmans, 1957), 229.

of our Lord Himself, perfect and without sin, that he feared God, how much more ought not the repeated injunction to live in fear be impressed upon our souls? It is perhaps this very lack of fear in our present generation which, in large measure, explains the low state of morals, the worldliness and carnality, the pleasure-madness and ethical perversion, which characterize our times.

There are, however, in both the Old and the New Testaments two senses in which the word 'fear' is used in the Scriptures. This must become clear to us, for our understanding of these uses stands at the very heart of our calling to worship God in fear.

There are many passages in Scripture which speak of fear as that terror of God and His just judgments upon sin which seize the soul of the sinner and make him live in dread and anxiety. There are many passages which use the word 'fear' in this sense. When God appeared to Israel on Mt. Sinai in clouds of darkness, thunders and lightnings, and the sound of a trumpet, He appeared as One Who is terrible in judgment. It was to be expected that the Israelites, called to assemble before the mount, would be terror-stricken. Moses, therefore, said to them: "Fear not: for God is come to prove you, and that his fear may be before your faces, that ye sin not" (Ex. 20:20). The reference is very obviously to the fear of terror incited in the people by the dreadful appearance of God on the mount. The same meaning is to be applied to the words of the Lord in Matthew 10:28: "And fear not them which kill the body, but are not able to kill the soul: but rather fear him which is able to destroy both soul and body in hell."

God is a righteous and holy God. He is so perfectly holy that He cannot look on sin without great displeasure and fiery indignation. He must, to maintain His own holiness, punish the sinner with the judgments of His righteous anger. When men sin against Him, they sin against the One who will surely vindicate His own Name and protect His holiness, for He is jealous of His honor. It is this judgment against sin which invokes terror in the heart of the sinner. It can be nothing else. It is true that the sinner may, while in this life, suppress that terror with impunity; he may mock at the thought of judgment and rail against the infinitely holy God; he may harden himself to spiritual insensibility against the thought of judgment; but for all that, he knows, in the depths of his heart, that God is judge and that He will surely render just judgment upon the ungodly. Even in worship this is true. The preaching of the Word of the gospel, with its blessed promises to the elect, is also a proclamation of God's just judgment against all who remain unconverted. While, therefore, the godly see the greatness of God's everlasting grace, the judgments of a holy God against sin fill the soul of the unconverted with terror. And when Christ appears at the end of time as the Judge of the living and of the dead, the sinner can only shrink in terror before the Judge of all the earth. Jesus Himself reminds us of this when on the way to His cross He spoke these words to the daughters of Jerusalem:

> "Weep not for me, but weep for yourselves, and for your children. For, behold, the days are coming, in the which they shall say, Blessed are the barren, and the wombs that never bare, and the paps which never gave suck. Then shall they begin to say to the mountains, Fall on us; and to the hills, Cover us. For if they do these things in a green tree, what shall be done in the dry?" (Luke 23:28-31).

This terror can only strike dread and anguish in the soul of the sinner. Surely it is true that the sinner has every reason to live in such terror before the face of the Holy God.

But God's people are delivered from that fear of terror by grace through the atoning sacrifice of our Lord Jesus Christ. He bore all the judgments of God against the sins and guilt of His sheep for whom He died, so that no anger, no wrath, no judgment remain to be brought upon their heads. And so it is that the word 'fear' in Scripture comes to have another meaning, the meaning of reverential awe and adoration.

There are also many texts which speak of fear in this sense of the word. We need quote only a few. In his letter to the Philippians, Paul admonishes the Church: "Work out your own salvation with fear and trembling, for it is God which worketh in you both to will and to do of his good pleasure" (2:12, 13). The Psalmist sings of this fear in Psalm 19:9: "The fear of the Lord is clean, enduring for ever: the judgments of the Lord are true and righteous altogether." It is obvious that these and many other texts speak of a different fear than that of terror.

This fear of awe and reverence characterizes even the angels in heaven. We read, for example, in Isaiah 6:1-3:

> "In the year that king Uzziah died I saw also the Lord sitting upon a throne, high and lifted up, and his train filled the temple. Above it stood the seraphim: each one had six wings; with twain he covered his face, and with twain he covered his feet, and with twain he did fly. And one cried unto another, and said, Holy, holy, holy, is the Lord of hosts: the whole earth is full of his glory."

It is clear from this that fear arises, first of all, from a sense of God's greatness. If even angels in heaven, who stand in the presence of God Himself, are filled with awe at His greatness and glory, how much more ought not this to characterize us? But this same fear arises also from the fact that we are constantly in God's presence, that we cannot escape from it even for a moment. The sweet singer of Israel was moved deeply by this when he sang: "Whither shall I go from thy spirit? or whither shall I flee from thy presence: If I ascend up into heaven, thou art there: if I make bed in hell [Sheol], behold, thou art there. If I take the wings of the morning, and dwell in the uttermost parts of the sea; even there shall thy hand lead me, and thy right hand shall hold me" (Ps. 139:7-10). But no less does this fear arise from a consciousness of our smallness in comparison with the greatness of Him who dwells far above the heavens. The twenty-four elders who fall down before God and worship Him shout: "Thou art worthy, O Lord, to receive glory and honor and power: for thou hast created all things, and for thy pleasure they are and were created" (Rev. 4:10, 11).

Though the fear of terror may bring anguish and dread into the hearts of the wicked, so does the fear of awe and reverence bring forth many virtues in the elect as a fountain pours out a stream of clear water. This fear, when found in the child of God, brings into his consciousness an awareness of and sorrow for sin. After all, fear in the sense of reverence and awe is also a profound concern that we have provoked God by our sins. It is a deep desire not to offend the Holy One of Israel. And when we do sin, it evokes in us this consciousness of our sins and a deep sorrow for them. For this reason, fear also humbles us before God. It humbles us not only because we, so small and insignificant, stand before the face of the Holy God; but also because we are sinners, worthy of only His great wrath against us. Fear brings about a deep and profound humility without which no man can come to God.

Yet we know too that God has redeemed us, unworthy sinners that we are. That God should, in great grace and mercy, in boundless love and compassion, save us, fills our souls with wonder and awe. We, when captured by this great salvation He has provided for us in Jesus Christ our Lord, can only fall before Him in amazement and wonder, in awe and reverence to praise and extol Him who has been so merciful to us. This can only lead to reverence before Him and praise to His holy Name.

> "Blessed be the God and Father of our Lord Jesus Christ, who hath blessed us with all spiritual blessings in heavenly places in Christ: According as he hath chosen us in him before the foundation of the world, that we should be holy and without blame before him" (Eph. 1:3, 4). "O the depth of the riches both of the wisdom and knowledge of God! how unsearchable are his judgments, and his ways past finding out! For who hath known the mind of the Lord? or who hath been his counsellor? Or who hath first given to him, and it shall be recompensed unto him again? For of him, and through him, and to him, are all things: to whom be glory for ever. Amen" (Rom. 11:33-36).

Thus when we live in the assurance by faith that we are God's people, redeemed through the blood of the cross, destined to live forever in the everlasting tabernacle of God's covenant, we are so overwhelmed with the greatness of this gracious salvation, that we are filled with awe and wonder. Fear floods our souls at the greatness of such grace and love.

Those who live in the fear of awe before God, need be afraid of nothing. Repeatedly Scripture reminds us of this. God told Abraham, surrounded as he was by hostile people, "Fear not, Abram: I am thy shield, and thy exceeding great reward" (Gen. 15:1). Exultantly, the Psalmist sings: "The Lord is my light and my salvation; whom shall I fear?" (Ps. 27:1). And our Lord, in words of tenderest concern, reminds His flock of sheep: "Fear not, little flock; for it is your Father's good pleasure to give you the kingdom" (Luke 12:32). It has been rightly said: "He who fears God is afraid of no man."

Though there is a clear distinction made in Scripture between the fear of terror and the fear of awe, the two, nevertheless, are related. They are related because the greatness of God and His supreme holiness require of us awe before His presence. When the wicked refuse to live in awe before Him, they are terrorized because they know they are the objects of His just judgment. When the righteous are delivered from such just judgment, to their awe at the greatness of God they add the awe of wonder at such a great salvation as God has provided for them.

At the same time, this awe is of such a kind that the people of God are deeply concerned that they live lives of obedience to God. They are afraid that they will offend God by their sins. The Psalmist speaks of this in Psalm 119:120: "My flesh trembleth for fear of thee; and I am afraid of thy judgments." And this fear is a profound motivation to strive to live according to the will of our God Who has saved us. Yet, in the consciousness of their salvation in Christ, they no longer have terror of God's wrath. In this sense the apostle John clearly states: "There is no fear in love; but perfect love casteth out fear; because fear hath torment. He that feareth is not made perfect in love." (I John 4:18).

It is clear from all this that the man who attempts to come into God's presence without fear is guilty of grievous sin. When he assumes an attitude of familiarity, when he speaks to God and of Him as he speaks to his fellow man, when he, without any semblance of awe and reverence in his voice and words, addresses the holy God, he is profane and blasphemous. It is precisely to this sin that God refers in the Third Commandment: "Thou shalt not take the name of the Lord thy God in vain, for the Lord will not hold him guiltless that taketh his name in vain." In worship we take God's holy name upon our lips. When the fear of awe is lacking, we use this name of our God in vain. He who does this is guilty of intolerable presumption and almost unbelievable arrogance. He drags God down from His high throne above the heavens and molds Him in his own filthy hands, making God in the likeness of his own evil thoughts. It is a presumption and pride that God will not allow to go unpunished. He will not hold him guiltless who takes His name in vain. God is God! He is jealous of His honor. He will maintain His own greatness and glory. Puny man may rail and rant, may mock and curse, may blaspheme and ridicule, may seek to pull Him from His throne; but such dreadful sin can only bring curses upon him who does it.

This is, of course, true in the whole of our lives. How much more, therefore, ought not this to be true in our worship?

As we have already pointed out, God has graciously taken people into His covenant fellowship to live with Him in friendship, to talk with Him and enjoy His companionship. But this very blessing does not breed in man an air of familiarity; quite the contrary. When we know what great depths of mercy and love, what great oceans of compassion and pity are involved in God coming down to us in Christ to take us into His own covenant fellowship, the reaction in the heart of every saved man can be nothing else but awe and profound wonder at the greatness of it all. It is almost too good to be true. It is almost more than we can bear. Has the living God indeed done this for us?--poor, wretched, undeserving sinners? He has! Praise to His glorious Name.

That awe and reverence is an essential characteristic of all worship. This is true in the service we give God in all our lives. If it does not characterize our prayers, these become a mockery. If it is not the deepest principle of all our lives, we will not have the spiritual motivation to walk in the ways of the precepts of our God.

But if this is true in all our life, it ought especially to be true when we come together with God's people to worship Him in His house. All of worship must reflect this fear, or it is no worship at all. An atmosphere of reverence must pervade all the worship of God's people. The prayers that are made, the songs that are sung, the words of the minister or of the congregation must all express that awe without which it is impossible to please God.

And then, when fear, true fear, is present, we will enjoy the blessedness of God's favor and love, the great wonder of His grace in taking us into His own covenant fellowship. The wonder of this is so great that eternity itself will not be long enough to give praise to Him who has so abundantly blessed us.

3 - THE DIALOGICAL NATURE OF WORSHIP IN THE OLD TESTAMENT

E. Clark Copeland

Man's worship is response to God and progresses with the revelation of God from Old to New Testaments. To examine this presupposition we shall undertake a Biblical-theological study of the Old Testament. Our purpose will be to let the Scriptures in their historical order unfold for us that response of man to God that pleases Him.

The Bible is the record of God's self-revelation. It is not, however, a book that God has, so to speak, dropped out of heaven into man's hand. Biblical revelation is covenantal in character. The Bible records for us the fact that God entered into a union with man. In this union God revealed to man the knowledge of Himself, of the creation and of His purpose for the creation. It was in this way that man understood his place in the creation and his relation to God; in other words, what God wanted him to do. Thus man was not left alone to search for God, who He is and how he may please Him; or even to read the Book and do by himself what he was commanded. He has been brought into union with God so that all of his life and work is accomplished in union with God and by His power. He has been made God's partner for the accomplishment of His purpose. His whole life is, therefore, to be lived out as response within this covenant union with God. This is the basic presupposition of revelation that is borne out in all of Scripture.

Revelation is also progressive. God has revealed Himself at various times (in fragmentary fashion, Heb. 1:1, NEB). The covenants mark significant steps ('epochs,' to use Geerhardus Vos' term) in the revelation of God and His adminstration of His eternal purpose towards the full manifestation of Himself and the final accomplishment of His purpose. Thus there is an eschatological expectation that is increasingly unfolded from beginning to end of the Bible. We shall note the development of worship within this covenantal framework.

The Creation Covenant

The Bible begins with the account of creation, displaying the magnificent wisdom and power of God's person, His kingship over the universe. By His word God not only created--He established the bounds of earth's activities, fixed its course, determined its inter-relatedness and mutual support. Indeed, "The heavens declare the glory of God" (Ps. 19:1).

At last "God created man in his own image, . . . male and female . . ." (Gen. 1:27). In the image of God, man was a self-conscious person, like God, with spiritual qualities that enabled him to know, fellowship with and respond to God in love, faithfulness, righteousness and honor, recognizing his creaturely relation to his Creator.[1]

The creation mandate (Gen. 1:28) made man ruler over every created thing (see Heb. 2:8), and it subjected him to God in perfect obedience. As the Hebrew text of Psalm 8 says, "For thou hast made him a little lower than *God*, and hast crowned him with glory and honor" (v. 5). A measure of God's kingly honor and majesty was given to man. Thus he was confronted immediately with God's wisdom and greatness as Creator, calling for adoration and worship. He was also confronted with God's kingship of the universe, and so with his own position as vassal to give loving submission and due honor to the Lord God (Gen. 2:4). David expressed man's spontaneous response, "O LORD our Lord, how excellent is thy name in all the earth" (Ps. 8:1, 9).

God ended creation by resting on the seventh day and by blessing and hallowing it for man (Gen. 2:1-3). God was anticipating the consummation of creation, and He called man to join Him in this

---

[1] *Cf.* C. F. Keil and F. Delitzsch, *Biblical Commentary on the Old Testament, The Pentateuch* (rpt. Grand Rapids: Eerdmans, 1971), I, 64.

expectation by resting on the seventh day as God did.[2] It should be noted here that, although the Sabbath is not mentioned again until God gave Israel manna in the wilderness, it was then acknowledged as an established day of rest before the giving of the Fourth Commandment at Sinai (Ex. 16:24-30). The Sabbath is part of the cosmic order of God for man's joyful celebration of the creation and his anticipation of its glorious consummation. And so it will remain through all time until the hope is realized.[3]

Man's life began in Eden, "the garden of God" (Ezek. 28:13). Man was to dwell with God in unbroken fellowship with Him. In the center of the garden was the Tree of Life, representing the fact that life was not inherent in man, but flowed to him from God. By his revolt, man's fellowship with God was broken. He was put out of the garden. The tree was preserved and hedged about by cherubim and a flaming sword "to guard the way to the Tree of Life" (Gen. 3:24). God will keep the way to the tree open and will eventually bring man to it. Satan had tried hard, but he did not, nor can he, succeed in preventing man from coming to the tree. As we shall see, Adam eventually believed the word of God and received life. The covenant, however, had been broken; the penalty was death; in meting out the sentence, God would confront the sinner.

The Covenant of Grace

In guilty shame Adam and Even tried to hide their nakedness and to hide from God. God's "Where are you?" was both a convicting and a gracious call. In this first court scene in history, God passed sentence on the guilty and announced victory over the Serpent by the seed of the woman. All mankind in all of history was included in the sentence and would be involved in the ensuing struggle. There will be two groups of men in the earth: the seed of the woman--God's kingdom, and the seed of the serpent--

---

[2] *Cf.* G. Ch. Aalders, *Bible Student's Commentary, Genesis* (Grand Rapids: Zondervan, 1981), I, 76-77.

[3] *Cf.* Keil and Delitzsch *op. cit.*, 69-70.

Satan's kingdom. They will be locked in perpetual warfare as God has fixed enmity between them. But the outcome is certain. The head of the Serpent will be crushed. The seed of the woman will suffer at the hand of the Serpent and his seed. All creation groans under the curse of futility and death. But there is hope of redemption (Rom. 8:18-24).

"Adam called his wife's name Eve, because she is the mother of all living" (Gen. 3:20). Thus the account records that our first parents believed the promise of God and began to build their lives on it, on God's covenant of grace. Then God dealt with their guilty consciences by giving them clothing of animal skins instead of their fragile, self-made fig-leaf girdles. The commentators are not agreed on the meaning of this act of God. Kidner says that God showed them how to protect their bodies. Leupold concedes that God's provision of proper clothing for man's body "does suggest and does render reasonable the conclusion that He will provide the proper covering for man's guilty soul." But he adds, "It is difficult to say whether the slaying of beasts for the purposes of clothing in Adam's day already involved sacrifice." Keil is a little more positive as he says that in showing them "how they might use the sovereignty they possessed over the animals for their own good . . . this act of God laid the foundation for the sacrifices."[4] The inference of the text seems clear: since God's action in providing clothing (v. 20) replaces the covering Adam and Eve had made (v. 7) in response to their guilty consciences, God was dealing with the real problem, not just with clothing for their bodies. Guilt and being afraid of God is not dealt with by leather jackets, but by a substitionary death for the sinner. Adam and Eve (mankind) must always wear clothing, but they need no longer be afraid of God.

Outside the garden Adam and Eve begin to build their life based on the covenant. They recognized the hand of God in the birth of their sons. At the birth of Cain, Eve said, "with the help of the LORD I have brought

---

[4]Derek Kidner, *Genesis* (Downers Grove, IL: Intervarsity Press, 1972), 72; see H. C. Leupold, *Genesis* (Grand Rapids: Baker, 1942), I, 178-9; Keil, and Delitzsch, *op. cit.*, 106.

forth a man" (Gen. 4:1, NIV[5]). This is her personal response to the God of love and mercy who had fulfilled His covenant promise to her. Thus man knew God by His covenant name from the very beginning.

The sons began to subdue the earth and rule over it, Abel raising livestock and Cain cultivating the earth. It became a part of their life to acknowledge God's goodness to them, and so "the day came" (NEB) when each brought his offering to the Lord. We are not to see this as the beginning of presenting offerings to God, but as what was their custom as begun by their parents. Each brought the produce of his labor: Cain, the fruit of the ground; and Abel, "the firstlings of his flock and of the fat thereof" (Gen. 4:2, 3). The Lord was pleased with Abel and his offering, but He did not look with favor on Cain and his offering. God first observed the person, then his offering. The offering reveals the character of the person. Abel brought the best animal, the first born, and the best portions of the choice animal, thus revealing his desire to please God. Cain "brought of the fruit of the ground." No comment is made in respect of quality. When he understood that he was not accepted, nor his offering, he was angry.

The Hebrew word for offering used here means "gift, tribute, offering, whether of grain or animal."[6] After the Mosaic institutions of sacrifice at Sinai, this word became a technical term for the various forms of grain offering (cf. Ex. 30:9; Lev. 7:37; etc.), but not exclusively so, as these references will show. There is no record of specific command concerning sacrifice given previously. Even if we are correct in our conclusion concerning God's provision of clothing for Adam and Eve in Genesis 3:21, that example of sacrifice was related to guilt. The purpose of Cain and Abel's offering was not related to guilt--though man is always a guilty sinner before God. They were bringing a present, a gift, offering it spontaneously.

God's response to Cain was, "If thou doest well, shalt thou not be accepted? and if thou doest not well, sin lieth at the door. And unto thee

---

[5]The NIV more correctly reflects the Hebrew than the KJV, "from the LORD."

[6]Francis Brown, S. R. Driver, and Charles A. Briggs, *Hebrew English Lexicon of the Old Testament* (rpt.; Oxford: The Clarendon Press, 1942), 585; cf. I Sam. 2:29b; Isa. 1:11, 13.

shall be his desire, and thou shalt rule over him" (Gen. 4:7). That is, sin's desire is to control Cain, but Cain must rule over sin, personified. Cain's pouting indicates that he blamed God for not accepting his offering. When God addressed him telling him how to remedy the situation, he only became jealous of his brother and slew him. It becomes clear that he had expected to buy God's favor with his offering. He did not come as God's humble servant in worship, but as an arrogant impostor. Cain, the man, was unacceptable to God; so nothing he might offerd would be pleasing to God. He did not come with a spontaneous gift of thanksgiving and adoration, but with a bribe. That was a sacrilegious affront to the holy, gracious, loving God.

We are confirmed in this conclusion when we read in Hebrews that it was faith that made Abel's offering to differ from Cain's. Cain lacked the one thing by which he could please God, faith. God looks upon the heart (I Sam. 16:7). The heart of man, vile by nature, is made pure by faith (Acts 15:9). Cain's evil heart was fully displayed in his jealous murder of his brother. Thus we have our first lesson in private worship.

God gave Adam and Eve another son in place of Abel whom Cain slew. It is through this line that the covenant promise was passed on to succeeding generations, as we are now to learn. Seth named his son Enosh, seeing the weakness and fraility of man because of the corruption of sin. "Then began men to call upon the name of the LORD" (Gen. 4:26). The conjunction "then" explicitly calls attention to the connection between Seth's acknowledgement in naming his son and the beginning of "calling on the name of the LORD," the covenant God of grace and mercy. The name Enosh appears to call attention to what is taking place in the rest of mankind, the family of Cain, and to cry out for reversal. The next sentence announces the reversal.

The phrase, "to call on the name of the LORD," may signify prayer as the New English Bible implies in its translation, "to invoke the LORD by name." This is clearly the meaning in I Kings 18:24, when Elijah says to the priests of Baal, "And call ye on the name of your gods, and I will call on the name of the LORD; and the God that answereth by fire, let him be God" (*cf.* II Kings 5:11).

It frequently refers to public worship, as in Psalm 116:17-18:

"I will offer to thee the sacrifice of thanksgiving,
and will call upon the name of the Lord.
I will pay my vows unto the LORD now
in the presence of all his people.
In the courts of the LORD's house
in the midst of thee, O Jerusalem.
Praise ye the LORD."[7]

The same Hebrew phrase may also have the specific meaning of "to proclaim," as in Exodus 33:19 where God told Moses He would pass by in front of him and "proclaim the name of the LORD before thee." God's doing it is recorded in verse 5 of the next chapter, "And the LORD descended in the cloud, and stood with him there, and proclaimed the name of the LORD."

It must be recognized that this statement in Genesis 4:26 does not mark the beginning of prayer. As Aalders says, "The emphasis must fall on the public character of this worship. What was intended at this time, the time of Enosh, was communal worship."[8] The Cainites were known for their lines of cultural development: tent making and livestock raising, music and metallurgy, marked by blatant paganism. The Sethites, on the contrary, were to be known as worshippers of the covenant God, the LORD. This name had been known and used since Eve acknowledged that it was with the help of the LORD that she had begotten Cain. The Sethites believed and publicly proclaimed the covenant promise and passed it on from generation to generation. Their "cultural development took an entirely different direction than it did among the Cainites."[9]

We may say, then, that Seth and his descendents proclaimed the

---

[7] *Cf.* Psalm 79:6=Jer. 10:25; Zeph. 3:9; II Sam. 6:2=I Chron. 13:6.

[8] Aalders, *op.cit.*, 135.

[9] *Ibid.*, 136.

covenant of the LORD in worship, and their culture reflected the LORD's ownership and man's stewardship of the creation. They looked for the fulfillment of the promise of victory and liberation from the curse. Among them the arts and sciences would serve the LORD's purposes, as will be seen in the building of the ark by Noah.

Public worship in the line of Seth was accompanied by strong personal fellowship with God. It is recorded of Enoch that "he walked with God" (Gen. 5:22). This expression is used elsewhere only of Noah (6:9) and of Levi (Mal. 2:6). It describes intimacy of fellowship with God in a righteous, blameless life, as in the case of Noah (Gen. 6:9). The description of Levi in Malachi 2:5-6 gives the broad significance of the expression.

> "My covenant was with him of life and peace; and I gave
> them to him for the fear wherewith he feared me, and was
> afraid of my name. The law of truth was in his mouth, and
> iniquity was not found in his lips; he walked with me in
> peace and equity, and did turn many away from iniquity."

The Septuagint translates "he walked with God" as "he pleased God." This is what is said of Enoch in Hebrews 11:5. He pleased God, not by ascetic pursuit, but by being occupied with his family as the rest of the men of his time: "Enoch walked with God after he begat Methuselah three hundred years and begat sons and daughters." The life that pleases God is one that honors Him in the whole of life's involvements.

The fact that Enoch walked with God is related by its repetition in God's taking him from the earth. Aalders renders it "God took him to Himself," explaining that the word means "separation from its prior environment" and "implies a being brought near to the subject doing the taking."[10] Thus the man who lived in the presence of God on earth was taken into the presence of God forever. In this way God gave a witness to that age before the flood that life lived in fellowship with Him is eternal life:

---

[10] *Ibid.*, 141.

there is life after death (*cf.* John 11:26).

That the line of Seth lived by the covenant of grace is clear from the statement of Lamech in naming his son Noah: "This same shall comfort us concerning the work and toil of our hands, because of the ground which the LORD has cursed" (Gen. 5:29). They bore the curse in hope of deliverance, in hope that God would give a deliverer through "the seed of the woman" (*cf.* Rom. 8:20-22).

After the flood Noah built an altar to the Lord and offered a burnt offering of clean animals and birds on it. This is the first recorded instance of building an altar, of burning the sacrifice, and of the choice of clean animals for sacrifice (*cf.* Gen. 7:2). This differs from the offering of Cain and Abel also in that it is a "burnt offering," not a "gift." "Burnt offering" comes from a word meaning "to go up," and signifies that the offering ascends to God in fire and smoke. Though it is a first in these several ways, since no explanation is given in connection with this sacrifice, we may assume that it was a common kind of sacrifice offered in the usual way.

We are to recognize the offering as thanksgiving for preservation in the flood, and as supplication for God's blessing as Noah and his family went out to a new life on the earth. As Kidner says, "Homage, dedication and atonement are all expressed in the *burnt offerings*: the new earth is to be God's, if He will have it."[11]

"The LORD smelled a sweet savour" (Gen. 8:21). God was pleased with Noah's offering. His wrath was appeased, and He covenanted with Noah and "with every living creature that is with you, for perpetual generations" (9:12) that he would never again destroy the earth with a flood as he had done. Man worshipped; God responded with a covenant sign, the rainbow, in confirmation of His promised mercy (8:21; 9:8-17). God had judged the ancient world, destroying it save for four pairs of men and one or seven pairs of animals and birds. From now on His judgment would be tempered with mercy for the purification of creation rather than its destruction (*cf.* II Pet. 3:5-15a).

---

[11]Kidner, *op.cit.*, 93. See Aalders, *op.cit.*, 179, and Keil, *op.cit.*, 150f.

The Covenant with Abraham

By the covenant with Noah, God promised to withhold universal judgment until He had accomplished His purpose of universal salvation by the seed of the woman, setting the stage for the special work of redemption which God was about to begin with Abraham and his family. By this covenant He would bring salvation to all nations of the earth.

God began to move in a special way to fulfil the covenant of grace when He called Abraham to leave Ur of the Chaldees for the land God would show him. There He promised to make him a great nation, to bless him and to make him a blessing to all the peoples of the earth. God confirmed this promise by a covenant, swearing by Himself to accomplish it (Gen. 15:17-18; Heb. 6:13-19). "And he believed in the LORD; and he counted it to him for righteousness" (Gen. 15:6). So he became the father of all who believe (Rom. 6:11, 12). Faith is the mark of all God's people, being the only way of approach to Him, the only way to please Him (Heb. 11:6). This statement about Abraham is important because faith is the basic characteristic of worship.

Abraham's life was marked by intimate fellowship with God. God showed him the land of promise, that is, He went with him, leading him by the hand, as it were (cf. Isa. 41:8-9; Jer. 31:32). He was called the friend of God (Isa. 41:8; James 2:23). Friends communicate and respond to one another. Where God is one of the parties, that means revelation from Him, a blameless walk before Him, and worship of Him (John 15:14, 15). "Abraham fell on his face: and God talked with him" (Gen. 17:30). Thus Abraham acknowledged the master-servant footing of the covenant. Hence, "the relationship could grow into the full stature of friendship."[12]

Abraham's tent sites were marked by altars. At Shechem the Lord appeared to Abraham and said, "Unto thy seed will I give this land" (Gen. 12:7). Abraham responded by building an altar to the Lord who had appeared to him. So also he did at Bethel (v. 8) and at Hebron (13:18). An

---

[12]Kidner, op.cit., 129.

altar is the place of animal sacrifice. No extensive ritual is described, but two things developed in Abraham's worship. He built altars at the places where God appeared to him. Place became important, the place of revelation. This is the place he had been called to seek as home for himself and his descendents forever. His whole life and mission is to be here. Here he will die and be buried, here in the place to which God had called him, because the Lord is here.

Secondly, the altar and the presence of God is also the place of public worship. "There [at Bethel] he builded an altar unto the Lord and called upon the name of the Lord" (12:8; so also Isaac at Beersheba, 26:23). We have already seen above that "to call on the name of the Lord" signifies to proclaim the name of the Lord in public worship. Remarking that Abraham's camp included a considerable number of people (318 armed men--14:14), Aalders comments, "Abraham gathered his entire entourage together and led them in public prayers to God."[13] This is not just a pious guess by Aalders. In Genesis 18:19 God says of Abraham, "For I have known him, that he will command his children and his household after him, and they shall keep the way of the Lord, to do justice and judgment; that the Lord may bring upon Abraham that which he hath spoke of him." When we consider that Abraham was to bring all his hired servants into the covenant by circumcision (17:12-13), no mere outward sign (Deut. 10:16; Jer. 4:4), we see that proclamation of the covenant, as well as prayers, must have been a regular part of Abraham's household worship. A strong case in point is the way Abraham's servant, whom he sent to find a wife for his son Isaac, prayed for guidance, and then thanked the Lord for leading him to the house of Laban to Rebecca, just as Abraham would have done.[14]

The verb most frequently translated "to worship" in the Old Testament is first used of Abraham when he went to offer Isaac in sacrifice to God. As he left the young men with the donkey to go on alone with

---

[13] Aalders, op.cit., 272.

[14] It is worth noting that altars were the only permanent markers of their camps to which the patriarchs returned.

Isaac, he said to them, "Abide ye here with the ass; and I and the lad will go yonder and worship, and come again to you" (22:5). Abraham's servant, just mentioned, when Rebecca watered his camels and invited him to her father's house, "bowed down his head and worshipped the Lord" (24:26, 48). The verb means to bow down in courtesy, respect, homage, reverence, submission, and carried all of these ideas when used in respect of God. It is often used with other expressions that mean to bow down, often to the earth, to bend the knee, and to fall flat on one's face in show of humility and submission. The patriarchs clearly associated the ideas of humility, reverence, and submission with their bowing down before God.

Sacrifice takes on more specific form when it is related to covenant making. In Genesis 15 God swore to make Abraham's seed as numerous as the stars and to give him a land from the river of Egypt to the Euphrates. He was to take a heifer, a goat and a ram, each three years old, and a dove and a young pigeon. The animals were to be divided and the parts laid out opposite each other; the birds were to remain whole. Abraham fell into a deep sleep in which he beheld God as a "smoking furnace and a burning lamp that passed between those pieces" (v. 17). Thus God acted out before Abraham a self-imposed death oath to provide the promised seed and to accomplish His blessing upon Abraham and the nations. Here we have the first intimation that the covenant Maker will give His life to accomplish the covenant. Thus God drew Abraham into an amazing act of worship to behold the condescending mercy of the Lord.

Abraham was given the covenant sign of circumcision in which he should present himself, his children and his whole household in solemn life-death commitment to God and receive from God the seal of His work in them. God would circumcise their hearts, giving them new hearts (cf. Deut. 30:6).

The offering of Isaac came as the supreme test of Abraham's love for God. "Take now thy son, thine only son Isaac, whom thou lovest . . . and sacrifice him there as a burnt offering" (Gen. 22:2). Abraham believed the promise that his seed would be through Isaac, and proceeded to the sacrifice of the promised seed. The one through whom the covenant promise is to be realized is condemned to die. God spared his life by providing a ram in the place of Isaac. Thus Abraham learned more specifically the substitutionary character of sacrifice. Isaac, being born in the image of his father (*cf.* Gen. 5:3), is under condemnation of death, but is spared at the altar by a substitute, the ram. That is the law of sacrifice. The seed of Abraham, now alive, having been delivered from death (or through death) is the instrument of blessing to the nations. Thus Isaac, the first covenant heir, represents the future Seed of Abraham, who will give His life that the covenant promise of blessing may come on all nations.

Abraham would not again offer Isaac, but he and his descendents will continue to offer rams, goats, heifers, and birds as he had done before. In the worship acts of His people God is hiding the representations of the covenant realities. He is making clearer what He wants from His people and what the acts He asks from them mean. It is also becoming clearer that man's approach to God in worship is in response to the call, presence and direction of God; and that man can come to Him only through sacrifice.

Isaac and Jacob followed the pattern set for them by Abraham. God illustrates more specifically His calling and election in the birth of Isaac and the choice of Jacob. God appeared to each to renew the covenant with them (Gen. 26:1-5; 28:10-13), and to bless them and direct their lives in the covenant (26:23-24; 31:3, 10-13; 32:24-31; 35:1, 9-13; 46:2-4). They responded by building altars and worshipping the Lord (26:25; 33:20; 35:7-20) as Abraham had done. Isaac prayed for a child, and God answered; Rebecca became pregnant (25:21). Rebecca "inquired of the Lord" about her distress in the pregnancy and the Lord told her His plans for the twins in her womb (25:22, 23). The patriarchs were made prophets to guide their descendents (27:27-29; 35:5-6, 9; 48:14-22; 49:1-27). Jacob marked the place where God appeared to him and blessed him by erecting a stone pillar and anointing it with oil (28:18, 22; 35:14-15), proclaiming it as God's house and naming it Bethel. He also made a vow to give God the tithe of his possessions as a token of thanksgiving and submission when God had kept him in his journey and brought him back in peace. This is the first mention of vowing to God. Jacob's full commitment to God came later in a struggle with the angel at Peniel (Gen. 32:24-32). With wounded thigh and tears (Hosea 12:4), he begged for mercy, not willing to let go until God, whom he had offended by cheating Esau, deceiving Isaac, and cleverly outwitting Laban, should bless him. Thus Jacob was brought to repentance for his sins, and to trust only in God's grace. Worship that "prevails with God" changes the life-style of the worshipper.[15] He called upon God who had shepherded him all his life and the angel who delivered him from all harm to bless the sons of Joseph (Gen. 48:15-16). He was confessing at last that God had provided for and guarded him in all those years of struggling for position and family and wealth.

We cannot close our account of worship in patriarchal times without noting two men completely outside the covenant: Melchizedek and Job. The former was a Canaanite, "priest of God Most High, Creator of heaven and earth," whom Abraham also worshipped and by whom he swore (Gen. 14:18-24). Abraham paid to Melchizedek "the tithe of all," which was later recognized to belong to God to be given to the priests for their service to the Lord (Lev. 27:30-32; Num. 18:21-24). Melchizedek exceeds Aaron as a type of Messiah (Ps. 110; Heb. 7).

Job is described as a blameless and upright man who "feared God and shunned evil" (1:1, NIV). He had a keen sense of the need to be right with God. Fearing that his sons may have "sinned and cursed God in their hearts" in their merry-making, he regularly sacrificed a burnt offering for each of them (vv. 4-5, NIV). In grief at the loss of family and property "he fell down on the ground and worshipped, . . . [and] blessed the name of the Lord." He did not sin by charging God with wrongdoing (vv. 21-22). His cry for vindication in his intense suffering was answered by the Lord from a whirlwind. God spoke of His inscrutable ways and the unfathomable wisdom of His works. Job heard, his soul was quieted and he "repented in dust and ashes" (42:5-6). Thus he is in a position to pray for his three erring friends (42:8-9). Job gave evidence throughout that he lived in piety, confidently trusting in God, caring for widow and orphan and showing mercy to the poor. He greatly resembles the patriarchs, though it appears that God's communication with him was less personal and more indefinite

---

[15]See Aalders, *op.cit.*, 142-45.

than with them.

Thus there was universal knowledge and worship of God based on the covenant of grace from the time of Noah and Shem. There was common knowledge of animal sacrifice for sin and of the function of priesthood. But God was beginning a special work of grace through his call of Abraham. The patriarchs as head of the household performed the offices of priest and prophet, leading them in worship, and speaking God's revealed word to them. On occasions God reached out through them to those around them. God was beginning to make Himself known to the Canaanites and the Egyptians, and to leave them without excuse through His chosen people. The knowledge of God would be present in the world through them.

The Mosaic Covenant

This is the period of the most concentrated self-revelation of God, giving the most specific directions how man may approach Him. God draws near to Israel as the God who had covenanted with their fathers Abraham, Isaac and Jacob (Ex. 2:23-24). His name is LORD, Jehovah (3:5). This name had been used by Adam and Eve and the patriarchs, but only now is its meaning declared. The LORD comes to Israel to fulfil His covenant promises by redeeming them from slavery in Egypt and by bringing them to live with Him in His land (6:6-9; 15:17-18). "I will take you to me for a people, and I will be to you a God; and ye shall know that I am the LORD your God" (6:7). "I brought you to myself" (19:3). The Sinai Covenant drew Israel into a union of love and fidelity with the LORD God. It demanded commitment of heart and body in loving service to God, to accomplish His eternal purpose that all the nations of earth should serve Him. God sealed the covenant by giving them the tabernacle where He dwelt among them and received them in worship (25:8; 29:44-45; 40:34). Above all else, Israel was distinct from the nations in that God dwelt among them (33:16).

As the model of God's heavenly sanctuary, the tabernacle was to be made with the greatest care following the model God showed Moses (25:9, 40; and frequently). The workmen executed the plan precisely (39:42-43).

Moses set it up "just as the Lord commanded" (40:16 and eight times). The book of Leviticus is the detailed prescription of sacrifices and how they were to be performed, of the mediating ministry of the priests, of purification ceremonies, of the requirement of holiness "as I am holy" in every sphere of life, of the festivals of worship showing men when and how they might approach God with assurance that He would receive them graciously.

"The place will be consecrated by my glory" (Ex. 29:43). God is infinitely holy and cannot look upon sin. No man can see His face and live (Ex. 33:20; 19:21; cf. Gen. 16:13; 35:30; Isa. 6:5). But God is gracious and comes to man. He hid the brilliance of His face from Israel at Sinai by the cloud (Ex. 19:14-19; 20:21; Deut. 5:22-26). In the tabernacle He dwelt among His people, yet hid Himself behind the curtain, His presence guarded by cherubim as was the tree of life when man was driven from the Garden (Ex. 25:18-22; Gen. 3:24). The whole tabernacle was most carefully guarded by the Levites from improper, unauthorized approach (Num. 1:51-53). Only Aaron, the High Priest, and his sons the priests and Levites could serve at the tabernacle (Num. 3:5-10; 17). The High Priest only could enter the presence of God behind the curtain, and he only once a year, with the blood of sacrifice on the Day of Atonement (Lev. 16:1-17). Thus the curtain prevented Israel's entrance to God's presence, but it also assured them that God was there and that they could enter through the High Priest in the appointed manner and at the set time. The bells on his garments made a joyful sound, announcing that God had accepted him as he performed his service in the Holy of Holies and returned to the waiting people outside (Ex. 28:33-35). Thus all Israel rejoiced in meeting God.

Israel was called to worship at the tabernacle. Burnt offerings were presented by the priests morning and evening for the whole congregation of Israel (Num. 28:3-8). The individual presented his offerings in confession of sin and self-dedication to God with assurance that his offering was accepted to make atonement for him, and that he was forgiven (Lev. 1:34; 4:26, 31, 35). A "holy convocation" was to be held each Sabbath (Lev. 23:2-3). When Israel was settled in the land, this could not be at the central sanctuary each week, but all males were called to worship there three times a year, at the feasts of Unleavened Bread, First Fruits of the harvest, and Tabernacles or

Ingathering (Ex. 23:15-17). And none was to come "empty handed," that is, without an offering. In these feasts they celebrated the saving acts of the Lord in Egypt and the wilderness, and His provision of the annual crops. This reminded them that they belonged to the Lord and that all they had was the gift of His grace to them.

Besides the offering of the first fruit of every crop, every seventh and fiftieth year the land was to lie idle in remembrance that it belonged to God, and that He gave the crops yearly. They could eat what grew, but they could not store it up; the poor were to gather it. Thus the poor, the widow and orphan, the Levite and stranger were to share in their tithes (Deut. 26:12-13), in the abundance God gave in the seventh and fiftieth years. Those who had no one to provide for them, or were foreigners living in the land, were to have opportunity to join in the joyful celebration of God's goodness in creating them a people and in providing abundantly for them daily.

These ceremonial observances were signs and seals of the covenant, marking their union with God and reminding them of His sanctifying grace in them, calling them to be holy instruments of His rest and peace to the nations (Lev. 19:1; 20:7, 8; Ex. 19:5-6). These ceremonies were more than ordinances of the Mosaic Covenant. They joined it with the creation covenant and the covenant of grace (Gen. 1:28; 2:3, 4; 3:15-19). They were the object lessons of the holiness of God, the awfulness of sin, and the need of a substitutionary death for the sinner to experience forgiveness. The repetition of sacrifice on the Day of Atonement demonstrated the fact that the daily burnt offerings and the sin and trespass offerings had not actually accomplished what they represented--for animal sacrifice cannot take away sin. Israel rested in the promise of God, "It shall be forgiven him" (Lev. 5:10, 16), and they knew the assurance of forgiveness (Ps. 32:1-5). But their eyes were turned toward a sacrifice that would take sin away. These ceremonies that were to be carried out exactly as prescribed (note the consequences of unauthorized performance, Lev. 10:1-3), because they represented Divine action (see Heb. 8-10), would someday be displaced by that accomplishment. The seeds of this hope were present in and stimulated by the ceremonies themselves, and in the promised blessings and curses of

the covenant: in spite of Israel's unfaithfulness and God's judgment, God
will redeem them (Lev. 26:40-45) and His glory will indeed fill the earth
(Num. 14:20).

These ceremonies were not dead rituals. They were more than
instructive observances. They were the way by which Israel spontaneously
responded to God, confident that they were accepted by Him. The making
of offerings and the celebration of the festivals were times of great rejoicing
(Lev. 23:40; Deut. 12:7, 12, 18; etc.). There was great joy in the observance
of the Passover in the days of Hezekiah, so that they doubled the time of the
feast of Unleavened Bread: "their voice was heard, and their prayer came up
to his holy dwelling place, even unto heaven" (II Chron. 30:23-27). In Asa's
time all the people rejoiced at the revival of true religion with "shouting,
trumpets and horns" (II Chron. 15:11-15). At the dedication of the walls in
Nehemiah's time there was great rejoicing and celebration in the offering of
sacrifices and the renewal of the covenant (Neh. 8-11). The reality of their
joy was manifest in their provision for the priests and Levites according to
the law, a matter they had previously neglected (12:43-47).

The law was given as part of the covenant to the redeemed people
(Ex. 20:2) to show them how to live in thankfulness as the people of God
(Deut. 4:1; 5:33, and frequently). God freely loved Israel (Deut. 7:6-10), and
Israel was called to respond by loving Him with heart and body, by keeping
His commandments with all their heart (6:4-9). The moral and the
ceremonial were all part of one inseparable whole of God's way of life for
His people.

Pleasing worship began in fearing God and keeping His
commandments. It continued in the offering of sacrifices in a broken spirit
and a contrite heart (Ps. 51). As Samuel said to Saul, the Lord delights in
obedience more than in sacrifices, "For rebellion is as the sin of witchcraft,
and stubbornness is as iniquity and idolatry" (I Sam. 15:22-23). God hates
meaningless offerings, evil assemblies, keeping feasts by wrong doers, said
Isaiah (1:11-17). Wicked men cannot buy God's favour by sacrifices (Ps.
50:7-13). God warned that if men desecrated His dwelling place, He would
destroy it (I Ki. 9:6-9). Since Abraham the core of covenant religion has
been blameless walk before God (Gen. 17:1). Covenant life is walking

humbly with God and doing justice and mercy with men. This is more desirable to God than sacrifices and burnt offerings (Hosea 6:6; Micah 6:8; Deut. 10:10-12).

The first of Israel's songs comes from the pen of Moses, celebrating God's victory at the Red Sea (Ex. 15).

> "The Lord is my strength and song
>   and he is become my salvation;
> he is my God, and I will praise him,
>   my father's God, and I will exult him." (v. 3, KJV)

The song continues to laud the incomparable greatness of the Lord's works, His majestic holiness and awesome glory. Israel may have sung this at the annual festivals, particularly the Passover and Tabernacles, although nothing is mentioned of this. Phrases of it re-occur in Israel's later hymns of praise (*cf.* Is. 12).

As they neared the end of the wilderness journey, song breaks forth again as they find water in digging a well in the desert, as they reach the Arnon after the weary jouney around Moab, and as they have victory in Trans-Jordan (Num. 21). This is a refreshing breath after their all too frequent murmurings against Moses and God during those forty years. It must be to those songs that Hosea refers when he says that restored Israel will again sing as she sang in the days of her youth when she came out of Egypt (2:15).

At God's command Moses wrote a song of "witness for Me against the children of Israel" when they turn to other gods (Deut. 31:19-22). Moses recited the song in the hearing of all the congregation (32). We do not hear of Israel singing it, but it may have been used to bring Israel to repentance in the days of the judges and in the defections of the kings of Israel and Judah. It contains seed thoughts often developed by later prophets: God the Rock, the Creator of Israel, their Saviour, jealous of His own worship, and of Israel His chosen inheritance from among the nations. It is a song of judgment, but also of deliverance and salvation for Israel and the nations.

A notable worship experience of Israel occurred at the inauguration of the covenant at Sinai (Ex. 24). Moses wrote all the words of the Lord in the book of the covenant. He offered twelve bulls. He read the book of the covenant and the people said, "All that the Lord hath said will we do, and be obedient." Moses sprinkled the blood on the people, saying, "Behold the blood of the covenant which the Lord hath made with you concerning these words." Then Moses, Aaron, Nadab and Abihu and seventy of the elders of Israel ascended Mt. Sinai where they saw God in all His heavenly splendor and glory. They ate and drank with Him, and God received them graciously (note v. 11). God was not yet fully revealed to Israel. Only representatives of the congregation could eat and drink with the Lord; but what a foretaste of the day when the whole congregation should eat and drink with the Lord of the church, Jesus Christ; and of the yet future day when the redeemed shall partake of the wedding feast of the Lamb! The Sinai Covenant continually opened up to Israel the glories that should follow (I Pet. 1:11). Israel saw God from a distance, and they worshipped in hope. This covenant continued to direct the worship of Israel throughout the Old Testament, but it is supplemented and enlarged through the covenant with David.

The Davidic Covenant

God took David from feeding sheep to "be the shepherd of his people Jacob, of Israel his inheritance" (Ps. 78:71). More than that, he "sat on the throne of the Lord as king" (*cf.* I Chron. 29:23), in the understanding that it was God's eternal throne, a law for all mankind (II Sam. 7:19, Hebrew text). David was the regal authority of the Kingdom of God visible. Besides, he was a prophet, a poet and a musician, and as such greatly influenced the broad spectrum of kingdom life, especially worship.

David had a great desire to build a house for God in keeping with his own house. Although he was not permitted to do that, he made considerable preparations for the temple which his son Solomon should build, organizing the priestly service by courses and initiating the use of instrumental music and choirs in the temple service.

The sounding of the ram's horn trumpet, a divine, not human, blast,[16] called Israel out of the camp to meet God at Sinai (Ex. 19:13, 16, 19). Later the trumpet announced the annual Day of Atonement, various assemblies and festivals and to proclaim liberty in the year of Jubilee (Num. 10:1-10; Lev. 25:9). The priests blew trumpets over the burnt offerings and peace offerings as "a memorial for you before the Lord." All this had the effect of announcement rather than the making of music.

Tambourines accompanied the joyful singing of the women in celebrating the victory of God over the Egyptians at the Red Sea (Ex. 15:20-21). When the ark of God was brought to Jerusalem, David asked the chief of the Levites to appoint their brethren "to be singers with instruments of music, psalteries and harps and cymbals, sounding, by lifting up the voice with joy" (I Chron. 15:16). David gave to Asaph and his choir a psalm of thanks to the Lord, to which all the people responded, "Amen, praise the Lord" (16:7-36).

This use of instruments and choirs was to become permanent in the temple as David appointed musicians, choirs and choir leaders (I Chron. 25). Asaph, Heman and Jeduthan and their sons were set apart "for the ministry of prophesying by harps, lyres and cymbals" under the supervision of the king. Delitzsch understands the meaning of "prophesy" here to be "in its wider signification of the singing and playing to the praise of God performed in the power of the Divine Spirit."[17] The prophets Gad and Nathan were associated with David in this prescription of temple worship (II Chron. 29:25).

The description of worship in Hezekiah's renewal of the temple after the defection of Ahaz is especially instructive. There was apparently a renewal of the covenant, although it is not described (II Chron. 29:10). The Levites prepared, at Hezekiah's command, to do the service according to the prescription of David, Gad and Nathan "as the Lord had commanded" (v.

---

[16]See W. H. Gispen, *Bible Students' Commentary, Exodus* (Grand Rapids: Zondervan, 1982), 182.

[17]Keil and Delitzsch, *Chronicles*, 270.

27). As the offering began, singing began, accompanied by instrumental music. This continued until the sacrifices of burnt offering were completed. As the singers sang and the instruments played the congregation bowed in worship. When the offering was completed the king and the whole assembly knelt down and worshipped, "the Levites [praised] the Lord with the words of David and Asaph and bowed their heads and worshipped" (v. 30). The whole assembly then brought sacrifices and thank offerings with willing hearts (v. 31).

Thus the instrumental music and singing by choirs was a part of the sacrificial service of mediated atonement. In itself, the sacrifice could not take away sin, for sins were remembered on the Day of Atonement every year. The sacrificial service anticipated a sacrifice that would cause sin to be remembered no more. It was a "copy" of the reality yet to be revealed (*cf.* Heb. 8:5). But it must also be noted that the sacrificial service was not just representative of a future reality. By it men genuinely approached God with willing hearts as they knelt down, bowed their heads and worshipped. They were confident that they were meeting with God, that they had been received into His presence, and that their sins had been forgiven (Ps. 103:3-5; 66:16-20; 73:23-28; 84; etc.).

The Book of Psalms was given for the whole congregation, not just for the Levitical choirs. In it Israel called the whole world to join with them in praise to God. Hence there is in the Psalter a strong eschatological anticipation of the achievements of the Messianic, the gospel age, which are yet to be realized. Believing Israel, as represented in the Psalms, was truly a missionary people looking forward to the day when the peoples of every nation and tongue would join in the praise of the one true God.

That there is a complete book given to the subject of praise is worthy of note, indicating the divine intention to direct praise. The formation of the Psalter is not at all clear. The expression "of the choirmaster," found in 55 titles (all but two of which are accompanied by other significations, such as "of David" or "of Asaph"), suggests that a temple song leader collected songs by these authors for use by his choir. The Psalms of David and of Asaph and of the sons of Korah may have already been known in groups. They would have been available by the time of Hezekiah's reformation, already mentioned, which may have spurred on the collection already in process.[18] Psalms 113 to 118 have traditionally been connected with the Passover observance. Samuel Cox may be correct in his suggestion that the "Songs of Decrees" or "Ascents" were songs sung by the pilgrims on their way to and from the annual feasts at Jerusalm, since they frequently mention Jerusalem and the going to or coming from the Lord's house.[19]

The earliest is Psalm 90, "A Prayer of Moses the man of God." The latest (126) describes the return from captivity,[20] but with the people still in distress (see v. 4). The psalms cover the length and breadth of the revealed purpose of God from creation to the judgment; the flood, the call to Abraham, Jacob, Joseph, the exodus, Moses, the giving of the law at Sinai, the conquest of Canaan, David, the temple, the captivity and the restoration. It touches the gamut of human experience from conception in the womb to old age, death and decay in the grave. It describes the home and family, prosperity, persecution of the righteous man, the wicked. A large place is given to the greatness and glory of God, His kingdom and law, the Messiah, His suffering and distress, the cry of hope and the joyful shout of deliverance. And there are communal songs of distress and victory. Choirs had a significant part in temple worship, as we have observed above, but the psalms are not addressed to them, nor do they arise in their artistry. They express the broad experiences of individual and communal life of the people of God under God's call in a world of sin and evil, the kingdom of God against the kingdom of Satan. Like the rest of Scripture the Psalter was given for the consolation and strength of the whole people of God, to be stored in the heart and mind and to guide the feet in the ways of peace.

There were other songs in Scripture that did not find a place in the Book of Psalms. We have already mentioned songs from the time of Moses.

---

[18] Note that Hezekiah's men copied out Proverbs by Solomon and added them to an already existing collection (II Chron. 25).

[19] Samuel Cox, *The Pilgrim Psalms* (London: R. D. Dickinson, 1885).

[20] For another view, see Derek Kidner, *Psalms*, II, and the *New Bible Commentary*.

We may mention also the song of Deborah and Barak in Judges 5, the song of Habakkuk (ch. 3), the song of Hezekiah (Is. 38:9-20), and the songs of Isaiah (*e.g.*, 42:10-13). The books of the Old Testament were recognized to be the Word of God when they appeared, and so were accepted as authoritative in the life of His people. This was undoubtedly the case with the Book of Psalms, as indicated by Jesus' recognition of it as having authority upon His life with the rest of Scripture (Luke 24:44). What effect this had on the use of those songs in Scripture which were not in the Book of Psalms is difficult to determine. However it is not difficult to recognize that the existence of a Book of Praises within the recognized books had considerable weight in determining the songs used in worship.

There is another act of worship in the Old Testament that must not be overlooked. Israel's relation to God was covenantal. This required commitment by all who approached God. "Walk before me and be thou perfect. And I will make my covenant between me and thee, . . . " (Gen. 17:1, 2). God renewed covenant with Isaac and Jacob when they became head of their households. In the plains of Moab, just before they were to cross the Jordan, God renewed covenant with the new generation of Israel that had grown up in the wilderness. Joshua gathered all Israel at Shechem and renewed the covenant.

> "And the people said to Joshua, The Lord our God will we
> serve, and his voice will we obey. So Joshua made a
> covenant with the people that day, and set them a statute
> and an ordinance in Shechem. And Joshua wrote these
> words in the book of the law of God, and took a great
> stone, and set it up there under an oak that was by the
> sanctuary of the Lord." (Joshua 24:24-26)

In the time of King Asa after the evil reigns of Rehoboam and Abijah, the prophet Azariah the son of Oded encouraged Asa to seek the Lord: "[I]f you seek him, he will be found of you" (II Chron. 15:2). He called all Judah and Benjamin to Jerusalem. They were joined by people from Ephraim, Manasseh and Simeon who recognized that the Lord was with Asa. "They entered into a covenant to seek the Lord God of their fathers with all their heart and with all their soul." There was great rejoicing at the oath, "for they had sworn with all their heart, and sought him with their whole desire, and he was found of them" (vv. 12, 14). Similar experiences are recorded in the time of Hezekiah (29:10), Josiah (34:30-33) and Ezra and Nehemiah (Neh. 9, 10). In each case the covenant was followed by significant reforms appropriate to the times of defection that preceeded them.

Old Testament worship was defined in minute detail, and God guarded His presence with jealousy because the acts of worship were instructive of the character of God, the Holy One, of the nature of man and sin, and of how God deals with sinners through Christ. At the same time God called for loving obedience and worship and gave room for man's whole-hearted response. One cannot read the Old Testament, either in the writings or its historical or prophetic sections, without recognizing that, while Israel failed miserably and rebelled most stubbornly, there was always a remnant of grace, God's faithful 7,000 who loved Him, served Him joyfully and spontaneously worshipped and adored Him because they knew His forgiveness and abundant and loving provision for them. Only one thing was lacking, the promise that they awaited: "The Lord, whom ye seek, shall suddenly come to his temple, even the messenger of the covenant, whom ye delight in" (Mal. 3:1).

4 - "HEAR YE HIM":
WORSHIP IN THE NEW TESTAMENT

Sherman Isbell

The Zurich reformer Heinrich Bullinger placed on the title page of several of his books the words, "This is my beloved Son, in whom I am well pleased; hear ye him"(Mt. 17:5), as indicative of the source of authority for the gospel doctrines Bullinger published. These are words particularly pertinent to New Testament worship, because they direct us to the "One" whose voice is the sole rule for appropriate worship. In our brief essay our purpose is not to encompass the full scope of New Testament teaching on worship. Rather we shall center our thoughts on aspects of continuity and discontinuity between Old and New Testaments.

WORSHIP ACTIVITY

Throughout Biblical history God has given His church ordinances of worship by which He is to be approached. Certain solemn forms and ceremonies have been invested by God's Word with significance for worship. God has been glorified as His people obeyed His instructions, employing these rites as the vehicles for rendering praise to Him. Indeed, observance of these ordinances has been a test of the submission of God's people to His revealed will. In the garden of Eden, the tree of the knowledge of good and evil was given to put Adam's obedience under trial. Circumcising the males of his household was the responsibility of Abraham. Remembering the Lord's death by the giving and receiving of bread and wine is a duty which no believer may ignore.

The Lord's designation of certain ordinances for worship continues in the New Testament church. No doubt the New Testament apostles use the language of an Old Testament ordinance figuratively to describe the believer seeking to honor God in all the course of life (Rom. 12:1-2, I Pet.

2:5). But far more commonly in the New Testament we read of worship ordinances which are to be kept when the church comes together in its assemblies: prayer, reading the Word, preaching, congregational singing of Psalms, baptism, the Lord's Supper.

What is it, then, that gives legitimacy to any particular activity, for it to be included in worship? Is it the experience of God's people, who find over a period of time that some practices are conducive to feelings of reverence and adoration? Is it the value God's people see in them for dramatizing the truths of the gospel? Is it the likelihood of drawing unbelievers who might be impressed with activities that seem to be as sophisticated or entertaining as something they might see in the secular world? Is it the consensus judgment of the church's governing elders which should determine what is appropriate ceremonies for us in worship?

In Mark 7:3-13, Jesus instructs us that worship is vain when its practices are based on the traditions of men, and do not have a warrant in God's Word. "In vain do they worship me, teaching for doctrines the commandments of men." Jesus cites these words from the book of the prophet Isaiah, disclosing that there is a continuity of principle here between Old and New Testament. It is in the commandments of God alone that we are to seek direction for acceptable worship. Worship has become misguided and has lost its value when it is not the result of obedience to an authorizing command from God. The authority of a human tradition cannot make an action righteous, nor make activity an ordinance of worship in Christ's church. Never in the Scriptures do men institute a practice for religious worship, and then meet with Divine approval of their conduct. In Mark 7 we have such an instance of Divine condemnation when men sanctioned religious practices not required by God.

What is it that has raised washing, eating, drinking and singing to the significance of being ordinances of worship for the New Testament church? Might painting, dancing and dramatic plays be given a similar standing? It is the Word of God alone which sanctions a sacramental association between the crucified body of Christ and the bread of the Lord's Supper. No other authority can draw that connection. Only the Word of

God can provide the warrant that transforms any activity into a worship ordinance. True worship is an act of obedience rendered to a Biblical command requiring the performance of that activity as a duty.

In this the sovereign Lord asserts His own wisdom and good pleasure in the determination of what will be acceptable elements of worship. According to Mark 7, worship activity is only glorifying to God when it is sanctioned by His command. Without God's word of institution for the service we offer Him, what we do in worship is fruitless. In passing from the Old Testament to the New, God has not surrendered His exclusive prerogative as the determiner of worship ordinances. The differences between Old and New Testament worship lie elsewhere.

John 4:23-24 may reflect, in part, the need for inwardness in worship. Jesus frequently inculcates the necessity of inward integrity in worship (Mt. 5:23-24; 6:16-18; 12:7). This integrity is envisaged as showing itself in behavior. But central in John 4 is the imperative that worship be consonant with the nature of God. "God is Spirit, and those who worship him must worship in spirit and truth." Truth in worship means that the content and mode of our worship must correspond to the reality of who God is (Acts 17:16, 24-25, 29). It is this requisite which is provided for by Divine revelation, and by Divine prescription of such worship activities as are in accord with the glory of God. There would be changes in some of the specific forms as the church passed from Old to New Testament, and some of these changes would reflect the temporary character of old covenant type and shadow. What abides is that true worship is consonant with God's nature, and that the religious practices appropriate to the worship of the living and true God are derived from His revealed Word rather than from human judgment (Col. 2:18-23, Rom. 1:21-25).

Why is it such a common feature of church life in our day that activities never required by God in the Scriptures are introduced into worship? Is it not because men fear that the few and simple practices prescribed in Scripture will be insufficient to build the church? Is there not an underlying anxiety that further means beyond the Biblical ordinances must be devised in order to secure the welfare and prosperity of the church?

Jesus sent the apostles to disciple and baptize the nations, and specified that the instruction they would give should be "to observe all things that I have commanded you." The risen Savior accompanied this injunction with the assurance that His presence in grace and power would attend His church as it acted in observance of His commands. "All authority has been given to me in heaven and on earth, and lo, I am with you always, even to the end of the age." (Mt. 28:18-20). Christ has provided in the New Testament the institution of such ordinances of worship, and an eldership to dispense them, as will sufficiently minister to the holiness and comfort of His people and the increase of His kingdom, through His gracious presence in their midst (Mt. 18:20; Acts 1:8; 5:31-32).

Indeed the building of Christ's church may proceed by means of such suffering, humiliation and hardship as men would not choose (Mt. 16:21-23), and much is often done to avoid the pain, the humbling and the shame which God has always used in the growth of the kingdom. It was in the humiliation of God's Son that the kingdom was brought to birth, and the kingdom will not be built without painful self-denial, crucifying the flesh and losing of one's life in following Christ (Mt. 16:24-26, Mark 10:39, Col. 1:24, I Cor. 4:9-13).

Nevertheless Christ has given us His pledge that as His servants fulfill his mandate, conforming their teaching and practice to His requirements, Christ will be with the church, with all the redemptive blessings implicit in His Divine presence. It is He who nourishes and cherishes the church, sanctifying it with the washing of water by the Word. He does this in part by supplying gifts and officers to His body, causing growth of the body for the edifying of itself in love (Eph. 5:25-29, 4:7-16; Mt. 16:16-19). The institutions in Scripture, coupled with the presence of the Savior among His people, are sufficient to attain the Savior's purpose for His church.

What, then, are we to make of efforts to add institutions of worship not required by God? Will Christ be present to bless what His people ingeniously contrive as supplements to His institutions? Can God's benediction be secured for the variety of new worship activities devised by men for securing the church's property? When we adhere to Christ's commands, we may expectantly rely upon God's promised presence, confident that the seed of His Word will bring forth fruit. But can we conjure the blessing of God upon our own inventions? When the Lord's few and simple ordinances must vie with human traditions in worship, human fancy may be satisfied, and there may be increase in numbers of people attending, in financial resources, in construction of facilities, and in ministry enterprises. But to the extent that this increase is not occurring through the observance of Christ's commands, it is not the expansion of the kingdom of God. The kingdom is not furthered by eschewing the prescriptions of Christ in the Scripture.

The rebuke to our generation's fascination with extra-Scriptural worship practices is the apostles' persuasion that insufficient as they were in themselves, the ministry Christ commissioned them to carry out would be accompanied by the power of the Holy Spirit. As the apostles preached, the Holy Spirit would take the things of Christ and show them to men, bringing conviction and conversion. Through the Spirit alone will they be able ministers of the new testament (II Cor. 3:2-12, I Cor. 5:1-5, John 15:7-15). New Testament churches prayerfully conducting the Biblical institutions of worship may trust in the ministry of the Spirit, who alone can regenerate and sanctify. Such undertakings, building with gold, silver and precious stones, will erect temples of eternal and enduring value, temples of godly character (I Cor. 3:9-17). When Biblical worship practices are altered to make the service more appealing to the spiritually uncommitted, what can be expected will be the character of the church being erected? But the comfort of following Biblical requirements in worship is the knowledge that God is glorified by our obedience, and the belief that God in His time will bring forth an unfading inheritance as a blessing upon our faithful worship.

Matthew 28:18-20 also discloses the function of church officers. The terms of their commission restrict them to practice and teach the commands of Christ. As Jesus the Messiah was set apart for a designated work which the Father sent Him to do, Christ sends the eldership to carry out a task He has assigned them. His faithfulness as the Servant of the Lord consisted in His careful performance of the mission laid upon Him. Likewise the elders have a responsibility delegated to them to dispense ordinances Christ has placed in their hands. Their authority is administrative and ministerial, not legislative. It is not for elders to make new rules and standards for worship and morals, but as stewards of the mysteries of God, theirs is faithfully to administer the institutions warranted by higher authority (I Cor. 4:1-4, 9:16-17, Col. 1:25, Titus 1:5-9). Biblical elders might be likened to judges and sheriffs, called not to make new laws, but to see that the provisions of existing legislation are fulfilled. Or like the trustees of a deed, they are entrusted with responsibility to see that the will of the testator is honored, and have no functions to add supplementary stipulations to the deed. Conformity to Christ's commands is the measure of an elder's fidelity to his stewardship.

This precludes the notion that elders have a permissive liberty to admit new worship practices, as long as all is done in a reverent and orderly manner. We may not go beyond Scripture and use our discretion to allow new activities not instituted in the Word of God. The wisdom which the Lord of the church has given to elders is not a wisdom to contrive or approve new practices, but the wisdom to administer Biblical institutions in an edifying manner. The rule for what may be permitted in worship has not been changed to whatever may seem reasonable to the supervising elders. Rather the apostles are content to hand on to the church the institutions which they received from the Lord (I Cor. 11:1-2, 23). Paul's injunction in I Corinthians 14 that the church's worship be conducted decently and in order, and his directions that men addressing the church in Corinth do so each in succession and always in a known tongue, are not a permission to devise new act of worship, for the activity of the men is a given: they had a psalm, a doctrine, a tongue, a revelation, an interpretation. They were teaching from already extant Scripture, or delivering new revelation by tongues and prophesying. Who can be asked to submit to the contrivances of elders who impose themselves on other men's consciences by going beyond Biblical ordinances, intruding themselves, instead of administering Christ's institutions? The primary responsibility of the eldership is to see that the church discharges the commands of Christ, without adding to them or departing from them.

THE HEAVENLY SANCTUARY

Worship in the Scriptures presupposes a priest mediating between sinners and a righteous God. In the Old Testament, tabernacle worship revolved around the Levitical priesthood. Clearly the temple service would be inoperative if the officiating priests were removed. Now Christ is revealed as the priest through whom our worship is mediated (Heb. 2:17, 7:25, 10:19-22, Eph. 2:13, 17-18, I Tim. 2:5-6, I John 2:1-2). The church could never come before God in worship except by virtue of Christ having died, and now ever living to make intercession for us. Without the merits of His sacrifice, and without this continuing advocacy on our behalf, there could be no standing before God, nor acceptance of the church's prayers. It is to be feared that when the church assembles for worship we are not always as conscious as we ought to be of Christ's key position in the acceptance of what we offer to God.

The service of the Levitical priests was played out in an earthly sanctuary, modeled upon realities in heaven. While the Mosaic tabernacle, a copy of heavenly things, was still standing, the way for sinners into the true tabernacle in heaven was not yet made manifest. But Christ ministers not in a shadow temple, simulating an approach into God's presence. "Christ has not entered the holy places made with hands, which are copies of the true, but into heaven itself, now to appear in the presence of God for us" (Heb. 9:24; 8:1-2; 9:11-12; 10:11-13; 1:3-4; 4:14; 6:19-20; 7:26). In the Epistle to the Hebrews we learn that this has the most far-reaching significance for the prayers and worship of the New Testament church.

Whenever the church assembles, wherever believing hearts are lifted to God in prayer, we ourselves enter with boldness into the holiest in the heavenly sanctuary, through that blood of Jesus which has consecrated for us a new and living way of access to God (Heb. 10:19-22; 12:18-24; 4:14-16; 6:19-20; 7:17-19, 25; Eph. 3:11-12). Jesus is the forerunner who has entered for us the presence within the veil, and behind Him we follow, with liberty of access to obtain mercy and find grace to help in time of need. In prayer we place our confidence in our great high priest who has passed through the heavens--the mediator through whom alone we may draw near to God. With such prayer all the ordinances of worship are to be administered. Thus the cross of Christ and His present advocacy in heaven ought surely to be in the mind of every worshipper as we come to God in prayer. How can the church worship God acceptably without the people's hearts being directed in faith to its priest ministering in the heavenly sanctuary? When the priest Zacharias went into the temple, the people prayed outside, awaiting his return (Luke 1:8-10). Their prayers centered upon the priestly service he was performing. Can anything less be true of New Testament Christians with respect to the focal-point which Christ's priestly activity should have for their worship?

From the days when David took the tabernacle up to Jerusalem, that city was the seat of divine worship. When the people prayed toward Jerusalem, spreading out their hands toward the city and the temple, it was in expectation that their prayers would come before God, for there in Jerusalem the appointed sacrifices were offered and God met with His people over the mercy seat. Even when the temple and the sacrifices had been cut off during the exile in Babylon, prayer was still directed toward Jerusalem, and answers came at the time of the evening offering (I Kings 8:29-30, 37-38, 44-49; Dan. 6:10; 9:21; Ezra 9:5).

There is a New Testament equivalence to this, for now the seat of worship is the true sanctuary in heaven, where Christ our priest is active. We are not come to the fearful intimidation of Mount Sinai, but to Mount Zion, the heavenly Jerusalem, where the angels worship, where the church is registered in heaven, to God the Judge, the spirits of just men made perfect, to Jesus the Mediator of the new covenant, and to His blood of sprinkling. Christ's entrance into the most holy place, and our entrance there by the blood of Jesus, mean that nothing less than the throne room of God in heaven is the seat of New Testament worship (Heb. 12:18-24; Rev.4:1-5:14; 7:9-17; 15:2-8). Christ appears in heaven garbed as a priest, and there the angels bring the golden censors which are the prayers of the

saints (Rev. 1:13, 5:8, 8:3-5). New Testament worship is always directed to
the greater and more perfect tabernacle, not of this creation, where Jesus
Christ is our advocate with the Father (I John 1:9-2:2). Believers draw near
with their hearts sprinkled from an evil conscience, and therefore with
freedom of access and full assurance of faith. This contrasts with coming to
the Mount Sinai which gives birth to bondage, and which corresponds to the
Jerusalem which now is, whose repeated sacrifices are a remainder of sins
every year. "But the Jerusalem above is free, which is the mother of us all"
(Gal. 4:22-26: Heb. 10:1-3, 22). This Jerusalem above is the nub of the New
Testament church's worship. Congregations everywhere in the world enter
the holiest by the blood of Jesus. Our prayers are directed to heaven not
only because it is God's dwelling place, but because our priest and tabernacle
are situated there.

  This Jerusalem above is the place where the Lamb of God is
opening the scroll and loosing its seals, bringing about the realization in time
of God's redemptive design for the church. The Lamb has been slain and
has prevailed, and is worthy to bring redemption to its fullest application.
Such is the glory of the risen Christ that John falls at his feet as dead. We
ourselves bow in wonder and join in worship as we read in Revelation of the
throne room in heaven, where the Lion of the tribe of Judah is in the midst
of the throne and triumphant, the angels singing His praises: "Worthy is
the Lamb who was slain to receive power and riches and wisdom, and
strength and honor and glory and blessing!" (Rev. 4:1-5:14; 1:10-20). Surely
our priest and savior is surrounded here with undimmed glory.

  The service of the Levitical priests in the earthly tabernacle was
encompassed with a wealth of symbolic representation. Such symbols were
types of the more excellent glory of a future priest. There was a splendor
expressed in outward pomp and aesthetic display which the Lord mandated
as the setting for the activity of the Levitical priesthood. Such were their
ephod, the breastplate embedded with precious stones, and the turban (Ex.
28), the ark of the testimony and other tabernacle furniture overlaid with
pure gold--the ark being topped by the two cherubim of gold at either end
of the mercy seat (Ex. 25), the uniquely composed incense and holy
anointing oil made of sweet spices (Ex. 30), the paneling with Lebanon cedar

and the lavish employment of gold in Solomon's temple, the architectural cube for the temple's inner sanctuary, and the temple's wood relief of cherubim, palm trees and open flowers (I Kings 6). There was also the blast of the trumpets by the priests, and the instrumental and vocal choirs of assisting Levites, who made music during the offering of sacrifices and when the ark was being taken up into Jerusalem (Num. 10:10; I Chron. 15:16-26; II Chron. 29:25-30). Truly there was a glory and a beauty in Old Testament worship, a beauty attached to the seat of worship where the Levitical priests ministered (Ex. 28:2, 40).

There is a corresponding glory which attaches to the seat of New Testament worship. What can excel the glory of the exalted Christ entering heaven itself, now to appear in the presence of God for us, continuing forever with an unchangeable priesthood? As with the Old Testament, the glory of New Testament worship is the glory of its priest. But while the glory of the Levitical priests is a symbolism in outward pomp and aesthetic display, the glory of Christ's priesthood is its efficacy to purge the conscience of sin and to constitute the ungodly righteous. The Old Testament symbols were unable to put away sin, and their very repetition was reminder of sins unremoved. The Levitical priesthood had inadequacy written all over it (Heb. 7:11, 18-19, 23-24, 26-28; 9:6-10, 23-26; 10:1-4, 11). How superior is the glory of the priest who finished the work the Father had given him to do, who consequently has been given authority to give eternal life to many, and who could look to the Father to glorify Him with the glory He had with the Father before the world was (John 17:1-5: Eph. 1:19-23; Phil. 2:9-11; Acts 2:33-36; 5:31)! The glory of this priest is the worthiness of the Lamb, who has prevailed to put away sin by the sacrifice of Himself. And the glory which He lends to worship in the New Testament church is the freedom of access consecrated for us by our priest's efficacious sacrifice.

When the Levitical priesthood was superseded by the coming of Christ, there was also a termination of the gifts, sacrifices and temple ordinances of which the old priesthood was the focus (Heb. 7:11-12, 15-19; 8:13-9:10; Gal. 3:15-4:11, Eph. 2:11-18). Not everything in the Old Testament forms of worship is still appointed for use in the church today; much was imposed until the time of reformation, when an effectual sacrifice would displace the old forms. The old order passed away with the accomplishment of Christ's mediatory work.

What is it of the temple worship which is gone forever? Substantial elements like prayer are continued in the New Testament Scriptures. But what of the permanence of a temple structure, the priestly garments, the animal sacrifices, the lavish overlay of gold, and the instrumental and vocal choirs? None of these is continued in the New Testament record of the church.

The temple, with its altar, sacrifice, priest and many fixtures, was a shadow of the good things to come, but Jesus Christ is the substance. He Himself is the fulfillment of all that they typologically depicted (John 2:18-22; Col. 2:16-17; Heb. 8:4-5; 10:1). The strength of Christ's offering was to dissolve the Mosaic institutions, and to introduce new ordinances of worship for the church. The old forms pictorially represented the glory and efficacy of the new covenant priest. Now we have in heaven the reality of Christ's glorious entrance into the throne room, rather than a shadow portrayal of it on earth. Though the picture show is abolished, and the glory of our worship is not visible to the eye, the power of the Spirit conforming us to the likeness of Christ (II Cor. 3:7-18), and the freedom of access to the presence within the veil, surpasses anything known in the Old Testament forms of worship. The passing away of an aesthetic representation of Christ's glory, in favor of the reality of His undimmed glory in the heavenly sanctuary, leaves a marked simplicity in the worship forms of the New Testament church. But this is not a lesser glory, unless glory is measured by outward pomp rather than by redemptive blessings.

There is a distinction between Old Testament and New Testament worship in the manner of our access to God. Old Testament believers dealt with altars, tabernacles, veils and animal sacrifices, shadowy representations of approach into God's presence, rather than relating immediately to the true tabernacle in heaven. There is a directness of approach in New Testament worship, because we deal not in the realm of shadows, but come boldly to God's own throne of grace, the way into the most holy place now being manifest. The old covenant's copies of heavenly things were unable to

cleanse the conscience and remove the fear of death, and association with
these shadows left men with a spirit of bondage and a sense of
condemnation (Heb. 2:14-15; 9:9, 13-14; 10:3, 20-22; 12:18-21; Gal. 4:3-11).
The New Testament regards these shadows as a restraint in our bold
approach to God. Christ by His death has purchased for us a directness of
access, and a freedom from the typological pomp and ceremony of the
Levitical priesthood.   Do we cherish this liberty from the Mosaic
institutions? Christ shed His blood to acquire it for us.

The beauty of New Testament worship is not produced by aesthetic
display. When a congregation tries to worship God by making a creative
artistic program for its services, it is not only offering to God something He
has not commanded and never sought, it is also failing to appreciate the
nature of our access into God's very presence in heaven which was won for
us by the blood of Christ. The glory of our worship is the glory which
surrounds our priest in heaven. Does that suffice us? The pomp of heaven
is not to be independently recreated in a shadow on earth, for the shadows
and copies (even those once authorized by God) have been abolished by the
death of Christ. Now we go by faith into the true tabernacle, which is
immeasurably superior. We participate not in symbols but in the realities in
heaven when we worship.   The simplicity of New Testament forms of
worship--the absence of outward pomp and aesthetic exhibition--speaks
volumes. It tells of the complete reality of our entrance into the holiest of
all in heaven. We are no longer playing with models, but have come to the
new Jerusalem itself. New Testament worship is not an imaginative aesthetic
production offered to God.

The Old Testament temple worship was a pictorial spectacle of the
prefigured entrance of Christ into the true sanctuary.   When what was
foreshadowed has arrived, it is inconsistent to perpetuate the depiction of its
awaited debut. Are we being unduly fascinated with sensory displays like
those of the temple? A bride does not continue to hold wedding rehearsals
after the marriage has taken place. Now she has something better to enjoy,
namely the actuality of the marriage relationship. Or, as the Basel reformer
Johannes Oecolampadius put it, the Old Testament ceremonies were like the

lighting of candles, which in the hours before dawn serve their own purpose. But after the sun has risen in the morning and ascended to the height of its noonday position, it is a strange lack of appreciation for the sunshine when we continue to burn candles. Appreciation for the efficacy of Christ's sacrifice should show itself by not seeking to return to a shadow notion of glory in worship.

In Acts and in the Epistle to the Hebrews we see indications that the Jews clung to the temple service in Jerusalem because they did not recognize the superior glory of Christ as the New Testament mediator (Acts 6:13-14; 21:27-28). Worshippers before the coming of Christ were meant to inquire into the meaning of the temple typology as it pointed forward to Him, but now believers look to Christ fully revealed as the savior who has been exalted and has entered heaven itself (cf. I Pet. 1:10-12; Luke 24:26-27, 44-45). We should not pray with our faces to Jerusalem, hankering after the outward pomp of the temple ordinances. Rather, may we absorbed with the glory of our Redeemer's intercessory ministry in the heavenly throne room. May we pray toward heaven where Christ mediates so competently for us, and where we enter by believing prayer into the holiest of all. May the worship services in our churches bespeak the efficacy of Christ's priestly ministry in heaven, and the immediacy of our approach to God.

5 - THE SECOND COMMANDMENT: THE PRINCIPLE THAT GOD IS TO BE WORSHIPPED ONLY IN WAYS PRESCRIBED IN HOLY SCRIPTURE AND THAT THE HOLY SCRIPTURE PRESCRIBES THE WHOLE CONTENT OF WORSHIP, TAUGHT BY SCRIPTURE ITSELF

William Young

Before inquiring into the Scripture warrant for the principle in question, it may be in the interest of clarity and accuracy to attempt a more precise formulation of the principle than that provided in the sub-title of this chapter. We may first state the principle positively, then set it in contrast to other views, then mention certain qualifications of the principle.

The statement of the principle in the sub-title is redundant. That God is to be worshipped only in ways prescribed in Holy Scripture is implied in the statement that the Holy Scripture prescribes the whole content of worship. The principle in question may then be stated simply by the latter proposition, i.e. "The Holy Scripture prescribes the whole content of worship." By this is meant that all elements or parts of worship are prescribed by God Himself in His Word. This principle has universal reference to worship performed by men since the fall. In other words it has equal application to the Old and the New Testament. It is also universal in that it is regulative of all types of worship, whether public, family or private. It is in order to observe the universality of the principle, although our special concern is with public worship under the New Testament.

This principle has been formulated in contrast to other views, particularly to the principle that anything not expressly forbidden in the Word of God is allowable in the worship of God. QUOD SCRIPTURA NON VETAT, PERMITTIT   (What Scripture does not forbid, it permits): This is the principle of the Romish Church, also of Lutherans and Anglicans embodied in the 20th Article of the Church of England: "The church has power to decree rites and ceremonies . . . and yet it is not lawful for the church to ordain any thing contrary to God's Word written." The doctrine of the Calvinistic churches clearly formulated in the Westminster Standards is sharply opposed to this: QUOD SCRIPTURA NON IUBET, VETAT   (What Scripture does not command, it forbids). "The silence of Scripture is as real a prohibition as a positive injunction to abstain."

We may also contrast this principle with the ambiguously stated principle that God is to be worshipped according to His Word. Of course it is true that God is to be worshipped according to His Word, but it is also true that the civil magistrate should administer his office according to the Word. In this sense, the worship of God would not be in principle regulated more directly than the conduct of civil government.   Such is not the Calvinistic view of the character of the worship of God. Neither may we say that God's Word provides us with general principles of worship, but leaves the particulars of practice to the discretion of the Church. The whole content of worship includes specific acts of worship as well as the broad principial basis of these acts.   The Word of God, moreover, obviously prescribes specific acts of worship even in quite minute detail, in addition to laying down the general principles of worship. This principle may not be construed as admitting that Scripture itself opens up in the New Testament economy an area of liberty in the worship of God within which area nothing is prescribed by God and everything left to the judgment of men.   The admission of such an area of liberty is tantamount to asserting the un-Reformed principle that anything not expressly forbidden in Scripture is allowable in the worship of God. On the Reformed principle no part of the content of God's worship can be regarded as belonging to the *adiaphora*, to the class of actions neither required nor forbidden by divine commandment. Whatever has not been commanded is prohibited.

That no misunderstanding may exist with respect to this principle it is necessary to make two qualifications, both of which are stated in section 6 of the first chapter of the Westminster Confession of Faith. First, that which may be derived by good and necessary consequences from the express statements of Scripture is no less binding than an express command itself. Approved example has equal validity with a direct command, and even where approved example and express command may both be lacking or uncertain, as in the baptism of infants, necessary inference from the doctrine and commandments plainly set forth in Scripture may sufficiently warrant a practice of worship. Secondly, there are "some circumstances concerning the worship of God . . . common to human actions and societies which are to be ordered by the light of nature and Christian prudence according to the general rules of the word which are always to be observed."

That these circumstances constitute no part of the content of worship is clear from the following quotation from Gillespie, who writes of the conditions "requisite in such a thing as the church hath power to prescribe by her laws."

> First, it must be only a circumstance of divine worship; no substantial part of it; no sacred, significant and efficacious ceremony. For the order and decency left to the definition for the church, as concerning the particulars of it, comprehendeth no more but mere circumstances.

Again he writes,

> We say truly of those several and changeable circumstances which are left to the determination of the church, that, being almost infinite, they were not particularly determinable in Scripture; for the particular determination of those occurring circumstances which were to be rightly ordered in the works of God's service to the end of the world, and that ever according to the exigency of every present occasion and different case, should have filled the whole world with books. But as for other things pertaining to God's worship which are not be reckoned among the circumstances of it,

they being in number neither many, nor in change various, were most easily and conveniently determinable in Scripture.[1]

An even more precise definition of the circumstances that may be ordered by the church in connection with God's worship is given by John Owen in his "Discourse Concerning Liturgies."   Owen distinguishes circumstances "which follow actions as actions from circumstances which do not of their own accord, nor naturally nor necessarily attend them." The former kind of circumstances "not determined by divine institution may be ordered, disposed of and regulated by the prudence of men."

As the action cannot be without them, so their regulation is arbitrary, if they come not under some divine disposition and order, as that of time in general doth. There are also some things which men call circumstances, also that no way belong of themselves to the actions whereof they are said to be the circumstances, nor do attend them, but are imposed on them, or annexed to them, by the arbitrary authority of those who take upon them to give order and rules in such cases; such as to pray before an image, or toward the East, or to use that form of prayer in the gospel administrations, and no other. These are not circumstances attending the nature of the thing itself but are arbitrarily super-added to the things they are appointed to accompany. Whatever men may call such additions, they are no less parts of the whole wherein they serve than the things themselves whereunto they are adjoined. The school men tell us that which is made so the condition of an action, that without it the action is not to be done, is not a circumstance of it, but such an adjunct as is a necessary part. But not to contend about the word, such additionals that are called circumstantial, are made parts of

---

[1] George Gillespie, *A Dispute Against the English-Popish Ceremonies, Obtruded upon the Church of Scotland* . . . (1637), 224, 226 (Part III, Ch. 7, Sect. 5, 6).

worship as are made necessary by virtue of command to be observed.[2]

The qualification with respect to circumstances far from weakening the force of the regulative principle of worship rather sets in the sharpest focus the position that everything properly belonging to the content of worship must be the matter of divine commandment, not of human devising.

Having attempted a precise formulation of the principle regulative of worship, we may now turn to inquire as to the Scripture warrant for this principle. Before appealing to particular texts in which the principle is asserted, we should observe that it is a principle involved in several cardinal doctrines of the Word of God. The case for this principle rests not on a string of isolated proof texts, but upon the central concepts and doctrines of the Word of God. We shall content ourselves with stating five fundamental articles of our faith, from which this principle follows as a good and necessary consequence.

First: The Scriptures are the only infallible rule of faith and practice, and are therefore sufficient for all the needs of the church (II Tim. 3:16, 17). It clearly follows from the accepted Reformed doctrine of the authority and sufficiency of Scripture, that Scripture is the sole and sufficient rule for worship, particularly the worship of the Church. If the prescriptions of worship contained in Holy Writ are sufficient, why add ordinances of worship for which there is no need?

The attempt to avoid the force of this argument by the assertion that Scripture itself opens up an area of liberty in which it prescribes nothing as to the content of worship is vain. Such a position is a virtual denial of the sufficiency of Scripture and is certainly not the view of Scripture on which the Calvinistic reformation in Geneva, France, and Low Countries, and the British Isles proceeded. Just such an idea of liberty would make allowance

---

[2]William H. Goold, ed., *The Works of John Owen* (rpt.; Edinburgh: The Banner of Truth Trust, 1965), XV, 35, 36.

for Romish ceremonies retained by Lutherans and Anglicans but rejected universally by the Calvinists. The Calvinistic conception of the sufficiency of Scripture, which I trust my readers are prepared to acknowledge to be the Scriptural conception, thus involves the regulative principle of worship. It is no accident that the regulative principle of worship makes its first appearance in the Westminster Confession in connection with the discussion of the sufficiency of Scripture.

Second: The sole object of worship is the absolutely Sovereign God. The basic conception of Calvinism, God's absolute sovereignty, excludes worship of human devising. In anthropocentric systems of doctrine like Lutheranism, or Arminianism, the human will may be allowed to define the content of worship at least in part, even as it contributes in part to man's salvation. But in the theocentric system of Calvinism, the autonomy of man's will is rejected in the face of God's absolute sovereignty. This is true at every step of the way, with respect to worship as well as to the plan of salvation. Man's will may contribute nothing more to God's worship than to God's plan of salvation, and it is no accident that will-worship and rejection of the doctrine of salvation by grace alone flourish together. As Sovereign, God is the supreme Law-giver. As His sovereignty extends to His worship, so it is His sole prerogative to appoint the laws of His worship, to command of His subjects the way they ought to worship Him. Can it be anything other than presumption in a subject of the absolute Sovereign to offer as worship anything which has not been commanded? Can the inventions of the human will be set on the same level as the commands of the Divine Will as proper material of worship? That God shall allow worship other than what He has commanded is contrary to reason itself. Gillespie writes, "How absurd a tenet is this, which holdeth that there is some particular worship of God allowed and not commanded? What new light is this which maketh all our divines to have been in the mist, who have acknowledged no worship of God, but that which God hath commanded?

Who ever heard of commanded and allowed worship?"[3] The question raised by the Lord in Isaiah 1:12 thus applies to all worship offered to Him: "When ye come to appear before me, who hath required this at your hand . . .?"

Third: The total corruption and deceitfulness of the human heart disqualifies man from judging what is to be admitted into the worship of God. It may be that before the fall, our first parents had written on their hearts the law of worship and by looking within the depth of their own beings, could read off the commandments of God. Yet even then, they were not without direct external communication of the will of Him who walked and talked with them in the garden.

Since the fall, however, though the human conscience still witnesses in all men that worship is due to the supreme Being, no information can be gained from the heart of man as to how God is to be worshipped.

The idolatry and superstition not only of the heathen in their blindness but of the professing Christian Church enjoying the full light of God's Word sufficiently demonstrates this to be the case. It goes without saying that the unregenerate consciousness, blind to spiritual things, is unfit to determine matters concerning the worship of God. Worship that is the invention of the heart of men, every imagination of the thoughts of which is only evil continually, in the nature of the case cannot be acceptable to a holy God.

What requires, however, to be emphasized is that the regenerate consciousness is no more fit than the unregenerate to decide what may be introduced into God's worship. The regenerate, it must be remembered, ever groan under the burden of sin that dwells in them, and therefore should well know that their understanding and will are not to be trusted to determine what is acceptable worship before God. The enlightened understanding is content to learn God's precepts and the renewed will to walk in them, but the regenerate heart as such cannot desire to make the slightest addition to God's commandments. Whenever true believers have acted inconsistently in

---

[3]Gillespie, *op.cit.*, 93 (Part III, Ch. 6, Sect. 2).

this respect, they have invariably allowed great corruption to be introduced into God's sanctuary.

Fourth: Christ is the sole Head and King over His body, the Church. In the exercise of His headship and kingship, the Lord Jesus Christ has appointed the ordinances of His house. This applies in particular to the public worship of the New Testament Church. How may a minister of Christ with a clear conscience administer any rite or ceremony of worship in the Lord's house without warrant from his Lord and King? To add human inventions to Christ's express commands is to usurp an authority which is not ministerial, but which is tantamount to placing the doctrines and commandments of men upon the same level as the commands of the Lord Jesus. The pretense that the humanly invented modes of worship are optional, whereas Christ's commands are mandatory, is to no avail. We have already noted the absurdity of distinguishing two kinds of worship, prescribed and allowed. It is also worthy of note that in practice no difference is made between the two types of worship. Hymns of human composition and divinely inspired Psalms are sung the one after the other, as if the one were offered to God in obedience to the Lord's appointment as much as the other. Furthermore, the people are led to feel that the one type of worship is of the same character as the other and that they are no less bound to engage in the one than in the other. Quite apart from the evil of singing the word of man alongside of God's Word, we would now stress the inevitable binding of the conscience of the ordinary worshipper by the inventions of men, as soon as those inventions are given the same place as divine institutions which truly bind the conscience.

In this connection it should be observed that the regulative principle of worship, far from abridging the scope of genuine Christian liberty, is the preeminent safeguard of Christian liberty in matters of worship. It is this principle that has again and again liberated Christ's little flock from the impositions of man in the worship of God. Deliverance from human tyranny and complete subjection to Christ's commands are involved in one another, and these two are but the negative and positive elements of Christian liberty in the worship of God.

Fifth: In the same connection the character of the Church's constitution should be kept in view. Even as the doctrine, government and discipline of the Church have been prescribed by Christ, so also has its worship. May any doctrine be taught which the great Prophet has not revealed? May any new office or function be added to the government of the Christ's Church that the Head of the Church has not provided for? May anything be counted an offense but that which Christ has declared to be such from His Word? So also may anything be added to the content of His worship that He has not prescribed?

We may sum up the above argument from the central teachings of Scripture in the words of William Cunningham:

> The truth of the principle, as a general rule for the guidance of the Church, is plainly enough involved in what Scripture teaches concerning its own sufficiency and perfection as a rule of faith and practice, concerning God's exclusive right to determine in what ways He ought to be worshipped, concerning Christ's exclusive right to settle the constitution, laws and arrangements of His kingdom, concerning the unlawfulness of will-worship and concerning the utter unfitness of men for the function which they have so often and so boldly usurped in this matter.[4]

In adducing Scripture warrant for the regulative principle of our Reformed worship, we will not confine ourselves to inferences, as good and necessary as these inferences are. The inferences prove the principle by bringing to light that it is part and parcel of the Calvinistic system. But that system itself rests on Scripture revelation and so also does this principle which we may defend by direct appeal to Scripture passages. Let us first consider a number of passages expressly asserting this principle and then observe certain Scripture examples confirming it.

---

[4]William Cunningham, referenced in *Psalm Singer's Conference* (Belfast: Fountain Printing Works, 1903), 71, 72.

The first passage we may consider in this connection is the Second Commandment, Exodus 20:4, 5. It might be said that the Second Commandment contains an express prohibition of idolatry and nothing more and thus has no bearing upon the question. From the point of view of historic Presbyterianism, however, this is not the case. Our Larger Catechism states, among other rules to be observed for the right understanding of the Ten Commandments, "that under one sin or duty, all of the same kind are forbidden or commanded, together with all the causes, means, occasions, and appearances thereof, and provocations thereunto."[5] The Larger Catechism further includes among the sins forbidden in the Second Commandment, "all devising, counseling, commanding, using and any wise approving any religious worship not instituted by God himself. . . all superstitious devices, corrupting the worship of God, adding to it, or taking from it, whether invented and taken up of ourselves, or received by tradition from others, though under the title of antiquity, custom, devotion, good intent, or any other pretense whatsoever."[6]

The prohibition of idolatry is thus understood to involve the regulative principle. As John Knox expressed the matter pointedly: "All worshipping, honoring, or service invented by the brain of man in the religion of God, without his own express commandment, is idolatry."[7] One might view the matter this way. Idols are the work of men's hand. Men make them unto themselves for the worship of God as fit means for the worship of God. Deeper even than the fact that the idol is unfit to represent the invisible God, is the fact that it is the product of man's own brain and hand. And every product of man's brain and hand introduced into God's worship is, in the very nature of the case, an idol.

The correctness of the historic Presbyterian doctrine of the Second Commandment is verified by several other passages of the Mosaic Law, in

---

[5]Westminster Larger Catechism, Q. 99.

[6]Westminster Larger Catechism, Q. 109.

[7]John Knox, "A Vindication of the Doctrine that the Sacrifice of the Mass is Idolatry," in *The Works of John Knox* (ed. by David Laing; Edinburgh: T. G. Stevenson, 1864), III, 34.

which the Church is expressly forbidden to add anything to the commandments of God respecting His worship and service (Deut. 4:2; 12:32; cf. Prov. 30:6). When Moses was about to make the tabernacle, he was admonished by God, "And look that thou make them after their pattern, which was showed thee in the mount" (Ex. 25:40; Heb. 8:5).

The minuteness of detail in the divine prescriptions as the construction of the tabernacle and as to the practice of worship to be performed in it made it perfectly plain to God's ancient people that whatever was not commanded was forbidden. Those who, contrary to such clear light, worshipped God with their own inventions, as we shall see, became the object of the fearful vengeance of a jealous God. In this connection observe that the jealousy of God is revealed against idolatrous corruptions of and superstitious additions to His worship. Meditation on this much forgotten attribute of God should impress us with the grave importance of the purity of God's sanctuary. The Lord will not suffer His bride to seek after her own heart and eyes, after which she is accustomed to go a whoring (Num. 15:39, 40), but visits such unfaithfulness with the severest rebukes.

A most remarkable passage bearing on the question is Jeremiah 7:31: "They have built the high places of Tophet, which is in the valley of the Son of Hinnom, to burn their sons and their daughters in the fire: which I commanded them not, neither came it into my heart." How clearly does this passage show that God does not view sin as does man. Man would revolt at the unnatural and inhuman cruelty of the burning of the fruit of one's own body before an idol. But in God's mind this is but secondary, the essential evil being that it is worship which He did not command, neither came it into His heart.

Owen writes in this connection:

Moreover to testify what weight He laid on the observance of these general prohibitions, when men found out other ways of worship than what He had appointed, though the particulars were such as fell under other special interdictions, yet the Lord was pleased to place the great aggravation of their sin in the contempt of those general rules mentioned. This is that He urgeth them with, that they did things by Him not appointed; of not observing anything in religion but what He requires,that He presseth them withal. The command is general. 'Ye shall add nothing to what I have instituted.' And the aggravation of the sin pressed by Him relates not to the specific nature of it, but to the general command or prohibition, 'ye have done what I commanded ye not.' That the particular evil condemned was also against other commands of God, is merely accidental to the general nature of the crime they were urged withal. And whereas God hath given out these general rules and precepts, 'you shall do whatever I command you, and according as I command you; you shall add nothing thereunto, nor take anything therefrom,' can the transgression of this rule be any otherwise expressed but this, 'They did the thing which He commanded them not, nor did it ever come into His heart?'[8]

As Gillespie puts it briefly, "howsoever manifold wickedness might have been challenged in that which they did, yet if any would dispute with God upon the matter, He stoppeth their mouths with this one answer: 'I commanded it not, neither came it into my heart.'"[9]

The objection may be raised that, while it became the state of the Church in the Old Testament to have all ordinances of worship prescribed even in minute detail, the New Testament economy is free from such restriction. The Church, it may be said, has passed from childhood to years of maturity where it can exercise discretion and liberty in determining its own worship.

In reply, it must be said that this would be contrary to the identity of the covenant of grace in both the old and the new dispensation. The principle regulating the worship of God's people belongs to the substance of the covenant of grace. With reference to the heavenly Father, the most

---

[8]Owen, op.cit., 4 (Part III, Ch. 7, Sect. 15).

[9]Gillespie, op.cit., 234.

mature saint remains a covenant child, and the most mature state of the Church itself remains subject to the ordinances imposed by the Church's Head and Lord. Notwithstanding the changes involved in abrogation of the ceremonial law, there is no change in the divine prerogative of appointing the worship to be rendered by the Church. The teaching of our Lord and His apostles on this matter is quite express. In condemning the Pharisees for their tradition as to eating bread with unwashen hands, the Lord quotes the words of Isaiah: "In vain do they worship me, teaching for doctrines the commandments of men" (Mark 7:7) and comments, "For laying aside the commandments of God, ye hold the tradition of men, as the washing of pots and cups: and many other such like things ye do" (v. 8). The Lord goes on to show that human traditions added to God's Word have the effect of making the Word of none effect. Additions to the Word of God in worship will not allow the Word itself to stand. Professor Petticrew observes:

> Laying aside the commandments of God, that they may keep their own tradition! Is there not a close likeness between this action, thus condemned by Christ, and the action of those in modern times who lay aside the Divine Ordinance of the singing of the Psalms that they may keep their own man-appointed ordinance of the singing of uninspired hymns in the place of the Psalms?[10]

Observe also the terms of the Great Commission: "Teaching them to observe whatsoever I have commanded you" (Mt. 28:20). Here there is to be found authority by the means appointed by the Church's Lord. But there is no authority for anything besides those appointed means. Observe the Lord does not give authority to His disciples to teach man to observe what He has not forbidden, but only what He has commanded them. The charter of the New Testament Church at this point is expressed in identical terms as those of the Mosaic economy which we have seen so expressly to exclude the inventions of men from the worship of God. No addition to or

---

[10] *Psalm Singer's Conference*, 73.

subtraction from Christ's commands may be allowed in the New Testament any more than with respect to the commands given on Mount Sinai in the Old. As we read concerning Moses again and again that he did all as the Lord commanded him, so the Apostles organized the worship and government of the Christian Church according to Christ's commands. We have no more right to alter that divinely instituted pattern of ordinances for the New Testament Church than Nadab and Abihu, Saul, Jereboam, or any others in the Old. The apostle Paul expressly condemns will-worship, worship according to the doctrines and commandments of men (Col. 2:22, 23). The will of God, not the will of man, is the rule of the worship of the New Testament Church.

The examples by which Scripture enforces this principle may occupy our attention briefly. First: The sacrifices of Cain and Abel. Though Abel was accepted as coming in true faith which was lacking in the case of Cain, yet it would appear that Abel's offering was also intrinsically more excellent than his brother's. True faith will bring to God the offering of penitence and praise that He has appointed as He has appointed, while unbelief brings an offering of its own choosing in a perfunctory manner. Cain appears not to have brought the best of what he had as did Abel (Gen. 4:3, 4). Equally striking is the reference to the atoning blood in Abel's offering for which he had the precedent of the animals slain by the Lord's own hand to provide coats of skin to cover the nakedness of our parents (Gen. 3:21). From the beginning, acknowledgement of the imputed righteousness of the Lamb slain from the foundation of the world and meticulous observance of divinely instituted methods of worship appear to be yoked inseparably.

Second: If there be doubt as to the case of Cain and Abel, there is no obscurity in the least in the instance of Nadab and Abihu (Lev. 10:1, 7). The strange fire they offered before the Lord "Wherefore the Lord had given to them no charge" was "a common fire and not of that fire which God had commanded to burn day and might before the altar of burnt sacrifice, which only ought to have been offered unto God."[11] Nadab and Abihu were

---

[11]Knox, *op. cit.*, 38.

Aaron's sons, priests next to himself. They seem to have had no unworthy
motive in their offering, they desired no earthly gain but only to honor God,
and that in a way He had not expressly forbidden. They did nothing more
than substitute fire of their own for that which the Lord had commanded.
Yet for this act they were instantaneously consumed by fire from the Lord.

John Knox comments further:

> Whereof it is plain, that neither the pre-eminence of the person of
> man that maketh or setteth up any religion, without the express
> commandment of God, nor yet the intent whereof he doeth the
> same is accepted before God. For nothing in his religion will he
> admit without his own Word, but all that is added hereto doth he
> abhor, and punisheth the inventors and doers thereof, as you have
> heard in Nadab and Abihu, whereof they had no express
> commandment.[12]

Can the Lord be pleased with the fire of strange praise on the lips
of men, which He has not commanded, any more than with the strange fire
offered by Nadab and Abihu? Disrespect for His command and neglect of
His own provision in the interest of our inventions cannot but provoke His
indignation.

Third: Reference may be made also to (a) Korah, Dathan and
Abiram, Numbers 16; (b) Moses smiting the rock at Kadesh, Numbers 20;
(c) The rejection of Saul, I Samuel 13; (d) The handling of the ark, I
Chronicles 15:13, as a few instances chosen from among many.

We may conclude this discussion with following quotation from
James Begg:

> The first thing necessary is to fix the principle which regulates New
> Testament worship. There is a tremendous emphasis in the question
> of the king of Moab, 'Wherewithal shall I come before God, and

---

[12] *Ibid.*

bow myself before the Most High?' To hear many speak at present, one would suppose that there was nothing less solemn than an act of worship, and that, instead of raising the question, 'What in worship is pleasing and acceptable to God?' they have simply to consider, 'What is pleasing and acceptable to themselves and each other?' They perfectly well understand that they must study the most minute rules of the court before they can dare to be permitted to approach an earthly sovereign; but they presumptuously imagine that it is, and ought to be, the easiest thing possible to enter in the presence of the King of kings, before whose awful majesty angels veil their faces whilst they adore. They forget that it is in connection with His own worship that God proclaims Himself in the second commandment to be 'a jealous God,' and that it has been in the same connection with His worship that this jealousy has most frequently flamed forth in the past history of the Church--in the case of Cain, of Korah, of Uzzah, of the buyers and sellers in the temple. Corruption here is corruption at the fountain head, fitted to cause the withdrawal of the Holy Spirit of God, and thus to leave the Church to sink under deeper and more hopeless evils; whilst, if we consider the relation of the thrice holy God to fallen sinners, the wonder is not that our mode of access into His presence is strictly regulated, but that any such access is permitted to us at all.[13]

[13]James Begg, *The Use of Organs and other Instruments of Music in Christian worship Indefensible* (Glasgow: W. R. M'Phun & Son, 1866), 11, 12.

6 - CHRISTIAN LIBERTY AND WORSHIP

David C. Lachman

"Stand fast therefore in the liberty by which Christ has made us free and do not be entangled again with a yoke of bondage" (Gal. 5:1). Although the context here is circumcision and attempts to be justified by the works of the law, that there is an extensive liberty in the gospel surely is taught in the New Testament. We are delivered from the bondage of sin into the glorious liberty of the children of God (Rom. 8:21). There is liberty where the Spirit of the Lord is (II Cor. 3:17).

But it is a serious error--and an error all too many have made and still make--to suppose that gospel liberty is freedom to do as we please. Pleasing ourselves rather than God is the bondage to which we as sinners have been enslaved. "I did it my way" is not the song of the redeemed, but of the lost. Rather, the nature of gospel liberty is that described by Jesus in His invitation to those who labor and are heavy laden: "Take my yoke upon you, and learn from me, for I am gentle and humble in heart; and you shall find rest for your souls. For my yoke is easy and my load is light" (Mt. 11:29, 30).

Gospel liberty *is freedom from* the bondage of sin and freedom *to* serve God. In general this involves a loving, willing obedience: first loving God with all our hearts, minds, and souls and our neighbor as ourselves and then a seeking to know and to do His will in all of life. While, without qualification, we are justified by faith, without reference to our works of any kind, all who truly have been justified will be sanctified. This involves a practical, progressive death to sin and a life of obedience, both in word and deed.

What is true in general of the Christian life is also true of worship. Christian liberty in worship is not freedom to serve God as *we* please, but as *He* pleases. It is undoubtedly true that God is pleased--and indeed *only* pleased--by worship which is heartfelt and sincere. Those who honor God with their lips while their hearts are far from Him (Mt. 15:8) are hypocrites and are in no way pleasing to Him. Nothing in Scripture even so much as hints that God is pleased by a formal worship, however correct the form, in which the heart of the worshipper is not fully involved. If we have not listened to His words and have rejected His law, even the incense and sacrifices He has prescribed are not pleasing to God (Jer. 6:19, 20). If we do not show compassion, do justice and love mercy and if we live lives which demonstrate that our hearts are far from Him, no amount of formal obedience will be pleasing to Him (*cf.* Micah 6:8; Hosea 6:6; Mt. 9:13 and 12:7), Our worship must reflect the true state of our hearts and lives if it is to please God.

But that this is true and of primary importance in no way lessens our obligation to seek diligently to bring our lives in general and our worship in particular into harmony with His revealed will. True love and obedience do not seek to see how little they can get away with doing, but rather how much they can do to please Him. This certainly involves positive obedience to God's commands. Much emphasis is placed on such obedience throughout Scripture, even down to jot and tittle (Mt. 5:18). "Has the Lord as much delight in burnt offerings and sacrifices As in obeying the voice of the Lord? Behold, to obey is better than sacrifice, And to heed than the fat of rams" (I Sam. 15:22). But such obedience nevertheless includes worship. As in the rest of life, we ought to seek His will and His will alone as we try to worship Him in a way which pleases Him. The commandments or traditions of men (Is. 29:13) are to have nothing to do with our worship of God (*cf.* also Mt. 9:13, where Jesus repeats this); it is His word alone to which we must look.

The Old Testament makes it plain that God wishes to be obeyed even in points of minor detail; this is as true in worship as in all of life. Nadab and Abihu, Aaron's sons, were consumed by fire from the Lord when they ventured to offer strange fire--that is, fire from their own fire pans, rather that that which had come out from the Lord (Lev. 9:14-10:7). Again, when David arranged to move the ark to Jerusalem, God's arrangements for carrying it were ignored (poles are specified in Ex. 25:10ff) and the ark was placed on a new cart pulled by oxen. When the ark was nearly upset by the oxen, Uzzah reached out to steady it. Though his intention was surely good, we read that God's anger burned against Uzzah and that He struck him dead. Even in such a situation, God meant to be obeyed according to the detail of Numbers 4, in which the sons of Kohath were instructed not to touch the holy objects lest they die. David's plans were disrupted and at first he was angry. But, on learning why God was angry, he ordered no one to carry the ark but the Levites and, in explaining the matter to them, said God's anger was aroused because "we did not seek him according to the ordinance" (I Chron. 15:2, 13).

Again, when we read in Jeremiah 7:30, 31 that the sons of Judah did evil in the Lord's sight by setting detestable things in the house called by His name, to defile it, and building "the high places of Topeth, which is in the valley of the son of Hinnom, to burn their sons and daughters in the fire," we are not told it is evil in the Lord's sight because it is a wicked and horrible thing to do (though it surely is) or because it breaks the Sixth Commandment (though it certainly does). But we are told that it is wrong because the Lord did not command it or even think it. The conclusion rightly drawn from this is that worship, if it is to be pleasing to God, must be worship which He has commanded.

The worship of a golden calf, both as created by Aaron (Ex. 32) and as repeated by Jeroboam (I Ki. 12:25ff), was a clear violation of the Second Commandment, even though the golden calf was apparently intended in each instance to represent God himself and not to be another god. It is clear that God was angered by the worship of an idol, even one meant to depict himself. "A craftsman made it, so it is not God" (Hosea 8:6). But Jeroboam is also condemned in the same context for devising a feast, and a time for its celebration, in his own heart and for sacrificing on his own altar to the Lord. It would appear from this that worship is unacceptable both if it violates God's express command and if it is of man's devising rather than God's. God is offended with worship He has not commanded as much as He is with worship He has expressly forbidden.

Under the New Covenant, the regulations which governed the worship of God in the temple, including the entire sacrificial system, were entirely abolished. Although such worship had been prescribed in detail by

God, it was only a shadow of the good things to come in Christ. With His one sacrifice for sin for all time the sacrificial system of the Old Covenant was fulfilled. Since this is the case, the worship of the temple is now forbidden to us. To continue it would be to deny that the offering Jesus made of himself is sufficient (*cf.* Heb. 8-10). Therefore none of the regulations governing the worship of the temple remains in force. And we are not merely free from their binding power, but, since Christ has come and fulfilled the whole of it, we are prohibited from using any of them. There is not only nothing in Scripture which warrants our emulation of any portion of temple worship, but we are forbidden to return to it. That the temple was razed to the ground in A. D. 70 by Titus and its worship thereby terminated was not an accident of history, but a forceful prevention of a continuation of the sacrifices of the Old Testament, the continuation of which would have been offensive to God. Christian liberty did not allow the Apostolic church to continue, and does not allow us to return to, a system God has abolished. This is true both of the sacrifices which were central to the worship of the temple and of such incidental elements as the incense which, though prescribed in detail, was relatively peripheral. All has been abolished. Whatever else it may be, New Testament worship may not be that of the temple.

Of what, then, does worship under the New Covenant consist? As Christians it is certain we are meant to worship God. We are not only to honor Him in the general way we live our lives, but we are instructed to gather together as His people, as a church, to worship Him. How is this worship regulated by the yoke of Christ and to what extent is it left to our own discretion? It is clear that there is no detailed systematic instruction given us. As a consequence many have urged that the church, being freed from the law and from the sacrificial worship of the Old Covenant, is now free in regard to its worship, Roman Catholics, the Eastern Orthodox Churches, Episcopalians and Lutherans believe that they are free to impose ceremonies in worship, conceiving of them as beneficial to the worship of the church. Many, if not most, others today believe that the church has been given freedom, perhaps within very broad limits, to worship God as it pleases. Usually this involves those elements which are found in the New

Testament, but administered in such a way as the church chooses, on the (usually implicit) assumption that God will be pleased whatever the church does, as long as it is done in faith and with a right heart.

There is, however, no indication in the New Testament that the church has been given the privilege of worshipping God as it pleases, or imposing its ideas of how He is best worshipped on others or even of applying broad principles as it sees fit. In worship, as in much else, the want of systematic presentation in Scripture does not mean the mind of God is not made plain.

Apostolic precept and example, particularly in conjunction with what we know of the worship of the synagogue in the first century, which was clearly used as a model by the Apostolic or primitive church, makes it plain what was the norm for the New Testament church. Every indication is that the worship of the New Testament church was essentially a continuation of the worship of the synagogue, with only such modifications as were necessitated by the transition from the Old Covenant to the New. Synagogue worship had been in Israel at least since the return from Exile and possibly (perhaps probably and some would argue certainly) from remote antiquity. Surely both Jesus and His disciples endorsed the worship of the synagogue by their regular participation in it. The worship of the Apostolic church was modeled closely upon it. It was only much later and very gradually that ritualistic innovations were added to it. The worship of the Roman church, both as it existed in the later Middle Ages and as it exists today, has almost no affinity to the worship of the church of the New Testament. Rather it is the worship of the Reformers, particularly that of Calvin and the Reformed churches, which closely reflects the worship of the Apostolic church (though the Reformed churches have largely departed from such worship over the last century and a half, with many moving toward ritualism).

The historic practice of the Reformed churches, as summarized in the Westminster Confession of Faith, Chapter 21, is an attempt to follow the practice of the New Testament church. Thus prayer (I Tim. 2:1), the reading of the Scripture (Acts 15:21), the preaching of God's word (II Tim. 4:2), the singing of praise (Col. 3:16) and the administration of the sacraments (Acts

21:42) are all part of the ordinary public worship of God. It is beyond doubt that these were elements of the worship of the New Testament church. It is not clear that anything else was included in the ordinary worship of the New Testament church, though certainly it was corporately engaged in a variety of other activities. These included the collection and distribution of alms, a fellowship which involved a measure of sharing of material possessions, love feasts and mutual comfort and counsel. But there is no evidence that the ongoing worship of God, as practiced in the synagogue and in the first century church, included anything beyond the elements first mentioned.

Various claims have been made in regard to the nature of the worship of the New Testament Church. Although this is not the proper place to consider it fully, it should be said that it is a serious error to suppose that the events of Pentecost in general, and a speaking in tongues in particular, were anything more than extraordinary manifestations of the Spirit's power, attesting the truth and reality of the claims of Christ at the beginning of the Christian era. Thus speaking in tongues has no place in the ongoing worship of God by the church; we are not free to attempt to imitate that which the Spirit no longer bestows. This is true of services of 'healing' as well; the essentially fraudulent healing so prevalent today never results in the blind receiving their sight or the withered hand being restored, but is confined to that which can not be readily verified. The miracles which accompanied Jesus and the Apostles are not possible for us to duplicate by our own power and have without question been withdrawn since the conclusion of the age in which Jesus came.

Nor should we mistake the figurative language of Revelation for instruction or example to us for our worship. That the twenty-four elders in 5:8 had a harp and golden bowls full of incense and proceeded to sing a new song is no more intended for our imitation in worship than are the pearly gates or golden streets of the heavenly Jerusalem (9:21) intended for the church to imitate in constructing buildings in which to worship or cities in which to live. The worship of the glorified saints in heaven is no more normative for the Christian church than the worship of the temple or the extraordinary manifestations of the Spirit's power which accompanied the coming of Christ and the initial spread of the gospel, but is confined to the precept and practice of the Apostolic church itself, as it is recorded for us in Scripture.

While positively, gospel liberty in worship is freedom to worship God as He would be worshipped, negatively it is freedom from being forced to worship God in ways devised by human invention. It takes away our liberty in Christ to be forced to sit and watch while a priest goes through some sort of mumbo jumbo or hocus pocus, with gestures, incense and the like. It equally curtails our liberty to be forced to sit and watch while 'the fat lady sings', while doting parents admire (and perhaps applaud) a children's choir, while a dance troupe performs or while a dramatic production is presented. It does not matter if the performance is well or badly done. It does not matter if the performers are talented or not. It does not even mater if the performers intend in their hearts to honor God. For none of these things is required of us in Scripture; there is no indication God wishes to be worshipped in these ways. And to impose such worship on believers gathered together to worship God is to force on them worship of human invention. Whether or not they recognize that this is being done, the gospel liberty given us in Christ is thereby taken away.

It will not do to say that the individual believer whose liberty is thus taken away is free to leave and worship elsewhere, where there is a more congenial style of worship. This assumes an urban, suburban or large town setting in which there will be a church which worships without the offending practice. It does not cover a situation in a rural or small town environment (or a state church in which non-Biblical forms of worship are prescribed) in which the abridgement of liberty can not--or at least can not easily--be remedied.

Nor does it justify those who would impose their ideas of how God ought to be worshipped on others. A church--any church--ought to order its affairs in general and its worship in particular in such a way that any believer who comes together with it should immediately feel at home and should no more be forced to worship in ways not found in Scripture than he should be compelled to hear erroneous or heretical doctrine in the preaching and teaching or fail to receive the basic love and hospitality due a fellow believer. Those who believe themselves free to impose their ideas on other believers are seriously out of accord with New Testament teaching. We are not Lords and Masters in the church of Christ, but are only servants and ambassadors for Him; we have only powers which are ministerial and declarative, not legislative. There is nothing in Scripture which gives us power to innovate in worship; we are as restricted in this as we are in matters of doctrine and, without the authority of Scripture, are no more free to invent ways of worshipping God than we are free to invent teaching about Him.

Some have maintained that it is appropriate for different churches to have differing worship styles, often citing cultural differences. In practice this tends to mean catering to a variety of musical tastes (classical, folk, gospel, rock, etc.) and often is just various kinds of entertainment, frequently with an emphasis on instrumental accompaniment. Indeed, much of what goes on under the guise of worship today is essentially entertainment. The applause which increasingly frequently accompanies the performance of, for example, a musical or dramatic presentation is illustrative of this and those who attempt to excuse it as an expression of appreciation to God are simply deluding themselves, while justifying a practice which is essentially blasphemous, giving as it does honor to man in a service supposedly designed to worship God. Of course there is no indication in the New Testament that God is pleased by such a man-centered, entertainment-oriented worship, whatever the musical orientation; there is no indication in Scripture that worship is to vary from church to church or that the aesthetic, musical or cultural taste of believers should have any influence on worship. New Testament worship is spiritual worship and, as such, like the worship of the synagogue, is devoid of signs, symbols and ceremonies (apart from the two instituted by our Lord, baptism and the Supper); it is a worship in which cultural differences are minimized to the circumstantial and are not allowed to intrude into the substance of worship. Thus it is wrong to expect that we should have dancing in aisles in one culture and ceremonies and vestments in another. While such externals as dress (as long as it does not signify anything and thus enter into the substance of worship), type of building and seats (if indeed there are seats at all), and time of meeting are circumstantial and vary from place to place and time to time, the substance of worship ought to be such that Christians from any time or place ought to feel immediately at home--and ought not to find anything which would surprise them. Those who urge the expression of cultural differences generally do so because they also urge the inclusion in worship of practices which God has not commanded and which by their very nature are culture oriented. Gospel liberty in worship is such that cultural barriers are minimized; restricting our worship simply to what God has commanded enables this. Emphasis on different styles and on cultural differences separates Christians, both from each other and from God.

Much ingeneuity has been exercised in attempting to justify various worship practices. Some have even argued that music is a spiritual gift, claiming that the lists of spiritual gifts given in Scripture are not exhaustive, but rather only illustrative. But such arguments generally contend only for a few other supposed gifts, usually including such artistic accomplishments as dance, drama and even magic. Beyond these and similar forms of entertainment, no one ever suggests that a surgeon perform some particularly difficult operation or a plumber clear a clogged drain as part of worship, however talented each may be. Although all these may be legitimate parts of our lives, Scripture nowhere suggests that God is pleased by any of them when they are included as part of our worship.[1] What we may well do to the glory of God in our lives in general is not thereby given any warrant to be intrude into our worship of Him.

Others have sought to obtain freedom to worship God as they please by saying that only principles are taught in Scripture (e.g., that we are to praise God is clearly taught, but not *how* we are to praise Him; thus we may do so in prayer, drama or whatever suits us. We are not confined to song).

---

[1]This is not to say that singing is not mandated as part of God's worship, but that it is not a matter which relates to spiritual gifts or even musical talent. The 1867 Old School General Assembly rightly reminded "the churches that the Scriptures nowhere recognize the service of song as to be performed by the few in behalf of the many; but teach us that the Lord delights in the 'praise of all the people.'" *The Presbyterian Digest of 1886* . . ., compiled by William E. Moore (Philadelphia: Presbyterian Board of Publication, 1886), 781.

But although it is true that the praise of God ought to permeate our prayer and preaching, for example, as well as our song, it can not legitimately be concluded that the primary form of praise, that of song by the whole church, is not commanded as much as is the principle of praise. It is true that principles are taught, but that this is the case does not mean that forms are not prescribed as well. Saying that it is left to our judgement as mature Christians how we will render praise to God sounds noble, but if it leads to practice contrary to God's revealed will it is nevertheless simple will-worship and rebellion, however artfully disguised by fine-sounding words.

How has the church been led into the non-Scriptural practices so common today? It is probable that the modern failure to consider God's commands rather than human desires in worship stems largely from nineteenth century Revivalism which, working on semi-Pelagian or Arminian principles, sought to concentrate first the Revival meeting and then worship in general on the sinner and his conversion rather than on God. The result has been a worship oriented to the worshipper rather than the One worshipped. As the potential convert seemed to respond to gospel songs and extended emotional appeals and anxious seats, these were emphasized. Soon they became institutionalized in worship. It was reasoned that people were influenced for good by the use of such means; surely therefore God would be pleased. The progression to the present day, in which worship is largely entertainment, has been gradual, but really is little more than the logical result of such a premise. If it pleases people and attracts them to hear the gospel (often itself adjusted so as not to offend), we assume God will be pleased by it and that we are therefore free so to worship Him.

All this makes it plain that, as the Westminster Confession of Faith puts it in the matter of divorce, "the corruption of man be such as is apt to study arguments" that will enable him to worship God in a way that pleases him, without concern as to how God wants to be worshipped. This was true in the case of Cain and is equally true today. In my own experience, there is little as likely to get many, ostensibly spiritually mature, Christian people really angry than to suggest that they ought to consider if what they are doing in worship is really pleasing to God, according to Scripture. If we are genuinely seeking to worship God, if our worship is not to be will-worship, if it is not to be primarily oriented to entertain ourselves, surely we ought to focus on what will please God. For therein lies not only the right and only safe course of action, but also the only true path of liberty, the freedom given us in the gospel truly to love God and serve Him as He would be served, forever.

7 - FAMILY WORSHIP: BIBLICAL, REFORMED, AND VIABLE FOR TODAY

Douglas F. Kelly

Scriptural Basis

To understand the Scriptural teaching on family worship, we must begin by looking at the basic purpose for which God created man. God's purpose for man can only be understood in light of who God is. The Bible teaches that the One God who is "infinite and eternal" in His being and attributes has always existed as three persons "the same in substance, equal in power and glory." According to Richard of Saint Victor, a great theologian of twelfth century France, God's triune life is related to His being love, as I John teaches us. That is, love is outgoing and overflowing, seeking another with whom it may share its blessedness and have it reflected back by an appropriate respondent. Love is never self-centered, isolated and solitary. Thus, as Richard explains, God has never been a solitary, lonely individual who was lacking anything outside of Himself, but rather has always lived in what we may call the family life of Father, Son and Holy Spirit with an eternal sharing of the fullness of life, light and love among these utterly happy and holy persons. Our very family life on earth is in some sense a pale reflection of the Holy Trinity, for Ephesians 3:14-15 speaks of Him as "Father . . . of whom the whole family in heaven and on earth is named."

From hints we have in John chapter 17 and elsewhere, we have the impression that the Father so loved the Son that from all eternity he purposed to create a world that would then be peopled with a race who would be like His Son in having personalities (but unlike Him in being finite creatures). This race then being like the Son could share -- in a way appropriate to finite, personal creatures -- in the blessed happiness and holiness of the family life of the Trinity.

Therefore God created Adam in His own image and from Adam's side created Eve, from whom the whole human family was to come. Genesis makes it clear that God created our first parents -- and their future progeny -- for fellowship with Himself. God had personal communication with Adam, and "walked in the garden in the cool of the day" (Gen. 3:8). We may surely assume that the fellowship Adam and Eve had with God involved reverential worship of His person.

This 'native' reverential worship of and delightful fellowship with God however was soon to be turned into fear and dread as Adam sinned against God and so brought infinite guilt, divine wrath and endless separation between himself -- and all his descendants -- and the God who created him for fellowship and joy. But God's purpose to have a vast multitude of Adam's seed in the endless joy of family life and fellowship with Himself was not to be thwarted by this sin -- terrible as it was. From all eternity the Father had appointed the Son "as the lamb slain from the foundation of the world" (Rev. 13:8) to come to earth as the God/man "in the fullness of the time" (Gal. 4:4) in order to redeem "the seed of the woman" (Gen. 3:15).

The whole Bible is the true story of the eternally planned, historical development and future triumph of the Father's purpose to redeem the chosen myriad millions of Adam's race through His Son and Spirit back into the holy joy of living communion with and unceasing worship of Himself. Some have thought that the coats of skin with which God clothed Adam and Eve after they realized the nakedness of their fallen condition (Gen. 3:21) may be the first hint of the blood sacrifice of animals, which in pointing to "the lamb of God that takes away the sin of the world" (John 1:29) covers guilt (see Heb. 8, 9, and 10) so sinners can come back into the gracious favor of God and resume the real goal of their existence, which is to know, worship and glorify Him.

As the story of redemption is unfolded, we find that God deals with the human race through the principles of covenant and representation. That is, God has so structured the world that human beings must inevitably relate to Him and to one another in terms of divinely imposed arrangements and consequences. Central to this inescapable covenant structure by which the world and humanity must always operate is the principle of representation, according to which the many are affected by what a few do on their behalf and in their place.

Romans 5, 1 Corinthians 15 and other texts indicate that every human being who shall ever live is directly related to and represented by either the first Adam or the last Adam (the Lord Jesus Christ). As an old Puritan said, "there are two and only two Adams, and every man hangs from the belt of one of these two." Adam represented -- and thus implicated -- me (and every other human being) in sin, guilt and death. The Last Adam represents -- and thus implicates -- me (and every other sinner who is chosen to be united to Him by grace through faith) in his holy life, atoning death and victorious resurrection. Put in other terms, all persons are represented by Adam in the original probation (or Covenant of Works), and many persons -- past our counting -- are represented by Christ in the Covenant of Grace.

But the principle of representation is much broader than the matter of my identification (and hence my ultimate salvation or damnation) with the first or the last Adam. God has for his covenant purposes so structured this world and its history that the principle of representation runs through -- and indeed makes possible -- the effective functioning of every major human institution such as family, church, and state. The parents represent the children, and father represents wife and children; the elders represent the members of the church, and various civil magistrates represent the citizens of the state. In the plan of God, what these representative leaders do directly and seriously affects the lives -- and sometimes destinies -- of those whom they represent.

We must now look specifically at how the principle of representation was at work in the life and particularly the worship of the chosen families of the Bible. We find Cain and Abel offering sacrifice to God (Gen. 4); whether they may have been representing wives and children at that stage is not revealed to us. The Patriarch Job (who presumably lived between the time of Adam and Noah) sanctified his children by "rising up early in the morning and offering burnt offerings according to the number of them all: for Job said, "It may be that my sons sinned and cursed God in their hearts"

(Job 1:5). When the same text tells us, "thus did Job continually," we would infer that this was a representative duty of godly fathers of that time. Job represented his children before God in worship, pleading for their sanctification so that the family could remain rightly related to God and so fulfill the purpose of its creation -- to glorify (as Job 2:3) and worship Him (as Job 1:20).

During these ancient times, true worship seems to have been passed down through generations of godly families, even while rebellion against God was communicated through an ungodly line of descent. B.M. Palmer asks:

> But was not piety preserved in the line of Seth, under the denomination of "the sons of God" as distinguished from the ungodly descendants of Cain, who were designated as "the daughters of men"? And through what channel was true religion kept alive and transmitted, until that sad commingling of the two lines brought on the enormous wickedness which terminated in the judgment of the flood? Was not the first act of Noah in coming forth from the ark, the resumption of the patriarchal prerogative in offering burnt sacrifices for himself and for his household?[1]

At this stage of human history, God was not dealing with men through the later institutions of church and state (the state appears not to have been instituted until after the Flood, when the death penalty is given in Genesis 9). The race was organized in terms of families and probably tribes, and so God's primary dealing with the race was through the offices of the father.

> The patriarchal blessing, too, was priestly and official in its nature. And the birthright which the profane Esau rejected, and which the supple Jacob acquired, was the investiture of the first-born with all the patriarchal privileges, magisterial and priestly, which death

---

[1] B.M Palmer, *The Family in its Civil and Churchly Aspects* (Richmond: Presbyterian Committee of Publication, 1876), 203.

conveyed from father to son. . . . When the church came to be more distinctly constituted, with enlarged promises and with new seals, in the days of Abraham, it was still founded in the house of the patriarch. A covenant was made with him, which included a twofold blessing. "I will make of thee a great nation," said Jehovah to him; "and in thee shall all the families of the earth be blessed." It is a double promise, of temporal enlargement and of spiritual preferment. In the former, we find the Hebrew nation in its germ; in the latter, the Christian Church.   By virtue of the first, he becomes the father of all the tribes of Israel; by virtue of the last, he becomes the father of the faithful through all generations. . . . The seal of this ecclesiastical covenant was put into the flesh according to the law of natural descent. . . . Thus visibly was the Church set up in the family of Abraham for a time, even more conspicuous than the Hebrew State which should issue from his loins.[2]

The principle of the father representing the family in worship to God and of God dealing with the family on the basis of the standing and action of the father continues under the Mosaic economy. Before Moses it would appear that the first-born was set aside for God and in some sense became the priest to represent the family to God, but that upon the institution of the Levitical system, the tribe of Levi replaces the first-born as the representative priesthood for all Israel.   Yet the principle of the representation in worship of the first-born is remembered as silver redemption money is given to the Tabernacle (and Temple) as in Numbers chapters 3 and 8.

The representative duties of the father for family worship and standing with God were still not eclipsed by the substitution of the tribe of Levi and commutative tax for the first-born. The father was to lead the family in Passover worship and specifically instruct the children in its meaning. After the land was conquered, families were to go up to Jerusalem

---

[2]*Ibid.*, 204-205.

three times a year to worship together. Family religious instruction is laid
upon the parents in Deuteronomy 11:18-19: "Therefore shall ye lay up these
my words in your heart and in your soul, and bind them for a sign upon
your hand, that they may be as frontlets between your eyes; and ye shall
teach them your children, speaking of them when thou sittest in thine house,
and when thou walkest by the way, when thou liest down, and when thou
risest up."

The period of the monarchy saw no diminution of the duty of the
head of the household to lead his family in divine worship, and thus by his
life and service, to bring blessing or cursing upon them. The spirit of David,
king, father and Psalmist, is well summarized by Alexander Fletcher:

> David, after bringing the ark from the house of Obededom to the
> place prepared for it, returned at night, and blessed his household;
> which was nothing else than engaging in the work of domestic
> worship. His own acknowledgment and resolution prove that he
> regularly maintained the observances of family religion. Psalm
> 101:1-2: "I will sing of mercy and judgment: unto thee, O Lord, will
> I sing. I will behave myself wisely in a perfect way. O when wilt
> thou come unto me! I will walk within my house with a perfect
> heart." Surely none will venture to assert that he could have done
> all this without the regular discharge of the duty of domestic
> worship.[3]

As the Old Testament people are about to enter the blessings of life
in the promised land, Joshua reminds them of the importance of family
religion: "As for me and my house, we will serve the Lord" (Josh. 24:15).
And as the descendants of these Old Testament people will one day enter the
blessings of life in the promised Spirit of Christ, Zechariah 12:12-14 predicts
that as He is poured out upon them, they will experience the spirit of
brokenness, grace and supplication, family by family: "The land shall mourn,
every family apart; the family of David apart, and their wives apart; the

---

[3]Alexander Fletcher, *A Guide to Family Devotion* (London: George Virtue, n.d.), xiv.

family of Nathan apart, and their wives apart; the family of Levi apart, and their wives apart; the family of Shimei apart, and their wives apart; all the families that remain, apart, and their wives apart."

The New Testament, which is based on the coming of the promised Messiah and the long awaited outpouring of the Spirit of God on all flesh, testifies to a continuance of the sacred bonds between religious worship and household life as well as to an increase (rather than a reduction) of the representative, priestly influence of the parents upon their offspring. In the words of Palmer:

> . . . [in] the ancient promise made to the father of the faithful, the Family lies couched as the germ of the Church: "In thee shall all the families of the earth be blessed." Observe how this is recognized by Peter in the first proclamation of the gospel, after the day of Pentecost, when he says to the Jews, "the promise is unto you and to your children, and to all that are afar off." The line of the Church is through the household; and the fundamental law is assumed in its application to the Gentiles, that the ecclesiastical position of the child shall be determined by that of the parent. It is upon this identical principle the Apostle settles the controversy which arose upon the continuance of the marriage relation between believers and unbelievers, when he says, "The unbelieving husband is sanctified by the wife and the unbelieving wife is sanctified by the husband; else were your children unclean, but now are they holy" (1 Cor. vii:14). The faith of either party determines the status of the offspring, as being within the covenant of God, and thus constitutionally entitled to the privileges of Church upon earth. The household baptisms in the New Testament proceed upon the same fundamental idea, recognizing the law of birth fixing the fact of Church relationship, as still unrepealed. It is difficult to see how this cumulative evidence could be stronger than it is -- all the more

valuable because so incidental -- that God designed the Family to be the radix of the Church.[4]

The history book of the early church, Acts, tells of the Roman officer, Cornelius, "a devout man and one that feared God with all his house, who gave much alms to the people and prayed to God always" (10:1-2). Aquila and Priscilla, Paul's "helpers in Christ Jesus," had a "church in their house" (Acts 18:26; Rom. 16:3, 5). The family religion of Timothy's mother exercised its ancient and beneficent covenant sway over her son. Paul speaks of: " . . . the unfeigned faith that is in thee, which dwelt first in thy grandmother Lois, and thy mother Eunice. . ." (II Tim. 1:5).

J.W. Alexander reminds us of the centrality of family religion and duties to New Testament ethics:

> It was doubtless recognized in regard to spiritual as well as in regard to temporal things, that 'if any provide not for his own, and especially for those of his own household, he hath denied the faith, and is worse than an infidel' (I Tim. v.3). That spirit of social prayer which led disciples to join in supplication or praise, in upper chambers, in prisons, in the stocks and on the sea-beach (Acts i.13; xvi.25; Gal. iv.12; 2 Tim. i.3), could not but have manifested itself in daily household devotion.[5]

A reverent reading of Old and New Testament will leave us with this unmistakable conclusion: family religion, which depends not a little on the household head daily leading the family before God in worship, is one of the most powerful structures that the covenant-keeping God has given for the expansion of redemption through the generations, so that countless multitudes may be brought into communion with and worship of the One who is worthy "to receive glory and honor and power: for thou hast created

---

[4]Palmer, op.cit., 208-209.

[5]James W. Alexander, Thoughts on Family Worship (Philadelphia: Presbyterian Board of Publication, 1847), 17.

all things, and for thy pleasure they are and were created" (Rev. 4:11). Given the importance of family worship, we are not surprised that the covenant God has clearly laid down in the Scriptures the exact terms of the covenant obligations binding on all generations of household heads, who have the awesome privilege of representing their dependents before the Living God. A structure so potent in the winning of untold millions as the parental influence exercised through daily family worship has not been left to the whim of human imagination. God has definitely regulated this matter in His Word.

How careful, tenderly sensitive and joyfully confident we should therefore be as we seek the wisdom of God properly to carry out this tremendous privilege and responsibility! In order to serve the God of the covenant as he deserves, we must always say: "To the law and to the testimony" (Is. 8:20); "The entrance of thy words giveth light" (Ps. 119:130).

Commenting on Christ's words to the woman of Samaria in John 4:23-24, Professor John Murray has written:

> The principle "in spirit and truth" bears directly upon the content of worship. If worship must be consonant with the nature of God, it must be in accord with what God has revealed himself to be and regulated as to content and mode by the revelation God has given in holy Scripture. The sanction enunciated ("in spirit and truth") excludes all human invention and imagination and warns us against the offense and peril of offering strange fire unto the Lord. No principle more than this inculcates jealousy to ascertain that what we offer has the warrant of divine authority.[6]

---

[6]John Murray, "The Worship of God in the Four Gospels," in *The Biblical Doctrine of Worship*, eds. Martin, McMillan, et al. (Pittsburgh: The Reformed Presbyterian Church of North America, 1974), 93-94.

Family Worship in the Modern World: A Continuing Duty

Our brief study of the history of God's redemptive dealings with men shows that regular household worship is a covenant duty of every believing family. We must now, from a very practical viewpoint, consider the obligatory nature of this duty, and then survey its content, its spirit, its difficulties, and finally, its blessings.

A Commanded Duty

Daily divine worship is a household duty which our covenant God holds the head of the house responsible for instituting and maintaining. In the chaste words of the Westminster Confession of Faith, "God . . . is to be worshipped . . . in private families daily . . ." (XXI.6). The head of each household is never an independent or absolute head; he is merely a steward, an undershepherd whose covenant duty it is to bring the sheep, day by day, to pledge their love and loyalty and to receive their needed blessings from "the chief Shepherd" (I Pet. 5:4). The representative principle inherent in God's covenant dealings with our race indicates that the head of each family is to represent his family before God in divine worship and that the spiritual atmosphere and longterm personal welfare of that family will be affected in large measure by the fidelity--or failure--of the family head in this area. Authority is always in order to responsibility: this is basic to every human institution -- business, government, church and family. To possess authority by virtue of one's covenant position and to fail to exercise it, is an appalling failure of stewardship, as the parable of the talents reminds us. But, on the contrary, to exercise one's authority properly is a way of subduing the earth for the Lord, extending His kingdom among men, defeating sin and sowing seed for a harvest of goodness, beauty and truth.

One of the reasons God gives for the immense trust he reposed in Abraham and for the lasting blessings He placed upon his seed is this: "For I know him, that he will command his children and his household after him . . ." (Gen. 18:19). Concerning this text, Andrew Murray has written:

The spirit of modern so-called liberty has penetrated even into our family life; and there are parents who, some from a mistaken view of duty, some from want of thought as to their sacred calling, some from love of ease, have no place for such a word as "command." They have not seen the heavenly harmony between authority and love, between obedience and liberty. Parents are more than friends and advisers: they have been clothed by God with a holy authority to be exercised in leading their children in the way of the Lord. There is an age when the will of the child is to a great extent in their hands, and when the quiet, loving exercise of that authority will have mighty influence.[7]

Precisely how does a father command his offspring into the ways of the Lord? Granted that the family is a community of life, the first way that the father and mother command their family will surely be by their lives. Sincerity (though not perfection) of parental life is the necessary background for meaningful family worship if that worship is to bear heavenly, commanding authority on the young.

J.W. Alexander has written very movingly in this regard:

The example of a father is acknowledged to be all-important. The stream must not be expected to rise higher than the fountain. The Christian householder will feel himself constrained to say: I am leading my family in solemn addresses to God; what manner of man should I be! how wise, holy, and exemplary![8]

He is their head. He is such by a divine and unalterable constitution. These are duties and prerogatives which he cannot alienate. There is something more than mere precedence in age, knowledge, or substance. He is the father and the master. No act

---

[7]Andrew Murray, *How to Raise Your Children For Christ* (Minneapolis, Minn.: Bethany Fellowship, Inc., 1975), 46.

[8]J.W. Alexander, *op.cit.*, 49.

of his, and nothing in his character can fail to leave a mark on those around him. . . . Though all priesthood, in the proper sense, is now done away on earth and absorbed in the functions of the great High Priest, there is still something like a priestly intervention in the service of the Christian patriarch.[9]

Especially where the head of the family is one who grows in grace and Christian knowledge, he will by his very presence lift up the hearts of his household. . . . Where the head of the family is a man of faith, of affection and of zeal, consecrating all his works and life to Christ, it is very rare to find all his household otherwise-minded.[10]

Lest we parents be totally discouraged at this high calling, let it be added here that parental perfection in daily life is *not* required for the observation of anointed family worship. The Bible nowhere teaches sinless perfection of believers -- whether parents or children, and it is perfectly clear that Abraham, Moses, Joshua, David and all of the others who are our Biblical examples of headship in household piety were far from perfect. Weaknesses, inconsistencies, and even sins in the parents will not "turn off" their children so long as the parents are sincerely seeking to follow the Lord and are honest enough to admit and confess these faults in front of the children, as together they seek God's mercy in family prayer. A.W. Pink said it well: "It is not the sins of a Christian, but his *unconfessed* sins, which choke the channel of blessing and cause so many to miss God's best."[11] While it is true that those closest to us in the family circle know best our personal weaknesses, it is also true that they will be the best able to perceive our heart sincerity. Children are excellent readers of the heart, and they will follow us -- imperfect though they know us to be -- when our hearts are set on following our Good Shepherd, and on doing His -- and our -- sheep

---

[9]*Ibid.*, 44.

[10]*Ibid.*, 32-33.

[11]Arthur W. Pink, *Pink Jewels* (MacDill AFB, Florida: Tyndale Bible Society, n.d.), 91.

good. After all, the Old Testament high priest had first to offer sacrifice for his own sin before he was in a position to sacrifice for the sins of the people (cf. Heb. 5). Human infirmity and failure did not disqualify him from mediating the blessing of God to his people; nor do they do so today. Our sufficiency is in the Great High Priest, not in ourselves.

Content of our Duty

God, who commanded corporate and family worship, and provided the sacrifice of His Son to make it possible, has also provided us with specific instruction by way of principles and examples -- as to how our families are profitably to worship Him. We have Scriptural guidance both as to frequency and times of worship and also as to the elements of worship in the household.

During long periods of the Old Testament economy, and on into the New Testament, official worship was conducted twice a day: the beginning and close of each day were sanctified by the offering of morning and evening sacrifices in tabernacle and temple. It seems likely that home worship in the Hebrew commonwealth and in the early Church would have followed this pattern of morning and evening prayer. There are morning and evening Psalms (though these do not exclude the idea of praising God three times a day, seven times a day, or continually -- cf. Ps. 55:17; 119:164; and 34:1). Perhaps we would be safe in thinking the exhortation to praise God seven times a day, for instance, or 'continually' might refer to one's inner spirit and attitude (rather like 'secret prayer'), whereas corporate prayer (in temple, synagogue and family) would fit into the twofold daily rhythm of morning and evening. The fact that "evening and morning were the first day" suggests a rhythm of life for God's image-bearers, and the universal necessity of going to bed at night and getting up in the morning reminds us of our dependence upon God for His blessing upon our rest and our work. Thus, from ancient times, morning and evening have been considered appropriate times for corporate worship of the God who created, redeemed and sustains us and ours.

During much of the Middle Ages, the duty of family worship seems to have been largely eclipsed by the church's emphasis on the daily public mass in the sanctuary, but at the Reformation -- and especially in Puritan times -- it was realized that:

> God's grace could be as well exercised in the family as in the cloister. Neither can it be claimed that discipline and communion with God demand withdrawal from family life. The family was called 'a school of Christ,' and there we learn all necessary virtues and practice all needful spiritual exercises.[12]

Some of the writers such as Matthew Henry give us helpful guidance as to the differing content between morning and evening household worship. According to Henry and other Puritan writers, both morning and evening praise consisted of the same basic elements. The Westminster Directory for Worship states them plainly: "Family worship, which ought to be performed by every family, ordinarily morning and evening, consists in prayer, reading the Scriptures, and singing praises."

While the elements were the same, the emphasis differed between morning and evening prayers in the Puritan household. Hughes Old has beautifully summarized the teaching of Matthew Henry in this regard (taken from Henry's 1694 Family Hymns, and three of his published sermons on Family Worship)[13] and isolates three emphases in Henry's teaching on morning prayer:

> First, the morning is a time of praise. He comments: "Every day we have reason to bless him, for every day he is blessing us; and therefore, as he is giving out to us the fruits of his favor, which are said to be 'new every morning,' . . . so we should be still returning

---

[12]Gordon Stevens Wakefield, *Puritan Devotion* (London: The Epworth Press, 1957), 55.

[13]Hughes O. Old, "The Reformed Daily Office: a Puritan Perspective," in *Reformed Liturgy and Music* 12:4 (1978), 9-18. Cf. Matthew Henry, *Family-Hymns. Gather'd (mostly) out of the best Translations of David's Psalms* (London: Tho. Parkhurst, 1695).

the expression of our gratitude to him, and other pious and devout affections, which like fire on the altar, must be new every morning." The morning is a time to take notice of the bounty of God's gifts to observe how "the heavens declare the glory of God." It is a time to remember the story of creation and the promise God gave to Noah, the covenant with the day and the night.

Second, Henry reminds us of how Job rose up early in the morning to make sacrifices for his children. In the morning, prayer should be made for our families, remembering each person by name. . . .

Third, we are to pray that God would strengthen us to perform the duties of relation and vocation. By the duties of relation were meant the duties of a father to a son, a husband to a wife. . . . The duties of vocation had to do with one's work.[14]

Henry also had a threefold emphasis for evening prayer in the family: thankfulness to God, penitent reflections upon the sins of the day, and humble supplications for the mercies of the night.[15] Somewhat more simply, the nineteenth century Scottish minister, W.B. Clark, summarized the respective duties of morning and evening prayer as follows: "Every morning, we should supplicate God's protection throughout the day, and his blessing on our labors; and in the evening, we should implore his preservation of us, during the night, and such sleep as is necessary for the refreshment of the body."[16]

Without specifying whether for morning or evening, the 1647 Church of Scotland *Directory For Family Worship* reminds the family to pray not only for personal and familial, but also for national and ecclesiastical concerns: "First, Prayer and praises performed with a special reference, as well to the public condition of the kirk of God and this kingdom, as to the present case of the family, and every member thereof" (par. II).

---

[14]*Ibid.*, 15-16.

[15]*Ibid.*, 16-17.

[16]W.B. Clark, *Book of Family Worship* (London: T. Nelson and Sons, 1852), 208.

A large part of the sweet power that family worship exercises over its participants lies in its peculiarly personal nature. As J.W. Alexander says:

> Many things may be proper here, which would be out of place in a promiscuous assembly, or even a small meeting. There is no domestic want, danger, sorrow, or dispensation, which may not be remembered. Special cases in the household will be faithfully and affectionately commended to God. . . our Heavenly Father permits us to spread before him our minutest trials, and this is one of the principal blessings of domestic religion.[17]

Those of us who were raised in Christian homes where there was daily worship can never get far from our minds the sounds of our parents' and grandparents' loved voices lifting our very names in intercession and calling on the Lord to bless us in large and small matters. There is probably no more effective way to influence our teenaged and adult children for God than to let them hear us praying for them -- by name and specific need -- on a daily basis while they are young. This says: "you are important to your parents and you are important to God. God is the One who will help you." If young parents will pray with and for their children now, while they are small, it may pay rich dividends in preventing grief and alienation during teenage and adult years.

Many a sincere Christian parent, however -- particularly those who are not teachers or preachers -- will be daunted at the thought of leading others in prayer, even in the family circle. The 1647 Church of Scotland *Directory For Family Worship* wisely suggests that those who are "rude and weaker" may "begin at a set form of prayer" (par. IX). "John Knox's Liturgy" contains a "Form of Prayers" to be used in family worship, morning and evening. John Calvin wrote "Several Godly Prayers" to help individuals and families, including one for "Preparing to go to school."[18]

------

[17]J.W. Alexander, *op.cit.*, 196.

[18]"Several Godly Prayers," in John Calvin, *Tracts* (Edinburgh: Calvin Translation Society, 1849), II, 96-97.

In sum, there are numerous books of prayer which are theologically sound and would prove helpful to those who feel shy about praying out loud in the family.

And yet, as the 1647 Church of Scotland Directory adds, if those who may feel 'rude and weak' in articulating public prayers will do two things, then they will by and by become able to pray freely out loud. First, let them keep using the set forms of prayer publicly, and secondly, let them in secret, ". . . be more fervent and frequent . . . to God, for enabling of their hearts to conceive, and their tongues to express convenient desires to God for their family" (par. IX). In other words, the only way to learn how to pray is to start praying. The Holy Spirit is still given in answer to prayer (Luke 11:13); God will pour the "Spirit of grace and of supplications" upon his people (Zech. 12:10). The more we seek God's face in secret, the more our tongues will be loosed in public.

Reading the Scriptures

After prayer, the second element of family worship mentioned by such classical guides as The Westminster Directory For Worship is the reading of the Scriptures. Probably it will add interest to read from one portion of Scripture in the morning (such as the Old Testament) and another in the evening (such as the New: or vice versa). Many families read consecutively through the Testaments in this way, covering several verses, or perhaps a chapter at a time each worship session.

While it is not absolutely necessary, it is certainly appropriate for the head of the house to make some comments or applications related to the passage he has read which will speak to the current situation of the family, church, or nation. Here it will be helpful for us to quote at large the 1647 Church of Scotland Directory:

> . . . in every family where there is any that can read, the holy scriptures should be read ordinarily to the family; and it is commendable, that thereafter they confer, and by way of conference, make some good use of what hath been read and heard. As, for

example, if any sin be reproved in the word read, use may be made thereof to make all the family circumspect and watchful against the same; or if any judgment be threatened or mentioned to have been inflicted, in that portion of scripture which is read, use may be made to make all the family fear lest the same or a worse judgment befall them, unless they beware of the sin that procured it: and finally, if any duty be required, or comfort held forth in a promise, use may be made to stir up themselves to employ Christ for strength to enable them for doing the commanded duty, and to apply the offered comfort. In all which the master of the family is to have the chief hand; and any member of the family may propone a question or doubt for resolution (par. III).

We note from the last quoted sentence that dialogue is in order here: *i.e.* the children may certainly be encouraged to ask questions, and of course the father or mother may ask the children questions to see what they have learned from the reading and application. This family dialogue around God's Word is very much in line with the Hebraic procedure of household question and answer (*cf.* Ex. 12; Deut. 6; Ps. 78, etc.).

Again, the same question arises here as in the matter of public prayer: how shall those who are not naturally gifted or formally trained in Scriptural teaching manage to comment on them and apply them -- even in the family circle? First of all, look at the passage beforehand, pray over it and ask the Holy Spirit to help you understand and apply it. It is often helpful to purchase some good commentaries on the text which are suitable for laymen. Or one may prefer to begin by quoting directly from some devotional guide for a period of time until one becomes more accustomed to dealing with various texts in family instruction. Remember this significant fact: a few direct, simple, and heartfelt words from one's own parent make far more impression on any child than the most eloquent flow of fine instruction from an outsider. Our real problem as parents is not our lack of ability in praying, reading or commenting, but is rather our underestimation of the immense power and influence God has given us to shape our offspring for His glory simply by virtue of the representative covenant relationship that is ours as parents who are "in Christ."

Singing

The third traditional element of family worship, and one that is deeply embedded in both the private and corporate life of God's covenant people through the ages, is singing. Both Psalmist and New Testament writers command us to sing and give plentiful examples. "Sing praises to God, sing praises: sing praises unto our King, sing praises" (Ps. 47:6). "I will sing of the mercies of the LORD forever: with my mouth will I make known thy faithfulness to all generations" (Ps. 89:1). "Speaking to yourselves in psalms and hymns and spiritual songs, singing and making melody in your heart to the Lord . . ." (Eph. 5:19).

An old writer describes the beauty and drawing power of this part of the service:

> Singing the praises of God is a peculiarly pleasing and animating part of religious worship. . . . Great are the advantages arising from this part of worship. It shows the ungodly and profane the cheerful and animating nature of true religion, and the sublime superiority of the songs of Zion above the boisterous songs of carnal and unhallowed mirth. This part of worship is calculated, in a very eminent degree, to deliver the soul from despondency and gloom, and to impart those delights which bear a close resemblance to the enjoyments of the celestial state. Little children are much pleased with this part of the service, and even before they could speak they have attempted to join in this holy and animating exercise.[19]

This is a grand opportunity to teach our children to sing and love the Psalms of David, an element long neglected in most of our modern

---

[19]Fletcher, *op.cit.*, x.

Presbyterian worship services. In this writer's opinion, the Scottish metrical version of the Psalms is still a highly usable, rich repository of the deepest and broadest and most living Scriptural piety available to the human soul. There are other more modern versions of metrical Psalms as well, which may be easier to understand and more appealing to those not brought up in the Scottish tradition. Some of the contemporary "Scripture songs," which set various verses of the Psalms to pleasing tunes and cadences, may well be appropriate in family worship. "This is the Day which the Lord hath made," "Evening and morning and at noon will I pray" (made famous by the ministry of the late Pastor Lester Roloff), "Thy lovingkindness is better than life," and "The word of the Lord is pure" are all good examples of short, lively and singable texts for family praise.

Catechism

In addition to these major elements of prayer, Scripture reading and singing, it has been a tradition over the years to replace one of the Sabbath family worship services with a time for catechizing the children. In a sense, this is merely a variation on the element of Scripture reading and commentary. To guide our children in memorization of, for instance, the Westminster Shorter Catechism is a matter which requires us to spend considerable time with them -- and that in itself may be one of the greatest benefits that comes to the frenzied and fractured existence of modern American parents and children alike. The fact that a busy, and perhaps tired, father or mother in our society exerts himself or herself to devote personal time each Sunday afternoon or evening to each child individually, and that this precious time is centered on memorizing the great doctrines of the Christian faith in a personal setting, speaks volumes to the child about the true priorities of their parent.

In addition to the purely spiritual impact made on the child by committing the catechism to memory, Professor Thomas F. Torrance has pointed to research done among Scottish school children, which indicates that the catechized child has a greater capacity for conceptual thought than the noncatechized child (who, as a rule, finds it more difficult to think in

concepts as opposed to images).[20]   Obedience to our divinely-imposed
responsibility to teach the Faith to our children thus has its hidden, as well
as obvious, blessings. How better can a parent fulfill the requirements and
reap the promises of such covenant instructions as Psalm 78, than by
regular, time-consuming Sunday catechizing?

"His testimony and his law
in Isr'el he did place,
And charg'd our fathers it to show
to their succeeding race;

That so the race which was to come
might well them learn and know;
And sons unborn, who should arise,
might to their sons them show:

That they might set their hope in God,
And suffer not to fall
His mighty works out of their mind,
but keep his precepts all"
(Psalm 78:5-7, Scottish Metrical Version).

Proper Spirit of Family Worship

Prayer, Scripture, singing and catechism will ultimately avail little
unless family worship is conducted in a proper spirit. Forms -- even good
and Scripturally-based forms -- without life and grace will soon be dropped
by the younger generation. It is never easy, nor is it fully possible, to
describe the 'spirit' of a person, place or duty. Perhaps the best we can do
is to list some of the vital elements that are present where there is an
atmosphere of faithful, lively, and loving family worship.

----

[20]Thomas F. Torrance, *The School of Faith* (London, James Clarke & Co., Ltd., 1959),
xxvii-xxix.

First, let the parents be persuaded that they are ushering their children into the very presence of the Living God. This is not an external, meritorious, works' righteousness sort of ritual, nor is it a tiresome formal treadmill we walk to keep from feeling guilty, nor is it a sort of substitute penance, nor is it anything at all that we do in our own name and strength. Instead, it is a genuine entrance into the presence of God through the worthy blood and continuing prayers of the Lord Jesus Christ, the Mediator of the New Covenant.

The spirit manifested by the seeking Gentile, Cornelius, in his own household must permeate our Christian family worship: "Now therefore are we all here present before God . . ." (Acts 10:33). Our covenant God has spoken to his Old Testament people (and He changes not): "I said not unto the seed of Jacob, seek ye me in vain" (Is. 45:19). Let parents reply with the Psalmist: "When thou saidst, Seek ye my face; my heart said unto thee, Thy face, LORD, will I seek" (Ps. 27:8). Let us ask the Spirit to impress us with the truth that as finite persons, we are coming into direct communication and close dealing with the infinite, personal, Triune God.

Thus, in our worship we will not be primarily echoing liturgical externalities, nor cleverly rearranging and "serving up" theological propositions: we are here to meet with a Person -- the most important person in the universe. The grace and life we need for proper spiritual atmosphere in worship can only be given by God Himself in the person of the Holy Spirit. HE is the atmosphere we seek in which to worship with our loved ones.

It will powerfully add life to our family devotions if we remember that every time we go to our knees, we are doing so in the atmosphere and presence of God, the Holy Spirit. But we must keep in the forefront of our minds that we are not dealing with an impersonal force or atmosphere (however supernatural or beneficial), but with a living, sensitive Person. John Owen properly reminds us:

> He is an intelligent, voluntary, divine agent; he knoweth, he worketh as he will. . . . The sum is, that the Holy Ghost is a divine, distinct

person, and neither merely the power or virtue of God, nor any created Spirit whatever.[21]

He is not a mere instrument or servant, disposing of the things wherein he hath no concern but in what we receive from him and by him, no less to acknowledge His love, kindness, and sovereign grace, than we do those of the Father and the Son.[22]

Granted that we are seeking in the power of the Holy Spirit nothing less than the face of God for us and our children, certain other related elements are vital to an effective family worship service. A vital command for gracious and lively family praise of God is: be friendly! Rev. Richard Cecil, last century, wrote:

Gloominess or austerity of devotion will make them think it a hard service. Let them be met with smiles. Let them be met as friends. Let them be met as for the most delightful service in which they can be engaged. Let them find it short, savory, simple, plain, tender, heavenly. I find it easy to keep the attention of a congregation, compared with that of my family.[23]

Even in a gracious and friendly atmosphere of worship, sometimes our children will wriggle, interrupt, and in other ways act rudely. We must tell ourselves ahead of time that when such takes place, we will not lose our temper, but will calmly, fairly and deliberately deal with the little offender. We obviously use our common sense to decide whether a serious look or word will suffice for the time being, or whether procedures must be halted until the rowdy one is removed from the room and properly dealt with. And then we pick up where we left off. If we handle offenders with sufficient

---

[21]"A Brief Declaration and Vindication of the Doctrine the Trinity" in John Owen, *Works* (London: The Banner of Truth Trust, 1967), II, 403.

[22]"A Discourse Concerning the Holy Spirit" in *ibid.*, III, 202.

[23]J.W. Alexander, *op.cit.*, 195.

firmness the first time, it will not be necessary to take them out very often. If we manage these inevitable occasional disruptions in the proper spirit, the consciences of the little ones will tell them that we were right, and they will approve. Therefore, if we are prepared ahead of time, little annoyments will not destroy the friendly, caring atmosphere of the household at worship.

In addition to friendliness, brevity is called for if family worship is to be practical in these days. If we set our goals too high, try to accomplish too much, and make the services too long and tedious, then everyone in the family -- ourselves as parents included -- will become discouraged, frustrated, and the entire effort will either be dropped or resented. Let us be realistic about the personalities, as well as the demands and rhythms of the particular household and times in which God has providentially chosen for us to live. It was no more spiritual to have lived in the sixteenth century than in the twentieth, and an agricultural society with its slower pattern of life and greater amount of free time was not inherently more spiritual than our post-industrial society with its increased speed and stress.

Given the inescapable round of activities of most normal, Christian families in our own society, it is surely realistic -- and not in the least lacking in true spirituality -- to have a goal of keeping evening worship (maybe immediately after supper) to ten or fifteen minutes in length, and morning worship (maybe immediately before breakfast) to about five minutes. In the morning, for instance, the father could be reading consecutively five or ten verses through the New Testament without much comment. Then he could thank God for His morning mercies, and pray for the particular needs of each child that day, and have everyone at table sing together the Doxology or a brief "Scripture Song" from the Psalms, or perhaps one verse from Psalm 100, 23, 1, etc., and then next morning sing the second verse and so on. That can easily be done within five minutes. In the evening, one can take more time for commenting, let the children more actively participate, and have somewhat longer prayer and song. If family worship is actually going to be observed through the years, orderliness and brevity are absolutely essential.

Variety is another ingredient which is usually found where there is a good spirit of household praise. In the evening prayers, for example, the father can take requests one night, everyone can pray another night, the Lord's Prayer could be prayed another night, and again, pictures of missionaries, churches, Christian schools, absent family members, national leaders, and so forth could be passed round to the children so they can select one or two and then pray for them. What a wonderful way to learn geography and politics! Sometimes -- especially when one's children are very young -- it adds interest to substitute stories from a good children's story Bible for the Scripture reading and comment. Any caring parent can think of a number of ways to vary the routine so as to hold the child's attention. There is, after all, nothing wrong with being interesting!

Blessings Upon Family Worship

Tremendous blessings are in store across unnumbered future years for those households where father and mother (or either, or guardian) will expend persistent energy, thought, time and love to gather their children together, strive to hold their attention to the things that matter most, in order that together on their knees they may seek the presence and blessing of God, who created them for fellowship with Himself in the first place. Scripture is insistent that God loves to bless the houses of the righteous, where He is worshipped. "He blesses the habitation of the just" (Prov. 3:33). They are "like a tree planted by the rivers of water that brings forth its fruit in its season . . . whatever he does shall prosper" (Ps. 1); "The voice of rejoicing and salvation is in the tabernacles of the righteous" (Ps. 118:15); "Blessed is every one that feareth the Lord; that walketh in his ways. For thou shalt eat the labor of thine hands: happy shalt thou be, and it shall be well with thee" (Ps. 128:1-2); "Then they that feared the Lord, spake often one to another; and the Lord hearkened, and heard it; and a book of remembrance was written before him, for them that feared the Lord, and that thought upon his name. And they shall be mine, saith the Lord of hosts, in that day when I make up my jewels; and I will spare them as a man spareth his own son that serveth him" (Mal. 3:16-17).

We must conclude by mentioning briefly a few of these blessings on worshipping families. First, there is the simple truth that "we have not because we ask not" (Jam. 4:2). God does answer prayer, and families that ask for more, get more. Family worship, in the second place, does much to build an atmosphere of Christ-centered piety in the home. True life is to know God in Christ (John 17:3), and family worship assists us in knowing Him who is the true meaning and goal of our immortal existence. During a lifetime we may teach our children many things and give them many things, but if we do not teach them to know God in vivid and practical ways, then by what stretch of the imagination could we conceive all our other efforts to be worthwhile? Daily household piety bodily manifests the practical value of Christianity in an otherwise materialistic, secular setting. James W. Alexander wrote: "Family-worship has a direct and manifest tendency to make religion a matter of every-day interest."[24]   Without a family altar, many children may, in a sense, be excused for thinking that the regular evening news, *The Wall Street Journal*, and a hundred other parental interests are really more important than the Word of God with its solemn warnings and glorious promises.

Not least of the blessings attending the family altar in this frenetic generation, is the calm security of at least a somewhat regular and orderly household schedule. To set aside even a little time to worship God morning and evening will inevitably cause us to begin thinking through our day more carefully.   It may lead us to eliminate some activities, and--almost unconsciously--to organize more effectively those many and varied activities that do remain.

John Calvin said: "Fixed hours can save our prayer life."[25]   In the words of J.W. Alexander:

> That which is most important in regard to the time of Family-Worship, is that it should be *fixed*. We ascribe great value to this particular. . . . It saves the time of the household; and it tends to

---

[24] *Ibid.*, 36.

[25] John Calvin, *Commentary on Psalms*, ch.55:17-18.

that method and punctuality in domestic affairs, which is a chief ornament of a Christian house.[26]

It brings a stated regulation into the house, and gathers the inmates by a fixed law. It sets up a wholesome barrier against wanton irregularity, sloth, and night-wandering. It encourages early hours, thoughtfulness, and affection; and above all it adds strength to the principle of subordination and obedience; a point which we dare not pass lightly.[27]

It would be missing the point, and indeed, unnecessarily discouraging ourselves from taking action, to think that starting a family altar requires parents to become overly anxious and overly precise about everyone's schedule: in a word, to become 'fussy.' On the contrary, quietly and simply doing the best we can to begin observing morning and evening family praise, will gradually, silently and sweetly extend an influence through the house and through the day that unconsciously tends to promote greater order and calm. Some days we may well miss morning or evening worship. Some times we may fail to have either for a number of days. It is important that we not become discouraged and give it all up. The thing to do is to start over afresh. Press towards the future. Be realistic enough not to expect perfection from your own performances or from your children's responses. Your -- and their -- perfection is in Christ, the Great High Priest, who even now is interceding for you and is "waiting to be gracious" (Is. 30:18) to you and to your seed, whom He purchased with His blood to join in His triune life, blessings and praises forever.

---

[26]J.W. Alexander, op.cit., 190.

[27]Ibid., 165-66.

PART II

THE ELEMENTS OF WORSHIP

8 - AN INTRODUCTION TO THE ELEMENTS OF WORSHIP

Frank J. Smith

Now that we have explored the nature of worship, we turn to look at the implications of some of these principles in terms of the proper elements of worship.

One of the keys to understanding worship is an appreciation for its dialogical nature. We have noted that, in worship, God speaks and men respond.

The forms of God's verbal expression to His people in public worship are the audible reading of the Scripture and the preaching of the Word. The reading of the Word is God's direct address to His people. As such, it should be performed by someone who is specifically a leader in the Church--that is, by someone who has been ordained to the gospel ministry (including ruling elders), or who has been licensed to preach, or who is at least an eligible candidate for the ministry. The reading of the Word in public worship is an aspect of the pastoral ministry which should not be done by just anyone, even as preaching should not be (see I Tim. 4:13ff).

The sermon is to be derived directly from God's holy and inspired Word. Preaching is a form of teaching, but it is a special kind of teaching. Preaching is the authoritative, ambassadorial declaration of the Word of God. It is basically a spoken presentation. Gestures by the preacher are legitimate, but this is because they are natural to speaking, and are consonant with the whole of the man being involved in the message.

But not only is preaching primarily spoken, it is also one-way. When the king's herald proclaims the royal message, there is to be no discussion during the message. The dialogue of worship is not between the preacher and the people, it is between God and the people. This is not to say that there is to be no rapport between the preacher and the people--

indeed, such is necessary to good preaching--, but merely that the dialogical nature of worship means that it is God Who is speaking and therefore the people, as part of this particular act of worship, listen with awe and reverence. With the eyes of faith, we perceive that it is the words of Jesus Christ which come through the preacher as he is led by the Holy Spirit to speak.

The reading of the Word and the preaching of the Word are, of course, two separate and distinct elements of worship. They differ in terms of form (reading/preaching), purpose (preaching is somewhat more direct in its application), and content (the infallible Word of God/words which God uses to address us which may not be inerrant and are not infallible). These two related elements are discussed in the next two chapters of this section.

God's people are to respond, then, in the royal court, in the way in which God desires them to respond: in the praying of prayers and the singing of praise. These, too, form two separate and distinct elements of worship, and they are covered in three chapters in this section.

The sacraments are also ordinary elements of worship. In these particular means of grace God declares His love for His people not only by means of giving physical signs for our encouragement and edification, but also because He seals His love toward us by means of them. The sacraments are also communal times of the Church, expressing her loyalty and therefore confessing her faith. The essay on the sacraments considers them particularly from the perspective of their administration: why do we employ certain sacramental actions in worship?

Besides the ordinary elements of worship, there are the occasional elements of worship, which are "religious oaths, and vows, solemn fastings, and thanksgivings upon special occasions; which are, in their several times and seasons, to be used in a holy and religious manner" (Westminster Confession of Faith, XXI.5). What must be noted is that these elements are 'occasional,' that is, they are to be engaged in when Providence dictates. When a famine or earthquake or war or some other such disaster strikes, it is appropriate to be called to solemn fasting. When delivered from such like oppression, it is appropriate to be called to special thanksgiving (like the Pilgrims in Plymouth Colony in 1621). When in His grace God has raised up Church officers, it is proper to have them make solemn oaths and vows before God and men. But to establish perennial days and seasons is to violate the occasional nature of these occasional elements of worship. Nor is the observance of special religious holidays (other than the weekly Sabbath) authorized by Scripture. Thus the use of an ecclesiastical calendar is forbidden. The final chapter in this section deals with the occasional elements.

As we consider what is appropriate for worship, the words of Ecclesiastes 5:1-2 serve as good reminders for us:

> "Keep your foot when you go to the house of God, and be more ready to hear, than to the give the sacrifice of fools: for they consider not that they do evil. Be not rash with your mouth, and let not your heart be hasty to utter anything before God: for God is in heaven, and you upon earth: therefore let your words be few."

Implicit in this text is the notion of a worship service--a definite gathering in Heaven's presence for a period of time. Public worship, then, does not consist of a series of disjointed acts; it is an organic whole, which from beginning to end must reflect an awareness of the Almighty.

There are other considerations that indicate that a service of worship is a Biblical concept. The Old Testament contains many examples of various services. Acts 20 describes a service at which Paul preached and the Lord's Supper was administered. The very nature of worship--that it is special, dialogical, and prescribed--would be called into question, unless there is such a thing as a worship service.

One of the privileges of a worship service is that of coming into the special presence of God and communing with Him. Anything which detracts from this clearly should not be allowed. If we were to be in the royal presence of the Queen of England, it would not be proper protocol to interrupt that audience with the monarch in order to talk with one another. How much more important it is that we do not interrupt our audience with the King of kings by trivial items which center on ourselves.

But it is also necessary that we do not bring before the King that which He has not required, even when we may be directing that activity towards Him. Such action would likewise violate protocol and disrupt the flow of the service.

Following the teaching of the Westminister Standards, it is this author's belief that the only items which properly belong in a worship service are the ones presented here in this section, as they alone have been demonstrated to be acts appropriate and commanded for New Covenant worship.

Whether or not the reader agrees with the exclusion of other elements or practices from worship, we trust he will benefit from the ensuing discussions on these elements which all agree are indeed a part of worship.

9 THE READING OF THE SCRIPTURES

Louis DeBoer

INTRODUCTION

What could be more important than the reading of the Holy Scriptures? The Apostle Paul said of them that they are able to make us "wise unto salvation." Jesus said to the Pharisees, "Search the scriptures; for in them ye think ye have eternal life: and they are they which testify of me." Our knowledge of Jesus of Nazareth, the Christ, the Son of the Living God, comes through the agency of the Spirit of Truth, and the means used are the Holy Scriptures. Without them we would have no meaningful, and certainly no saving, knowledge of our Lord. Without the Scriptures, calling on the name of Jesus would be reduced to an exercise in magic, mysticism, and superstition. This is exactly what happened in the Dark Ages when Romish superstition replaced the Christian faith, and the priest's Latin "hocus pocus" (Hoc est corpus meum) replaced true knowledge of God and of his Christ. Spurgeon, arguing against the close communion principles of his fellow Baptists, stated that, "The pulse of Christ is communion; and woe to the church that seeks to cure the ills of Christ's church by stopping its pulse." But the pulse of Christ's Church is His Word. Without the Word we have no knowledge of Christ, we have no church, and we indeed have no sacrament. The sacrament is founded on the Word, takes its meaning and significance from the Word, and symbolizes the great truths of the Word. Reformed theologians have always stressed the connection between the word and the sacrament, and indeed without the word the sacrament degenerates into an exercise in mysticism and superstition.

The strength of the Christian faith is the strength of the word of God. Christianity is a revealed religion, a divinely revealed religion, and the revelation that establishes it is a written one, the Holy Scriptures. Christians are not mystics, and they are warned not to dabble in dreams and visions and other additions to the Word of God. Whenever the Christian faith has mired itself in such subjectivism it has soon corrupted itself almost beyond recognition. And by contrast whenever she was so corrupted she has only been restored by a faithful return to the Word of God as her only rule of faith and practice. Thus it was that while mysticism, superstition, and pagan traditions could usher in the Dark Ages, only the light of God's word could bring about the Reformation. More than anything else it was the publication of the Greek New Testament and the translation of the Scriptures into the common languages of the peoples of Europe that brought about the great Protestant Reformation. During that reformation the Word was so central that it touched and affected everything including church architecture. The altar was swept away along with the idolatrous mass and in its place was the lectern, where a great Bible was placed. The focal point was the pulpit, where the Word of God was read and expounded to the people in their own tongue. The importance of the Scriptures to the Christian faith cannot be overstated or overemphasized, and their being publicly read as the very word of God, as a separate and distinct act of worship to that God, is a quintessential part of the Christian faith.

WORSHIP

The centrality of worship and its overwhelming importance in the life of the Christian should never be overlooked. The very purpose of man's existence is that he might glorify God, that he might worship and honor his Creator. The entire creation was called into existence by the word of His power for the sole purpose of magnifying and glorifying the Creator. Man preeminently, as the apex of God's creation, fashioned in His own image, is to worship God.

THE PRINCIPLE

Having asserted the importance of worship we must next ask how should we worship. If we are to read the Scriptures as an act of worship, how are we to read them? The who, when, where, and why of all worship, including this particular act of worship, must be answered if we are to be able to worship at all. But the same Lord that has issued the command to worship does not leave us without an answer to this question. For the Lord is sovereign over both the end and the means. God who has ordained that we should worship has also appointed the appropriate and acceptable forms, means, and acts of worship. God commanded us to pray and he gave us a model prayer. The great principle is that it is God, not man, who defines what is acceptable worship. God did not form the entire Creation to praise Him and glorify His name only to have that creation itself define what worship is. The same God who ordained the proper object of worship when he declared, "Thou shalt have no other gods before me," also ordained the acceptable means of worship when he declared, "Thou shalt not make unto thee any graven image."

Now if this be true of worship in general, it also holds true for the doctrine of reading the Scriptures. Men may reason, and have reasoned: What could possibly be wrong with reading the Scriptures? Can there really be any significant restrictions or controls on such a good thing? Can we really do wrong when we are trying to do something so good? But God's ways are higher than our ways and God's thoughts than our thoughts. We must adhere to the regulative principle in order to establish the Scripture doctrine of how we ought to read and handle the Word of God.

THE COMMAND

God has through His very word given us an abundant testimony not only that we are to read His Word but also how, when, where and by whom it is to be read. Moses included in his writings several explicit commands to read the Scriptures. In Deuteronomy 17:18-20 the king is commanded to "write him a copy of this law in a book. . . . And it shall be with him, and he shall read therein all the days of his life: that he may learn to fear the LORD his God, to keep all the words of this law and these statutes, to do them." The Word of God containing His law is to be read daily by the highest civil magistrate in the land that it may be an effective guide both to the entire nation in its national conduct and in the personal conduct of the king. But important as it is for the civil magistrates of a kingdom daily to read the Word of God and conduct their affairs in its light, yet Moses is far from stopping at that. In Deuteronomy 31:11-13 it is commanded that all Israel is to come under the public reading of the Scriptures. Moses commands the priests,

> "When all Israel is come to appear before the LORD thy God in the place which he shall choose, thou shalt read this law before all Israel in their hearing. Gather the people together, men, and women, and children, and thy stranger that is within thy gates, that they may hear, and that they may learn, and fear the LORD your God, and observe to do all the words of this law: And that their children, which have not known anything, may hear, and learn to fear the LORD your God, as long as ye live in the land whither ye go over Jordan to possess it."

But the commands to read the Scriptures do not stop with all Israel, or with Israel's king, but include the stranger and the foreigner. The prophets Isaiah and Jeremiah amplified this theme, restating the command that all men are to read the word of the Lord. Isaiah addresses all men when he commands, "Come near, ye nations, to hear; and hearken, ye people: let the earth hear, and all that is therein; the world and all things that come forth of it" and "Seek ye out of the book of the LORD, and read" (Is. 34:1,16). And Jeremiah echoes the universality of the command when he declares "O earth, earth, earth, hear the word of the LORD" (Jer. 22:29). Jeremiah's pronouncements concerning the seed of David were of such earth-shaking significance that all men were to hear them; that all men ought to know them and ponder them. Surely all men should read them as well.

Now since this was true under the Old Covenant, then it certainly is true under the New Covenant, with the Gentiles grafted into the true Israel of God and the middle wall of partition broken down. And so we find the commands of the New Covenant echoing and reaffirming the commands of the Old. In John 5:39 Christ confronts the representative men, the elders and leaders of the nation, and commands them to "Search the scriptures" for "they are they which testify of me" paralleling the instructions of Deuteronomy 17. Likewise the instructions in Colossians 4:16, "And when this epistle is read among you, cause that it be read also in the church of the Laodiceans; and that ye likewise read the epistle from Laodicea" and in I Thessalonians 5:27, "I charge you by the Lord that this epistle be read unto all the holy brethren," renew the command publicly to read the Word of God to the covenant people--of every race and tribe and kindred and people on the face of the earth.

THE EXAMPLE

The Scriptures teach us not only by precept but also by example. It is not only the explicit command but the godly example that bears fruit and brings blessing that instructs us in the way of righteousness. In Exodus 24:7, at the very beginning of the Old Covenant, in the very process of Israel ratifying its covenant with God, we have Moses publicly reading the word of the Lord to the people. "And he took the book of the covenant, and read in the audience of the people: and they said, All that the LORD hath said will we do, and be obedient." The informed consent of the people, essential to the covenant, was established by the public reading of the Scriptures. But that generation apostatized at Kadesh-Barnea and they all died in the wilderness. A new generation came up led by Joshua, who renewed the covenant on the plains of Moab and entered into the land of promise. And to that generation Joshua also publicly read the law. "And afterward he read all the words of the law, the blessings and cursings, according to all that is written in the book of the law. There was not a word of all that Moses commanded, which Joshua read not before all the congregation of Israel, with the women, and the little ones, and the strangers that were conversant among them" (Josh. 8:34-35). The reading of the Scriptures was commanded at the inception of the nation and was fundamental to its establishment and preservation.

THE IMPORTANCE OF READING THE SCRIPTURES

The importance of reading the Scriptures cannot be overstressed. If one thinks that this is so obvious it need not be stated then one only has to study contemporary church practice to see the fallacy of that naive assumption. Men, especially preachers, are often so infatuated with their own words that they give short shrift to the reading of the Word of God. It is typical in many churches for the minister to read a few, a very few, verses, his text, and then proceed right into the sermon. If one is fortunate he might actually stick to those few verses and give an exposition of them. All too often that is almost the last one hears of even those few verses.

But as we have seen we are commanded to read the Word of God. If we crowd it out because we don't want to weary the people with a long service and the speaker doesn't want to surrender his time, then we are dishonoring, displeasing, and disobeying God. Reformed churches have a sound and Biblical tradition of giving adequate attention to the reading of the Word of God to the people. Most of them, if they dusted off their Directories for Worship, would discover that they are required to read a significant portion each service. Personally, I like to read two full chapters, one from each Testament, that go with the theme of the sermon. If the Word of God does not have an honored place in our services than we are neither Biblical nor Reformed.

Another problem with which we must deal is the balance of Scripture. Often error is not a bold untruth but just a truth stressed out of proportion. Error may consist of persistently ignoring a particular truth or of stressing a truth at the expense of other truth. Ministers are fallible human creatures. They have their opinions and their moods. They have their pet subjects and favorite hobby horses, all of which pose a threat to maintaining the balance of Scripture. In preaching, as the Puritans pointed out, this is best avoided by preaching expositionally through an entire book of the Bible. That way one is almost bound to maintain the balance of Scripture. Next best would be to preach doctrinally (*i.e.*, a series of sermons on baptism, etc.) and the worst system, short of ignoring Scripture entirely, is to allow the minister to pick a favorite verse each week at his own impulse and preach on that. In the reading of the Scriptures the same dangers need to be avoided and the remedy again is simple. If one reads only a few verses each Sabbath then it is very easy to direct those few verses to stress the balance of priorities in the minister's mind. But if one reads two entire chapters each service, totaling four each Sabbath, then obviously the balance of Scripture is more likely to be kept. And if the minister is expected to read two chapters that support and expound his theme he will have even more difficulty violating the balance of Scripture. If he cannot find two chapters that support his theme he ought to reconsider whether in the mind of the Spirit this is really what the people need to hear!

Finally, without the proper reading of the Scripture there can be little blessing and fruit in the ministry and life of the church. This is true not only because God honors those who honor Him and not only because he deals with those who dishonor Him and His Word, but it is especially true because God has appointed the simple reading of His Word as a means of grace. The Scriptures, the Word of God, are the seed whereby we are born again. The Spirit works through the word. Christ himself taught in the Parable of the Sower that the word is the seed that bears fruit unto eternal life. The Apostle Peter declares the same, stating, "Being born again, not of corruptible seed, but of incorruptible, by the word of God, which liveth and abideth ever" (I Pet. 1:23). Paul affirms that, "Faith cometh by hearing, and hearing by the word of God." It is a Scripture truth that if we sow sparingly we shall reap sparingly. If we would sow bountifully we ought bountifully to read the Scriptures in our services. How often we need to be reminded that men are saved by the sovereign, irresistible grace of God and that God has sovereignly chosen to channel that grace through certain covenants and through certain divinely appointed means of grace. It is not the eloquence of the preacher, it is not the appeal to fickle human emotions, it is not the logic of the sermon; but it is the Word of God itself that is the seed that bears fruit unto eternal life. If we really believe that, then we will never be sparing in the reading of generous portions of the word as we feed the flock of the Lord Jesus Christ when they assemble to hear it.

EXAMPLES OF THE IMPORTANCE OF
READING THE SCRIPTURES

We have already seen the part played by both the giving and the public reading of the Word of God at Mount Sinai and in the land of promise under Joshua. But not only did the Word of God play a major part in the origins of the life and the land of Israel, it also played a critical part in sustaining them in their national life and keeping them in that land. If they wandered too far from the terms of the covenant the land would spue them out as it had the original inhabitants, the Canaanites. Then they would fall from being a nation to being a dispersion of rootless wanderers. It was the commanded public reading of the Scriptures from generation to generation, the instruction in the word of God from father to son, that was the divinely appointed means to sustain the nation and deliver it from national decay and destruction.

In the days of Ahaz, King of Judah, apostasy and idolatry had nigh brought Judah to ruin. God in judgment had precipitated a destructive fraticidal war with Israel, and Ahaz in desperation sought Assyrian assistance in his troubles, bringing that imperialistic power into the politics of Palestine. Judah was spared, and survived an Assyrian invasion under Sennacherib because Ahaz's heir, Hezekiah, reformed the land according to all the commandments of the Word of the Lord. Such reformation is impossible without extensive reading and application of the Word of God. It literally means a reforming of all things to bring them into conformity with that word. It was just such a submissive and reverent reading of God's Word by Judah's king, and ultimately by the priests, the Levites, and the people, that led to Judah's deliverance from the abyss into which Ahaz's apostasy had almost precipitated it.

Similarly a few generations later the apostasy and wickedness of Hezekiah's heirs, Mannaseh and Amon, had again brought the Southern Kingdom to ruin. God's wrath and judgment were so provoked that the Lord declared by the mouth of His prophets,

"Behold I am bringing such evil upon Jerusalem and Judah, that whosoever heareth of it, both his ears shall tingle. And I will stretch over Jerusalem the line of Samaria, and the plummet of the house of Ahab: and I will wipe Jerusalem as a man wipeth a dish, wiping it, and turning it upside down. And I will forsake the remnant of mine inheritance, and deliver them into the hand of their enemies" (II Ki. 21:12-14).

The nation underwent a Babylonian invasion, the captivity of their king, Mannaseh, and the assassination of his heir, Amon. At this critical juncture the nation was again spared, and drawn back from the abyss of final destruction by a reformation that was led by Josiah, their king, reformation that was precipitated by the discovery and the reading of a scroll of the word of the Lord. As Scripture records it,

"And Hilkiah the high priest said unto Shaphan the scribe, I have found the book of the law in the house of the LORD. And Hilkiah gave the book to Shaphan, and he read it. . . And Shaphan the scribe shewed the king, saying, Hilkiah the priest hath delivered me a book. And Shaphan read it before the king. And it came to pass, when the king had heard the words of the book of the law, that he rent his clothes. And the king commanded. . . Go ye, enquire of the LORD for me, and for the people, and for all Judah, concerning the words of this book that is found: for great is the wrath of the LORD that is kindled against us, because our fathers have not hearkened unto the words of this book, to do according unto all that which is written concerning us" (II Ki. 22:8-13).

Josiah, the king, then enacted a thorough reformation of the worship of the land in which he mercilessly extirpated idolatry, destroying it root and branch, as he reestablished the pure worship and service of Jahweh. This reformation commenced with a public reading of the scripture and a public commitment to the word read. The very foundation of this reformation was in the acts of Josiah recorded for us as follows,

"And the king sent, and they gathered unto him all the elders of
Judah and of Jerusalem. And the king went up into the house of the
LORD, and all the men of Judah and all the inhabitants of
Jerusalem with him, and the priests, and the prophets, and all the
people, both small and great: and he read in their ears all the
words of the book of the covenant which was found in the house of
the LORD. And the king stood by a pillar, and made a covenant
before the LORD, to walk after the LORD, and to keep his
commandments and his testimonies and his statutes with all their
heart and all their soul, to perform the words of this covenant that
were written in this book. And all the people stood to the
covenant" (II Ki. 23:1-3).

Not only does the reading of the Word of God provide the very
foundation for the existence of the nation but the contrary is also true. The
refusal to read the word of the Lord can be the specific cause of national
destruction. We see a graphic illustration of this truth in the life of
Jehoiakim, the king of Judah. Jehoiakim, the second son of the godly
Josiah, continued the evil reign of his brother Jehoahaz. But although his
idolatry and abominations wearied the Lord, the capstone of his iniquity was
his willful destruction of the Scriptures. The nation was again on the brink
of cataclysmic judgments and the Lord in His mercy again appointed the
reading of His Word as a means of grace. He instructed Jeremiah,

"Take thee a roll of a book, and write therein all the words that I
have spoken unto thee against Israel, and against Judah, and against
all the nations, from the day I spake unto thee, unto the days of
Josiah, even unto this day. It may be that the house of Judah will
hear all the evil which I purpose to do unto them; that they may
return everyman from his evil way; that I may forgive their iniquity
and their sin" (Jer. 36:2-3).

Jeremiah obeyed the Lord and called the scribe Baruch who

"wrote from the mouth of Jeremiah all the words of the LORD,
which he had spoken unto him, upon a roll of a book. And
Jeremiah commanded Baruch, saying, I am shut up; I cannot go
into the house of the LORD. Therefore go thou, and read in the
roll, which thou hast written from my mouth, the words of the
LORD in the ears of the people in the LORD's house upon the
fasting day: and also thou shalt read them in the ears of all Judah
that come out of their cities. It may be they will present their
supplication before the LORD, and will return everyone from his
evil way: for great is the anger and the fury that the LORD hath
pronounced against this people" (Jer. 36:4-7).

Here we have a testimony to the power of the reading of the Scriptures.
Baruch faithfully discharges his commission and reads ". . . the words of
Jeremiah in the house of the LORD. . . at the entry of the new gate of the
LORD'S house, in the ears of all the people." The result is that a certain
individual, Michaiah, became so affected when he "heard out of the book all
the words of the LORD" that he hastened to the king's house where he
found the princes assembled. "Then Michaiah declared unto them all the
words that he had heard when Baruch read the book in the ears of the
people". The result, as God graciously again honors His appointed means
of grace, is that the princes ". . . when they had heard all the words, they
were afraid both one and other, and said unto Baruch, We will surely tell the
king of all these words." All of this set the stage for the final act in this
national tragedy and the culmination of Jehoiakim's wickedness.

"And they went in to the king into the court, but they laid up the
roll in the chamber of Elishama the scribe, and told all the words
in the ears of the king. So the king sent Jehudi to fetch the roll:
and he took it out of Elishama the scribe's chamber. And Jehudi
read it in the ears of the king, and in the ears of all the princes
which stood beside the king. Now the king sat in the winterhouse
in the ninth month: and there was a fire on the hearth burning
before him. And it came to pass, that when Jehudi had read three

or four leaves, he [Jehoiakim] cut it with the penknife, and cast it into the fire that was on the hearth, until all the roll was consumed."

The result was predictable as Jeremiah again prophesied saying,

"Therefore thus saith the LORD of Jehoiakim king of Judah; He shall have none to sit upon the throne of David: and his dead body shall be cast out in the day to the heat, and in the night to the frost. And I will punish him and his seed and his servants for their iniquity; and I will bring upon them, and upon the inhabitants of Jerusalem, and upon the men of Judah, all the evil that I have pronounced against them."

A clearer example of the power of the reading of the Word of God both as a savor of life unto life or a savor of death unto death can scarcely be found.

The power of God's Word is not limited to the life of the nation but also operates powerfully in the life of the individual. Faith comes by hearing and hearing by the Word of God. Each child of God is regenerated by the Spirit operating through the Word, the seed by which which we are born again. Every Christian comes to know that it is the Holy Scriptures "which are able to make thee wise unto salvation through faith which is in Christ Jesus". And the Word not only is the seed that begins our spiritual life as new creatures in Christ but it is also the bread that sustains that life. Each day again the Christian is strengthened, renewed in the inner man, edified, and built up in the faith by the ministry of the Word of God. It is the Scriptures that are "profitable for doctrine, for reproof, for correction, for instruction in righteousness: That the man of God may be perfect, throughly furnished unto all good works" (II Tim. 3:16-17). A good example of the ministry of the reading of God's Word in the life of the believer is the story of the Ethiopian eunuch. We are told of him that he was returning from Jerusalem where he had come to worship and "sitting in his chariot read Esaias the prophet." He was reading in Isaiah 53 of the substitutionary death and suffering of the Lamb of God that takes away the sin of the world. And the result was that he was baptized, confessing, and believing with all his heart "that Jesus Christ is the Son of God."

HOW TO READ THE SCRIPTURES

It is not only necessary that the Word of God be read but that it be read properly. That means first of all that it is to be read as the word of God. It is to be read with reverence and solemnity. It is to read with respect. And it is to be read with authority. Christ's ministry, from His first public sermon, was remarkable, "For he taught them as one having authority." When read publicly Scripture ought to be read by those in authority, who have been ordained and set apart to the ministry of the word, and are clothed with the authority of church office as ministers of Jesus Christ.

But if the foremost issue be that it be read as the Word of God, we ought not to lose sight of the fact that it is the word of God to men. It therefore ought to be read so as to promote human understanding. The keeping of the Scriptures in the Latin tongue by the Church of Rome may have promoted a superstitious reverence for the Scriptures but was totally destructive of its God given purpose. The example of Ezra at the return from the Babylonian captivity is instructive in this regard. The Scriptures record that

"Ezra the priest brought the law before the congregation both of men and women, and all that could hear with understanding, . . . and he read therein . . . from the morning until midday, before the men and the women, and those that could understand; and the ears of all the people were attentive unto the book of the law. And Ezra the scribe stood upon a pulpit of wood, which they had made for the purpose . . . . And Ezra opened the book in the sight of all the people; (for he was above all the people;) and when he opened it, all the people stood up: and Ezra blessed the LORD, the great God. And all the people answered, Amen, Amen, with lifting up their hands: and they bowed their heads, and worshiped the LORD with their faces to the ground" (Neh. 8:2-7).

Note first of all the authority of the reading. The Word is read publicly in the gate, the place of civil authority in the Old Testament Hebrew Commonwealth. It is read by one in authority, Ezra, the scribe, a priest of the line of Aaron, clothed with authority not only by virtue of his priestly office, but commissioned by Artaxerxes to aid in the restoration, to instruct the people in the law of God, and to "set magistrates and judges, which may judge all the people that are beyond the river" (Ezra 7:25). He is flanked on the left and on the right by others in authority, officers of the theocracy, probably priests. And he stands over and above the people on a wooden platform from which vantage point he proclaims the word of God. It is an imposing sight and an authoritative setting.

Secondly we note the reverence the reading inspires in the people. They listen attentively, and when the divinely inspired scroll is opened they rise and stand reverently. They remain standing as Ezra blesses Jahweh their God and join with him with uplifted hands. Then they bow their heads and worship their God.

And finally we note that the reading is directed to their understanding. We read that they "caused the people to understand the law: and the people stood in their place. So they read in the book in the law of God distinctly, and gave the sense, and caused them to understand the reading" (Neh. 8:7-8). The reading was distinct. It was not mystically intoned or ritually chanted. It was in the plain ordinary everyday language of the people. It was a plain, clear, and understandable reading of the text.

THE ACCURACY OF THE READING

The Bible is an inspired book. It is a work of God. It is the work of the Holy Spirit of Truth. As such it is perfect, and any deviation from perfection must mar that perfection and introduce potential error. Therefore the reading must be precise and as perfect as fallible men are capable of. The Word of God must be handled as just that, the Word of God. A word whose every jot and tittle shall come to pass; a word that shall never change, mutate, or pass away, but shall stand forever, through time and eternity. This is the way Christ and the apostles handled the word and we should profit by their example. Christ in His ministry had to contend not only with the Pharisees, but also with the Saducees, who denied a physical resurrection. In His debate with them on just that point Christ showed His absolute reverence for and confidence in the Word of God. He demonstrated its absolute authority and perfection. He was willing to hang the whole doctrine of the resurrection on the tense of a verb when He declared to the Saducees,

> "Ye do err not knowing the scriptures, nor the power of God. . . . But as touching the resurrection of the dead, have ye not read that which was spoken unto you by God saying, I am the God of Abraham, and the God of Isaac, and the God of Jacob? God is not the God of the dead, but of the living" (Mt. 22:29-32).

The tense of a verb, that the Scriptures taught that God "is," that He still "is" the God of Abraham, Isaac, and Jacob, that He says "I am" and not "I was" is sufficient for Christ to maintain the doctrine of the resurrection on that point of grammar alone. Similarly the Apostle Paul while wrestling with one of the greatest theological issues of the Apostolic Church, the relationship of the Gentile converts to the Jewish Church, argues his case on another point of grammar, the singularity of a noun. He argues in Galatians 3 that the Gentiles are included in the Abrahamic Covenant. This is because the covenant was made with Abraham and his seed. Seed being singular refers to one particular seed of Abraham, Jesus Christ, and that if we have the faith of Abraham, then, being united to Christ by faith, we are in Christ and "heirs according to the promise." Now if major doctrines can be hung on the authority of singular points of scripture than we can see the perfection and authority of the word that God has given. Then we can see that all paraphrases and loose renderings are anathema. Then we can see the absolute importance of reading the scriptures with power, authority and precision. The accuracy of the reading must be maintained to the best of our ability.

THE CONTEXT OF THE READING

Not only must the text be read with power and authority, distinctly, clearly and accurately with a view to proper understanding, but it must be read in context. This includes both the context in which it is placed in the Scriptures and the context of the circumstances in which it is read. A prime example of this is the public reading of the Scriptures by our Lord Jesus Christ in the synagogue of Nazareth. We read,

> "And he came to Nazareth, where he had been brought up: and, as his custom was, he went into the synagogue on the sabbath day, and stood up for to read. And there was delivered unto him the book of the prophet Esaias. And when he had opened the book, he found the place where it was written, The Spirit of the Lord is upon me, because he hath anointed me to preach the gospel to the poor; he hath sent me to heal the brokenhearted, to preach deliverance to the captives, and recovering of sight to the blind, to set at liberty them that are bruised, To preach the acceptable year of the Lord. And he closed the book, and he gave it again to the minister, and sat down. And the eyes of all them that were in the synagogue were fastened on him. And he began to say unto them, This day is this scripture fulfilled in your ears" (Luke 4:16-21).

The reading fits perfectly into the context of the historical situation. Jesus of Nazareth had come of age at thirty, He had been baptized, had withstood the temptation in the wilderness, and He had commenced His messianic ministry. Now He appeared in his home town of Galilee, read a messianic passage in the scroll of the prophet Isaiah, and revealed Himself as the Lord's Anointed, the long awaited, the prophesied Messiah. The citizens of Nazareth had with great anticipation and curiosity come to the synagogue to see this native son whose fame had gone out throughout all Galilee, and

Jesus in that sense did not disappoint them. He clearly revealed, in the application to Himself of Isaiah's prophecy, the significance of His activities and ministry. He perfectly read the word to suit the context of the situation.

This is an important lesson. Martin Luther is credited with a statement to the effect that if the Word of God is under attack on a certain point then no matter how faithfully one teaches and preaches other portions of Scripture he is not really faithful if he doesn't defend the challenged point of truth. We must faithfully read the Word in its Scriptural and in its historical context. For instance at an ecumenical gathering where infidels and apostates are present it would be horribly wrong to read the blessing from Psalm 133 ("Behold, how good and how pleasant it is for brethren to dwell together in unity"), when what is properly called for is Jehu's rebuke of Jehoshaphat for his alliance with the House of Omri in II Chronicles 19:2 ("Shouldest thou help the ungodly, and love them that hate the LORD? therefore is wrath upon thee from before the LORD"). We have to be careful not only how we read the Scriptures, but also what we read. The devil quoted Scripture in the temptation in the wilderness and he can certainly read it too. We have to be certain we are doing God's work not the devil's when we use the sword of the Word of God. We are commanded not to "cast our pearls before swine." We are commanded not to "sew pillows to all armholes." We are rebuked for saying, "Peace, peace, when there is no peace," when we ought to have been saying "What peace, so long as the whoredoms of thy mother Jezebel and her witchcrafts are so many." God requires a faithful reading lest the salt should lose its savor and Christianity its sting. No wonder our faith has fallen into public contempt and disrespect when so often its blessings and comforts are prostituted to tickle the itching ears of infidels; when the comforts of the Shepherd's Psalm are offered to those who care little for the Shepherd and have no intention of walking in the paths of righteousness. The Word of God must be faithfully read, true to its entire context, before it can be a means of grace and be the seed of life everlasting.

THE POWER OF THE READING

It is all too easy to underestimate the power of the reading of the Word of God. In our day when the Bible seems to have lost any relevance to our public life and is banned from certain public instititions, it is easy to conclude that the reading of the Scriptures seems to be impotent. However this is not the doctrine of the Word of God. According to the Scriptures, every time that they are read it is with power and with effect. God Himself declares, "So shall my word be that goeth forth out of my mouth: it shall not return unto me void, but it shall accomplish that which I please, and it shall prosper in the thing whereto I sent it" (Is. 55:11).

What we have to keep in mind is that God accomplishes His purposes every time that He in His providence causes His Word to be read. We have to remember that His thoughts are higher than our thoughts and His ways than our ways. And we have to recognize that we cannot know His secret purpose. As Moses taught, "The secret things belong unto the LORD our God: but those things which are revealed belong unto us and to our children for ever, that we may do all the words of this law" (Deut. 29:29). We know that it is God's revealed will that all men should hear His Word, and repent in faith, believing in the Lord Jesus Christ. But we do not know His secret will, His secret counsel, that He is bringing to pass each time His Word is read. All we know is that each time the Word of God is read it is being read with power and effect to bring about the secret purpose of God. That is certainly the way the Apostle Paul viewed his ministry. It was never in vain but always in the Lord, "For we are unto God a sweet savour of Christ, in them that are saved, and in them that perish: To the one we are a savour of death unto death; and to the othe the savour of life unto life" (II Cor. 2:15-16). Paul was always a sweet savour unto God as a faithful witness. It was God's business to work His secret will in the labors of His servant Paul. And that secret counsel could be to pile up judgment upon judgment against the great Day of the Lord, to vindicate His final disposition of the wicked, so that they as David would be compelled to confess that God is just in His judgment and right in His sentence.

But whether as a savour of life unto life or as a savour of death unto death we ought to be assured that the reading of the Word of God never leaves men the same as they were before the hearing of it. They are either progressing on the road to eternal life or they are progressing on the road to eternal damnation. Either way each time they hear the word and react to it they are never the same again. The Word has operated with power in their lives. They are either growing in grace, sanctification, and edification, or they are progressively hardening themselves against it and piling up wrath and a multitude of stripes against the evil day. It will have an effect on each soul that hears it, each time it is heard. Such is the power of the Word of God. It should be publicly read with the recognition that it has such power. We ought never to be timid and apologetic in our public readings, as if our ministry were weak and ineffectual. We are handling a word that is sharper than a two edged sword and each swing will have eternal consequenses.

WHO MAY READ THE SCRIPTURES

Who may read the Scriptures? In our antinomian age that probably seems like a ridiculous question. What could possibly be wrong with reading the Scriptures? But that was the doctrine of Cain. He too thought what could possibly be wrong with bringing a sacrifice. That was also the doctrine of Korah, Dathan, and Abiram who rebelled against Moses and Aaron and intruded into the priesthood. It was also part of the arrogant apostasy of later Kings of Israel and Judah such as Jereboam and Uzziah. The Westminster Larger Catechism (Q/A 156) answers the question, "Is the word of God to be read by all?" with "Although all are not to be permitted to read the word publickly to the congregation, yet all sorts of people are bound to read it apart by themselves." That is, while all ought to read the Scriptures privately, not everyone is allowed to read them publicly. As we have noted earlier, it is God who regulates all the details of His worship and it is God not man who decides who is authorized to do what in His public worship. But from Cain to modern antinomians this does not sit well. Like Korah, Dathan, and Abiram they think they are just as good as any ordained to that task, failing to see it is not an issue of ability, but rather of authority. Indeed in their presumption they elevate themselves even over the Lord Jesus Christ. When the author of the Hebrews states, "No man taketh this honour unto himself, but he that is called of God, as was Aaron," he includes Jesus Christ, stating "So also Christ glorified not himself to be made an high priest; but he that said unto him, Thou art my Son, today have I begotton thee. As he saith also in another place, Thou art a priest forever after the order of Melchisedec" (Heb. 5:4-6). Christ's authority for His ministry came not only from His divine nature, which made Him equal with God, but also from His human nature which was fully ordained and consecrated to the work the Father had given Him to do. So much so that when the Pharisees and the temple rulers challenged His authority to cleanse the temple he responded by questioning them concerning the legitimacy of John the Baptist's prophetic ministry. The inference is clear. John baptized Jesus and if his ministry was from God then Jesus was properly consecrated and ordained to His work and had lawful authority in the Jewish Church. From Moses, who delegated the public reading of the Scriptures to the sons of Levi, to Christ who by example publicly read the sacred scroll in the synagogue of Nazareth, we see that by both precept and example the Scriptures teach that only those ordained and set apart to that office may publicly read the word of God.

The Bible ought to be read. It ought to be read with power, authority, reverence, and accuracy. It ought to be honored and prayerfully used as a divinely appointed means of grace. It ought to be read boldly without apology as an effective means of God's working His will in the eternal destiny of His creatures. And it ought always to be read as the very Word of God and nothing less. Then and then alone will it be "quick, and powerful, and sharper than any two-edged sword," a means of grace to the elect, a savour of life unto life to God's covenant people, and a means of wrath to the enemies of our Lord Jesus Christ. Let us boldly and skillfully use it by God's grace to those ends.

10 - WORSHIP AND PREACHING

Henry Krabbendam

If worship can be defined as the activity of ascribing the proper worth to God and, then, of extolling that worth, the preaching of the Word is foundational for it. The Bible, after all, is essentially the story of God, His person, His perfections, His plan, His purposes, His works and His words. And preaching is the first and foremost means to make this story known in its totality and in its details. So Scripture is indispensable for a full view or a glimpse, for that matter, of the worth of God. And preaching is of the highest significance if one is to enjoy that view or catch that glimpse. In a nutshell, in the Word of God the worth of God is on display and through the preaching of the Word that worth is grasped in its full-orbed totality and in its many facets. This explains not only the perennial devotion of the Church to the Scriptures, but also its consistent preoccupation with preaching as the major means to convey its content.

WORSHIP

According to Revelation 4:8-11, further corroborated by Revelation 5:9-14, Biblical worship has at least two preparatory aspects along with a heart-felt attitude. These will now be introduced.

1. The Vision of the Holiness of God

The first preparatory aspect is a vision of the holiness of God and the exultation of God in His holiness (Rev. 4:8). The vision is perfect, in more than one way. Full of eyes around and within, the four living creatures are not only 'all eye,' but also have eyes only for God. This, of course, precipitates exultation. If the vision is perfect, the exultation is awesome. Since these creatures continue day and night, their exultation of God in His holiness is endless.

Holiness may well be the hub of the divine perfections. No other attribute is repeated three times, let alone in two texts, Isaiah 6:3 and Revelation 4:8. This includes attributes such as love, grace and mercy. Furthermore, only holiness can be combined with all other perfections. There is holy love and holy wrath, a holy heaven and a holy hell. But loving wrath is a contradiction in terms. So is a heavenly hell. In this light the observation of Jonathan Edwards must be endorsed that someone who has not loved God for His holiness has never truly loved God.

When God is loved only for His love--necessary and noble as that is in itself--, the time will come when the 'why's' will rise up in one's heart. Divine providences, which tend to push all men to the breaking point at one time or another (Jam. 1:2), will precipitate cries such as "Why, oh God? Do You not love me anymore?"

Such cries, however tempting, are indicative of a man-centered attitude and preclude worship, which is God-centered. The 'why's' to God will silence the worship by definition. To love God centrally for His holiness is to escape that trap. In the light of the awesome purity of God, man sees himself in his ruined state (Is. 6:5), which admittedly deserves eternal damnation. In the face of any providence of God, even the kind that seemingly presses the last drop of blood out of an individual, the response of anyone who acknowledges his ruined state as his own fault and damnation as his just desert will never be 'Why?' but rather 'Why not?'. This response, and this response alone, which can not be produced except through a vision of God in His holiness, will pave the way for the worship that God seeks (John 4:23) and with which He is satisfied.

In fact, love for God in His holiness always goes hand in hand with a desire for holiness before God. That ultimately will produce thankfulness, not just in spite of or in the circumstances, but because of the circumstances. After all, everything in the lives of those who love God aims at their 'good,' that is, their transformation into the image of Christ, their sanctification (Rom. 8:28-29). Never do 'bad' things happen to good people. To complain that something bad is happening to 'me' is to imply that 'I' am a bad person. For God's people there are literally no stumbling blocks to worship. Everything fosters it!

2. The Submission to the Dominion of God

The second preparatory aspect is to "fall down" before God (Rev. 4:10). This is routinely presented as introductory to the worship of God (Mt. 2:11; 4:9; Rev. 5:8, 14; 7:11; 11:16). It was also the customary procedure for anyone both in ancient and more contemporary times who appeared before absolute monarchs or emperors. It spelled total and radical submission. To lift up one's head in the presence of the ruler would mean a quick and certain death. Not only would 'why's' never be tolerated, but any kind of rebellion, whether opposition, refusal to obey or even a bad attitude in carrying out orders, would be dealt with in a summary fashion.

If the 'worship' of earthly rulers requires such submission, how much more should it be bound up with the worship of the Ruler of the Universe. Any reservation, any if, and or but, any question mark, is intolerable and unthinkable. It is needless to say that only total and radical submission is conducive to Biblical worship. Anything else will break up, if not destroy, the worship of God. Whenever man-centeredness prevails, anything God-centered and God-ward will vanish.

In terms of both of these preparatory aspects, preaching clearly has its task cut out for it. It may not be satisfied with anything less as its initital objective than a vision and exultation of the holiness of God as well as a radical and total submission to God in His holiness.

3. The Surrender of Everything to God

The heart-felt attitude of worship is to cast one's crowns before the throne (Rev. 4:10). This is worship in deed. Believers are crowned with many gifts. They may have received the 'crown' of health, of strength, of studies, of a vocation, of a profession, of a spouse, of children, of energy, of time, of reputation, of money, of luxury, of wealth, of possessions, of a home, of an automobile, of friendships, of vacation. The list is potentially endless. It should and does cover all that life has to offer.

In acceptable worship all those 'crowns' are handed over, indeed immediately returned to God upon receipt, unequivocally and without holding anything back. Nebuchadnezzar is a prime example. When his kingdom in all its 'golden' glory is restored to him, he for all practical purposes hands it right back to God (Dan. 4:34-37). He confesses God's sovereignty and does not ask, 'Why?'. He submits to His dominion and does not chafe under it, nor seek to escape it. No wonder that he concludes with worship.

In fact, when God removes anything from any believer at any time, from the simplest and minutest to the biggest and most precious item, projected event or even person, he simply says 'Thank You' for the 'crown' that had been presented to him in the first place. To be content (Phil. 4:11), yes to be thankful (I Thess. 5:18), indeed to rejoice (Phil. 4:4; I Thess. 5:16) in God's 'Thank you's' is the only evidence that a truly acceptable worship has taken place. Any other response does and will fall short of it.

These two preparatory aspects and this heart-felt attitude not only evidence the need for preaching. They also more than hint at the type of preaching that should prevail and the objectives that it must pursue. People are to gain a vision of the holiness of God with all that this entails. They are to submit to God's dominion in total and genuine submission with all that this implies. They are to function as stewards, and not as owners, with all that accompanies this. They are to ascribe all the worth to God with all that flows forth from this.

PREACHING

If the kind of preaching that will lead to the true and full worship of God is ever to become a reality, various concerns ought to be recognized and taken into account. These concerns are reflected in the following composite definition. Preaching is: (1) the authoritative, purposeful and timely communication of God's truth as deposited in the Scriptures of the Old and New Testaments; (2) based upon a thorough contextual and textual study and in the form of a carefully structured message; (3) through the personality of human instruments, commissioned by God, as a gift of Christ, anointed by the Spirit, molded by the Word and committed to prayer; (4) the Gospel of and the keys to the Kingdom with discriminating, applicatory and healing power with a view to regeneration, justification and sanctification; (5) through the minds, to the hearts and into the lives of any and all audiences, sinners and saints, men and women, old and young and presented in a well articulated, imaginative and persuasive fashion; and (6) all of these things in dependence upon, for the sake of and to the praise of the Triune God.

This definition with its sixfold focus, upon the Scripture, the preparation, the preacher, the proclamation, the audience, and last but not least upon God, will now be unpacked, be it in broad strokes only.

I. Focus upon Scripture

The minister of the Gospel is under a solemn obligation to preach the Scripture of the Old and New Testaments (II Tim. 4:2), to preach all of the Scripture (Acts 20:27) and to preach the Scripture exclusively (Gal. 1:8). For only Scripture is the inspired Word of God (II Tim. 3:16). Its very word is needed to produce and sustain life (Deut. 8:3). And no other word is on a par with it or can claim to be without error in whatever it asserts (John 10:35). If the preacher is a channel of the truth, the whole truth and nothing but the truth of Scripture, whether his emphasis is edificational or evangelistic, whether his method is expository, textual or topical, he will be able to speak with authority. For what he transmits in that case is not just an all-too-human message, but a word from God (I Thess. 2:13).

The minister of the Gospel is under the equally solemn obligation to handle the Scripture accurately (II Tim. 2:15) and to handle all of the Scripture accurately (II Pet. 3:16). The careful interpretation of Scripture and the presentation of its proper meaning are necessary for the truth to come to grips with the hearer (Acts 8:31). Even seemingly insignificant details can make a world of difference (Gal. 3:16). The most fundamental prerequisite for handling Scripture or any part of it accurately is to interpret it in the light of its own purpose. At times this is explicitly stated in the passage that is chosen as a preaching unit. At other times it must be inferred from the available clues found in that passage. But only this insures that the aim of the preacher in his preaching is identical with the purposes of God in the text. This must be so for the message of the preacher to be truly a word of God for the audience.

The minister of the Gospel has a similarly solemn obligation to bring out the significance of Scripture (Heb. 4:12) and to bring out the significance of all of Scripture (II Tim. 3:16). For the preaching of the Word of God can hardly be complete unless and until its truth is shown to have applicatory force and at times even a cutting edge (II Tim. 4:2). The aim ought to be that the truth of Scripture, and indeed all of its truth, is genuinely understood intellectually, experientially and practically (Neh. 8:8). In a word, it must be presented as timely, however timeless it may be. For a preacher to succeed in this he must, in the context of the purpose of the preaching unit, glean universal principles and patterns from the text. Then the exposition will flow into application, the old will show itself to be amazingly young, the venerable will prove to be ever fresh, and the timeless will appear to be quite timely.

In short, the minister of the Gospel must honor the Scripture of the Old and New Testaments for what it is, the inerrant and authoritative Word of God. The preacher ought to interpret and present the preaching unit's meaning according to its purpose, and should bring out its significance and apply its truth cogently.

By way of concluding observation, it is not without good reason that Paul cautions Timothy, and in Timothy all ministers of the Gospel, to "preach the Word." There may be times that call for a special emphasis upon God the Father, or God the Son, or God the Holy Spirit. There may be circumstances that require special attention to regeneration, or justification, or sanctification. There may be conditions that call for a special focus upon discipleship, or evangelism, or missions. There may be situations that invite special preoccupation with the sacraments, or the end times, or spiritual gifts. There may be a need for special instruction in the areas of divine sovereignty and human responsibility, promise and law, etc.

It may even be realistically admitted that at different times different preachers are gripped by different facets of the truth which they should not hesitate to preach.

But the Church will do well to heed the summons of the apostle Paul carefully. It must "preach the Word." If it does so, preferably, if not predominantly, in an expository fashion, it will safeguard itself against obscuring, impinging upon, or subtracting from the whole counsel of God by an unbecoming fascination with one or more favorite themes and so against an inevitable spiritual loss.

II. Focus upon Preparation

To understand the fundamental significance and indispensable character of preaching is to understand the importance of proper preparation. For a message to be Biblical in content and purpose it must reflect the content and purpose of the preaching unit. To arrive at such a message a thorough contextual and textual study of the preaching unit is necessary.

A contextual study inquires into the historical, cultural and geographical setting of a text and seeks to determine whether this is reflected in the particulars this text sets forth. It also researches its literary setting and seeks to establish the genre, author, date, audaim of the larger unit of which the text is only a part. Contextual studies often shed a remarkable light upon the text.

After the contextual studies have been completed, the meaning of the text must be established. This may be done with the assistance of dictionaries, grammars and other helps. At least two rules of thumb, however, ought to be kept in mind. For one, since the text is always directed to a specific audience, no meaning may be ascribed to any text that could not have been recognized by the original audience. For another, since the text is always truth applied to an audience in its specific situation, no meaning may be imposed upon the text beyond this truth as it is applied. In a word, the interpreter faces two inherent limits that he may not transgress. He may not wrest an answer to a question or a solution to a problem from a text when this text is not designed to answer that question or solve that problem in addressing its original audience in its circumstances.

Once the meaning of the text is established, the bedrock for relevant preaching is in place. The genius of such preaching is to glean the legitimate universal principles and patterns of God's dealings with man and of man's response to God from the text. To arrive at these principles and patterns an outline of the text in its literary context is indispensable. The theme and the main divisions will yield the more general and structural universal principles, the subdivisions the more particular and concrete principles.

The outline of the preaching unit, formulated in terms of these principles, should determine the structure of the body of the message. It must present and unpack the theme and divisions of the text. At no time may the audience hear anything else but, "Thus says the Lord." It is advisable for a preacher to state the theme and divisions of his message explicitly and at the outset, whether in the form of propositions, assertions, questions, etc. If he decides against that, the minimum requirement is that the audience clearly understands what the text wishes him to get across and is able to follow the flow of the message.

When the body of the message is ready to be presented, an introduction and conclusion should be added. The introduction must be just that, an introduction, short and to the point. However construed, it must arrest attention, awaken interest in the subject matter and produce an eagerness in the audience to listen to the message. Indeed, it must create a tension in the hearers that will not be released until the climax is reached and the presentation is completed. The conclusion should follow the climax. Again it should be short and to the point. Whether it consists of a summary, a series of questions, a plea, or a challenge, its aim should be to drive the message home, into the hearts and lives of the hearers.

III. Focus upon the Preacher

In a very fundamental sense God's message is God's man. The messenger must be the embodiment of the message. He must be truth personified. It is not just that the preacher must be God's mouthpiece, his

Master's voice, however much that should be the case. This is what the previous section was all about. When he speaks, he must be able to say with confidence that Christ speaks (Rom. 10:14). But there is more. As the Father is truth, Christ is truth and the Spirit is truth, so the preacher as the Father's representative, Christ's ambassador and the Spirit's instrument must in a sense be truth himself. How else could Paul have spoken with approval of the Thessalonians as "imitators of him" (I Thess. 1:6)?

For any preacher to be truth personified and to present himself with confidence as a model for believers, he must have proper credentials in terms of the origin of his ministry and the preparation for his task as well as of his walk with God and the execution of his duties.

God must have called and commissioned him (Heb. 5:4), and Christ must have presented him to the Church as His personal gift (Eph. 4:11). God's call to ministry can never be separated from his call to Christ. In fact, the latter is the foundation for the former. The call to Christ, is, first of all, experienced in the heart-rending and transforming reality of rebirth, accompanied by repentance and faith, evidenced by a thirst for God, and resulting in an appropriation of Christ. Then, in the refreshing reality of God's justifying verdict that yields forgiveness of sins, which is sealed by the indwelling of the Spirit. And, finally, in the enriching reality of sanctification through the energizing presence of the Spirit. From all this arises an inner desire to serve in the pastoral and preaching office, to extend the Gospel call to others, and so to see sinners saved and saints edified.

Already at this stage there is a curious intertwinement of the call of God to and the preparation of man for the ministry. The call is evidenced by the avenue of the preparation. In fact, the clarity of the call is commensurate with the progress in the preparation. Progressive sanctification and a desire to enter the ministry, however indispensable, are only the first steps in the preparatory process. By themselves they are far from definitive proof of a divine call and in a sense only the launching pad for the main and much more focused stage in the preparation. The focus of this stage is twofold, in line with both a divine and human aspect.

The human aspect is expressed in II Timothy 2:2, where a period of intensive training is ordered for future leadership. This is a straightforward directive. Historically it has often been quoted as the basis for seminary instruction. The curriculum of such an institution usually calls for a training period of three to four years. This is intensive, indeed. But it is not sufficient unless, hand-in-hand with the acquisition of the knowledge of the Word, there is a maturation in being molded by that Word. In short, the process of sanctification in the broadest sense of the word must be a priority. Anyone who wishes to be molded by the Word, that is to make progress in practical godliness, must not only be filled with what Word that directs, but also with the Spirit who empowers (Col. 3:16; Eph. 5:18). The former without the latter will leave emptiness in its wake, the latter without the former will have blindness as its net effect. It makes little difference whether one knows the way to reach a destination but lacks the wherewithal to get there, or possesses the wherewithal to get somewhere but does not know which destination one wishes to reach.

The divine side is somewhat more intricate. It is closely linked with the area of spiritual gifts. The presence of the Spirit is not just evidenced by a lifestyle that has the marks of holiness indelibly stamped upon it. According to Peter, the Spirit also furnishes every believer with a special gift, either in the area of speech or of action (I Pet. 4:10-11). These are identified by Paul as prophecy (indicating the recipient as God's mouthpiece) and ministry (characterizing the recipient as doing his footwork). This is further subdivided as teaching and exhorting in speech, and sharing, caring and showing mercy in action (Rom. 12:3-8). What emerges here is the connecting link, the bridge, between the call to Christ as the foundation and the call to the minstry as the crowning piece. The Christian who aspires to the pastoral/teaching ministry with its focus upon the Word should display a gift in speech before he ever may consider, or may be considered for, that ministry. Incidentally, the call to be a Christian and the identification of one's gift are intimately interwoven. Teaching and exhorting are activities in which all Christians should be involved as Christians (Heb. 5:12; 3:13). So are sharing, caring and showing mercy, for that matter (Luke 3:11; Rom. 16:2; Jam. 2:13). In the way of purposeful obedience, then, to God's explicit commands through the indwelling Spirit in all these areas every Christian will eventually be able to determine experientially that the same Spirit has given him something special in one area or another.

The intensive training and the identification of a spiritual gift of speech in the course of, or--preferably--prior to, that training, must now be capped off by the third and final phase of the preparatory process. The Church must determine whether the candidate is, indeed, called of God and a gift of Christ. Neither God the Father, nor the ascended Lord, grant only salvation to individuals. They also grant officers, not just offices, to the Church (Eph. 4:11). Officers are not man-made on earth, but gift-wrapped in heaven. The must be recognized as such. The Church does so by applying the standard of I Timothy 3 that, hardly surprisingly, fully honors the intertwining of call and preparation. Does the candidate have a fervent desire for the pastoral/teaching office? Does he have a track record of practical godliness, acknowledged by believers and unbelievers, and can he function as a model for the Church? Has he given evidence of possessing a teaching gift that will enable him to edify believers as well as promote and/or defend the Gospel before unbelievers?

If the answer to these questions is in the affirmative, and properly so, the way to his ordination is open. This ordination, then, will constitute a commission of God through the Church on behalf of God, once again blending the divine and human together while acknowledging the primacy of the divine. When an ordination comes about in this way, it can be expected that a resulting preaching ministry will be pursued in prayerful dependence upon divine grace and be executed with the anointing of the Spirit. Such dependence naturally flows forth from the recognition of the primacy of the divine. The pastor/teacher owes his origin to God's call and Christ's gift. Such anointing naturally flows forth from the recognition of the indispensable operation of the Spirit. The Spirit who sanctifies and the Spirit who endows with a special gift, in the first steps and the main stage of the preparatory process respectively, is also the Spirit who grants unction to the preacher in the proclamation of the Gospel. This is a curious reality that, just like so many other spiritual realities, transcends conceptualization. It must be experienced to be understood. Its presence produces a liberty and a power that transforms the proclamation into "rivers of living water" (John

7:37-39) that "make glad the city of God" (Ps. 46:4) and prevail over "the gates of hell" (Mt. 16:18).

IV. Focus upon Proclamation

The preaching of the Gospel is the first and foremost means of grace. Of the several parables that disclose features of the Kingdom which were unknown in the Old Testament era (Mt. 13:1-52), the one that heads the list brings this out with great force. In order to implement the Kingdom there is no other alternative than to sow the seed of the Word. This is further on display on the Day of Pentecost (Acts 2:17ff, 42) and set forth by Paul as a universal principle. People will not believe unless they hear the preached Word (Rom. 10:14).

The power of the spoken Word is clearly enormous. It guarantees that the Church of Christ has a great future. After all, it is specifically designated by Christ Himself as a key to the Kingdom. This ensures that the gates of hell will not prevail against the Church. With the weapon of proclamation of the Word it is invincible on the march. The picture is bright, indeed. But does it seem realistic? The facts look rather grim. They hardly seem to bear out a triumphant impact of the Church. Worldwide it does not keep up with the birthrate. Nationwide it barely appears to hold its own. And locally the Church is often in retreat! How does one square the promise of the Savior with the facts, the ideal with the real?

The reason for this should not be sought in the promise, as if that is too grand and too idealistic. The Church is always ill-advised to tinker with God's promises, to question them or scale them down. It would seal its doom, for they are its lifeline and its power. If the problem, then, is not to be sought in the promise of our Lord, it must be in the preaching of His Word. This, indeed, is the case. Preachers readily acknowledge that the keys to the Kingdom are to be identified as the multifaceted Word of God. But they rarely recognize that this multifaceted Word should be proclaimed as the keys to the Kingdom. Too often they solely address the mind and are satisfied with agreement, a mental nod, on the part of the audience. Of course, the mind matters. The next section will enlarge upon this. But proper preaching goes deeper. It reaches out to the heart and insists on repentance and/or submission. Here comes into view the contours of the kind of preaching that opens and closes the Kingdom (Mt. 16:19), that forgives and retains sin (John 20:23), the kind that is both prescribed and modelled in the Bible itself and conquers the very gates of hell.

This kind of preaching is discriminatory and applicatory, and so proves to have healing power. By virtue of this power it is the only kind that truly satisfies.

Discriminating preaching is evangelistic in nature. In addressing unbelievers or in expositing an evangelistic preaching unit, the preacher may not leave the hearers in the dark as to their standing before God. In confronting Nicodemus with his need for a new heart in John 3:5, the Samaritan woman with her need for a new record in John 4:18 and professing Jews with their need for a new life in John 8:31, Jesus makes it crystal clear that as they are they cannot lay claim to the Kingdom of God. When Peter on the day of Pentecost exposits the truth of Joel 2:28-32, his audience has no doubt as to where they stand. The messages of both Jesus and Peter have a cutting edge that is unmistakable. The hearers are not the jury that must give a mental and oral verdict. They are the accused that need to bow before God and cast themselves upon mercy alone. In discriminating preaching the preacher goes after the rebel heart of man. Under discriminatory preaching lost sinners know that they are lost before the preacher has completed his message, whatever their response may be.

Applicatory preaching is edificational in character. In expositing edificational preaching units or in addressing believers, the preacher will not leave his audience in the dark as to their status before God. When Jesus had finished His exposition of the law in the Sermon on the Mount, the disciples knew what kind of lifestyle would disqualify a man from membership in the Kingdom and what lifestyle was indispensable for that membership (Mt. 7:24-27). When James addressed his hearers in the area of practical godliness, he did not simply define it in terms of its origin, nature, implementation and range. He also left no doubt that it was neither optional nor negotiable. Professing believers who saw their disobedient lifestyle or ungodly conduct exposed had little choice. They either would have to clean up their act or conclude that they were not genuine believers. Again, the cutting edge is noticeable. The hearers are not a jury that makes the final determination, but they are the accused whenever and wherever their conduct is found wanting. In applicatory preaching the preacher sensitizes the hearts of his audience as to their lifestyle. Under applicatory preaching deficient saints recognize when and where they are deficient and must deal with it if they truly love God and if they wish their profession to remain credible to others and themselves.

This kind of preaching has healing power. It sets the stage for the application of the three benefits of the Gospel, regeneration, justification and sanctification both in the life of the unbeliever and the believer.

In discriminating preaching the unbeliever is ultimately confronted with his rebel heart (Nicodemus), his guilty record (the Samaritan woman) and his unholy life (the professing Jews). This sets the stage for the preacher to call the sinner to repentance unto the forgiveness of his sins and an obedient life (Acts 2:38), and for the sinner to call on the Lord for a new heart, a new record and a new life based upon God's promise to that effect (Ezek. 36:37, 25-27; Acts 2:39). The upshot will be the liberating reality of a heart that is freely devoted to God, the refreshing reality of a record that is fully cleansed before God, and the enriching reality of a life that blossoms up before God.

In applicatory preaching the believer is faced with shortcomings in his conduct. This paves the way for the preacher to call the saint to repentance unto the forgiveness of sins and practical godliness and for the saint to call in repentance on his Father for forgiveness and progressive sanctification. This will produce a renewed liberation, refreshment and enrichment.

Discriminating preaching under God effects the once-and-for-all realities of regeneration (John 3:5), justification (Rom. 5:1) and sanctification (Heb. 10:10, 14); applicatory preaching effects the continuing realities of daily repentance (II Cor. 7:8-10), daily forgiveness (I John 1:8-9), and daily renewal (II Cor. 7:11). Everyone who possesses the once-and-for-all realities will give evidence of it in the continuing realities, thus resting in God without presumption. Everyone who experiences the continuing realities may know through that experience the possession of the once-and-for-all realities, thus working out his salvation without doubt. Clearly, the healing waters that flow forth from discriminating preaching continue to flow through applicatory preaching.

That such preaching which proclaims the Word of God as the Gospel of and the keys to the Kingdom is deeply satisfying hardly needs to be stressed. It furnishes entrance into the presence of God, peace in the love of God and fellowship under the smile of God.

V. Focus upon the Audience

Preachers invariably face a great diversity of listeners among their audience. They can expect to encounter saints and sinners, men and women, old and young who come from a variety of backgrounds, live in a variety of circumstances, find themselves in a variety of situations, cope with a variety of problems, look forward to a variety of futures, etc. It is the genius of preaching that the preacher can touch any and all audiences, however diverse, simultaneously with the truth of the Word of God. In order to succeed he must, as the primary aim, reach out to their hearts through their minds. This is the necessary means to the overarching objective, their holiness of life. This is fully in line with the Scripture's distinction of a threefold understanding, an understanding of the mind (Ps. 73:16-17; Dan. 9:2), an understanding of the heart (I Ki. 3:9; Is. 6:10), and an understanding of life (Job 28:28; Prov. 15:21).

Although the heart is the preacher's primary aim, the mind matters. The truth of the Word of God will not reach the heart except through the mind. That is why Scripture is replete with references to the significance, indeed necessity, of the teaching activity. All Christians should be teachers (Heb. 5:12). Many Christians have received a special teaching gift (Rom. 12:7). An elder in the Church is called a pastor-teacher (Eph. 4:11).

Teaching is the channel through which the truth of God enters into and impacts the lives of people. It can be defined as the conveying of the truth that is and the truth that ought to be. The truth that is, the focus also of systematic theology, covers the doctrines of Scripture, of the Trinity, of predestination, creation, providence, of the Spirit, of Christ, of man, of regeneration, justification, sanctification, of the Church, of the consummation, etc. The truth that ought to be, the focus of ethics, deals with substance of the Ten Commandments, the Sermon on the Mount and the many directives for a godly and righteous conduct that are found in Scripture. The truth that is and the truth that ought to be are closely related. In fact, the former is the foundation for the latter. By way of illustration, only the fact that a fetus is a human being (Ps. 139:15) (the truth that is) justififes the struggle to outlaw abortion (the truth that ought to be). But because of this fact such struggle is also mandated.

This illustration does more than indicate the relationship of "systematic theology" and "ethics." It also drives home that the stakes in teaching are high. Improper teaching turns the Church into a rudderless ship, exposed to every wind of doctrine that is bound to shipwreck it (Eph. 4:14). Proper teaching, on the other hand, organizes the presentation of God's truth in a way that it is conveyed in its totality (Acts 20:27) according to the intake capacity, the comprehension level and the need factor of the audience (Acts 20:31). Such teaching will renew the mind (Rom. 12:2). This, in turn, will result in the unity of the faith, the knowledge of the Son of God and the full transformation into His image (Eph. 4:13). Clearly, the mind does matter.

The recognition of the immense significance of the intellect, however, should never deceive anyone into directing his message exclusively to the intellect. This would be a deadly mistake. It will unalterably lead to the intellectualizing of the Gospel, either in whole or in part. Man simply is not all mind. In fact, with the renewal of man's mind one has in a real sense only scratched man's surface. That is why a teaching ministry may not simply address the mind, may not solely take aim at the mind or make the mind its final destination.

Through the mind it must aim at the heart. Discriminating and applicatory preaching that will proclaim the Word as the key to the Kingdom will do just that (Acts 2:37; 7:54; II Cor. 12:7; Ps. 51:10). For here one touches man's deepest being. The heart in Scripture stands for man's inner core, in contrast to his outer appearance (I Sam. 16:7; I Pet. 3:3-4). It represents man's personhood, man's deepest self.

The counsel written over the entrance to the oracle of Delphi, "Know Youself," is one of the most profound ever given to man. But the problem is that man cannot know his deepest self by self-reflection. This noble task proves to be an impossibility (Jer. 17:9). True self-knowledge comes to a man only as he looks in the mirror of divine revelation. And since out of the heart are the issues of life (Prov. 4:23), he needs the divine revelation desperately. This is supplied in the preaching of the truth. It does and must go right to the heart precisely to ensure that the life that flows forth from it is truly life. The pattern on display in chapters such as John 3 and 4, Acts 2 and 7, to mention only these, leave no doubt about the Biblical model in this regard.

It is no coincidence that the term "heart" is a figure of speech. As the deepest core of man it represents a layer in him that can only be experienced and therefore transcends conceptualization. It, indeed, goes deeper than the intellect. It is the "I," that has thinking and willing and feeling as three of its functions. This, therefore, should be the primary target in all pastoral ministry, including preaching. Any type of ministry that addresses merely the mind or the will or the emotions will only remain on the surface. The core of man's being must be targeted, touched and secured for any ministry to be permanent.

To repeat, the mind is of incalculable significance. It should be saturated with all the truth of Scripture. In fact, intellectually, there should be no doubt about the meaning or significance of any passage, text or topic of Scripture after it has been preached. This requires that the message is delivered in a well-articulated and clear fashion, in words that are carefully chosen and befit both the subject matter and the audience. It must further be presented in an imaginative way, with vivid illustrations that make the subject matter come to life before the audience. But it must also come across with persuasiveness, with a personal and practical touch that makes the audience come to grips with the subject matter.

If the preacher applies himself to accomplish this, he will not be satisfied with just an intellectual deposit as the end product. That would be tantamount to turning the mind into a place that serves the sole purpose of storing agreeable data like ice cubes in a freezer. No, the mind should be a channel through which the truth penetrates into the heart. It will be like a stream of water that floods it. It will prick, jolt, cut, instruct, direct, empower, set in motion. The primary aim is not agreement of the mind, but repentance, faith and submission of the heart. The result? Holiness unto the Lord up to and including the last nook and cranny in the Church, the armament upon the army's tanks and pans in mother's kitchen (Zech. 14:20-21). Here the grand objective of Biblical preaching comes into view.

Holiness is the essence of God's being (Is. 6:3); it is also the scope of election (Eph. 1:4), of the covenant (Gen. 17:1; Ezek. 36:27), of the work of Christ (Mt. 1:21), of the operation of the Spirit (Rom. 15:16), of repentance (Acts 26:20), of faith (Acts 26:18), of the Church (Eph. 4:11-12), of the new earth (II Pet. 3:13-14), etc. It is also the major subject matter (Old Testament and New Testament) and objective (Ps. 119:11; II Tim. 3:15-17) of Scripture. Why, then, should it not be the grand objective of preaching? It puts on display just one more aspect of that God-centeredness which is so characteristic of all of Biblical faith and practice. However, God-centeredness must adorn the preacher in more than the objective of his preaching ministry.

VI. Focus upon God

When a preacher is truly God-centered, he displays this in at least three ways. He will execute his pastoral and teaching ministry in full dependence upon God, for the sake of God and to the glory of God.

While it is unmistakable in Scripture that the person of the preacher is the indispensable agent and the activity of preaching the indispensable channel through which the grace of God reaches into the life of the hearers, it is equally unmistakable that the hearer owes his salvation fully to the sovereign grace of God (Acts 13:48b), the efficacious work of Christ (Is. 53:10) and the operation of the Spirit (John 3:5). If the dependent clause spells 100% man and the main clause 100% God, the combination of both clauses spells 100% (God) + 100% (man) = 100% (salvation). That is to say, in the implementation of salvation the human 100% rests squarely upon the divine 100% for its effectiveness.

On the one hand, God works through man (per hominen: Rom. 10:14) and the Spirit works through the Word (per verbum: Jam. 1:18). This is so by divine appointment. It is the way in which the salvation that is promised by the Father and personified in the Son is personalized by the Spirit. There is no other avenue of salvation. Human instrumentality in person and word is, indeed, indispensable.

On the other hand, however, God works with man (cum homine: II Tim. 2:25) and the Spirit with the Word (cum verbo: Acts 16:14). While God works exclusively through human instrumentality to effect salvation, there is no guarantee that salvation ensues just because man exerts himself in the preaching ministry. Apparently, one man can be man-taught without being God-taught, and Word-taught without being Spirit-taught. Unless God constructs an edifice, the human laborers build in vain (Ps. 127:1).

Concretely, the 100% man requires that man "gives it a hundred percent" in his person and in his preaching. By the same token, the primacy of the 100% God demands from him a deep humility and a total dependence. In the face of his impotence pride vanishes quickly. Man can only regard it as a privilege and be grateful if God decides to use him. At the same time, when a passion for fruitfulness is kindled within him, he will turn to fervent and unceasing prayer. After all God must make the difference if there is going to be any difference at all! In a word, pride must be replaced by prayer.

But there is more. The deepest motivation for the preaching must also be God-centered. The preacher in the execution of his ministry should not be driven by a desire for a sense of fulfilment, a sense of accomplishment or any such motivation that centers in himself. Neither should his deepest motivation be simply to see sinners escape the gruesome reality of hell. No, the driving force should be the desire for God's electing purposes to come to fruition (Rom. 9:11, 23), for the Lord Jesus to enjoy the fruit of His labor (Is. 53:10-11) and for the Holy Spirit to see His love crowned in finished products (Rom. 15:30). This, of course, in no way denies that an effective ministry will leave a sense of accomplishment in its wake and will result in joy about the salvation of sinners.

Finally, there is the goal. If that is to be God-centered as well, the preacher may not seek to build his ministry around himself or his church, so as to cherish the acclaim he gets and the reputation his church enjoys. Neither may he make evangelism or the dominion mandate or any other worthy and necessary goal ultimate, consciously or unconsciously. No, God must fill the horizon of his life, his endeavors and his accomplishments. The total range of his ministry, the progress of the Kingdom, all must be purposefully pursued and manifestly serve the glory of the Triune God. That is and must be the grand and ultimate objective. It is the objective of Christ (I Cor. 15:28). It may be no less the objective of His people, let alone of the God-appointed, Christ-given leaders among them. "For of God and through God and unto God are all things" (Rom. 11:33).

Conclusion

When preaching is God-centered in the full-orbed sense of the word, the truth of the Word is communicated through a godly man as the Gospel of the Kingdom with a view to practical godliness in dependence upon, for the sake of and to the praise of God. Then--and only then--a full-orbed worship can be expected to come to fruition. Such preaching programmatically and systematically aims at it. As it reaches out to any and all audiences, it opens up vistas of the full worth of the Triune God, inviting worship.

When an audience does not have the Word snatched away from it by the Enemy, does not have it scorched under persecution, nor have it choked by everyday realities, but has it blossom out into a full-orbed holy life (Mt. 12:18-23), this "invitation" will not fall on deaf ears. The heart will respond. In the joy of the Spirit and with undivided devotion to its Lord, it will praise God (Acts 2:46-47).

Through the vision of the holiness of God and in the submission to His dominion, all the 'crowns' will end up at the foot of the throne, and the exaltation of the Triune God will ever expand. Of course, the implications of such worship in deed and word upon all of life can hardly be over emphasized, and the impact of such worship upon it can hardly be over estimated.

But even beyond all this, the Father seeks worship (John 4:23-24). And what the Father seeks, He will find. If humans ever fall silent, the stones will take their place and cry out in praise (Luke 19:40)!

11 - SONG IN PUBLIC WORSHIP[1]

John Murray

The Committee on Song in the Public Worship of God presented to the Thirteenth General Assembly a report bearing upon the question of the regulative principle of worship. This principle is to the effect that divine warrant or authorization is required for every element entering into the worship of God. In the words of the Confession of Faith of this Church, "The acceptable way of worshipping the true God in instituted by Himself, and so limited by His own revealed will, that He may not be worshipped according to the imaginations and devices of men, or the suggestions of Satan, under any visible representation, or any other way not prescribed in the holy Scripture" (Chap. XXI, Sect. I).

In terms of the commission given by the Eleventh General Assembly and in accordance with the regulative principle set forth in the report of the committee, presented to the Thirteenth General Assembly, the question with which this report is concerned is: What does the Scripture warrant or prescribe respecting the songs that may be sung in the public worship of God?

In dealing with this question it should be appreciated that the singing of God's praise is a distinct act of worship. It is to be distinguished, for example, from the reading of the Scripture and from the offering of prayer to God. It is, of course, true that songs of praise often include what is of the nature of prayer to God, as it is also true that in the offering of prayer to God there is much that is of the nature of praise and thanksgiving. But it is not proper to appeal to the divine authorization or warrant we possess as to the content of prayer in order to determine the question as to the content of song. Prayer is one element of worship, singing is another.

---

[1] This chapter is the Minority Report of the Committee on Song in the Public Worship of God, presented to the 14th General Assembly (1947) of the Orthodox Presbyterian Church. The Majority Report is found in Appendix B.

Similarity or even identity of content does not in the least obliterate the distinction between these two specific kinds of exercise in the worship of God. Because of this distinction we may not say that the offering of prayer and the singing of praise to God are the same thing and argue from the divine authorization we possess respecting the one to the authorization respecting the other. One or two examples may be given of the necessity and importance of guarding the distinctiveness of the several parts of worship and of determining from the Scripture what its prescriptions are respecting each element.

Both reports submitted by this committee are agreed that some Scripture songs may be sung in the public worship of God. But these Scripture songs may also be read as Scripture and they may be used in preaching. In such cases the actual materials are the same. But reading the Scripture is not the same exercise of worship as singing, and neither is preaching the same as singing or reading the Scripture. The same kind of distinction applies to the exercises of praying and singing even when the content is identical.

The Lord's Supper is an act of thanksgiving as well as one of commemoration and communion. But though the partaking of the bread and the wine includes thanksgiving just as prayer and singing do, yet the celebration of the Lord's Supper is an act of worship distinct from both prayer and singing, and the divine prescriptions respecting the celebration of the Lord's Supper cannot be determined by the divine prescriptions regarding prayer or singing but must rather be derived from the revelation God has given respecting the observance of that distinct element of the worship of God.

Consequently the minority contends that the argument used in the report of the committee, to wit, that, since we are not limited in our prayers to the words of Scripture or to the "prayers" given us in Scripture, therefore the same freedom is granted in song, is invalid. We may not argue thus from the divine warrant respecting one element to the divine warrant respecting another. The question of the divine prescription regarding the songs that may be sung in the public worship of God must be answered, therefore, on the basis of the teaching of Scripture with respect to that specific element of worship.

When we address ourselves to the question of the teaching of Scripture we find that the New Testament does not provide us with copious instruction on this matter. It is for that reason that we are placed under the necessity of exercising great care lest we overstep the limits of divine authorization and warrant. This report will deal with the evidence that is directly germane to the question.

The Scripture Evidence

I. Matthew 26:30; Mark 14:26. Here we are told that, on the occasion of the passover, Jesus and His disciples sang a hymn before going out to the Mount of Olives. The Greek is *humnesantes*, which literally means "having hymned." The evidence available to us from other sources is to the effect of indicating that the hymn sung on this occasion was what is known as the Hallel, consisting of Psalms 113-118. This instance evinces the following facts.

(1) No warrant whatsoever can be adduced from this for the singing of uninspired hymns. There is no evidence that an uninspired hymn was sung on this occasion.

(2) The evidence we do possess evinces that Jesus and His disciples sang a portion of the psalter.

(3) This singing took place in connection with the celebration of the Old Testament sacrament of the Passover and the New Testament sacrament of the Lord's Supper.

II. I Corinthians 14:15, 26. Paul is here dealing with the assembly of the saints for worship. He says, "I will sing with the spirit and I will sing with the understanding also" (vs. 15), "Each one hath a psalm" (vs. 26). From the verb that Paul uses in verse 15 we might quite properly translate as follows: "I will sing a psalm with the spirit and I will sing a psalm with the understanding also," just as in verse 26 he says, "Each one hath a psalm." We must conclude, therefore, that psalms were sung in the church at Corinth and such singing has, by obvious implication, the apostle's sanction and is confirmed by his example.

The question does arise: What were these psalms? It is possible that they were charismatic psalms. If so, one thing is certain--they were not uninspired compositions. If charismatic they were inspired or given by the Holy Spirit. If we today possessed such charismatic psalms, sung by the apostle himself in the assemblies of worship or sanctioned by him in the worship of the church, then we should have the proper authority for the use of them in the songs of the sanctuary. It so happens, however, that we do not have conclusive evidence to show that we have any of such alleged charismatic psalms. But even on the hypothesis that they were charismatic psalms and even on the hypothesis that we have examples of such in Acts 4:23-30 and I Timothy 3:16, we are not thereby furnished with any authorization for the use of uninspired songs in the worship of God.

On the hypothesis that they were not charismatic psalms we have to ask, what were they? To answer this question we have simply to ask another: what songs, in the usage of Scripture, fall into the category of psalms? There is one answer. The Book of Psalms is composed of psalms and, therefore, by the simplest principle of hermeneutics we can say that, in terms of Scripture language, the songs that are repeatedly called psalms perfectly satisfy the denotation and connotation of the word "psalm" as it is used here. If inspired Scripture says, "Each one hath a psalm," and Scripture also calls the "Psalms" psalms, then surely we may also sing a Psalm to the praise of God in His worship.

So far as these two texts are concerned we can say that they provide us with no warrant whatsoever for the use of uninspired hymns. We can also say that, since the psalms we possess in the psalter are certainly psalms in the terminology of Scripture itself, we are hereby provided with divine warrant for the singing of such in the worship of God.

III. Ephesians 5:19; Colossians 3:16. With respect to these two texts it should be noted, first of all, that Paul is not necessarily referring to the public worship of God. The context does not make clear that Paul is confining himself here to exhortation that concerns the behavior of believers in relation to one another in the assemblies of worship. Paul may very well be giving general exhortation. Indeed, the context in both passages would appear to show that he is exhorting to a certain kind of exercise in which believers should engage in reference to one another in the discharge of that mutual instruction and edification requisite to concerted advancement of one another's highest interests and of the glory of God. This consideration does not, however, remove these texts from relevancy to the question of the public worship of God. For, if Paul specifies psalms, hymns and Spiritual songs as the media through which believers may mutually promote the glory of God and one another's edification in those more generic Christian exercises, this fact has very close bearing upon the question of the apostolically sanctioned and authorized media of praise to God in the more specific worship of the sanctuary. In other words, if the apostolically enjoined media or materials of song in the more generic exercises of worship are psalms, hymns and Spiritual songs, then surely nothing inferior to psalms, hymns and Spiritual songs would be enjoined for use in the more specific exercises of worship in the assemblies of the church. If psalms, hymns and Spiritual songs are the limits of the materials of song in praise of God in less formal acts of worship, how much more are they the limits in more formal acts of worship. With respect to these two texts the following considerations are to be borne in mind.

(1) We cannot determine the denotation or connotation of psalms, hymns and Spiritual songs by any modern usage of these same words. The meaning and reference must be determined by the usage of Scripture.

(2) Some of the facts with reference to the usage of Scripture are very significant.

The word *psalmos* (psalm) occurs some 94 times in the Greek Scriptures, that is to say, some 87 times in the Septuagint version of the Old Testament and 7 times in the New Testament. In the Septuagint some 78 of these instances are in the Book of Psalms. In the great majority of instances in the Book of Psalms, some 67 in all, it occurs in the titles of the Psalms. In three of the seven instances in the New Testament the word is unmistakably used with reference to the Psalms, in two instances in the phrase the "Book of Psalms" (*biblos psalmon*) and in the other instance with reference to the second Psalm. It is surely significant, therefore, that in some 70 of the 94 instances the reference is clearly to the Book of Psalms or to Psalms in the Book of Psalms.

The word *humnos* (hymn) occurs some 19 times in the Greek Bible, 17 (?) times in the Old Testament and 2 times in the New (in the passages under consideration). Of the 17 Old Testament instances 13 occur in the Book of Psalms and 6 of these are in the titles. In the seven instances not occurring in the titles the reference is in each case to the praise of God or to the songs of Sion. The other four instances in the other books of the Old Testament have

likewise reference to the songs of praise to God.

The word *odee* (song) occurs some 86 times in the Greek Bible, some 80 times in the Old Testament and 6 times in the New. Apart from these two passages (Eph. 5:19; Col. 3:16), it occurs in the New Testament only in the Book of Revelation. Of the 80 occurrences in the Old Testament some 45 are in the Book of Psalms and 36 of these are in the titles of the Psalms.

It is surely apparent, therefore, how large a proportion of the occurrences of these words is in the Book of Psalms. These facts of themselves do not prove that the reference here in Ephesians 5:19 and Colossians 3:16 is to the Book of Psalms exclusively. But these facts must not be forgotten as we proceed to determine the character of the lyrical compositions mentioned in these two texts.

(3) In the New Testament the word *psalmos* occurs seven times, as was just stated. Two of these instances are in the texts we are considering. One of these instances is I Corinthians 14:26, a text dealt with already. Two instances (Luke 20:42; Acts 1:20) refer to the Book of Psalms (*biblos psalmon*). Luke 24:44 clearly refers to Old Testament inspired Scripture and probably to the book of Psalms. Acts 13:33 refers to the second Psalm. In none of these instances is there any warrant for supposing that "psalms" refer to uninspired human compositions. In the majority, without the least shadow of doubt, the reference is to inspired Scripture.

In the New Testament the word *humnos* occurs only in these two passages. The verb *humneo* (to hymn) occurs four times (Mt. 26:30; Mark 14:26; Acts 16:25; Heb. 2:12). As we found already, the synoptic passages most probably refer to the singing of the Hallel by our Lord and His disciples. Acts 16:25 refers to the singing of Paul and Silas in prison. Hebrews 2:12 is a quotation from the Old Testament (Ps. 22:23)--*en meso ekklesias humneso se.*

No evidence whatsoever can be adduced from the usage in support of the use of uninspired hymns.

Apart from these two instances the word *odee* occurs in the New Testament only in Revelation 5:9; 14:3 (2); 15:3. From the New Testament, then, no evidence can be derived to show that these words may be used here (Eph. 5:19; Col. 3:16) with reference to uninspired songs. Even though *odee* is used in the Book of Revelation with reference to songs other than those in the Book of Psalms it is not used there with reference to uninspired human compositions but with reference to inspired songs.

(4) We now come to the consideration of some facts which are even more significant than those already discussed. The Book of Psalms is composed of psalms, hymns and songs. We have already found that the overwhelming majority of the instances of these words in both Testaments has reference to the Book of Psalms. We now come to the discussion of the meaning of these words in the titles of the psalms.

In the Septuagint *psalmos* occurs some 67 times in the titles to the Psalms. In most cases it is the translation of the Hebrew *mismor,* but in a few cases it translates other Hebrew words. *Psalmos* means simply "song of praise." The frequency with which the word *psalmos* occurs in the titles is probably the reason why the Book of Psalms is called in the LXX version simply *psalmoi.* In the Hebrew it is called *tehillim.*

It is perfectly obvious, therefore, that the New Testament writers, familiar as they were with the Old Testament in Greek, would necessarily have the Book of Psalms in mind when they used this word *psalmos.* There is no other piece of evidence that even begins to take on the significance for the meaning of the word "psalm" in the New Testament that this simple fact takes on, namely, that the Book of Psalms was called simply "Psalms" (*psalmoi*). The usage of the New Testament itself puts this beyond all doubt. There the Psalms are called the Book of Psalms.

There is nothing in the context of these two passages requiring us to regard "psalms" as referring to uninspired compositions. On the other hand, there are abundant instances in the usage of Scripture elsewhere which show that the word "psalm" refers to an inspired composition. Furthermore, there is no instance in which the word "psalm," as used with reference to a song of praise to God, can be shown to refer to an uninspired song. It is therefore quite unwarranted to regard "psalms" in these two passages as referring to uninspired songs, whereas there is abundant warrant for regarding them as denoting inspired compositions. Consequently, if we are to follow the line of the evidence provided by the Scripture, we are forced to find the "psalms" here mentioned within the limits of inspiration.

As we found, the word *humnos* appears some 17 times in the Septuagint version. In thirteen cases it appears in the Book of Psalms. In five or six cases it appears in the titles of the Psalms as the translation of the Hebrew *neginoth* or *neginah*. It is significant that on several occasions in the text of the Psalms *humnos* translates the Hebrew word *tehillah* which is the word used to designate the Book of Psalms in the Hebrew. This shows that psalms may be called hymns and hymns are psalms. Psalms and hymns are not exclusive of one another. A psalm may be not only a psalm but also a hymn.

These facts show that when, in the usage of Scripture, we look for the type of composition meant by a "hymn," we find it in the Psalms. And we have no evidence whatsoever that a hymn, in the usage of Scripture, ever designates an uninspired human composition.

The word *odee* occurs much more frequently in the titles of the Psalms than does the word *humnos*, but not as frequently as does the word *psalmos*. There are some 36 instances. It usually translates the Hebrew word *shir* but not always. Occasionally it is the translation of *mismor*, the word generally translated by *psalmos*. *Odee* occurs so frequently in the titles of the psalms that its meaning would be definitely influenced by that usage.

The conclusion to which we are driven then is that the frequency with which these words occur in that book of the Old Testament that is unique in this respect that it is a collection of songs composed at various times and by various inspired writers, the book that stands out distinctively and uniquely as composed of psalms, hymns and songs, would tend most definitely to fix the meaning of these words in the usage of the inspired writers. The case is simply this, that beyond all dispute there is no other datum that compares with the significance of the language of the Septuagint in the resolution of this question. When taken in conjunction with the only positive evidence we have in the New Testament the evidence leads preponderantly to the conclusion that when Paul wrote "psalms, hymns and Spiritual songs" he would expect the minds of his readers to think of what were, in the terms of Scripture itself, "psalms, hymns and Spiritual songs," namely, the Book of Psalms.

(5) The evidence does not warrant the conclusion that the apostle meant by "psalms, hymns and Spiritual songs" to designate three distinct groups or types of lyrical compositions. It is significant in this connection that in a few cases in the titles of the Psalms all three of these words occur. In many cases the words "psalm" and "song" occur in the same title. This shows that a lyrical composition may be a psalm, hymn, and song at the same time.

The words, of course, have their own distinctive meanings and such distinctive meanings may intimate the variety and richness of the materials of song the apostle has in mind. Paul uses three words that in the established usage of Scripture designate the rich variety of such lyrical compositions as were suited for the worship of God in the service of song.

(6) Paul specifies the character of the songs as "Spiritual"--*odais pneumatikais*. If anything should be obvious from the use of the word *pneumatikos* in the New Testament it is that it has reference to the Holy Spirit and means, in such contexts as the present, "given by the Spirit." Its meaning is not at all, as Trench contends, "such as were composed by spiritual men, and moved in the sphere of spiritual things" (*Synonyms*, LXXVIII). It rather means, as Meyer points out, "proceeding from the Holy

Spirit, as *theopneustos*" (Com. on Eph. 5:19). In this context the word would mean "indited by the Spirit," just as in I Corinthians 2:13 *logois. . . pneumatikos* are "words inspired by the Spirit" and "taught by the Spirit" (*didaktois pneumatos*).

The question, of course, arises: why does the word *pneumatikos* qualify *odais* and not *psalmois* and *humnois*? A reasonable answer to this question is that *pneumatikais* qualifies all three datives and that its gender (fem.) is due to attraction to the gender of the noun that is closest to it. Another distinct possibility, made particularly plausible by the omission of the copulative in Colossians 3:16, is that "Spiritual songs" are the genus of which "psalms" and "hymns" are the species. This is the view of Meyer, for example.

On either of these assumptions the psalms, hymns and songs are all "Spiritual" and therefore all inspired by the Holy Spirit. The bearing of this upon the question at issue is perfectly apparent. Uninspired hymns are immediately excluded.

But we shall have to allow for the distinct possibility that the word "Spiritual," in the grammatical structure of the clause, is confined to the word "songs." On this hypothesis the "songs" are characterized as "Spiritual," and therefore characterized as inspired or indited by the Holy Spirit. This, at least, should be abundantly clear.

The question would arise then: is it merely the "songs" that need to be inspired while the "psalms" and "hymns" may be uninspired? The asking of the question shows the unreasonableness of such an hypothesis, especially when we bear in mind all that has already been shown with reference to the use of these words. On what conceivable ground would Paul have insisted that the "songs" needed to be divinely inspired while the "songs" and "hymns" did not need to be? In the usage of Scripture there was no hard and fast line of distinction between psalms and hymns, on the one hand, and songs on the other. It would be quite impossible to find any good ground for such discrimination in the apostolic prescription.

The unreasonableness of such a supposition appears all the more conclusive when we remember the Scripture usage with respect to the word "psalms." There is not the least bit of evidence to suppose that in such usage on the part of the apostle "psalm" could mean an uninspired human composition. All the evidence, rather, goes to establish the opposite conclusion.

We see then that psalms are inspired. Songs are inspired because they are characterized as "Spiritual." What then about the hymns? May they be uninspired? As already indicated, it would be an utterly unreasonable hypothesis to maintain that the apostle would require that songs be inspired while psalms and hymns might not. This becomes all the more cogent when we recognize, as we have established, that the psalms and songs were inspired. It would indeed be strange discrimination if hymns might be uninspired and psalms and songs inspired. But it would be strange to the point of absurdity if Paul should be supposed to insist that songs had to be inspired but hymns not. For what distinction can be drawn between a hymn and a song that would make it requisite for the latter to be inspired while the former might not be? We, indeed, cannot be sure that there is any distinction so far as actual denotation is concerned. Even if we do maintain the distinct colour of each word there is no discoverable reason why so radical a distinction as that between inspiration and non-inspiration could be maintained.

The only conclusion we can arrive at then is that "hymns" in Ephesians 5:19 and Colossians 3:16 must be accorded the same "Spiritual" quality as is accorded to "psalms" by obvious implication and to "songs" by express qualification, and that this was taken for granted by the apostle, either because the word "Spiritual" would be regarded as qualifying all three words, or because "Spiritual songs" were the genus of which "psalms" and "hymns" were the species, or because in the usage of the church "hymns" like "psalms" would be recognized in their own right and because of the context in which they are mentioned to be in no other category, as respects their "Spiritual" quality, than the category occupied by psalms and songs.

In reference to these two passages, then, we are compelled to conclude:

(a) There is no warrant for thinking that "psalms, hymns and Spiritual songs" can refer to uninspired human compositions. These texts provide us with no authorization whatsoever for the singing of uninspired songs in the worship of God.

(b) There is warrant for concluding that "psalms, hymns and Spiritual songs" refer to inspired compositions. These texts provide us, therefore, with warrant for the singing of inspired songs in the worship of God.

(c) The Book of Psalms provides us with psalms, hymns and songs that are inspired and therefore with the kind of compositions referred to in Ephesians 5:19 and Colossians 3:16.

General Conclusions

This survey of the evidence derived from Scripture shows, in the judgment of the minority, that there is no evidence from Scripture that can be adduced to warrant the singing of uninspired human compositions in the public worship of God. The report of the committee maintains that we do have warrant for the use of such songs. The minority is well aware of the plausibility of the arguments of the committee, to wit, the argument drawn from the analogy of prayer and the argument drawn from the necessity of expanding the content of song to keep pace with the expansion of the revelation given in the New Testament. The former of these arguments has been dealt with in the earlier part of this report. The latter is much more cogent. There are, however, two considerations that require to be mentioned by way of answer.

(1) We have no evidence either from the Old Testament or from the New that the expansion of revelation received expression in the devotional exercises of the church through the singing of uninspired songs of praise. This is a fact that cannot be discounted. If we possessed evidence that in the Old Testament period the church gave expression to revelation as it progressed by the singing of uninspired songs in the worship of God, then the argument from analogy would be rather conclusive, especially in view of the relative silence of the New Testament. But no evidence has been

produced to prove the use of uninspired songs in the worship of the Old Testament. Or, if instances of the use of uninspired songs in the worship of the New Testament could be adduced, then the argument of the committee would be established. But the very cases adduced by the committee to show that there was an expansion of song in the New Testament do not show that uninspired songs were employed. Hence we are compelled to conclude that, since there is no evidence to show that use of uninspired songs in the practice of the church in the New Testament, the argument of the committee cannot plead authorization from the Scriptures. The church of God must in this matter, as in all other matters concerned with the actual content of worship, confine itself to the limits of Scripture authorization, and it is the contention of the minority that we do not possess evidence on the basis of which to plead the use of uninspired songs in the public worship of God.

The argument of the committee that "the New Testament deals with conditions in the early church which have not been continued and which cannot be our present norm" fails to take due account of the normative character of Scripture. It is true that we today do not have the gift of inspiration and, therefore, we cannot compose inspired songs. But the Scripture does prescribe for us the way in which we are to worship God in the conditions that are permanent in the church. And since the Scripture does warrant and prescribe the use of inspired songs but does not warrant the use of uninspired songs, we are to restrict ourselves to those inspired materials made available to us by the Scripture itself. In other words, the Scripture does not provide us with any warrant for the exercising of those gifts the church now possesses in the composition of the actual content of song.

(2) If the argument drawn from the expansion of revelation is applied within the limits of Scripture authorization, then the utmost that can be established is the use of New Testament songs or of New Testament materials adapted to singing. Principially the minority is not jealous to insist that New Testament songs may not be used in the worship of God. What we are most jealous to maintain is that Scripture does authorize the use of inspired songs, that is, Scripture songs, and that the singing of other than

Scripture songs in the worship of God has no warrant from the Word of God and is therefore forbidden.

On the basis of these studies the minority respectfully submits to the Fourteenth General Assembly the following conclusions:

1.   There is no warrant in Scripture for the use of uninspired human compositions in the singing of God's praise in the public worship.

2.   There is explicit authority for the use of inspired songs.

3.   The songs of divine worship must therefore be limited to the songs of Scripture, for they alone are inspired.

4.   The Book of Psalms does provide us with the kind of compositions for which we have the authority of Scripture.

5.   We are therefore certain of divine sanction and approval in the singing of the Psalms.

6.   We are not certain that other inspired songs were intended to be sung in the worship of God, even though the use of other inspired songs does not violate the fundamental principle on which Scripture authorization is explicit, namely, the use of inspired songs.

7.   In view of uncertainty with respect to the use of other inspired songs, we should confine ourselves to the Book of Psalms.

12 - THE SINGING OF PRAISE

Frank J. Smith

Music is one of the Creator's good gifts to His creatures. Its employment in worship is almost universally recognized, but its nature and content have been matters of great controversy.

The proper content of worship-song can be understood only through a knowledge of the nature of the singing of praise. And, the nature of the singing of praise can be understood only if the nature of worship as a whole is understood. Accordingly, these topics will be taken up in reverse order in this essay in order to address this matter logically.

I. The Nature of Worship

This topic has been dealt with in the first section of this volume. Therefore, only a brief overview will be given here, along with appropriate application to the question of song in worship.

As has been noted, worship is special, dialogical, and prescribed. Several implications follow from this.

First, specific rules of Scripture apply to the singing of praise, as it is a part of worship. One may not appeal to general considerations, such as musical talents given by God, the aesthetic beauty of music, religious sentiments expressed in a song, and so forth, in order to justify the inclusion of material during the sung part of worship.

Second, the singing of praise is a distinct element of worship. Although it may be similar to other elements, it is governed strictly by the rules which apply to it and not necessarily by the considerations which inform the conduct of the rest of the elements of worship.

Along these lines, one can observe that only circumstantial details of the singing of praise are left to human discretion. By definition, the question of the content of worship-song is not a matter of circumstance, and therefore it must be determined by a direct appeal to Scripture. Similarly, the purpose and the form of the singing of praise are divinely determined. This is not to rationalize--the point is intended to emphasize the opposite, namely, that the elements of worship must be taken as 'package deals,' and that is why one may not change any substantive aspect of an element.

Third, in accordance with the dialogical nature of worship, the singing in worship is directed primarily to God, not primarily to man. This is one reason why this element is called the singing of praise. Therefore, one may not appeal to purported edifying effects of a particular song as justification for its inclusion in worship.

A final implication is that worship is a command performance, and therefore the singing done during it must be demonstrated to be commanded by God. Otherwise, such singing should not be allowed.

II. The Nature of the Singing of Praise

This topic will be approached from two perspectives--the singing of praise is both objective and subjective in nature.

A. Objective Nature

1. Trinitarian Nature
a. God the Father

Since God is the object of our praise, it should reflect His glory. Singing in worship should extol the attributes and acts of God.

Further, the point that must be maintained here is that God commands His people to sing praise. We are not to sing praise simply because we think it is a good idea to do so, or a good way to bring glory to the Lord. We sing praise because God has ordered us to sing praise. Singing in worship is a response, but it is a commanded response. All of the commands concerning it must be obeyed if faithfulness is to be exhibited, and God's Name glorified and praised as He desires.

b. God the Son

The Son of God, being the same in substance and equal in power and glory with the Father, is likewise the object of the singing of praise.

Jesus Christ is the One who orders singing in His presence, not only because He is God, but also by virtue of the fact that He is the God-man who has purchased His Bride with His own blood and thus gives her life and direction. King Jesus is the only law-giver in Zion.

But in the paradoxical nature of the God-man, Jesus Christ Himself also offers and did offer sung praise. What is ascribed in a metaphorical sense to God in such passages as Zephaniah 3:17, where the Almighty is pictured as singing over His people, has been fulfilled in a literal way by the Second Person of the Trinity.

Jesus sings today in the covenant assembly. The question immediately arises, What does He sing? Some people have taken this consideration of Jesus' singing to imply that He does not limit Himself to the words of the Psalter and therefore neither should we. But as one observer has noted, "after all, the Lord Jesus is not up in heaven singing [the songs of] Fanny Crosby." With all due respect to that dear elect lady, the point is that not only is a song of merely human origin not infallible--it also is not inspired.

What words grace the lips of our Saviour today in glory? Are they the words of men, or the words of God? Is it reasonable to expect that Jesus Christ is to be conformed to our image and to worship according to our pattern? Or is it not much more reasonable to expect that we are to be conformed to His image and to worship according to His pattern? To ask the question another way: in an evangelical setting, in the assembly of the saints, in the congregation of the righteous, when an uninspired hymn is sung in worship, does the Lord Jesus join with His people, or does He not rather remain silent?

Not only does Jesus Christ sing with His people the songs of Zion, but He has sung in their place. This beautiful Saviour has fulfilled all righteousness on behalf of all those who trust in Him, that righteousness being imputed to them. Part of this active obedience included the singing of praise, not only as an example, but also as a perfect sacrifice for sinners whose worship is unacceptable except in Him.

What did Jesus sing for His people? Why, of course, He sang the inspired Psalms. The Scripture says that Jesus went according to His custom into the synagogue each Sabbath Day. Therefore, during His lifetime on earth, and even during His ministry, He would have had ample opportunity to have sung all 150 Psalms on behalf of His chosen sheep.

This has implications for singing in worship today. Union with Christ (which, after all, is the theme of Ephesians and Colossians, epistles which contain very important passages to the matter at hand) means that those who have faith in Christ are joined with that which He has done for them. To sing an inspired Psalm is to sing "in Christ."

Beyond that, to sing any Psalm means implicitly, if not explicitly, that the singer is rejoicing in justification, and in sanctification, and even in adoption, for the Elder Brother has paved the way for His brethren to sing.

c. God the Holy Spirit

The Spirit, along with the Father and the Son, is properly the recipient of sung praise.

But the Holy Spirit has inspired the Psalms for use by God's people, and thus those songs have a holy and objective character. This is so because of the moral perfection of the Psalter. But it is even more so because of the 'set-apartness' of the Psalter (using the concept of holiness in its more basic sense of 'separateness'). The Psalter has the stamp of approval of the Holy Spirit upon it--the Psalms have been 'approved for use.'

2. Covenantal
a. covenantal response

In worship, the covenantal community is responding to the Lord of the covenant.

As has just been noted, the covenant community does not engage in the singing of praise simply because it thinks that that is a good idea, or because it has freedom to respond in any way it likes. The injunction to "sing!" is indeed an order.

The manner as well as the fact of singing is objective. Singing in worship is to be "with joyfulness." Joy is deeper than happiness, of course, and praise can sometimes be bitter-sweet. But there should be a godly joy permeating our singing.

Scripture speaks of the shouting of praise. The picture is that of willing subjects rejoicing in the reign of a great King (Ps. 47). This figure of speech does not mean a literal 'hollering,' but it does imply a certain vim and vigor during singing. Concommitant with that, note that God is more interested in singing issued from people with broken hearts even if they cannot carry a tune in a bucket, than with professionalism and aesthetic beauty. This is not to say that there is anything wrong with trying to do one's musical best. It is simply to note that God is more interested in the shouting of praise and lively singing, than He is in beautiful four-part harmony. If that fervor is not present, the congregation has not been obedient to God with regard to the manner of singing which He has commanded.

b. covenantal universality

The Church is Universal and is One. There is "one Lord, one faith, one baptism." There is one authority structure, one set of doctrines to believe, and one way in which to worship.

Negatively, there is no indication that each culture should develop its own way to worship. The divinely mandated wall of partition between Jew and Gentile has been abolished through the Messiah. Now that the Church is One, there is no evidence to suggest that she should be held captive by cultural forms, and certainly not by forms which God has not authorized.

This observation applies to denominations as well as to cultures. The worship of the Church in one part of the world should be essentially the same as in every other part of the world--geographically and doctrinally.

Beyond that, the Church and her worship are grounded in the history of redemption. As Johannes Vos wrote, we should not be "ashamed of the tents of Shem"--that is, we should gratefully acknowledge the fact that our salvation is not some ethereal something that has no more actual truth in it than a fairy tale or a religious myth. Rather our salvation is rooted in history and in the history of Israel in particular. This means that all believers are one with each other because of common 'roots' or heritage. This is reflected in the Psalter. Even more deeply, we must see that we have this unity with believers in every age, and our worship indicates this when we use the Psalms for our sung praise.

c. covenantal identification

The "I" of the Psalter is the "I" of the covenant. One of the implications of this is that one does not have to be able to 'identify' with the Psalmist in order to sing praise from any particular Psalm.

A prime example of this idea can be found by looking at Psalm 37:25. There the Psalmist says, "I have been young, and now am old; yet I have not seen the righteous forsaken, nor his seed begging bread." Any member of the covenant community, whether he is eight or eighty, can confidently sing these words without violating the Ninth Commandment. He can do so, not because he necessarily is old and has gray hair, but because he is covenantally bound and identified with that old man who did see God's faithfulness. To sing Psalm 37 is to praise God's faithfulness that is so great that even when one is advanced in years he can be assured that he still will never have seen an incident of God leaving His own.

Without this objective understanding of the Psalter, and the historical distance between its writers and us, there is very little of the Book of Psalms that would be appropriate for public worship. For example, Psalm 71 would be limited only to people to gray hair. Psalms 74 and 79 would be limited only to those who experienced the ruins of the holy city and the Temple. Psalm 80 would be limited only to those who lived in the Old Covenant era when God dwelled between the cherubim. Psalm 84 would similarly be limited. Many of the Psalms are written from the "I" rather than the "we" perspective.

This factor of historical distance combines with the fact that the purpose of singing in worship is praise rather than petition, so that even the Psalms where we can easily put ourselves in the Psalmist's position should also be seen as being objectively related to us. The prayers found in the Psalter, though greatly informative for our own prayer life, do not function as prayers as they actually exist in the canon of Scripture. For example, when we read John 17, Christ's High Priestly prayer for His elect, we are not praying--we are reading Scripture. When we read Psalm 51, David's prayer of repentance over his sin with Bathsheba, we are not praying--we are reading Scripture. When we sing Psalm 51, we still are not praying--we are singing praise to the God who does forgive sin.

The entire covenant community not only sings Psalms which may seem on the surface to relate to only some of the people, it also sings Psalms which are, on the surface, 'individualistic.' The Church praises the Lord for being the God of the individual. But more deeply, Jesus Christ, the God-man, has fulfilled all of Scripture. He is the suffering Servant. He is the Conquering Warrior. We sing of our Saviour and Lord when we sing the Psalms.

B. Subjective Nature

1. performance of the singing of praise

There are many items about the performance of singing in worship which are circumstantial and which are properly left to human discretion.

For example, which particular Psalms are to be sung on any given occasion is not determined directly by Scriptural command, even as which Scripture passages are to be read is a matter left up to those in charge of the service. Similary, how many Psalms are to be sung is a matter of circumstance.

Another circumstantial matter is that of which tunes to use. While some tunes may be more appropriate than others, and some be totally inappropriate, the actual choice is an area where the Lord has granted a great deal of liberty.

2. effects of the singing of praise

One of the effects of singing in worship is that of edification. As the music is directed to God, it is also secondarily directed to the people in the congregation.

Scripture says that singing should be one way in which teaching is accomplished. The Psalms, of course, contain much systematic and Biblical theology. One can always be sure that, since there is no incorrect theology in the Psalter, God's people will never be led astray be singing the Psalms.

Let us illustrate this fact of the godly instruction which the Psalter affords. In terms of systematic theology, think of the many doctrines which the psalms inculcate. One is the doctrine of God. "God is a spirit, infinite, eternal, and unchangeable, in his being, wisdom, power, holiness, justice, goodness, and truth." The Psalms can serve as proof texts for every truth of this classic statement.

Another doctrine is that of Creation: the 8th, 33rd, 96th, 104th are among the relevant psalms which extol the Lord for having made all things from nothing by the word of His power. Psalms 107 and 115 display the doctrines of providence and divine sovereignty--in the poignant refrain, "Oh that men would praise the Lord for his goodness, and for his wonderful works to the children of men!" set in the context of reeling sailors tossed on a stormy sea and of God's provision of food and shelter, as well as in the suitable rebuke, "But our God is in the heavens: he hath done whatsoever he hath pleased."

Psalms 6, 25, 51, and 58 speak graphically of man's sin. Psalms 32 and 143 shed light on justification: that it involves imputation, and that divine righteousness is necessary. Psalms 15, 24, 26, and 119 tell us about sanctification: that without holiness (as in clean hands and pure heart) no one will see the Lord. Psalm 103 comforts us with the truth of adoption:

that like as a father pities his children so the Lord pities those who fear Him.

The 23rd Psalm, along with the 4th, the 16th, the 63rd, and the 71st, communicate the doctrine of assurance to the soul. Psalms 19 and 119 drill home lessons regarding the importance of the Law of God. Psalms 115 and 135 emphasize the spiritual nature of worship. Psalms 2, 58, and 82 imply the proper role of civil magistrates: these human rulers, designated "gods," must rule in the fear of Him who places them in authority and judge righteously.

Psalms 45 and 48 portray the Church, which is the Bride of Christ and the city of God. Psalms 22, 31, and 69 reverently speak of Christ's suffering and humiliation. Psalms 2, 16, 45, and 110 shine forth the exaltation of our Saviour. Psalms 11, 75, 76, and 98 proclaim God's final judgment on the wicked.

In terms of Biblical theology, think of the many ways in which the Psalter sets forth the drama of the history of redemption. We have already noted that Creation is dealt with in the Psalms. God's dealings with the children of Israel are pictured in such Psalms as 78 and 105. God's concern for David's seed is manifest in numerous places, such as Psalms 89 and 132. Christ's coming to earth in seen in Psalm 40.

But it is perhaps in a more implicit manner that the Psalter is especially helpful in informing us regarding redemptive history. When the people sing the Songs of Ascent (Psalms 120 to 134), they are being taught truths about the return from Exile. When the congregation employs the Egyptian Hallel (Psalms 113 to 118), there is the reminder of the Exodus and of the Passover. When we sing of the various Old Testament practices which are evidently a part of the ceremonial law, we understand that we are living in a different day, a time of the New Covenant in which God's grace is communicated by forms which are simpler and have less outward glory. When we rejoice in the "new song," we apprehend the fact that it is the Spirit's song we sing, and that the former ways of God's revelation have now ceased.

Whether systematic or Biblical theology, truth is being conveyed. Doctrine is edifying God's people.

Singing is also a means of admonishing one another. These inspired odes tell us how to live. They rebuke us when we break God's Law. This author often enjoys singing while driving along; well, it is awfully hard to put on one's lips the words, "Oh how I love Thy law, it is my study all the day," while going 60 through a school zone. Not only does singing in private have this effect, but there is also a residual effect that carries over from the congregational gathering to one's private and family life, as the Word of God begins to permeate the very core of our being. And, one finds the rebuke in specific as well as general terms: Psalm 15 gives particular guidance for the believer--he must not backbite with his tongue, charge usury, nor change his oath once he has given his word even if keeping his word works to his own disadvantage.

The Psalms are also songs of comfort. They speak of a God of love, mercy, and grace. They tell of the One who builds up Jerusalem, brings back the captives, and heals the brokenhearted (Ps. 147). The fact of our historical nature of our holy religion and its Psalter is a great encouragement, too: in a time when "New Age" thought is so prevalent, we can be assured that Christianity is not just another mystery religion, but is rooted and grounded in history.

In terms of apologetics, the Psalms form a cutting edge. Historically, they have been called "The Battle Hymns of the Reformation." They were on the lips of Reformed soldiers as they went to war; they rose with power from throngs of Scotsmen who kept Queen Mary up half the night as she was 'serenaded' with the songs of King David. Even today, it is possible for psalm singing to be a sharp sword outside the confines of the church. (We will not expand on that thought but will leave it to the reader's sanctified imagination.)

But it is particularly regarding public worship that psalmody is a convicting force. And it is such both explicitly and implicitly.

Explicitly, the psalms crash in on the complacency of the unbeliever, strip him naked, and call him to repentance. Consider all the references to ungodliness and to judgment. The Psalter begins on a note of contrast: "Blessed is the man that walketh not in the counsel of the ungodly, nor standeth in the way of sinner, nor sitteth in the seat of the scornful. . . . the ungodly shall not stand in the judgment, nor sinners in the congregation of the righteous. For the Lord knoweth the way of the righteous, but the way of the ungodly shall perish." Notice that the words establish the contrast for both the different types of 'walk' or life, and for the destination. When a person outside of Jesus takes these words upon his lips in the congregation, he is singing of his own destruction, unless he repents and believes the gospel. Psalm 11 declares, "Upon the wicked he [the Lord] shall rain snares, fire and brimstone, and an horrible tempest: this shall be the portion of their cup." Psalm 75 states, "A cup is in Jehovah's hand; It foaming wine contains; Of mixture full, He pours it forth; The dregs each sinner drains." Psalm 76 rhetorically asks, "Who may stand in Thy sight, when once Thou art angry?"

Think of Psalms 14 and 53, which state, "The fool is saying in his heart, There surely is no God; Corrupt are they, their deeds are vile, Not one of them does good." Ponder God's brilliant holiness which Psalm 99 focuses for our attention: "Holy is He!" Meditate on Psalms 64 and 59 which paint an unflattering view of man in his prideful rebellion.

Whether we consider the folly and sinfulness of man, his just condemnation, or the holiness of God, the Psalter contains many expressions which pierce the souls of the unconverted. This author has personally witnessed non-Christians be cut to the quick as they either sing or refuse to sing of their own damnation.

More than the content *per se*, psalmody in public worship can convict rebels just from the nature of it. Implicitly, the psalms have their effect. The Word of God is as a searing light--a brilliance which in and of itself causes men to run for cover.

But even more than that, psalmody, along with the rest of public worship, works on those who are yet in their sins. It does so because it emulates the Second Commandment and implicitly maintains that man dare not approach God according to his whims and fancies, but according to divine precept and command. Yes, the Psalter comes out of a different culture and time; yes, it has hard-to-pronouce names and obscure references--yet those very facts point to the transcendent One with whom we have to do, and who has revealed Himself in history and who is jealous for His worship; those very facts serve to condemn those who refuse to bow to Him.

Psalmody, and the rest of public worship, function much like the preaching of the gospel itself--a savor of life unto life to the elect, and a savor of death unto death to those that are perishing. If you want to be evangelistic in your worship, be sure to sing the psalms, for both explicitly and implicitly they drive sinners--either further into their sin, or to Christ.

C. Overview

So we see that there is an objective and a subjective side to psalm singing. What we must press home at this moment is the fact that we do not engage in psalmody because of its beneficial effects; nor do we sing psalms in public worship fundamentally because by doing so we identify covenantally with God's people, rejoice in the Spirit's good gifts, or express liturgically our union with Christ. We sing psalms in public worship principially because our Sovereign Triune God has ordained that we do so. Thus we underscore the essential objectivity of the singing of praise.

The objective considerations always take precedence over the subjective ones. And, the subjective nature does not, according to Scripture, address itself to the issue of the content of worship-song. What should be sung in worship is determined on an explicitly objective basis.

III. The Content of Worship-Song

The preceding discussion has focused on the nature of the singing of praise and on implications drawn from general considerations as to the proper content of worship-song. It has to a certain extent assumed the validity of psalm-singing, though not necessarily exclusive psalmody, in arriving at various conclusions. This section focuses on the specific Scriptural data relating to the proper content of this element of worship. Because Colossians 3:16 is perhaps the clearest of all passages in aiding one's understanding of this issue, that text will be used as a take-off point for discussing all of the relevant texts.

A. "Let the Word of Christ dwell in you richly in all wisdom"

The term "the Word of Christ" has been subject to various interpretations. In a theoretical way, one could contend that this means that more than inspired words are intended. But that contention depends upon a distinction between "Word of God" and "Word of Christ." Beyond that, it also depends upon a virtual ignoring of the way the Bible talks.

It is far more Biblical to connect this term with verses such as Psalm 119:11 ("Thy Word have I hid in my heart, that I might not sin against Thee") and Jeremiah 31:33 ("I will put My law in their inward parts, and in their heart will I write it"). This is especially the case since the term is connected with the notion of dwelling in people.

Positively, "the Word of Christ" must include Scripture, even if other materal is intended. Negatively, one would be hard-pressed to demonstrate conclusively that anything else was intended. Logically, that which follows must be a sub-set of "the Word of Christ" (one would not be allowing this Word to indwell by means of singing something else).

This indwelling is to be done "in all wisdom." Again, from where does wisdom? Does it come from man, or from above?

B. "teaching and admonishing one another . . . singing with grace in your hearts unto God"

God's people are taught and admonished by means of (instrumental participle) singing praise to God. We would note in passing that, no matter what content is employed, praise must come from the heart that has been touched by God's grace.

C. "with psalms, hymns, songs which are spiritual"

The adjective "spiritual" (*pneumatikos*) most likely comes back and modifies all three nouns. As will be seen, whether it affects directly all three nouns or only the last one does not in the least affect the argument.

This word means driven by or energized by the Holy Spirit. It is used of things: Romans 7:14 ("the law is Spiritual"), I Corinthians 15:44a (the resurrected body is "Spiritual"), Romans 15:27 and I Corinthians 9:11 ("Spiritual things"), I Corinthians 12:1 and 14:1 ("Spiritual gifts"), I Peter 2:5 ("Spiritual house" and "Spiritual sacrifices"). It is used of people: I Corinthians 2:15, 3:1, 14:37, 15:46; Galatians 6:1.

Given this basic meaning of the word, the conclusion is inescapable that these songs must be "filled with the Spirit." Note that the Bible does not refer to people being filled with the Spirit and thus "inspired" to write songs. Rather, the songs themselves are "Spiritual" and thus inspired. (In Ephesians 5:19, the injunction corresponding to "Let the Word of Christ dwell in you richly . . ." is "Be filled with the Spirit"--this may explain why *pneumatikos* is used rather than *theopneustos*).

A study of the three nouns employed here also point to inspired material. The word for song is *ode*. It is seen in passages such as Revelation 5:9 and 14:3 where there is no indication that anything other than inspired compositions are in view. The word for hymn is *humnos*, the verb form is *humneo*. These words appear in several places in the New Testament. Acts 16:25 says that they sang praises at midnight. There is no reason to believe that anything other than the Psalms on which those two prisoners grew up were employed at that time. Matthew 26:30 and Mark 14:26 are in the accounts of the Last Supper. The hymn which the Lord Jesus and His disciples sang undoubtedly was the Egyptian Hallel (Psalms 113-118) or the last section of it (Psalms 115-118). Hebrews 2:12 uses this term in order to translate Psalm 22:22.

The word for psalm is *psalmos*. In places like Luke 20:42 and 24:44, and Acts 1:20 and 13:33, the reference is obviously to one or more of the 150 Psalms of the Old Testament. I Corinthians 14:26 cannot be demonstrated to be anything other than a reference to the Psalms of Scripture--even if this verse refers to a charismatic song, that song, by definition, could not be uninspired.

Not only do these three terms refer to inspired compositions generically, they refer specifically to the material of the Psalter. Various Hebrew terms for the Psalms, particularly as found in the titles of them,

207

have been translated as "psalm" and "song" in English. However, those responsible for the Greek translation of the Old Testament, the Septuagint, utilized three terms: psalm, hymn, and song. The audience to which Paul was writing would immediately associate these three terms with the Old Testament Psalter. No one has ever produced conclusive evidence that these terms must refer to something else.

C. Conclusion

We may conclude several things. One is that the Psalter is the hymnbook of the covenant community. The inductive evidence points in that direction. Two, that the phrase, "psalms, hymns, and songs which are Spiritual," does indeed refer to inspired songs, and specifically to those of the Psalter. Three, there is no evidence that anything else was ever intended by means of these words or of this phrase.

IV. Possible Objections Explained and Answered

This section is divided into two parts, the first dealing with objections of a more technical nature the second dealing with common objections heard from the 'man in the pew.'

A. Technical Objections

1. the Orthodox Presbyterian Church "Majority Report"

The General Assembly of the Orthodox Presbyterian Church commissioned a committee to study the question of worship-song. The final report was given at the 14th Assembly in 1947. The position of the minority on that committee, representing the views of John Murray and William Young, appears in this volume, and the views of the majority are dealt with in that article. However, it is important to give at least a brief answer to the Majority Report in order to set the stage for the consideration of the next potential objection. (See Appendix B.)

The Majority Report contended that new revelation means that God's people will respond with "free," uninspired compositions. Specifically, the new revelation of Jesus Christ means that such Christian songs should be composed. As Murray points out, however, there is no Scriptural warrant for believing that this is the case. The very examples cited by the majority may not be used to demonstrate that thesis--if anything, they prove the opposite.

The other major consideration advanced by the majority was that of the great similarity between prayer and singing praise. The immediate answer is that of course there are similarities between these two--both are directed to God, they often have the same or similar content--but the argument from analogy is weak at best.

However, the majority persisted in its argumentation, and said that the freedom of prayer implied freedom in the singing of praise as well. Two things need to be said in reply.

First, the form of an element is as important as is the content. Therefore, even though there is a continuum of speech, there is a definite difference between singing and speaking (or, if you will, 'praying'). The point, again, is not to be rationalistic--we would gladly receive the elements simply as they are, 'package deals.' When forced to analyze them in this way, however, we must recognize that they do indeed contain both 'form' and 'content,' and that the form among them differs according to Scripture. Therefore, we too must recognize this distinction.

Secondly, the majority's argumentation essentially wipes out any meaningful distinction between prayer and praise, and thereby establishes a hymnbook's validity on the basis that it is a prayerbook. The 'guilt-by-association' reply to this is that we are supposed to be Puritans not Anglicans. The more substantial reply is that the majority apparently misunderstood the nature of free prayer. Freedom in prayer means freedom to pray without human imposition and with the direct leading of the Holy Spirit. Both of these concerns are contradicted by the forced use of a prayerbook, whether its content is spoken or sung, granted that, unlike the Psalter, no inspired collection of prayers exists.. Finally, the majority's appeal to Acts 4 and 16:25 is quite unconvincing. In the former, most commentators agree that the Church is being led in prayer by one of its leaders. In the latter, to argue an important position upon the interpretation of a participle is tenuous indeed. In any case, the translation "when they had prayed [or, because they had prayed], they sang praises to God" is consonant with the teaching of James 5:13, as well as maintains the distinction which Scripture itself is affirming.

2. the "worship chart"

This confusion of elements of worship, against which the Minority Report warned so strongly, has come to fruition in new ways in recent years. This thinking goes this way. 'Elements' of worship are the 'what' one does during worship, 'circumstances' of worship are 'the way' in which he performs these elements. Since circumstances are not specifically prescribed in Scripture, there is liberty as to which mode is to be selected for this or that particular element. Therefore, not only may a person sing a prayer, he may also sing a sermon.

However, the proponents of this view are not content to leave things there. Rather, they go on to explain that the model they have in mind is one in which any art form may be used to express the various 'elements' of worship. Therefore, 'preaching,' dancing, singing, responsive reading, and anything else which tickles one's fancy may be used to convey the 'elements' of worship.

However, these proponents go one step further. They maintain that there are really no 'elements' of worship, but merely 'aspects' of worship, with no clearly defined boundaries between them. Indeed, any such lines must be regarded as merely arbitrary.

The theological basis for this position is that of Christ's mediatorial kingship: since He is both Head of the Church and also its Priest, the Word which He speaks is both to God and on behalf of God, and the two often melt into each other.

The model which is thereby effected can be thought of as a simple chart or graph. At the top is a continuum of 'aspects' of worship; at the side is a continuum of ways of expressing these aspects. Therefore, one may place a check-mark where any two categories intersect, and whatever he comes up with is valid for worship. For example, in this system, dancing a sermon is perfectly legitimate.

But there is fluidity in this system, too. Instead of merely punctiliar events, allowance should be made for sliding sideways--slipping from exhortation to praising, for example, or praising during the exhortation; and also vertically--slipping from preaching a sermon to singing it, if the occasion demands; and also on slopes--slipping from responsive reading of praise to dancing a prayer. Indeed, all sorts of interesting patters may be developed on this worship-chart.[1]

In response to this view, several things must be said. As has already been noted, this viewpoint continues the confusion engendered in the Majority Report at the 1947 General Assembly. But this confusion is expanded not only in terms of the form (not only singing praise and praying prayer, but all of the elements are now being involved as to their form), but also with regard to the content (one can be exhorting and all of a sudden shift into praise). People who naively claim, "I may sing anything I may preach," should realize that that alleged aphorism has been built on this theoretical base.

All sorts of theoretical objections immediately arise. For example, on this basis, no one could any longer object to a person 'preaching' during a prayer. There is no proper understanding of the dialogical nature of worship, including, the nature of ecclesiastical authority by which elders and/or other male leaders speak authoritatively the Word of God.

Dangerous trends arise necessarily from this argumentation. One which is explicitly taught is that, because of the continuum existing between

---

[1]Note that this author does not intend to be unfair to the gentlemen who propound this theory by polemicizing against something which they do not advocate. Without question, however, they do openly espouse this model of a worship-chart (even if they do not call it that), and, in private conversation and open classroom discussion, they have unabashedly stated that dancing a sermon or dancing a prayer would be perfectly legitimate. Therefore, although they themselves may not have actually advanced the notion of sliding vertically or on a slope, one is hard-pressed to see why such conclusions must not be drawn once the basic motifs have been establihed. There definitely is advocacy of sliding sideways.

translating the Scriptures and preaching a sermon, there is no meaningful distinction between reading the Word and preaching the Word, either in terms of form or content. Therefore, a person could legitimately stand up and say, "Hear now God's Word as it comes to us from the Confession of Faith [or Karl Barth, or *Time* magazine] . . . ." Even though admitting that that might be "confusing," at least one advocate of this position sees nothing wrong with that.

Notice also how this position essentially does away with the Protestant notion of *sola Scriptura*. Not only that, but it virtually views worship as a subjective response rather than something which is ordained by God.

This viewpoint tries to boil everything down to meaningless principles which can be twisted anyway one likes. If one were to apply its methodology to other areas, disaster would result. For example, one could say that the essence of the Pauline prohibition against women's ordination was that all things be done decently and in order--now that we live in a society in which women are accepted in places of authority, we can let the antiquated 'form' pass by and hold to the kernel of the truth which Paul was stating. Or, a person could say that the essence of the Seventh Commandment is covenant faithfulness, and on that basis homosexual marriage is acceptable because the two partners are agreeing to be faithful to each other. If we are shocked at this type of thinking being used with regard to the Fifth and Seventh Commandments, why should we not be equally shocked at its being used with regard to the Second Commandment?

Finally, we can say that there is no real basis at all for this position. The appeal to Christ's dual role as the basis for confusing the 'elements' of worship should be seen as amusing at best. The argument that all of the 'elements' of worship are 'organically' tied together and therefore are 'aspects' of worship rather than being 'distinguishable parts' is ludicrous. Of course worship is one organic whole--which is precisely why foreign elements should not be introduced into this 'body' of worship. But to say that worship is an organic whole is not to argue for a protoplasmic entity. The organs of the human body are organically related to each other, and imply each other, but they are clearly distinguishable both in terms of substance and function. Even so, the elements are organically related, yet are definitely distinguishable as to purpose, form, and necessary content.

In conclusion of our consideration of this position, one may confidently say that it is essentially a denial of the regulative principle of worship. In principle, nothing could be prevented from entering into 'worship.' Not only dancing, but strobe lights (expressing "joy in the Lord"), model railroad exhibits (a 'heavenly train' could be set up with 'J-E-S-U-S' on the locomotive), magic tricks (illustrating the nature of parables, or the mysteries of an incomprehensible God), pet parades (demonstrating divine love for us, or man's dominion over creation), and so forth, all would have to be allowed. Since 'circumstances' are not the 'what' of worship, but the 'how,' communion consisting of Coke and chocolate chip cookies would be welcomed as a contextualized Lord's Supper (or, cheese could be served along with the bread and wine). The degrading practices of Montreat, North Carolina, in 1968, where young people, under the auspices of the increasingly-liberal Presbyterian Church in the United States, snake danced in the aisles, wore face masks, and served Coke and chocolate chip cookies at a hand-clapping communion service, are by this position given a theoretical base on which to stand.[2]

3. the didactic use of worship-song

One of the contentions of the position just discussed is that whatever may be preached may also be sung in worship. Somewhat independently of this previously-discussed position, a similar contention has been maintained, mostly on the basis of the relevant Ephesians and Colossians passages. For example, it is argued that Paul's use of "spiritual" in these texts points to something other than inspiration. The answer to that contention is simply to refer the person to the Minority Report of Murray and Young, and/or to any Greek lexicon.

---

[2] "Coke" is a trademark of the Coca-Cola Company.

Beyond that, the particular didactic role of these songs is argued as the basis for saying that whatever is true and edifying may be sung during worship.

Two areas of objection need to be raised under the general topic of the 'dialogical nature of worship.' In the first place, women are to keep silent in the Church; if the focus of this singing is instruction of the people, may women participate? If this instruction is thought of as being the authoritative, ambassadorial proclamation of the Word of God, then clearly they may not. If it is merely a general sort of edification, then presumably they may; but, by what right does that singing have a place in worship (which should consist of elements which reflect its dialogical--that is, between, God and man--character)?

Second, as has already been implied here and stated explicitly elsewhere, the nature of that which is sung in worship is such that it is to be directed to God in praise of Him. This fact is seen in the passages cited: no matter how the participles of the last clauses are interpreted (causally, temporally, etc.), the basic meaning cannot be escaped, namely, that the focus of the singing is God-ward ("singing and making melody in your hearts to the Lord"). Even as edification and teaching occur in public prayer, so also in singing Psalms do these things take place--as the people sing to God, they also sing to each other. But even as it would be wrong to determine the content of prayer on the basis of the fact that it functions in an edifying way (though its purpose is that of addressing God), even so it is wrong to determine the content of worship-song, the purpose of which is to address God, by an appeal to its edifying and/or convicting effects. The purpose of singing in worship is not to convey any and every bit of redemptive truth-- the purpose is to praise God by means of that which He has given us to do so, the Psalter. The purpose is to delight our jealous God who wants to hear His people sing His praises with those (implicit and explicit) declarations of His greatness which He Himself has prescribed.

Sung praise is objective in terms of content not only because it describes God as He has revealed Himself, but also in that it is that which God Himself specifically desires. All of this is to say, again, that there is a sacred nature to all of worship, including the singing of praise. It is just as illegitimate to determine the content of worship-song by asking the questions, "Are the sentiments true in this hymn? Is this composition based on Scripture?", as it is to determine the elements of the Lord's Supper on the basis of the question, "Is this food nourishing?"

4. the "confession of faith" argument

The argument has been advanced that the Church confesses her faith in various ways, and that singing is one of these ways. Therefore, although the Psalter, since it is the very Word of God, may be quite appropriate for this sung confession, any portion of God's Word, or any other edifying body of truth, may properly be used.

It is true that the Church is to confess her faith, but the question is, What is meant by that? Such confession is implicit in the very gathering for worship, and is explicit at other times (including church membership or full communion vows). But to raise up a 'principle' of confession as a basis for singing songs not explicitly authorized in Scripture is to open a Pandora's box, for nothing could then be prevented in worship. Explicit warrant for explicit confession by song must be exhibited before such may be required or performed.

5. the charismatic song argument

It has been claimed that even as charismatic, revelatory prophecy and tongues are replaced by exposition of Scripture, even as we would see the providential wonders of science and medicine as a replacement of the miraculous, charismatic gift of healing, even as the church has not lost any power through the cessation of these things but rather matured out of them, that which is more mature having come, even so the uninspired, but sound, beautiful, spiritual hymns of the church 'replace' the charismatic psalms, hymns, and spiritual songs which Paul mentions.

As far as this author is concerned, this is probably the most cogent argument in favor of 'hymn singing.' But several things can be said in response.

First, there is no mention in Scripture of our composing worship songs today.

Second, note that the argument is based on a twin set of inferences, neither of which is necessarily true. There is no conclusive proof from Scriptural evidence, either by the words of Scripture themselves or by compulsion therefrom, that there were charismatic songs composed in the early stages of the New Covenant. Similarly, there is no compelling force with regard to the conclusion that, on the (purported) basis of charismatic songs composed during that apostolic age, we may therefore compose worship songs today.

It is both a good and necessary inference (*i.e.*, it is logically valid and Scripturally compelling) that the charismatic gifts have ceased. It may be a good inference, but it is not a necessary one, that charismatic songs were composed during that stage of the Church and that we may therefore compose doctrinally sound songs today for worship. To illustrate this point, we need only look at the argumentation in the suggestion. The replacement of the charismatic gift of healing with the science of medicine may be a 'good' inference, but who is to say that it is a necessary one? Let us say that anointing with oil was a part of the charismatic gift of healing and thus not a legitimate practice for the contemporary church. Even if 'anointing with oil' is not valid for today, and thus not valid as a replacement, could not 'praying over the sick' be inferred just as well as the 'science of medicine'?

Third, note that there is more at stake here than the matter of inspiration. A more specific issue is that of the 'fixed-free' distinctions. The reading of the Word and the singing of praise are 'fixed.' The preaching of the Word and the praying of prayer are 'free.' The very fact that there were extra-Scriptural (and non-canonical) utterances indeed points to the fact that that activity is an analog for preaching ('prophesying') today. Similarly, charismatic tongues correspond today to praying, but not necessarily to the singing of praise. Again, there is no specific warrant for composing worship-songs today, while there is Scriptural basis for praying prayers and preaching the Word under the direct, immediate leading of the Holy Spirit. The 'freedom' in these two elements is never arbitrary--rather, one is led in the moment of action to pray or to preach. The advocate of this position must show how this requirement of freedom is met if the contemporarily-composed worship songs are set down, rigidly, in hymnals.

6. arguments from the Psalter's "inappropriateness"

Some people question the appropriateness of the Psalter for singing in worship. The first of these arguments is that there are many sentiments and images in the Psalter which are not fitting for Christian worship.

One would hope that this viewpoint would not need much refutation. Even on the surface, it smacks of Marcionism. Since there is no contradiction in Scripture, pleas for vengeance are entirely consonant with our Lord's command to pray for our enemies. Such pleas may be understood, for example, eschatologically, but not in a way which dictates that their present application implies private vengeance (which they never really indicated). Also, the references to sacrifices and many other Old Covenant things should be understood from a Biblical theological perspective. They should thus be seen as having their fulfillment in Jesus Christ--they point to Him in graphic style and are therefore very appropriate for praising God for redemptive history.

Others hold that not all the contents of the Psalter were designed originally to be sung. Therefore, if a person wants to sing these materials from the Psalter which were not originally sung, then he also should allow for other materials to be sung in worship as well.

In response, we can note that even if material in the Psalter were properly excluded on this basis, there would be no warrant to deny that conclusion in order to include in the singing during worship materials which should not be allowed, whether from the Psalter or not.

Second, one should be aware that the basis on which this argument was established was motivated by a concern to express liturgically various Scriptures in the same manner in which they were given. For example, if Psalm 118 is seen as originally being material which was 'acted out' with the king, the priest(s), and the people each having lines to say, then of course we today should (or at least could) present that material in worship in similar fashion. However, if this concern is allowed to be the determining factor, then all sorts of problems would necessarily arise. For example, on this basis, the 'sacrifice' of bulls and goats would be perfectly legitimate, since it was in that context that revelation came (I Kings 8, if not Leviticus). If a person tries to refine that argument by making only verbal entities legitimate, then a problem still remains, for having a congregation to shout, "Crucify Him! Crucify Him!" would be unpreventable, as that is the manner in which those portions of Scripture were recorded.[3] The over-riding concern in worship is not a 'drama,' but rather a dialogue.

If the argument were refined still further so that only those portions of Scripture which were originally presented as liturgical rites should be so used, then this is somewhat begging the question. This is so not only because there is no clear-cut requirement that these passages be used in this manner, but also because Biblical theology, if anything, works in the opposite direction, that is, for the exclusion of things that are from the past because of living in a different historical context.

Third, there are legitimate Biblical theological concerns with regard to worship. Biblical theology does help to inform us that there is historical differentiation between the Old Covenant and us, and that the New Covenant literature is going to be most helpful in determining the various elements of worship. Systematic theology, by examining the relevant texts, will help us to apprehend the various categories--reading the Word, singing praise, and so forth. Biblical theology then helps again in determining the 'content' of these categories. We know inductively that Scripture possesses a songbook of praises--the Hebrew title of the Psalter is "songs of praises" (*tehellim*). No matter what their original use was, the materials of the Psalter, besides being read in worship as the Word of God, are also songs to be sung in praise of Him. This can be illustrated in at least two ways.

---

[3]Remember the ruckus over "It Was On a Friday Morning," a song that stirred the righteous anger of many in the Presbyterian Church in the United States when it was approved for use at a denominational youth meeting; this song, which expressed the viewpoint of the unrepentant thief on the cross, was finally replaced in the Armed Forces Hymnal after it had been included in a revision of that hymnbook in the 1970's.

First, there is historical differentiation within the Psalter itself. For example, Psalm 90 most likely did not function as canon when it was written by Moses--rather it was included in Scripture about 1000 years later, when the Psalter was compiled around 400 B.C. What, then, is Psalm 90's function? It is designed as God's Word to us, and also is to be used as our sung word to Him.

Second, there is also historical differentiation between Scripture and ourselves. We have already noted that John 17, as part of Scripture, does not function as a prayer, nor does Psalm 51, nor Psalm 37:25. We make these comments in order to emphasize that there is an objective purpose and nature of the singing of praise in worship.

Whatever enrichment of understanding Biblical theology can bring to various Scripture texts, and whatever bearing it may have on the performance of worship itself, there is no warrant for allowing it to determine the elements of worship. Systematic theology informs us that we are to sing praise to God, that this is to be done by the congregation, and that the Psalter is to be used, and Biblical theology may not be used to contradict any of that.

B. Common Objections

1. hymnic fragments

One of the arguments from theologians which has filtered down to the 'on the street' Christian is that of hymnic fragments. The argument is that the Bible, in the New Testament, contains many fragments of hymns which were composed in New Testament times for use in public worship, and therefore we may likewise compose and use similar 'hymns' today.

At least four responses can be given to this argument. The first is that the inductive evidence is not at all conclusive. Nineteen scholars will have at least twenty different opinions as to what constitutes a 'hymnic fragment.' Beyond that, the most that could be shown is that there is a poetic, not a hymnic, fragment, since no musical notations are evident. Also, a careful study of these supposed hymnic fragments can be enlightening. Several chapters in *The Biblical Doctrine of Worship* deal with this matter and draw the conclusion that there is no necessary reason to believe that the Greek syntax indicates a different type of literature. More recently, Edward A. Robson has demonstrated that linguistically there is no basis for this belief in hymnic fragments.[4]

Second, the deductive evidence is virtually non-existent. Where in the Pauline epistles does it say, "as we sing in our assemblies," with I Timothy 3:16 or Philippians 2:5-11 following? This is just another way of saying that the argument begs the question.

Third, even if there are hymnic fragments, there is no evidence that they were uninspired--to assume otherwise also begs the question. The most that can be deduced would be that the Psalms and other inspired songs should be sung.

Fourth, even if there are hymnic fragments, that still does not necessarily mean that we are to sing them today. Making an exegetical observation does not necessarily mean drawing a systematic theological conclusion. The proof may be close, but it does not automatically or necessarily follow. We could say that the Old Testament has 'hymnic fragments' or even whole 'hymns,' but that does not necessarily mean that we should use Deuteronomy 32, Exodus 15, or II Samuel 22 in public worship today.

2. the coming of Christ

This position states that now that the Messiah has come, we should sing songs about Him. This viewpoint begs the question in at least two ways.

---

[4] Edward A. Robson, John W. McMillan, and Philip W. Martin, eds., *The Biblical Doctrine of Worship* (Pittsburgh, Pa.: Reformed Presbyterian Church of North America, 1974), 135-50, 156-91.

First, there does not seem to be any logical connection between the coming of Christ and the content of worship-song. Basically, the argument depends on a simple if/then or since/then statement: "If [since] Christ has come, then we ought to sing songs about Him." The problem is that this claim has never been proven. Logically, it is erroneous to assume a connection between the coming of Christ and the content of worship-song without ever proving it.

Second, even if this connection is demonstrated, the argument still begs the question, for there is no reason why the Psalter is not sufficient. Not only do the Psalms speak eloquently of the Messiah, even the personal name of Jesus is there. Psalm 98:3 sings of the great 'salvation'--Y'shua, or 'Jesus'--which is seen throughout all the earth.

3. "new song"

We are told in the Psalms about new songs, and how can a song be 'new' if it is 3,000 years old? As a matter of fact, it is said such passages give us warrant to compose our own worship songs today.

In reply, one should ask what do we know about the 'new songs' in Scripture. Are there any uninspired 'new songs' in the Bible? Assuming we are commanded to compose a new song, how often would we have to do so in order to fulfill the command? We are commanded to sing a new song, but where are we ordered to write one? The Bible does contain several new songs--but how can they be 'new' if they are 3,000 years old? From these questions, one should be able to see that what has commonly been assumed about new songs may not be correct.

Second, what is the Biblical concept of 'newness'? Think of all the new things found in Scripture--new creature, new creation, new heavens, new earth, new covenant, new testament, new life, new man, and so forth. From these, we can perceive several things. 'Newness' in the Bible refers to something done by God, not man. 'Newness' in the Bible is thus basically an objective concept, not a subjective one. This can be seen especially with regard to the history of redemption. Yes, we do sing a new song in Christ-- such as Psalm 96 or Psalm 98--, but it is a song which the Holy Spirit

Himself has composed for us to use in the new covenant, such praise coming out of a new heart which is rejoicing in the new life.

4. content not prescribed by God

It is claimed that the Bible, when it tells us to "sing praise," does not necessarily tell us what songs to use and therefore we may use whatever we like.

When the umpire yells, "Play ball!", may the pitcher throw any ball he wishes across the plate? Can you imagine the pitcher protesting, "But, ump, you didn't tell me what kind of ball to use!" The command to "play ball" does not address itself to the issue of what kind of ball to toss. However, if one wishes to find out the answer to that question, he can easily consult the rule book where such matters are dealt with. In a similar fashion, the command to "sing praise" does not address itself to the issue of which songs to use, but that does not mean that it is a matter of indifference. What a strange situation if rules governing an amateur softball game should be thought to be more precise than those divine rules governing worship!

5. hymn-singing has produced so much good

It is asked how can something be wrong that has so obviously been beneficial to so many people and brought glory to God?

In response, we would note that the purpose of singing in worship is not edification, it is praise.

Second, one should not argue pragmatically about these things. God, in His grace, has used cults, false churches, and other deviations, to bring people to Christ and glory to Himself. But the end does not justify the means. We must be more concerned about the glory of God than human convenience or pragmatism.

6. distortion of words of Scripture

The objection has been made that in order to sing the Psalms, the words of Scripture have to be twisted around in order to put them into rhyme and meter. If that can be done, then why not sing other words as well? And what about the fact that the actual Hebrew is not being sung?

It should be noted that the Bible in translation is still the Word of God. Also, the basic objection being raised here is that, by using metered and rhymed Psalms, we are doing a poor job of singing praise. Suppose someone said that the Church does a lousy job of preaching. Should the conclusion be--1. don't preach; 2. add to preaching another element of worship (slide shows, etc.), even without Scriptural authorization; 3. do a better job of preaching? Regarding the singing of praise, should the conclusion be--1. don't sing the Psalms; 2. add man-made hymns, without Biblical warrant, to the Psalms; 3. do a better job of singing the Psalms? This is not to say that considerations such as how better to sing praise and is it legitimate to put the Psalms in rhyme and meter should not be taken seriously. It is just to say that since the Psalms can be sung by means of chants and irregular tunes such considerations do not address themselves to the question of the propriety of psalm-singing itself.

7. difficult words and tunes

This objection is based on the fact that the words of the Psalms are hard to understand and deal with such things as judgment; and, that the tunes allegedly are atrocious.

This can be answered by saying that tunes can and should be worked on. However, this is a matter of circumstance, not substance.

Second, Scripture is difficult and has a lot of hard-to-pronounce names; but, we should not be ashamed of the tents of Shem. God has chosed to reveal Himself through the Semitic people, not through the peoples of Europe or America.

Third, the Psalms, like all of Scripture, are permeated with the theme of judgment. At least 87 (58%) of the Psalms have the theme of judgment in them. Of that number, 41 (27.3% of the total) have calls for vengeance in them. We must recognize that the Bible deals with serious things--heaven and hell, salvation and damnation, for eternity. Singing the Psalms should be viewed as a blessing in that such singing heightens one's awareness of the reality of coming judgment.

8. Christian liberty

The argument has been made that no one should dare to restrict Christian liberty by forbidding what the Bible does not. Such restriction seems awfully narrowminded and legalistic!

In response, note carefully that worship is an imposition, since we are required to gather with God's people in order to engage in public worship. Therefore, which is the legalistic position (and the one opposed to Christian liberty)--the one which thinks it does not need Biblical warrant to require this or that action to be performed in worship, or the one which makes strict appeal to Scripture and wishes not to impose anything upon God's precious flock unless it is found in His Word? In passing, we would note that the Reformed faith is at once the most strict and narrow, and also the broadest and most universal, because of its unwillingness to impose upon people anything unless it is Biblical. Also, if other songs were legitimate, which hymns or hymnbooks would the Church use? No one can accuse the Psalms of unwarranted theological bias. But to use a Methodist, Roman Catholic, Baptist, or Pentecostal hymnbook would legitimize a certain sectarian spirit rather than emphasize the Universality of the Body of Christ. Even in a Reformed church, which hymns should be imposed? Those authored by Romanists, liberals, and Unitarians? Those reflective of a deviant Christology, or a non-Reformed theology?

9. this is such a minority position

The objection has been made that 50 million evangelicals cannot be wrong!

First, note that truth is determined by Scripture, not by majority vote.

Second, in the current state of the Church, why should we expect the truth about psalm-singing to be widely recognized? We live in an irrational age, in which people are more concerned about comfort and convenience than with truth. Beyond that, if 50 million evangelicals cannot get the 'big' doctrines, such as predestination, baptism and the sacraments, ecclesiology, and so forth, what would make us think that they would not be confused about psalm-singing? Even in the Reformed church, there may be all sorts of reasons why people do not want to consider the Biblical evidence. An example of this would be traditionalism. Another would be that of vested interests, whether it be musical or financial. A standard reference work states, "The large displacement of the Psalter by other matter of praise in Protestant Churches during the last one hundred years has been due, not so much to lack of appreciation of the Psalms, as to the commercial enterprise of music publishers."[5]

Third, when one considers all of Church history, the 'hymn-singers' are in the minority. The Old Testament Church sang only inspired songs. The first 'hymn-singers' were heretics--the Greek gnostics, and Arius, who taught that Jesus is not God. The Council of Laodecia (AD 360) condemned singing uninspired hymns in worship. The Council of Chalcedon (AD 451) re-affirmed that tenet. The psalms were one of the keys of the Protestant Reformation. The Westminster Confessional Standards, considered by many the greatest confessional creed ever written, prescribe exclusive psalmody. As was just noted above, hymn-singing made great inroads only in the nineteenth century.

10. desire to sing hymns

A final objection that has been heard is, "But I *want* to sing hymns!"

We need to be very sympathetic regarding this. This is the way many people, including the present author, were brought up. It is interesting that the Synod of the Reformed Presbyterian Church of North America in

---

[5] *The International Standard Bible Encyclopedia*, cited in Robson, *op. cit.*, p. 103.

1983 affirmed that people may sing 'hymns' as expressions of fellowship, but not in worship. Although hymn-singing may not be pastorally wise (since hymns always tend to 'eat up' the Psalms), the line must be drawn at worship/non-worship. Therefore, the Church should not forbid people singing hymns as long as that is not done in or regarded as worship.

Second, tastes can be developed. Psalmody can become the natural, automatic, covenantal response it is meant to be. This author immediately bursts into Psalm 19 when gazing at a starry night, or Psalm 93 when strolling in ocean's breakers, or Psalm 106 or 150 when he is especially rejoicing in some Providence. The Psalms need to be learned and loved, so that they can be passed on to our sons and daughters to a thousand generations of those who love God and keep His commandments.

Summary and Conclusion

Psalm singing is a glorious truth. The Church has been unaware of it for several generations, and it needs to be re-discovered if she is to be faithful to her Lord. This doctrine is based upon a proper understanding of the nature of worship and the nature of the singing of praise in worship. Included in this proper understanding is the affirmation that there are elements of worship, not merely aspects of worship, with clear, Scripturally-determined lines between them.

Exclusive psalmody could, theoretically, be erroneous. That is to say, it is theoretically possible that someone, somewhere, somehow, will definitively prove that uninspired songs are acceptable to God in worship. However, that 'admission' is a double-edged sword that really cuts much more deeply the other way. The point is that the question in dispute is not whether or not the Church should sing Psalms, but whether or not anything else is acceptable. The burden of proof rests on those who advocate hymnody, not on those opposed to singing uninspired songs.

So, it is theoretically possible, but it is not very likely. In two thousand years of Christian worship, in two millennia of doing theology since the coming of Christ, no one has ever even come close to proving from

Scripture that God is pleased with the words of men during the sung part of worship.

In a 1948 article in the *Presbyterian Guardian*, Robert Marsden, who had been chairman of the Orthodox Presbyterian Church General Assembly's committee which studied the content of worship-song, stated, "it would . . . be imposssible to *prove* that uninspired songs are authorized in the Scripture, and to demand such proof before one can in good conscience sing uninspired is to demand the impossible!"[6] With that admission, of course, the jig is up. There is certainly nothing wrong or necessarily unhealthy in debating this issue of the content of praise in worship. But during that debate, unless and until a contrary position can be shown from Scripture to be correct, then all of us who acknowledge King Jesus as the only law-giver in Zion must submit to His Word and advocate that only the 150 Psalms be sung in worship.

---

[6] Cited in Robson, *op.cit.*, 274.

13 - PRAYER REGULATED BY GOD'S WORD

A. Michael Schneider, III

". . . the Lord may be said to love the gates of Zion before all the dwellings of Jacob (Psalm 87:2), because He prefers public worship before private. He loved all the dwellings of Jacob, wherein He was worshipped privately; but the gates of Zion He loved more than all the dwellings of Jacob, for there He was publicly worshipped. . . . Public worship is to be preferred before private. So it is by the Lord, so it should be by His people. So it was under the law, so it must be under the gospel." [1]

"At home in my own house there is no warmth or vigor in me, but in the church when the multitude is gathered together, a fire is kindled in my heart, and it breaks its way through." [2]

Statements like these seem utterly foreign to an age influenced by American individualism. What could seem more unnecessary than a discussion of public prayer? We are prone to move on to topics that are immediately "practical" and "personal." If we discuss prayer at all, it is likely to be in the context of personal devotional life. Christians in our era are interested in what applies to their job, their family, or the reformation of society.

But what could be more important from God's point of view than public prayer? God has promised particular blessings to corporate prayer: "Again I say to you that if two or you agree on earth concerning anything that they ask, it will be done for them by My Father in heaven. For where

---

[1] David Clarkson, *Works,* III, 187.

[2] Martin Luther, cited in Robert Rayburn, *O Come, Let Us Worship: Corporate Worship in the Evangelical Church* (Grand Rapids: Baker, 1980), 30.

two or three are gathered together in my name, I am there in the midst of them" (Mt. 18:19-20). These words, spoken in the context of the church's exercise of discipline, surely apply as well to all our praying. The disciples in the early New Testament church devoted themselves to "the prayers" (the article probably indicating set times of prayer), not just to prayer in their homes.

Jesus taught His disciples to pray together, "**Our** Father, Who art in heaven . . . give **us** this day our daily bread" (Mt. 6:9, 11), indicating "that we should pray with and for others" (Shorter Catechism, Q. 100).

Matthew Henry, commenting on Matthew 20:30, said, "The two blind men did not each of them say for himself, 'Have mercy on me,' but both for one another, 'Have mercy on us!'"

The Westminster Confession of Faith makes a distinction between "ordinary" elements of worship and "occasional" elements, such as oaths, vows, fastings, and thanksgivings (XXI.5). Foremost among the "ordinary" elements is prayer: "Prayer, with thanksgiving, being one special part of religious worship, is by God required of all men. . . . " (XXI.3; see also the Larger Catechism, Q. 108).

Consider, then, the Biblical teaching concerning:

   I. THE BASIS OF PUBLIC PRAYER
   II. THE ELEMENTS OF PRAYER
   III. THE QUESTION OF THE USE OF FORMS IN
       PUBLIC PRAYER
   IV. THE LANGUAGE USED IN PUBLIC PRAYER
   V. POSTURE IN PRAYER
   VI. THE PARTICIPATION OF THE PEOPLE IN
       PUBLIC PRAYER
   VII. THE ATTITUDE TO BE CULTIVATED IN
       PRAYER

I. THE BASIS OF PUBLIC PRAYER, and all prayer, is the Word of God.

It is the Scriptures that command us to pray. They tell us how we should pray and for what things we should pray. There are various ways that our public prayers may be based on Scripture.

First, in our worship services we may actually pray the prayers of Scripture. We find in the Bible prayers of Abraham, Jacob, Moses, Joshua, David, Solomon, Hezekiah, Ezra, Nehemiah, Daniel, Christ Himself, and Paul. For instance, in our prayer of adoration we might use these words:

"Lord, You have been our dwelling place in all generations.
Before the mountains were brought forth,
Or ever You had formed the earth and the world,
Even from everlasting to everlasting, You are God"
(Psalm 90:1-2).

"O Lord, our Lord,
How excellent is Your name in all the earth,
You who set Your glory above the heavens!"
(Psalm 8:1).

"In Your presence there is fulness of joy;
At Your right hand are pleasures forevermore"
(Psalm 16:11).

In our confession we might pray:

"If You, Lord, should mark iniquities,
O Lord, who could stand?
But there is forgiveness with You,
That You may be feared" (Psalm 130:3-4).

Among our petitons we might ask:

"Let the words of our mouths
                and the mediation of our hearts

Be acceptable in Your sight,
O Lord, our strength and our Redeemer" (Psalm 19:14).

A second way to pray Scripturally is to draw together various passages of Scripture into one prayer. For example, Daniel's prayer recorded in Daniel 9:1-23 contains many Scriptural references and allusions, especially from Deuteronomy and Jeremiah. Our prayers should also abound in the language of the Word of God. Our minds should be so saturated with Scripture that it flows naturally from our tongues when we approach the throne of grace.

A third method is to turn into prayers passages of Scripture which were not originally prayers. For example, from Psalm 19:1, instead of:

"The heavens declare the glory of God;
And the firmanent shows His handiwork;"

We would pray:

"The heavens declare **Your** glory, O God;
And the firmanent shows **Your** handiwork."

From I Timothy 3:1-4 we could pray, "Give us men who desire the office of elder, O Lord, men who are blameless, husbands of one wife, temperate, sober-minded, of good behavior, hospitable, able to teach . . .", etc.

Fourth, in one of our public prayers we might select one text and "pray through" that text, a practice often used by C. H. Spurgeon and recommended to his students. From the parable of the Pharisee and the Publican (Luke 18:9-14), we would praise God that He receives miserable sinners, thank Him for His justification of those who are unworthy, confess that we are too often proud like the Pharisee and look down on others whose sins are more outwardly gross and heinous than our own, and ask for the grace to cry, "God, be merciful to me, a sinner!"

I have made it a personal practice in private worship over the past ten years or so to "pray through the Bible" by writing down a brief passage or two from each chapter of Scripture and writing prayers based on those passages. My prayers would consist of more than those brief written words, of course, but the writing down of prayers has helped me to learn to pray Biblically. When we pray using this form publicly, the prayer would naturally cover other areas than those directly suggested by the passage at hand, but it would be grounded in and grow out of that one passage.

A fifth and final way to make the Bible the basis of our public prayers is to pray in a way that is **consistent** with Scripture. All prayer is to be Scriptural, whether we are using the actual words of Scripture or allusions to passages of Scripture. We do have Scriptural warrant for composing prayers that express the particular needs of God's people at one particular moment of their history. Solomon's great prayer at the dedication of the temple, for instance, does not consist of actual quotations from the law or the psalms (II Chron. 6:1-7:3). And we cannot simply pray the prayer he prayed on that occasion, because our circumstances are entirely different. We could pray, "Behold, heaven and the heaven of heavens cannot contain You," but we could not add, "how much less this temple which I have built!" (II Chron. 6:18), since we have not built the temple, and may not even have recently built a building for use by a church. We might add instead, "how much less a building made with human hands." When the publican prayed, "God, be merciful to me, a sinner" (Luke 18:13), he was not quoting directly an Old Testament passage, but his prayer was certainly a Scriptural prayer (Ps. 51:1, etc.).

Prayer, therefore, is not merely a string of verses linked together, but a calling upon God which is appropriate to the occasion. We may pray concerning the events of God's providence in the life of our own nation or congregation. If a president or king is undertaking a visit with another head of state to seek a just peace, we would pray specifically for his journey and the success of his mission. If a member of the congregation is seriously ill or undergoing some difficult trial, we should pray for that specific situation and that individual by name.

Nevertheless, all our prayers must be Scriptural prayers, in that they are instructed by the truth of God's Word. "Now this is the confidence that we have in Him, that if we ask anything **according to His will**, He hears us" (I John 5:14). God has revealed His will in His written word--His will for prayer as well as His will for every area of the Christian's life. From Scripture we learn **how** to pray (in what manner and with what attitude) and for what things we ought to ask. It would be better to spend an hour in the Word discovering whether what we desire is according to God's revealed will, and five minutes praying Biblical prayer, than to spend all day assaulting heaven for something God has not promised to give. Those who pray effectual prayers are those who know the Word of God. The Old Covenant saints were forbidden to offer "unholy incense" to God. They were to bring only that which God has prescribed and no substitute. So we too are to pray according to God's revealed will. Our prayers, public and private, are to be regulated by God's word.

II. THE ELEMENTS OF PRAYER.

We should study the prayers of the Bible to discover the things for which we should pray. "The whole word of God is of use to direct us in prayer; but the special rule of direction is that form of prayer which Christ taught His disciples, commonly called 'The Lord's Prayer'" (Shorter Catechism, Q. 99). The "Lord's Prayer" is a **model** for our prayers, not merely a **form** for us to repeat.

It **may** be used as a prayer which we actually pray together: "The Lord's Prayer is not only for direction, according to which we are to make other prayers; but may also be used as a prayer, so that it be done with understanding, faith, reverence, and other graces necessary to the right performance of the duty of prayer" (Larger Catechism, Q. 187). The Westminster Directory for the Public Worship of God says: ". . . because the prayer which Christ taught His disciples is not only a pattern of prayer, but is itself a most comprehensive prayer, we recommend it also be used in the prayers of the church." But the "Lord's Prayer" was given by Christ to His disciples primarily as a suggestive outline for their own prayers. It is like a "model house" shown to us, not so that we will live in it, but to help us build our own which we can live in. Notice the elements of prayer which it suggests:

ADORATION: "Our Father which art in heaven,
Hallowed be Thy name . . ."

SUPPLICATION: "Thy kingdom come.
Thy will be done in earth,
as it is in heaven.
Give us this day our daily bread . . ."

CONFESSION: "And forgive us our debts,
as we forgive our debtors.
And lead us not into temptation,
but deliver us from evil . . ."

ADORATION: "For Thine is the Kingdom,
and the power,
and the glory for ever. Amen."

The acrostic ACTS is often suggested as a succinct guide to remember basic elements in private and public prayer (Adoration, Confession, Thanksgiving, and Supplication--including intercession for others and petition for ourselves). The classic definition of prayer given in the Shorter Catechism also touches on such basic elements: "Prayer is the offering up of our desires unto God, for things agreeable to His will, in the name of Christ, with confession of our sins, and thankful acknowledgment of His mercies" (Q. 98).

Prayer, like all our worship, is to be done "decently and in order" (I Cor. 14:40). But these basic elements prayer will not necessarily always be in the **same** order in every prayer. (These elements are not always in the same order in the examples of prayer which are given in Scripture.) They will not all necessarily be found in the same prayer, nor will they be found in equal proportions. Our prayers may vary, emphasizing one element at one time and another element at another time. One prayer in a service of worship may be exclusively or largely a prayer of adoration, while another may be a prayer of confession or a prayer of thanksgiving and supplication.

When we interceed for others we should be specific, so that all may join together in intelligent prayer for a brother or sister; yet we need not be too detailed and may leave details for more lengthy private prayer. The Scriptural example is to concentrate on the **spiritual** needs of others, as is seen particularly in the prayers of the apostle Paul for the churches with which he corresponds (Rom. 1:8-10; I Cor. 1:4-8; Eph. 1:15-23; 3:14-21; Phil. 1:3-11; Col. 1:9-12; I Thess. 1:2-4; II Thess. 1:3-12; Philem. 4-7).

As a rule, our public prayers should be brief and our private prayers lengthy: "Walk prudently when you go to the house of God; and draw near to hear rather than to give the sacrifice of fools, for they do not know that they do evil. Do not be rash with your mouth, and let not your heart utter anything hastily before God. For God is in heaven, and you on earth; therefore let your words be few" (Eccl. 5:1-2). Many of the most striking and fervent prayers of the Bible are brief and pithy: Elijah at Mount Carmel (I Ki. 18:36, 37), Moses at the golden calf rebellion (Ex. 32:31, 32), Solomon's prayer for wisdom (I Ki. 3:7-9), Nehemiah's prayer in the presence of Artaxerxes (Neh. 2:4, 5), and the prayers of the publican (Luke 18:13) and the thief on the cross (Luke 23:42). However, long prayers in a formal setting are certainly not wrong, as is evidenced by the examples of Solomon (II Chron. 6:14-42), Ezra (Ezra 9:6-15; Neh. 9), David (Ps. 9, 18, 145), and Daniel (Dan. 9:4-19).

III. FORMS IN PRAYER.

Is it wrong to use forms in prayer, prayers prepared and written out or outlined beforehand and read during worship, or even prayers written by others? Great controversies have swirled around these questions. Objection raised to forms of prayer was usually limited to objection to **required** forms and objection to being **restricted** to them. Samuel Miller, the second professor of Princeton Seminary, wrote in 1835:

> We do not, indeed, consider the use of forms of prayer as in all cases unlawful. We do not doubt that they have been often useful, and that to many this mode of conducting public devotions is highly

edifying. If any minister of our Church should think proper to compose a form of prayer, or a variety of forms, for his own use, or to borrow those which have been prepared by others, he ought to be considered at perfect liberty to do so. But we object to being *confined* to forms of prayer. We contend that it is of great importance to the edification of the Church, that every minister be left at liberty to conduct the devotions of the sanctuary as his circumstances, and the dispensations of Providence, may demand.[3]

The objection, then, has not been to written prayers, but to the mandatory use of such prayers and to their use to the exclusion of prayers composed by God's ministers for particular occasions. The Westminster Directory for Worship suggests that such prescription detracts from the exercise of "the gift of prayer."[4]

We must guard against the danger of formalism. There was no "regulation" of prayers until the middle of the fifth century. There is no clear example of the use of a written liturgy in the New Testament, and there are examples of prayers which would seem to preclude the use of written forms, such as Paul's prayer with the Ephesian elders on the beach at Miletus (Acts 20:37) and the prayers of Paul and Silas in the Philippian prison at midnight (Acts 16:25).

But if there is a danger in the **misuse** of forms, there is also a great usefulness in the careful **preparation** of public prayers. Among "low churches" in our day there is a tendency to think of "spontaneous" or "free" prayer as more sanctified than planned prayer. The result has been that an unconscious liturgy often springs up, lacking depth and richness and plagued by hackneyed phrases often repeated and borrowed from the prayers of others. We may indeed learn a great deal from the best written prayers from various periods of church history, and the best public prayers are those which grow out of careful thought and preparation.

---

[3]Samuel Miller, *Presbyterianism the Truly Primitive and Apostolic Constitution of the Church of Christ* (Philadelphia: Presbyterian Board of Publications, 1835), 66-67.

[4]*The Preface of the Directory for the Publick Worship of God.*

IV. THE LANGUAGE USED IN PUBLIC PRAYER.

In modern evangelical churches there is a widespread form of "prayer language," namely, the use of worn and irritating cliches. For example, "we just pray" is often heard. (Does "just" mean "only," "barely," or "really"? No one really knows--it's just a habit!). Another example is "how we thank You" (calling attention to the manner or intensity of our prayers). "Dear Lord," a phrase not found in the Bible, has become the most common form of addressing God for many people. Even worse is the practice of punctuating our prayers with "Father," "Lord," or "Jesus." This practice borders on taking God's name in vain and the meaningless repetition which Christ condemned. We certainly should not discourage anyone from praying or encourage anyone to stop praying until they break these habits, but it would be best to purge our prayers of these phrases, particularly our public prayers.

What about the voice we use in public prayer? Should it be different from the voice we use in ordinary conversation (more hollow and hallowed-sounding)? The way a servant talks to his master is certainly different from the way he talks to his fellow servants, but his respect and humility are not shown by changing tone and modulation. Our public prayers will surely be louder than those prayed in private or in a small company of believers, and they may be more formal, but we need not effect an unnatural "holy voice" as many pastors do in prayer (and even in preaching). The other extreme of over-familiarity is to be avoided at all costs ("Hi, God, Bob again here!"--a prayer actually reported a few years ago!). We should come to God with a humble spirit, "with all reverence and confidence, as children to a father, able and ready to help us" (Shorter Catechism, Q. 100).

It must be kept in mind continually that in prayer we address God, not each other. We are praying together in public prayer, and we should be conscious of the corporate nature of our prayers ("we," "us," and "our" instead of "I," "me," and "my"), but we must guard against speaking primarily to be heard by our fellow worshippers. Prayer is not the time to preach or teach or flatter men ("We thank You for the great ministry of our visiting brother," etc.). A great deal may be learned from hearing godly men pray, but those prayers are not aimed at the ear of men but the ear of God. Charles Spurgeon once mentioned a newspaper report in the last century which spoke of "the most eloquent prayer ever offered to a Boston congregation." We must seek in our public praying to use the best and most proper language, but at the same time we must remember that God's first interest is not in eloquence or polish but in the state of our hearts.

V. POSTURE IN PRAYER.

Samuel Miller, in a chapter on "Posture in Public Prayer," wrote: "This is not essential. A prayer truly spiritual and acceptable may be offered up in any posture. And yet this is, undoubtedly, a point by no means unworthy of consideration and inquiry."[5]

Does it matter what physical position God's people assume when they engage in public prayer? The Scriptures specifically mention posture in prayer and indicate that it is not a matter of indifference or of little consequence. William Hendriksen, commenting on I Timothy 2:8-15, wrote:

Posture in prayer is never a matter of indifference. The slouching position of the body while one is supposed to be praying is an abomination to the Lord. On the other hand, it is also true that Scripture nowhere prescribes one, and only one, correct posture during prayer. Different positions of arms, hands, and of the body as a whole, are indicated. All of these are permissible as long as they symbolize different aspects of the worshipper's reverent attitude, and as long as they truly interpret the sentiments of the heart. . . . What is stressed, however, throughout Scripture . . . is

---

[5]Samuel Miller, *Thoughts on Public Prayer* (Philadelphia: Presbyterian Board of Publication, 1849; rpt. Harrisonburg, Va.: Sprinkle Publications, 1985), 116.

not the posture of the body or the position of the hands but *the inner attitude of the soul.*[6]

Hendriksen notes the following postures with their Scriptural references:

"1. *Standing.* Genesis 18:22; I Samuel 1:26; Matthew 6:5; Mark 11:25; Luke 18:11,13. (Note the contrast between the last two passages. It makes a difference even *how* and *where* one stands).
2. *Hands Spread Out or/and Lifted Heavenward.* Exodus 9:29; 17:11, 12; I Kings 8:22; Nehemiah 8:6; Psalm 63:4; 134:2; 141:2; Isaiah 1:15; Lamentations 2:19; 3:41; Habakkuk 3:10; Luke 24:50; I Timothy 2:8; James 4:8) . . . .
3. *Bowing the Head.* Genesis 24:48 (cf. verse 13); Exodus 12:27; II Chronicles 29:30; Luke 24:5).
4. *The Lifting Heavenward of the Eyes.* Psalm 25:15; 123:1, 2; 141:8; 145:15; John 11:41; 17:1; cf. Daniel 9:3; Acts 8:55.
5. *Kneeling.* II Chronicles 6:13; Psalm 95:6; Isaiah 45:23; Daniel 6:10; Matthew 17:14; Mark 1:40; Luke 22:41; Acts 7:60; 9:40; 20:36; 21:5; Ephesians 3:14.
6. *Falling Down with the Face Upon the Ground.* Genesis 17:3; 24:26; Numbers 14:5, 13; 16:4, 22, 45; 22:13, 34; Deuteronomy 9:18, 25, 26; Joshua 5:14; Judges 13:20; Nehemiah 8:6; Ezekiel 1:28; 3:23; 9:8; 11:13; 43:3; 44:4; Daniel 8:17; Matthew 26:39; Mark 7:25; 14:35; Luke 5:12; 17:16; Revelation 1:17; 11:16.
7. *Other postures.* I Kings 18:42 (bowing, with face between the knees): Luke 18:13 (standing from afar, striking the breast)."[7]

Prostration seems to be reserved "for days of special humiliation and mourning" (Joshua, David, Job, Christ). Kneeling would appear to be the

---

[6]William Hendriksen, *New Testament Commentary--Exposition of the Pastoral Epistles* (Grand Rapids: Baker, 1957).
    [7]*Ibid.*

most appropriate for individual devotions, family prayers or small group prayer (Daniel, Stephen, Paul, and Christ). Bowing of the head may be done at any time and in any circumstance, even while standing (Abram's servant, the elders in Egypt, Hezekiah). The most appropriate general position in public devotion would seem to be standing, an indication of respect and reverence (as we might rise to our feet if the president or king entered the room, out of respect for his office). The people stood while Solomon knelt to pray (II Chron. 6:3, 13). Standing appears to have been the common position for prayer at the temple, in the synagogue, and in the worship of the early New Testament church. It was the posture adopted in the Church of Scotland, among the Puritans of England, and by the descendents of both churches in America.[8] Miller wrote:

> The posture of **sitting** in public prayer has no countenance either from Scripture, from reason, or from respectable usage in any part of the Church's history. It was never allowed in the ancient Church, and was universally regarded as an irreverent and heathenish mode of engaging in public devotion. True, if there be any worshippers so infirm from age, or so feeble from disease, that standing would really incommode or distress them to a degree unfriendly to devotion, let them sit; not in a posture of indifference or indulgence; but with bowed heads, and fixed countenances, as becomes persons reluctantly constrained to retain such an attitude, and who are yet devoutly engaged in the service.[9]

An exception to Miller's generalization might be a brief mention of the fact that David "sat" before the Lord and prayed (II Sam. 7:18; I Chron. 17:16). The only other defense used for the practice of sitting during prayer is Acts 1:14 and 2:2, where the disciples are said to have "continued with one accord in prayer and supplication," and later that the sound from heaven "filled the whole house where they were **sitting**." But there is much

---

[8]Samuel Miller, *Public Prayer*, 121.

[9]*Ibid.*, 127-28.

intervening activity and no indication that they did not sit down after standing or kneeling for prayer. If sitting is to be occasionally allowed, it should be in the position and attitude which Miller suggests, "as persons . . . who are yet devoutly engaged in the service."

VI. PARTICIPATION IN PRAYER.

How is the congregation to pray **together** in public worship? Certainly not by all praying different prayers audibly, as is the practice in a growing branch of Christendom. "God is not the author of confusion, but of peace . . . ," therefore, "Let all things be done decently and in order" (I Cor. 14:33, 40).

The congregation prays by "one mouth speaking for all," by an elder leading the people to the throne of grace. Not all have a "gift" of prayer. Every Christian should pray in private, but not all should lead in public prayer. In fact, when some individuals pray publicly, it may be more a distraction than a help. But the ruling and teaching elders of the church must cultivate and develop that gift of prayer. They must carefully prepare for prayer beforehand, that their prayers will be Scriptural and that they will be appropriate prayers for the particular congregation which assembles for worship under their direction.

What should the worshipper do while the solitary voice is praying aloud? He may allow his mind to pray the same thing silently. He may say in his heart following each petition, "Yes, Lord, that is my prayer as well," or add his own brief petitions which are suggested by the petitions being offered. And at the conclusion of the prayer he should join audibly in saying the "Amen" as has been the practice of God's people in both the Old Covenant and the New (Neh. 8:6; I Cor. 14:16). Jerome said that the "Amen" following the prayers of the fourth century church was like a clap of thunder! This practice is much to be preferred over the common custom of interrupting or punctuating the prayers by audible "Amens" (or grunts or groans or other expressions such as, "Yes, Lord," or "Thank you, Jesus!"). Better to nod the head in silent agreement than to distract other worshippers or the one praying or to subject yourself to the temptation of attempting to appear more spiritual than others on the basis of the number or loudness of the audible responses.

The great danger, of course, in the time of public prayers is the inclination to allow the mind to wander. This danger is one reason why public prayers should be kept brief, and it is also an additional reason why the prayers should be saturated with the familiar language of Scripture. It is easier to follow the prayer and heartily join in praying it if the worshipper "knows where the pray-er is going."

VII. ATTITUDE IN PRAYER.

Finally, and most importantly, we must come in the right attitude of heart if our prayers are to be acceptable to God and agreeable to His word. "How are we to pray?" "We are to pray with an awful apprehension of the majesty of God, and deep sense of our own unworthiness, necessities, and sins; with penitent, thankful and enlarged hearts; with understanding, faith, sincerity, fervency, love and perseverance, waiting upon Him, with humble submission to His will" (Larger Catechism, Q. 185).

We must pray with awe and reverence to "the high and holy One who inhabits eternity, whose name is Holy" (Is. 57:15), with humility and submission to our Father "who art in **heaven**" (Mt. 6:9). Most wrong views about prayer are remedied by right thoughts about God.

We must pray with boldness and confidence to God, who is a Person. He is holy, yet He is also near. He is not only "the high and holy One who inhabits eternity," but also the One "who dwells with him who is of a humble and contrite spirit, to revive the spirit of the humble and to revive and heart of the contrite ones" (Is. 57:15). "The Lord is near to all who call upon Him, to all who call upon Him in truth" (Ps. 145:18). "The preface to the Lord's prayer (which is, 'Our Father who art in heaven') teacheth us to draw near to God with all holy reverence and confidence, as children to a Father, able and ready to help us; and that we should pray with and for others" (Shorter Catechism, Q. 100). "We do not have a High Priest who cannot be touched with the feelings of our imfirmities, but One who was tempted in all points as we are, yet without sin. Let us therefore draw near with boldness to the throne of grace, that we may receive mercy and find grace to help in time of need" (Heb. 4:15, 16). Is God **your** Father by adoption? Then say, "With confidence I now draw nigh, and, 'Father, Abba, Father!' cry."

We must pray with reliance upon the Person and Work of Jesus Christ. To pray "in Jesus' name" is not just to tack a formula on the end of our prayers, but to come to God through Christ, depending on His merit and intercession, for "no one comes to the Father except through Him" (John 14:6).

> "To pray in the name of Christ is, in obedience to His command, and in confidence on His promises, to ask mercy for His sake; not by bare mentioning of His name, but by drawing our encouragement to pray, and our boldness, strength, and hope of acceptance in prayer, from Christ and His mediation" (Larger Catechism, Q. 180).

We must at all cost beware of formalism and pray heartfelt prayer. Christ used Isaiah's condemnation of Judah's formalism to denounce the prayers of the Pharisees: "These people draw near to Me with their mouths and honor Me with their lips, while their hearts are far from Me" (Is. 29:13; Mt. 15:8, 9). Nothing is worse in God's sight than going through empty ritual without reality, having "the form of godliness but denying the power of it" (II Tim. 3:5).

How do we learn to pray in public worship and lead God's poeple to His throne? We must learn to pray in private devotions, spending much time alone with God and with His Word. When we come to lead God's people in prayer we must come "from the closet" with lips touched by coals from the altar (Is. 6:7). We must be lifted to heaven itself and worship with the countless multitude of the heavenly host of all the ages who surround God's throne and continually cry, "Blessing and honor and glory and power be to Him who sits on the throne, and to the Lamb, forever and ever!" (Rev. 5:13).

"For you have not come to the mountain that may be touched and that burned with fire, and to blackness and darkness and tempest. . . . But you have come to Mount Zion and to the city of the living God, the heavenly Jerusalem, to an innumerable company of angels, to the general assembly and church of the firstborn who are registered in heaven, to God the Judge of all, to the spirits of just men made perfect, to Jesus the Mediator of the new covenant, and to the blood of sprinkling that speaks better things than that of Abel" (Heb. 12:18, 22-24).

God has "blessed us with every blessing in the heavenly places in Christ" (Eph. 1:3).

Therefore, when God's people meet together for worship, that meeting is of more significance than a summit meeting of heads of state to decide on a treaty of peace between great nations. It is more important than a meeting of the city council or the state legislature, more important than a meeting or the United Nations or of Congress or Parliament. For in that meeting God Himself meets with His people. He has promised to dwell in their midst and inhabit their praise. We dare not treat that meeting lightly or forsake the assembling of ourselves together. Prayer to God is the most significant activity in which we can be engaged, and we must treat prayer with that reverence and esteem. It is the means which God Himself has chosen for His people to commune with Him. As we come, we have an intercessor in heaven, Jesus Christ, the Son of God, who "ever lives to make intercession for us" (Heb. 7:25). And we have an intercessor on earth, within our own hearts, "For we do not know how to pray as we ought, but the Spirit Himself makes intercession for us with groanings [longings, yearnings] which cannot be uttered" (Rom. 8:26).

Does prayer sometimes seem insignificant to us? Do we wonder what can be accomplished by a few words uttered by some insignificant people gathered together? Then we should look again at what happens when the incense of our prayers arises to God:

"Then another angel, having a golden censer, came and stood at the altar. And he was given much incense, that he should offer it with the prayers of all the saints upon the golden altar which was before the throne. And the smoke of the incense, with the prayers of the saints, ascended before God from the angel's hand. Then the angel took the censer, filled it with fire from the altar, and threw it to the earth. And there were noises, thunderings, lightnings, and an earthquake" (Rev. 8:3-5).

The earth is shaken in response to the prayers of God's people.

If a church is to be what it ought to be for the purposes of God, we must train it in the holy art of prayer. Churches without prayer meetings are grievously common. Even if there were only one such, it would be one to weep over. In many churches the prayer meeting is only the skeleton of a gathering: The form is kept up, but the people do not come. There is no interest, no power, in connection with the meeting. Oh, my brothers, let it not be so with you! Do train the people to continually meet together for prayer. Rouse them to incessant supplication. There is a holy art in it. Study to show yourselves approved by the prayerfulness of your people. If you pray yourself, you will want them to pray with you; and when they begin to pray with you, and for you, and for the work of the Lord, they will want more prayer themselves, and the appetite will grow. Believe me, if a church does not pray, it is dead. Instead of putting united prayer last, put it first. Everything will hinge upon the power of prayer in the church.

--Charles H. Spurgeon

14 - THE ADMINISTRATION OF THE SACRAMENTS

Kerry W. "Pete" Hurst

God has graciously given to His Church the sacraments of Baptism and the Lord's Supper. In their administration in the worship of His people, God declares and guarantees the reality of His gracious covenant with His people. As the sacraments are administered, His people see God's saving grace in Christ and the blessings which belong to those who are His. At His Table participants are visibly separated from those who are not of His Church and who belong to the world.

Additionally, when rightly used, the sacraments become instruments of God's grace whereby communicants are blessed by the Spirit of God unto their own growth in grace and do themselves pledge and rededicate themselves to the service of God in Jesus Christ.[1]

While public instruction and administration of the sacraments are led by an ordained minister of the Word, it should be recognized that ultimately elders of the local congregation together oversee their administration. For instance, the elders with Scripture and by examiniation determine who is or who is not permitted to come to the Lord's Table; it is these men who are responsible to instruct parents in their responsibility to present covenant children for baptism.

The minister does not lead because he and other elders belong to a special class of Christians higher than other believers, but by virtue of the fact that he is called of God to teach and this is what he does as the sacraments are administered. Reformed churches stress that the preaching of the Word and instruction regarding the sacraments should accompany their observance. While a person can experience what is felt, tasted, or outwardly observable, it is essential that the experience be understood and

---

[1] See the Westminster Confession of Faith, XXVII, "Of the Sacraments."

intrepreted as God intends.

This administration of the sacraments should be public, not private. Those receiving the Lord's Supper acknowledge their unity and communion with other believers; those being baptized are having the sign of God's people placed upon them. The congregation acknowledges new additions and agrees to the terms of God's covenant to walk together in the Lord. For those unable to gather regularly with God's people, perhaps because of illness, God's people can go to them. Public announcement can be made of worship and of the sacrament to be given to the one who is ill and all those who are able to attend should be invited.

Neither baptism nor any portion of the Lord's Supper is to be withheld from any among God's people who qualify to receive them. For instance, in the Lord's Supper, the cup is not to be withheld. The instruction of Christ is clear--those who eat also drink.

It is to be much lamented today that the sacraments are not understood Biblically and appreciated for their usefulness as given by Christ to the Church. Different extremes exist. Some treat the sacraments as magic, having power in and of themselves; these people believe that hearts are cleansed and sins forgiven apart from truth in Jesus Christ and faith in Him. Others regard them simply as quaint traditions to be observed, inventing "altar calls" and other worship practices whereby the sacraments are replaced with man's way of public confession and rededication to Christ.

BAPTISM

Christians universally agree that water is to be used in baptism; disagreement occurs over how much and the way it is applied. Word studies on *baptizo* do not prove its meaning to be immersion, but do point to union with Christ and cleansing from sin. Reformed theology has always stressed the idea or purification which was often symbolized in the history of God's people by sprinkling.[2]

Upon the occasion of someone being baptized, whether it be an adult or child, instruction should be given to all those present as to the meaning of baptism. Special care should taken both to emphasize what is needful and to correct what is erroneous as to the doctrine of baptism as it might relate to the congregation's understanding and to the Christian faith in the world.

At adult baptisms, vows are usually taken indicative of the individual's faith in Christ and commitment to follow Him within the body of Christ. At child baptisms, the Christian parents or guardians answer vows affirming their own faith in Christ, commitment to raise the child in the nurture and admonition of the Lord and the child's need of the saving grace of God and personal faith in the Lord Jesus. Often an admonition to faithfulness is given to adults and parents or guardians, as well as to the congregation, since the congregation is to welcome those being baptized to fulfill their Christian obligation towards them.

Baptism is administered in the name of the Father, the Son, and the Holy Spirit, even as Christ directed. Before and/or after baptism a prayer may be prayed seeking God's blessing upon the sacrament, that the one baptized would live unto Christ, look only in faith unto Him for salvation and follow Him as one bearing His name and separated from the World.

Apart from specific instruction on the sacrament itself, upon the occasion of baptism other instruction is most appropriate. An excellent opportunity is presented to preach the gospel to all who have not publicly professed their faith in Christ. Adults and children should be reminded of their sin and the only way of cleansing, which is through Christ. Baptized children should be reminded of their privilege to be within the Church but also of their responsibility to be believing upon Christ. Parents can be reminded of their obligation to raise their children in the nurture and

---

[2]It is not the purpose of this chapter to enter into a detailed discussion on the mode of baptism when books have been written on the subject. The reader can find a very concise statement of argument in Louis Berkhof's *Systematic Theology* (London: The Banner of Truth Trust, 1967), "Christian Baptism," 622f.

admonition of the Lord and of the promises and grace of God which will bless and attend their endeavors.

Finally, everyone baptized should be reminded that one's baptism, though occurring only once in one's life, is to be that which is "improved . . . all our life long."[3]

THE LORD'S SUPPER

Because the Lord's Supper is a means of grace for the Lord's people, it is appropriate that public notice be given so that those attending may properly prepare their hearts and lives and also seek God's blessing in the Supper for the whole body of believers. Some have found it beneficial to have a time of instruction prior to the meal to insure careful preparation and adequate understanding. Many local churches have designated either a particular Lord's Day each month or every Lord's Day for the Supper. This allows for preparation to be regularly before the people of God.[4]

The Scriptures teach that bread and wine were the elements of the Lord's Supper as Christ instituted it, representing His body and blood. It is foolish to argue that this wine was unfermented grape juice. Paul rebukes some at Corinth who drank so much of it that they became drunk (I Cor. 11:21). The practice of some weaker brethren in this area, who may insist on unfermented grape juice, is usually accepted because they are using the "fruit of the wine." However, it should be noted that the rich symbolism in Scripture in regard to the use of wine honors God, makes the heart glad and rejoices in salvation. Certainly this is in keeping with the joy that believers ought to experience as they meditate at the Lord's Table upon His great salvation. Unleavened bread is usually used because it is the bread Christ

---

[3] See the answer to Westminster Larger Catechism, Q. 167, which asks, "How is our baptism to be improved by us?"

[4] It is most unfortunate that some treat the occasion of the Lord's Supper as that time of worship when it is especially important to confess sin. The Scriptures teach confession and repentance as necessary preparation for all worship. See Matthew 5:23, 24; Psalm 66:18; Isaiah 66:2b.

used at the Passover feast when He instituted the Lord's Supper. However, some suggest that the common bread of daily life is suitable.[5] Again, in unleavened bread there is the symbol of God's people separated unto Him, which the Supper teaches and those participating declare.

The bread and wine are placed on a table located as much as possible on ground level with those gathered. It is a table of fellowship, not an altar. God and His people are reconciled in Christ; Christ is not being sacrificed. It is on ground level because both elders and congregation are the priesthood of believers.[6]

As God's people are gathered to receive the Lord's Supper, the minister should give instruction as to what is happening, the purpose for which Christ has appointed this meal, the benefits believers ought to receive, and the proper conduct and meditation of each communicant. He should be careful to invite only those who are allowed to come, as agreeable to the Scriptures.[7]

Resident communing members of the congregation have already been examined by the elders as to their faith in Christ and commitment to follow Him. These members are invited to come to the Table unless they personally know of some reason not to, or unless they are under a discipline which does not permit them to do so.

Due to our very mobile society and/or the sad disregard to some professing Christians for membership in a particular congregation of believers, it is not uncommon to have visitors present at those times when the Lord's Supper is received. Sometimes elders have the opportunity to meet for a brief examination of visitors before worship; some visitors carry written testimony from their church, that they are members in good standing. In either case, these should be allowed to participate in the

---

[5]A. A. Hodge, *Outlines of Theology* (New York: Robert Carter and Brothers, 1878), 633.

[6]William Childs Robinson, *Architecture Appropriate for Reformed Worship* (Weaverville, N.C.: Southern Presbyterian Journal, 1959), 4, 6.

[7]For an excellent explanation of the above areas, please see Westminster Confession of Faith, XXIX ("Of the Lord's Supper").

sacrament. However, time constraints on the Lord's Day or ignorance of the nature of the Lord's Supper itself usually dictate that the minister will give instruction carefully so that no one approaches the Supper who should not do so. This is further necessitated because of the actual administration of the elements: when people receive them seated in pews or in large groups, where it would be difficult to know everyone or to keep the elements from any who are disqualified. Professing Christians who are not actively faithful members of a congregation professing Biblical Christianity or who have not been examined as to their knowledge of Christ and the sacrament by elders or some governing board should not participate; such a lifestyle disregards the authority which Christ has instituted in His Church and the communion of saints, both of which are exemplified, among other things, in the Supper itself. Some are of the opinion that such public directives to visitors are insufficient and only after satisfactory private examination in these things should such ones be permitted to participate.

All professing Christ, but walking in known sin should be warned of the danger in which they live, and should be told that if they deliberately continue in sin, then they are without grounds for believing they belong to Christ. Those not believing on Christ should be reminded that He is God's provision and the only way of salvation. They are to believe upon Him, and if they do not, they remain rebels and enemies of God. Covenant children not coming to the Table should be encouraged to talk prayerfully about the meaning of the Supper with their parents and of their need to confess Christ at His table.

After prayer for God's blessing, the minister, in the name and authority of Christ, should distribute the bread and wine.

While Christ and the disciples ate and drank in a reclining position as was customary for meals in their day, there has never been any compelling reason advanced for that posture to be observed. Reformed churches have received the bread and wine standing, sitting around a table, sitting with the table before the congregation, kneeling, and even walking. Kneeling has been discouraged because of its association with the idolatry of the mass and its emphasis on humility instead of celebration which is stressed in the Supper. The Westminster Assembly had an extended debate as to whether people should come to the table or whether the elements could be taken from the table to where they were seated. It was finally decided that they could "sit about it, or at it," which allowed either. Because of the large number of people and time constraints, the practice of sitting "about it" has become normative.[8]

However, it its Act "for the Establishing and putting in Execution of the Directory for the Publick Worship of God," the General Assembly of the Church of Scotland, on February 3, 1645, approved this section of the Directory with the provision

> that the clause in the Directory, of the administration of the Lord's Supper, which mentioneth the communicants sitting about the table, or at it, be not interpreted, as if in the judgement of this Kirk it were indifferent and free for any of the communicants not to come to and receive at the table; or as if we did approve the distributing of the elements by the minister to each communicant, and not by the communicants among themselves.[9]

Seventeenth century Scottish Presbyterians believed that our Lord's example was meant to be followed, whatever inconvenience might be caused by the time involved in large numbers of people participating. Presbyterian churches, both in Scotland and abroad, continued this practice well into the nineteenth century.

If the congregation does not come to the table, it is left up to the elders to decide whether or not the bread and wine should be taken immediately when received or held until all have been served. Some zealously maintain that both must always be held until everyone is served so that the people can exhibit their unity and communion in one another by

---

[8]"The Posture of the Recipients at the Lord's Supper" in *Selected Shorter Writings of Benjamin B. Warfield*, ed. John E. Meeter (Nutley, N. J.: Presbyterian and Reformed Publishing Company, 1973), II, 351f.

[9]*Acts of the General Assembly of the Church of Scotland, M.DC.XXXVIII.-- M.DCCC.XLII.* (Edinburgh: The Edinburgh Printing and Publishing Company, 1843), 115-16.

eating and drinking at the same time. However, it must be remembered that unity and communion are always present because there is one Lord, one Table, and one Meal taken together. Moreover, Christ did not so instruct His disciples; to do so He would have had to tell them to hold the wine in their mouths until the common cup was passed around, and then to swallow at the same time.

After the distribution of the elements, prayer is usually offered in praise and thanksgiving to God for His salvation in Christ, after which a psalm may be sung following His example. Because the Church is celebrating God's grace, often churches will receive a collection for the poor.

From time to time, either in preparation before the day of the Lord's Supper, or on that day during the time of instruction or after the meal, those coming to the Table should be reminded to consider Question 175 of the Westminster Larger Catechism:

> Question: What is the duty of Christians, after they have received the sacrament of the Lord's Supper?
>
> Answer: The duty of Christians, after they have received the sacrament of the Lord's supper, is seriously to consider how they have behaved themselves therein, and with what success; if they find quickening and comfort, to bless God for it, to beg the continuance of it, watch against relapses, fulfil their vows, and encourage themselves to a frequent attendance on that ordinance: but if they find no present benefit, more exactly to review their preparation to, and carriage at, the sacrament; in both which, if they can approve themselves to God and their own consciences, they are to wait for the fruit of it in due time: but, if they see they have failed in either, they are to be humbled, and to attend upon it afterwards with more care and diligence.

15 - THE OCCASIONAL ELEMENTS OF WORSHIP

J. Cameron Fraser

Occasional elements of worship are defined by the Westminster Confession of Faith as "religious oaths, vows, solemn fastings and thanksgivings upon special occasions, which are in their several times and seasons, to be used in an holy and religious manner." They are distinguished from the ordinary elements of worship which are ". . . The reading of the Scriptures with godly fear; the sound preaching and conscionable hearing of the Word, in obedience unto God, with understanding, faith and reverence; singing of psalms with grace in the heart; as also, the due administration and worthy receiving of the sacraments instituted by Christ. . . . "[1] The purpose of this chapter will be to explore the Biblical basis and appropriate application of each of the 'occasional elements' listed above.

Religious Oaths and Vows

The Westminster Confession devotes an entire chapter to the subject "Of Lawful Oaths and Vows."[2] Although similar in form and purpose, oaths and vows are distinguishable in that oaths concern our duty to our fellow man, whereas vows have to do with our duty to God. Both are to be taken before God and in His name. They are binding except when they would oblige us to sin, as in the case of monastic vows.

It may seem strange to us that the Confession would not only include oaths and vows as an element of worship, but would devote a separate chapter to the subject. Oath-taking is no longer a common religious practice. Furthermore, it might appear that Jesus, in the Sermon

---

[1] Westminster Confession of Faith, XXI.5.

[2] Westminster Confession of Faith, XXII.

on the Mount, disallowed it entirely. This was certainly the understanding of most early church fathers, as well as of the Anabaptists at the time of the Reformation, and many Quakers and Brethren today. Why, then, did the Reformers and Puritans not only allow the practice, but give it so much emphasis?

Clearly, they did not accept the point of view that Jesus forbade the taking of oaths and vows in all circumstances. This was because of abundant New Testament evidence to the contrary. There would appear to be three categories of proof. First, there are those passages which quote Old Testament oaths in a favorable manner (Luke 1:73; Acts 2:30; Heb. 3:11, 18; 4:3; 6:11-18). Second, there are those instances in which Paul invokes the name of God as his witness (Rom. 10:2; II Cor. 1:23; Phil. 1:8; I Thess. 2:5, 10). Paul also took a vow on one occasion (Acts 18:18). Finally, Christ Himself used an oath-taking formula in His frequent use of "Verily, verily, I say unto you" (cf. Heb. 6:13, " . . . because He could sware by no greater, He sware by Himself"). When Christ appeared before the high priest at His trial and the high priest swore "I adjure you by the living God, tell us whether you are the Christ, the Son of God" (Mt. 26:63 NASB), Jesus not only did not rebuke him for swearing; He broke His own silence and, in effect, went on oath as testifying to the accuracy of the high priest's statement (Mt. 26:64). This would seem to be sufficient evidence to suggest that not all oath-taking was forbidden by our Lord.

Why, then, did Jesus so clearly denounce oath-taking in Matthew 5:33-37? The answer lies in a careful study of the passage in its context. Jesus prefaced this particular section of the Sermon on the Mount by stating clearly His relationship to the Old Testament law on the one hand and to the Pharisees' interpretation and teaching of the law on the other. In unequivocal terms, He affirmed that He had come not to destroy the Law and the Prophets, but to fulfill them (Mt. 5:17-19). At the same time, He distanced Himself from the sophistry and casuistical legalism of the Pharisees (Mt. 5:20). This set the stage for His teaching on anger, adultery, divorce, oath-taking, revenge and love (Mt. 5:21-48). As D. A. Carson writes:

[Jesus] cannot assume that everything the people have heard concerning the content of the Old Testament Scriptures was really in the Old Testament. This is because the Pharisees and the teachers of the law regarded certain oral traditions as equal in authority with the Scripture itself, thereby contaminating the teaching of Scripture with some fallacious but tenaciously-held interpretations. Therefore, in each of the five blocks of material which follows, Jesus says something like this, "You have heard that it was said . . . but I tell you . . . " He does not begin these contrasts by telling them what the Old Testament said but what they had heard it said. This is an important observation because Jesus is not negating something from the Old Testament, but something from their understanding of it.

In other words, Jesus appears to be concerned with two things: overthrowing erroneous traditions and indicating authoritatively the real direction towards which the Old Testament Scriptures point.[3]

Another important principle of interpretation is that Jesus would often make a relative point in an absolute manner. Thus, for instance, in Matthew 5:22 (according to the earlier manuscripts) He stated without qualification, "But I say to you that everyone who is angry with his brother shall be liable to judgement. . . ." (NASB), even though His own practice and other Scriptures make it clear that the qualification "without cause" (as in the KJV) is the true meaning of the statement (cf. Mt. 21:12, 13; Eph. 4:26; Heb. 3:10; etc.). Jesus' point was that it is not sufficient to hold back from the act of murder if the spirit of murder (ungodly anger and hostility) is in one's heart. Because He did not want His listeners to squirm out of the implications of His statement, He made it in the strongest possible manner. Many of Paul's seemingly contradictory statements about the law must be interpreted in a similar way. In each particular context, Paul (and Jesus) is concerned to make one particular point and he makes it forcibly, without

[3]D. A. Carson, *The Sermon on the Mount, An Evangelical Exposition of Matthew 5-7* (Grand Rapids: Baker, 1978), 39, 40.

bringing in the kinds of qualifications that might be appropriate in another context.

Applying the above to Matthew 5:33-37, we note that the passage must be understood against the background of Pharisaic practice. We know that in the *Mishnah*, the Jewish code of law, there is an entire tractate given over to the question of oaths, including detailed consideration of which oaths are binding and which are not. For example, according to one rabbi, if you swear *by* Jerusalem, your oath is not binding, but if you swear *toward* Jerusalem, it is binding. As Carson comments: "these oaths no longer foster truthfulness, but weaken the cause of truth and promote deceit. Swearing evasively becomes justification for lying."[4]

Jesus' main point, then, is to expose the evasiveness of this trivialized form of oath-taking. Since the law specified that swearing should be in God's name (Deut. 10:20) and also that His name should not be taken in vain (Ex. 20:7; *cf.* Lev. 19:12; Num. 30:2; Deut. 23:21), the Pharisees argued that to swear by something other than God's name both avoided the sin of taking His name in vain and freed the oath-taker from any obligation to keep the oath. Jesus exposed this hypocrisy by pointing out that it is impossible to avoid any reference to God in swearing, "for the whole world is God's world and you cannot eliminate him from any of it. If you vow by 'heaven' it is God's throne; if by 'earth' it is his foot-stool; if by Jerusalem it is his city, *the city of the great King.* If you swear by your head it is indeed yours in the sense that it is nobody else's and yet it is God's creation and under his control. You cannot even change the colour of a single hair, black in youth and white in old age."[5]

Jesus says that if the solemn ceremony of oath-taking is to be trivialized in this manner, it is far better not to swear at all. Indeed, the followers of Jesus should not need to resort to swearing, since swearing is, in any case, an accomodation to the sinfulness and fickleness of the human

---

[4] *Ibid.*, 47.

[5] John R. W. Stott, *Christian Counter-Culture, The Message of the Sermon on the Mount* (Downers Grove, Ill.: InterVarsity Press, 1978), 101.

heart. (By contrast with human swearing, divine oath-taking is not intended to enhance the trustworthiness of God, but to elicit and confirm our faith [*cf.* Heb. 6:13-20].) The Christian's word should be trustworthy to the point that his simple "yes" means "yes" and his "no" means "no."

In a parallel passage, Matthew 23:16-22, Jesus again exposes the hypocrisy of the Pharisees by pointing out that to distinguish between different kinds of oaths (*e.g.*, the temple as opposed to the gold of the temple) and to say that one is binding but the other is not, is to trivialize the seriousness of oath-taking and to make a mockery of truth and justice. The same essential point is made in James 5:12. False swearing brings only condemnation (*cf.* also Matt. 12:36, 37). Better by far simply to tell the truth and "swear not at all."

Swearing, therefore, is at best an accomodation to human frailty and its abuse is a very great evil. In the new heavens and new earth to which we look forward, perfect truth and righteousness will reign. There will be no liars or perjurers (Rev. 21:8, 17). It is that state of righteousness which Christians must seek (*cf.* Mt. 5:6). Meanwhile, oath-taking is a necessary concession to our state of sinful imperfection.

How are we to apply this Biblical teaching to the Westminster Confession and to contemporary church life? It is clear that the Westminster divines were correct in perceiving that not all oath-taking is sinful, provided that the oath be taken reverently in the name of God. Indeed, it would seem that they were close to the Spirit of Christ when they wrote that to

> swear vainly or rashly by that glorious and dreadful name or to swear by any other thing is sinful and to be abhorred. Yet, as in matters of weight and moment, an oath is warranted by the word of God under the New Testament as well as under the Old; so a lawful oath, being imposed by lawful authority, in such matters ought to be taken.[6]

---

[6]Westminster Confession of Faith, XXII. 2.

Thus, while Christians who refuse to take oaths of allegiance or swear in court are to be admired for their courage and integrity, it must be pointed out that their scruples are based more on a superficial reading of Christ's words in the Sermon on the Mount than on a careful study of their meaning in the context in which they were spoken and of Scripture as a whole.

But when the Westminster divines spoke of 'religious oaths and vows' as an 'element of worship,' the meaning was broader than an oath taken before a civil government or court, though, as we shall see, the 'religious' nature of civil oaths was more prominent in their day than ours.

In the historical context out of which the Westminster Confession of Faith arose, covenanting was a particularly prominent form of oath-taking whereby men bound themselves and their families to one another and vowed before God to uphold His cause. In 1581, at the instigation of King James VI, the people of Scotland had signed the King's Confession, in which Roman Catholicism was rejected and Protestantism was recognized as the national religion. The King's Confession became the basis of the National Covenant of 1638 whereby the Covenanters, pledging loyalty to the king's person and throne, reiterated the King's Confession in its rejection of Roman Catholicism and added to it their rejection of Episcopalian innovations which had been brought into the church under the rule of bishops. Presbyterianism was recognized as the established form of church government in Scotland. The National Covenant then continued:

> . . . we promise and sweare, that we shall, to the uttermost of our power, with our meanes and lives, stand to the defence of our dread Soveraigne, the Kings Majesty, his Person, and Authority, in the defence and preservation of the foresaid true Religion, Liberties and Lawes of the Kingdome: As also to the mutual defence and assistance, every one of us of another in the same cause of maintaining the true Religion and his Majesty's authority, with our

best counsel, our bodies, meanes, and whole power, against all sorts of persons whatsoever.[7]

Here we have a pledging of allegiance to both God and the king, performed as an act of religious worship. The need for personal piety is recognized in the conclusion of the National Covenant, which reads in part:

> And because we cannot look for a blessing from God upon our proceedings, except with our Profession and Subscription we joine such a life & conversation, as beseemeth Christians, who have renewed their Covenant with God; We, therefore, faithfully promise, for our selves, our followers, and all other under us, both in publick, in our particular families, and personal carriage, to endeavour to keep our selves within the bounds of Christian liberty, and to be good examples to others of all Godlinesse, Sobernesse, and Righteousness, and of every duety we owe to God and Man, . . .[8]

Prior to the meeting of the Westminster Assembly in 1643, Scottish Presbyterians and English Independents signed the Solemn League and Covenant. This was an attempt to bring "the Church of GOD in the three Kingdoms [of England, Scotland and Ireland] to the nearest conjunction and Uniformity in Religion, Confession of Faith, Form of Church government, Directory for Worship and Catechizing," and "mutually to preserve the Rights and Priviledges of the Parliaments, and the Liberties of the kingdoms; And to preserve and defend the Kings Majesty's Person and Authority, in the preservation and defence of the true Religion and Liberties of the Kingdoms; That the world may bear witness with our consciences of our

---

[7] James Aikman, *An Historical Account of Coveananting in Scotland* (Edinburgh: John Henderson and Co., 1848),

[8] 'The National Covenant' in J. King Hewison, *The Covenanters* (Glasgow: John Smith, 1913), I, 477-8.

Loyalty, and that we have no thoughts or intentions to diminish his Majesty's just power and greatnesse."[9]

Once again, we notice an interrelationship between church and state which is foreign to the modern situation, particularly in North America. Without entering the discussion as to whether the Westminster divines' understanding of church-state relations was sufficiently Biblical, we may simply point out that here we have no tension between a 'religious' vow before God and a 'secular' oath or pledge of allegiance to an earthly ruler-- provided that the ruler upheld the Biblical religion. Indeed, this very point underlay some fundamental differences between the English Parliamentarians and the Scottish Covenanters which resulted in the failure of the Solemn League and Covenant to achieve its professed goal. As Robert Baillie put it, "The English were for a civill League, we for a religious Covenant."[10] The result was that when, at the battle of Naseby in 1645, Cromwell's forces won a decisive victory over the Royalists, "the zeal of the English parliamentarians for the Solemn League and Covenant immediately abated, and the pressure which had been exerted upon them by the Scots in that connection was made a ground of accusation against them. They were imitating the king, it was said, against whose oppressive methods they had gone into revolt in their own country."[11]

Despite the failure of the Solemn League and Covenant, it did lead to the six year session of the historic Westminster Assembly of Divines, which produced the Westminster Confession of Faith (which has become the principal subordinate standard of Presbyterianism the world over.) Every member of the Westminster Assembly was required to take the following vow:

---

[9]'A Solemn League and Covenant' in *ibid.*, 479-80.

[10]Robert Baillie, *The Letters and Journals*, ed. David Laing (Edinburgh: Robert Ogle, 1841), II, 90.

[11]G. N. M. Collins, *The Heritage of Our Fathers* (Edinburgh: Knox Press, 1974), 24.

> I   do seriously promise and vow in the presence of Almighty
> GOD, that in this Assembly whereof I am a member I will maintain
> nothing in point of doctrine but what I believe to be most agreeable
> to the Word of GOD, nor in point of discipline but what may make
> most for GOD's glory, and the peace and good of His Church.[12]

The historical background of the Westminster Confession of Faith
has been dealt with at some length because it helps us understand what the
Confession means by 'religious oaths and vows' as well as why so much
prominence is given to the subject. But in addition to such public forms of
oath-taking, personal or private covenants with God were a characteristic of
Puritan and post-Puritan times. For instance, Philip Doddridge, in his *Rise
and Progress of Religion in the Soul*, recommends a solemn covenant
between the soul and God, to be signed and sealed with "full consideration
and serious reflection," if possible when it can be accompanied with "a day
of secret fasting and prayer."[13]   Besides private covenants of this nature, a
number of men might covenant together to pray for revival. Thus in
October, 1744, several ministers in Scotland agreed to join in prayer that
God "would deliver the nations from their miseries, and fill the whole earth
with His glory." The arrangement was to be binding for the next two years,
with a time of prayer set aside "every Saturday evening and Sabbath
morning, and a stated day every quarter to be spent in private, social or
public prayer; for the effusion of the Holy Spirit on the Church and the
world."[14]

---

[12] *Minutes of the Sessions of the Westminster Assembly of Divines*, ed. Alex. F. Mitchell
and John Struthers (Edinburgh: William Blackwood and Sons, 1874), lxxx.

[13] Philip Doddridge, 'The Rise and Progress of Religion in the Soul' in *The Works* (Leeds:
Edward Baines, 1802), I, 343 (chapter xvii). Referred to in C. H. Spurgeon, *Autobiography*,
Vol. I: *The Early Years* (Edinburgh: The Banner of Truth Trust, 1967), 148. Also found in the
Greenville Seminary Press edition (1991) of *The Rise and Progress of Religion in the Soul*, 169.

[14] Philip E. Howard, Jr., "A Biographical Sketch of the Life and Work of Jonathan
Edwards" in *David Brainerd: His Life and Diary*, ed. Jonathan Edwards (Chicago: Moody
Press, 1949), 31.

The ministers in question, led by the Rev. John McLaurin, invited Jonathan Edwards to join them. Edwards not only agreed to the suggestion; he persuaded a number of New England ministers to adopt the plan. The two year arrangement ended in November, 1746, at which time it was renewed, this time for seven years. At a later date, mainly at Edwards' instigation, ministers in the Netherlands were invited to participate.

Covenanting of this nature has fallen into relative disuse. However, along with the recovery of an emphasis on Biblical covenants in recent years there has been a renewed interest in the principle of covenanting. Thus for instance, in 1974 some of the world's leading missiologists and evangelists gathered in Lausanne, Switzerland, to sign the Lausanne Covenant, whereby they committed themselves to a common evangelical faith and promised to work and pray for world evangelization. In the more strictly covenanting tradition of the Reformed Presbyterian Church (descending from that branch of Scottish Presbyterianism which refused to accept the Revolution Settlement of 1690), there continues the practice of updating and subscribing to a Testimony which stands alongside of the Westminster Confession of Faith as a contemporary statement of Covenanter beliefs.

A form of religious oath-taking more familiar to modern day Christians would be the taking of baptismal, church membership, marriage and ordination vows. In the case of ordination vows, in particular, this includes swearing allegiance to a confessional statement. Such vows serve to underscore the seriousness of the commitments made, as well as to provide a basis for church discipline in the event of disobedience to the vows taken.

We may conclude from this that oaths and vows are necessary only in the present age and will be unnecessary in heaven, where perfect truth, justice and obedience will be the norm. Meanwhile, however, they serve a useful purpose in underscoring the seriousness of commitments made in the presence of God and men. These commitments are not to be entered into lightly. They are to be undertaken voluntarily in that no one should be coerced into them. But once made, under oath, commitments are binding, provided they are not discovered to be mandating sinful practices or binding the conscience beyond the Word of God.

Since oaths and vows are voluntary in nature, they are truly occasional and cannot be imposed in an arbitrary manner. They should not be undertaken in a purely formal way and a high degree of spiritual obedience is necessary to the faithful observance of them. The obligations which they represent may be and often would be desirable (cf. I Tim. 3:1). Christians may be exhorted to attain to and desire such duties and obligations. But the duties themselves and the oaths and vows binding Christians to the performance of the duties, should be undertaken only with the utmost care and prayerful forethought, under the guidance of the Holy Spirit through His Word. Oaths and vows become mandatory only following a voluntary commitment to undertake the duty or office required and all oaths and vows so taken must be subject to and qualified by God's Word.

Solemn Fastings

If the taking of oaths and vows has fallen into relative disuse compared to the practice of past days, so has fasting. Partly, this may be a reaction to the excessive asceticism of the Middle Ages where fasting was associated with the Roman Catholic religious calendar of feast days and fast days. More likely, at least in Western society, a lack of emphasis on fasting is related to our materialism and preoccupation with food. As Richard J. Foster writes,

> Anyone who seriously attempts to fast is bombarded with objections "I understand that fasting is injurious to your health"; "It will sap your strength so that you can't work"; "Won't it destroy body tissue?" All of this, of course, is utter nonsense based upon prejudice. While the human body can survive only a short time without air and water, it can go for many days before starvation begins. Without needing to subscribe to the inflated claims of some

groups, it is not an exaggeration to say that, when correctly done, fasting can have beneficial physicial effects.[15]

Foster offers some practical suggestions to those who might wish to fast. For instance, he points out that initial hunger pains are not symptoms of real hunger.

> Your stomach has been trained through the years of conditioning to give signals of hunger at certain hours. In many ways your stomach is like a spoiled child and spoiled children do not need indulgence, they need discipline. Martin Luther said " . . . the flesh was wont to grumble dreadfully." You must not give in to this grumbling. Ignore the signals . . . and in a brief time the hunger pains will pass. If not, sip another glass of water and the stomach will be satisfied.[16]

Headaches, coating of the tongue and bad breath as the body rids itself of toxic poisons that have built up over the years are side effects of lengthy fasts. The body will simply adjust and should be healthier as a result. It is possible to fast for several days at a time before genuine hunger pains set in.

Attempts have been made to distinguish between different kinds of fasts. For instance, Arthur Wallis suggests three basic kinds. First, there is the "normal fast" which consists of "abstaining from all food, solid or liquid, but not from water."[17] Wallis suggests that this was the kind of fast engaged in by our Lord since we are told that He ate nothing (but not that He drank nothing) and that after forty days He was hungry (but not thirsty) (Luke 4:2). Second, there is the "absolute fast" involving abstention from

---

[15]Richard J. Foster, *Celebration of Discipline: The Path to Spiritual Growth*, revised edition (San Francisco: Harper and Row, 1988), 57.

[16]*Ibid.*, 57.

[17]Arthur Wallis, *God's Chosen Fast* (Fort Washington, Pa.: Christian Literature Crusade, 1975), 14.

water as well. This kind of fast was engaged in quite frequently in Scripture: by Moses on two occasions (Ex. 34:18; Deut. 9:9, 18), Elijah (I Ki. 19:8), Mordecai (Est. 4:16), Ezra (Ezra 10:6). Third, there is the "partial fast" in which Daniel seems to have engaged, abstaining from only certain kinds of food and drink (Dan. 10:2, 3: cf. also Elijah in I Ki. 17). Wallis also points out that the Scriptures speak of fasts that were engaged in involuntarily because of unfavourable circumstances (cf. Dan. 6:18; Mt. 15:32; II Cor. 6:5, 11:27).

It is not certain that the Biblical evidence supports the kinds of distinctions that Wallis and others make. One thing, however, is sure. Biblical fasts, while of an essentially spiritual nature, involved literal abstention from food and drink (with the possible exception of water), sometimes for protracted periods of time. Thus, Wallis is perfectly correct when he states that we have widened the meaning of fasting to the point that its cutting edge is lost if we tell ourselves that to fast "is not simply or necessarily to abstain from food, but anything that hinders our communion with God," or that "fasting means to do without, to practice self denial."[18]

In addition to individual or personal fasts, the Bible records times of corporate or public--and sometimes national--fasting. Usually these were times of national disaster, imminent danger or mourning over sin, and the fast would be accompanied with fervent prayer for divine intervention and/or forgiveness (II Chron. 20:1-4; Est. 4:16; Ezra 8:21-23; Joel 2:15). The one public fast prescribed in the law of Moses was in connection with the Day of Atonement (Lev. 23:27), but by the time of Zechariah four regular fasts had developed (Zech. 8:19).

From being a spiritual exercise engaged in for specific reasons in times of special need, fasting came to be something regular and formal. The

---

[18] *Ibid.*, 13. Andrew Murray suggests that, "In nothing is man more closely conneted with the world of sense than in his need for and enjoyment of food. . . . We are creatures of our senses. Our minds are helped by what comes to us in concrete form. Fasting helps to express, to deepen, and to confirm the resolution that we are ready to sacrifice anything, even ourselves to attain the kingdom of God" (*With Christ in the School of Prayer*, Springdale, Pa.: Whitaker House, 1981, 100-101).

Pharisees of Jesus' day fasted twice a week (Luke 18:12). The *Didache* urged two weekly fasts on Wednesdays and Fridays. Regular fasting was made obligatory at the Second Council of Orleans in the sixth century.[19]

It was against the formalism and outward show of the Pharisees that Jesus was warning His disciples when He said in Matthew 6:16, 17,

> "And whenever you fast do not put on a gloomy face as the hypocrites do for they neglect their appearance in order to be seen fasting by men. Truly I say to you, they have their reward in full. But you, when you fast, anoint your head and wash your face so that you may not be seen fasting by men, but by your Father who is in secret and your Father who sees in secret will repay you."

It is true that the wearing of sackcloth and ashes and a general lack of attention to one's physical appearance often accompanied genuine fasting as an appropriate sign of mourning or repentance (*cf.* Esther 4:1ff; Dan. 9:3, 10:3--" . . . nor did I use any ointment at all . . ."). However, by the time of the Pharisees such outward signs of fasting had become formal rituals intended to draw attention to the person fasting rather than a genuine expression of humility. Therefore, it was necessary for the disciples of Jesus to avoid such outward signs of fasting altogether, lest they appear to be fasting before men as the Pharisees were. A similar concern that the outward signs of fasting were being substituted for the righteousness and repentance appropriate to such occasions is evident in the Old Testament prophets (*cf.* Is. 58:1ff; Joel 2:12ff).

The relationship between fasting and mourning is clear in Jesus' answer to the disciples of John when they asked Him, "Why do we and the Pharisees fast, but your disciples do not fast?" Jesus replied, "The attendants of the bridegroom cannot mourn as long as the bridegroom is with them, can they? But the days will come when the bridegroom is taken away from them and then they will fast" (Mt. 9:14, NASB). Some commentators refer

---

[19]Foster, *op. cit.*, 51.

these words to the period between the death and resurrection of Christ, but it seems more appropriate to understand them as referring to the period prior to our Lord's return at the end of the age (*cf.* Mt. 25:6, "Behold the bridegroom . . ."). The fact that Christ goes on to speak immediately of the new wine and the new wineskins of this gospel age appears to bear out this interpretation. Furthermore, the disciples quite simply did not fast in any literal sense between the death and resurrection of Christ (*cf.* Luke 24:41, 42), but Paul fasted following his Damascus Road experience and the church at Antioch fasted prior to sending Paul and Barnabas on their missionary journey (Acts 9:9, 13:3). Paul and Barnabas themselves prayed and fasted with the elders whom they appointed in every church (Acts 14:23).

The age of the Spirit is not to be one of perpetual fasting. But as those possessing the first fruits of the Spirit, yet, groaning in anticipation of our complete redemption (Rom. 8:23), it is surely appropriate that we fast on occasion as we long for the return of our divine Bridegroom (*cf.* Rev. 22:17-20). This is the age of the 'already but not yet.' In Christ we are already seated in the heavenlies, but we do not yet enjoy the full experience of the glory that is to be revealed at His second coming. Thus, as partakers in, yet also anticipators of, the spiritual blessings that are above, we fast and we pray as we "keep seeking those things above" (Col. 3:1-4, NASB).

In our fasting we join with the Old Testament saints in confession of sin, mourning over the low state of the church as well as of our own souls, and seeking that God would not judge us according to our sins, but rather that He would intervene with reviving power. However, fasting is also a positive exercise in terms of the establishment of Christ's kingdom on earth. The example of Paul and Barnabas suggests that fasting and prayer is appropriate to the establishment not only of the church in general, but of local churches in particular. Indeed, the examples of Moses and of Jesus before them suggest that fasting is appropriate prior to any notable work of God, as in the giving of the law or the commencement of Christ's ministry.

Fasting as it has been practiced in the history of the church, including and perhaps particularly in the Reformed tradition, exemplifies the above characteristics--repentance, mourning over sin, prayer for revival and a quiet confidence in God's power to advance His own cause on the earth.

The diaries and writings of men such as Martin Luther, John Calvin, John Knox, George Whitefield, Jonathan Edwards, David Brainard, and C. H. Spurgeon bear testimony to the importance and spiritual benefit of fasting in their lives. Spurgeon, for instance, writes: "Our seasons of fasting and prayer at the Tabernacle have been high days indeed--never has Heaven's gate stood wider, never have our hearts been nearer the central Glory."[20] David Brainard's diary includes several occasions of fasting, both in joyous anticipation of ministry and in sorrow over sin and personal failure.

The Old Testament practice of calling for a fast in times of national emergency also finds a parallel in modern history. In 1756 the King of Britain called for a day of solemn fasting to plead for divine intervention to prevent a threatened French invasion. The prayers were answered and, appropriately, a day of thanksgiving followed.[21] The need for similar times of fasting and prayer for the preservation and revival of the church should be apparent.

Thanksgivings

Whereas fasting and the taking of oaths and vows are, in the nature of the case, occasional elements of worship, thanksgiving is the constant accompaniment of all true worship. Furthermore, not only are we to give thanks in regular acts of public and private worship (cf. Ps. 35:18; 100:4; I Thess. 1:2; etc.): thanksgiving is an attitude of heart and mind that should characterize all of Christian experience (Phil. 4:6; I Thess. 5:18). Indeed, the consumated state of glory will be one of constant thanksgiving (Rev. 4:11; 5:9-14, etc.).

However, when the Confession speaks of "thanksgivings upon special occasions" it has in view more specific acts of thanksgiving for particular acts of providence and grace. An example would be annual harvest thanksgivings. Less regular and more truly occasional would be the

---

[20]E. M. Bounds, *Power Through Prayer* (Chicago: Moody Press, n. d.), 23.

[21]Wallis, *op. cit.*, 12, 29, 30.

times of thanksgiving for national deliverance in times of war or other emergencies. To what extent do special occasions such as these have Biblical support?

Thanksgiving was very much a part of Old Testament worship, particularly on feast days. The three major annual feasts, Passover, Pentecost, and the Feast of Tabernacles, had thanksgiving as an integral part of their celebration (cf. Ex. 23:14-16; Lev. 23:5-43). The Passover was a commemoration of Israel's deliverance from Egyptian bondage. Pentecost came at the completion of the wheat harvest and involved thanksgiving for the first-fruits of harvest as well as anticipation of God's continued faithfulness in providing His people with various harvests. The Feast of Tabernacles was a thanksgiving for completed harvests and a reminder of Israel's tent-dwelling days in the wilderness.

In addition to these major annual feasts, the most frequently celebrated feasts of the Sabbath, the New Moon Festival and the Feast of Trumpets (Num. 28:9-15; 29:1-6), involved both consecration and thanksgiving.

Among the feasts which developed later in Israel's history, the Feast of Purim was a commemoration of the Jews' deliverance in the time of Esther. It involved a day of fasting coupled with two days of rejoicing and celebrations, including the reading of Esther in synagogues.

Thus, thanksgiving for deliverance (as in the Passover) and for God's provision (as at Pentecost) was very much a part of Israel's stated acts of worship. The fact that these feast days ceased to be celebrated in New Testament times points to their fulfillment in Christ. Thus, for instance, the deliverance from Egypt, celebrated in the Passover, was a foreshadowing of the greater deliverance from sin in the death and resurrection of Christ. And it was on the day of Pentecost that the Holy Spirit was poured out on the Church, as the confirmation of Christ's finished work and the firstfruits of the harvest of redemption. Although some aspects of Old Testament worship lingered on till the destruction of the temple in A. D. 70, the New Testament emphasis from Pentecost on, is the gathering of God's people on the first day of the week, the memorial of Christ's resurrection for worship, edification and instruction. Because of this, the Confession of Faith includes in its chapter on "Religious Worship and the Sabbath Day" the statement that the first day of the week is now the Christian Sabbath.[22]   Not all Christians agree with this, some quoting passages such as Colossians 2:16 to argue that no special days exist in the Christian era.   However, Revelation 1:10, along with the practice of the early church (Acts 20:7; I Cor. 16:2), would seem to point to a recognition of the Lord's Day as a weekly celebration of Christ's resurrection and anticipation of the eternal Sabbath rest to which we look forward (Heb. 4:9).[23]

Besides the Lord's Day, there are no specific instances of thanksgiving days in the New Testament. However, one may point to Paul's response to God's providence on his journey to Rome as legitimate examples of special thanksgivings (Acts 27:35; 28:15), which give us warrant for such practice today. In any case, the principle of thanksgiving is clearly taught and this suggests the appropriateness of specific acts of thanksgiving, provided these occasions be truly occasional and do not become part of a religious calendar imposed on the church with binding authority.

In conclusion, then, the New Testament, as well as the Old, does provide examples of religious oaths and vows and fasting and thanksgiving upon appropriate occasions. Ironically, of the three occasional elements we have looked at, the one most comonly practiced, thanksgiving celebration, is the one with the least specific New Testament precedent. The other two, vows and fasting, though less commonly practiced, are clearly commended both by precept and example. The modern church would do well to give them closer consideration.

---

[22]Westminster Confession of Faith, XXI. 7.

[23]Part of the Lord's Day celebration is the remembrance of Christ's death which includes, among other elements, thanksgiving for Christ's atoning sacrifice (I Cor. 10:16; cf. Acts 2:46).

PART III

HISTORIC VIEWS AND PRACTICE OF WORSHIP

16 - HISTORY AND WORSHIP

Frank J. Smith

History can serve many purposes, including the illustration of what not to do and the ill effects that follow from wrongful actions. However, one can also use history to hold forth good examples of people performing that which the Lord requires. It is with this positive perspective that the following two historical essays were written.

Protestants generally agree that reforms implemented in the Reformation were crucial for the well-being of the Church. Sometimes less appreciated is the fact that in addition to revitalization of life and doctrine, reform of worship was also crucial. Indeed, one could argue that the famed Westminster Standards maintain proper worship as an essential characteristic of the Church (Westminster Confession of Faith, XXV.3-5). Or, perhaps we could say that the Church's marks are focused, dynamically, in three directions: inward (ecclesiastical discipline), outward (preaching of the gospel), and upward (worship, including administration of the sacraments).

The first essay of this section features an overview of the teachings of the Reformation and post-Reformation creeds and confessions with respect to worship. The findings may surprise officers and others in Calvinistic churches who profess allegiance to standard documents.

The second essay highlights the reformation of worship in Scotland under the guidance of John Knox. That small country's Presbyterian descendents have had a profound impact on much of the world, and the worship they practiced and promoted formed a substantial part of that influence.

All of the Reformed Protestant churches 'swept the house clean' with respect to worship, as the man-made liturgical practices of Romanism were eschewed. 'Aesthetics' was no longer the watchword: rather, the Reformers understood that the overarching structure of Biblical religion involves the covenant, including the principle that the New Covenant, in contrast with the Old, is administered "with more simplicity and less outward glory" (Westminster Confession of Faith, VII. 6).

Accordingly, elaborate rituals were 'out,' and simplicity, reflective of the humble believer's direct access and approach to God, was 'in.' Crosses, pictures, and images were viewed not only as non-essential, but as actual hindrances to piety. Morality plays obscured the light of the Gospel which plain preaching was able to convey, convictingly, to the heart. Priestly garb, burning of incense, candles, and musical instruments were all considered part of the old order which the coming of the Messiah had abrogated. The Bride was no longer to be in her 'childish' stage, but was to grow up into the glorious liberty of Christ who had set her free from human inventions and from the rigors of the ceremonial law (Westminster Confession of Faith, XIX.3, XX.2). The fullness of the Holy Spirit guaranteed that the outward signs and symbols of the Old Testament were unnecessary, and that all imitations were impotent.

One does not need a very lively imagination to perceive how these early Protestants would regard much of what passes today as 'worship'-- especially in churches that call themselves 'Reformed.'

The final essay of this section deals with bibliographical considerations, reflecting the more recent history of Reformed thought. This essay is a critique of many of the works which some folk have enthusiastically embraced. It helps to illustrate why the editors have felt that a volume such as this is so desparately needed.

Differences of culture and/or era are non-essential in terms of what does or does not constitute proper worship. History's light can therefore be of special relevance in aiding us in a reformation of worship as we head toward the twenty-first century.

17 - THE REFORMED CREEDS AND THE RECONSTRUCTION OF CHRISTIAN WORSHIP

C. Gregg Singer

The reformation of doctrine which took place during the era of the Reformation inherently and logically brought in its wake an equally thorough and even drastic reconstruction of the worship of the Church. Even as the worship of the Middle Ages reflected the theology of that era, so must the worship of the Reformed Churches reflect their theology. Both Luther and Calvin were well aware of the necessity of reshaping the worship of the Roman Church, but this awareness did not lead to an immediate realization of the changes which were demanded by their respective theologies. It was no easy task to restructure the worship of the faithful and to bring about changes in habitual forms of the liturgy, for these had been strongly ingrained in their minds and hearts.

Luther was alert to the necessity of making changes, but he was both theologically and liturgically timid, partly because of his own background and partly because of the peculiar political position in which he was placed. He was, therefore, unwilling to make any more liturgical changes than he felt were necessary to give expression to the central themes of his theology: justification by faith and the priesthood of the believer. The emerging forms of Lutheran worship reflected these two main emphases of Luther's theology, but stopped short of becoming a complete reformation of the worship of the Church. Luther basically held to the conviction that only those practices should be discarded which were openly forbidden by the Scriptures. As a result of this, there was much in the older form of worship which worked its way through into the Lutheran form of worship.

On the other hand, the Zwinglians and the Calvinists were much more critical of the Roman Church and were, therefore, much more insistent upon bringing about a more drastic change in the whole system, so that the resultant forms of worship would be in harmony with their theological positions.

However, neither Luther, Zwingli, or Calvin had been the first to issue such a call for reform. During the later Middle Ages, Wycliffe and Hus, as well as others of their day, had seen the necessity of such change, and had voiced their sentiments for it. But all these efforts had been in vain. Their calls had reflected their various theological positions and there was a rather close relationship between their views on theology and their efforts to reform the worship practices of the day. The Papacy was well aware of this close relationship and was thus unwilling to make any concessions which might endanger their sacerdotal theology.

Zwingli became an early champion of the reform of worship and he may well have been the first of the Reformers of the sixteenth century to issue such a call. His influence on the churches of Switzerland is quite evident in the Bernese Theses of 1528, in which the church at Berne declared that Christ is the only head of the Church. It therefore rejected the doctrine of the Mass on the ground that the essential and corporeal presence of the body and blood of Christ cannot be demonstrated from the Holy Scriptures. Hence, "the mass as now in use in which Christ is offered to God the Father for the sins of the dead is contrary to the Scriptures, a blasphemy against the most holy sacrifice and death of Christ and on account of its abuses an abomination before God."[1] Although this statement was rather timid, it did represent an important change in the thinking of the church at Berne and heralded those later changes in worship which would surely follow wherever Reformed doctrine was preached.

These "Theses," however, did not stop with this assertion and went on to declare that it was also contrary to the Word of God to invoke any other mediator than Jesus Christ. The authors of these theses were not unaware of the logic involved in their new position and they went on to insist that purgatorial fires, masses and all offices for the dead were useless. In assuming such a position, they were rejecting the heart of the Roman worship and they accordingly went on to abolish the worship of images in

---

[1]Philip Schaff, *The Creeds of Christendom* (New York, Harper & Brothers, 1877), III, 209.

Berne on the ground that such a practice was contrary to the Scriptures, since the images had been erected as objects of worship and adoration.[2]

Like the attacks of Luther, those of Berne were largely negative in character. But such negative attacks had to be made before new forms of worship could be introduced. However, their first impact was to create a kind of liturgical vacuum in the Zwinglian churches of Switzerland which Zwingli could not fill.

It is somewhat surprising to learn that this negative approach was also characteristic of the early Reformed creeds. For the most part, their authors were content to condemn the Roman Catholic liturgy and they were strangely silent as to what forms of worship would be acceptable in churches which held the Reformed theology.

If such a situation had been allowed to continue for any length of time, the changes in doctrine would not have brought about a robust and healthy church in Switzerland. Although it is not difficult to understand why the early Reformers were somewhat hesitant to introduce too many drastic changes into worship until the people had been thoroughly trained and made ready to receive them, it is more difficult to understand why they were apparently so hesitant to set forth some of the necessary changes into such creedal statements as the First Helvetic Confession of 1536. It is also true that a return to Augustinian theology, which must by its very nature awaken those who had accepted it to the great cleavage which existed between it and the theology and worship of the Roman Church, thus to a degree prepared them for the changes which would inevitably follow in those churches adhering to the Reformed doctrine.

The framers of the First Helvetic Confession showed some insight into what was involved in the reformation of theology in their discussion of the nature of the Church. Here we find a clear statement that Christ is its chief cornerstone and that only those rites which had been instituted by Christ, such as a legitimate and public discipline, should be allowed.[3]

---

[2] *Ibid.*, 209-10.
[3] *Ibid.*, 218-19.

It is interesting to note that a legitimate form of discipline should receive such specific attention. There is also a hint as to what direction the worship of the churches in Switzerland should take. It outlined the duties of the pastors and this section made it quite clear that they did not have any power to administer grace through the sacraments, for that power is in the hands of God alone.[4]

This confession also discussed the role of the minister in the worship of the Church. This was further defined by a very clear statement to the effect that the sacraments are only signs of grace invisibly received and their effects can be only spiritually perceived.

Beyond such statements, which were basically negative in character, this early confession of faith did not go. But with the death of Zwingli in 1531, the door was opened for further reform and the coming of Reformation in all of its fullness in the person of John Calvin. More than any other Reformer, Calvin saw the need for the thorough reformation of the Church in every aspect of its life: in its theology, in its government, in its worship and discipline. To be effective, reformation in theology had to be accompanied by a similar reform in worship and the Church had to be cleansed from all the accretions of the Middle Ages. The life of the Church in all its aspects must be based on the Scriptures and on them alone.

Calvin and Worship

Although Calvin had enunciated the basic principles of his theology as a guide for the reform of the Church in the first edition of the *Institutes of the Christian Religion* of 1536, he did not fill out their implications as he did in later editions, beginning with that of 1541. In this monumental work, along with his equally monumental commentaries, we find what is probably the most Biblical treatment of the role of worship in the life of mankind and those principles which must govern the worship of the Church.

He rightly saw that the duty of worship has its origin and frame of reference in the creation mandate--that man, created in the image of God as

---

[4]*Ibid.*, 220.

His viceregent on earth, was to be prophet, priest and king. In this capacity his supreme duty was to worship his sovereign creator. As a created being, he can do no less. "It will always be evident to persons of correct judgment, that the idea of a Deity impressed on the mind of man is indellible. That all have by nature an innate persuasion of the divine existence, a persuasion inseparable from their very constitution."[5]

Because of this innate conviction that God exists and that He must be worshipped, Calvin concluded that "the worship of God is therefore the only thing which renders man superior to brutes, and makes them aspire to immortality."[6] The great and all-important fact of this inbred sense of deity in man did not blind Calvin to the fact that sinful men do not and cannot fulfill this divinely imposed duty. "While experience testifies that the seeds of religion are sown by God in every heart, we scarcely find one man in a hundred who cherishes what he has received, and not one in whom they grow to maturity, much less bear fruit in due season. . . . The fact is, that no genuine piety remains in the world."[7]

Sinful men, conscious of the need to worship, cannot worship Him in spirit and in truth. Thus none of their consequent attempts for the worship of God can be considered as rendered to Him, "because they worship not him, but a figment of their own brains in his stead."[8] Man's blindness resulting from the fall of Adam in no way excuses his inability and failure to worship the true God as He must be worshipped, for the Scriptures reveal Him, and He is clearly distinguished from all fictitious deities by His creation of the world.

For this reason, Calvin took up the cudgels against all forms of idolatrous worship, pointing out that the worship of idols was not only forbidden to the children, but that this prohibition applied to all mankind. He summarized the Biblical teaching "that the Scripture, in order to direct us to the true God, expressly excludes and rejects all the gods of the heathen;

---

[5]*Institutes of the Christian Religion*, (trans. John Allen), I.III.3.

[6]*Ibid.*

[7]*Ibid.*, I.IV.1.

[8]*Ibid.*

because, in almost all ages, religion has been generally corrupted . . . [even] though the name of one supreme God has been universally known and celebrated."[9]

However, this general knowledge of God has not prevented mankind from corrupting that knowledge and their forms of worship. "But since all men, without exception, have by their own vanity been drawn into erroneous notions, and so their understandings have become vain, all their natural perception of the divine unity has only served to render them inexcusable."[10]

In his indictment and condemnation of idolatry, Calvin had not only the pagan forms of worship in view, but that of the Roman Church as well. In reference to the defense of the worship of images, Calvin had this to say: "If the papists have any shame, let them no longer use this subterfuge, that images are the books of the illiterate; which is so clearly refuted by numerous testimonies from Scripture. . . . What monsters they obtrude in place of diety is well known."[11]

Calvin continued his indictment of the worship of the Roman Church, particularly its use of images, with this admonition: "He [God] has commanded one common doctrine to be there proposed to all, in the preaching of his word, and in his sacred mysteries; to which they betray great inattention of mind, who are carried about by their eyes to the contemplation of idols."[12]

Even less was he impressed by the efforts of the Roman Church to deny the charge of idolatry by its clumsy efforts to distinguish between the respect (*eidolouleia*), which Rome claimed should be paid to images and that worship (*eudololatreia*) which must be rendered to God alone. Such a distinction, Calvin maintained, was nothing but a play on words, a distinction without any real meaning.

---

[9] *Ibid.*, I.X.3.

[10] *Ibid.*

[11] *Ibid.*, I.XI.7.

[12] *Ibid.*

It must not be supposed, however, that Calvin was merely negative in his treatment of worship. This is far from being the case. It must be remembered that all the Reformers were very much concerned with what they rightly felt to be the idolatry in the Roman worship. It was imperative for them, if their efforts to reform the Church according to the Biblical pattern were to be successful, that all the false debris had to be removed from both the worship services and the religious life of the people. Worship must be brought into conformity with the plain teachings of the Scriptures. Nothing less than this would be acceptable in the light of the great doctrines of the Reformation.

If at times their criticism of the Roman Church seems harsh and uncharitable, it must always be kept in mind that they were in combat with a liturgical tradition, the roots of which were deeply buried in a thousand years of tradition and were very difficult to remove. A frontal attack was necessary if this idolatry was to be removed and the worship of the Church purged of this monstrous evil.

Calvin was fully aware of the necessity of presenting a positive Biblical approach to proper worship in all of its aspects. For this reason he first insisted that all worship of God must be through Christ the Son, the Redeemer of men and their divine Mediator who is equal to God the Father in every respect. He charged that those who ascribe a lesser place to the Trinity are guilty of dishonoring Him and are not worshipping according to the Scriptural norm.

Having laid the foundation for all true worship, Calvin then embarked on a rather lengthy exposition of the various components of a Biblical worship service. In his *Institutes*, he devoted the whole of Chapter XX in Book III to this most important aspect in the life of the Church and of all believers, regarding it as the "principal exercise of faith and the medium of our daily reception of divine blessings." By prayer the Christian penetrates "to those riches which are reserved with our heavenly Father for our use. For between God and men there is a certain communication; by which they enter into the sanctuary of heaven, and in his immediate presence remind him of his promises, in order that his declarations, which they have implicitly believed, may . . . be verified in their presence."[13]

In his discussion of prayer, Calvin was much more precise than many evangelicals in his prescription as to how prayer should be offered to God. Even those who may feel that they are worshipping in accordance with Scripture may well be surprised by his discussion.

Calvin placed a great emphasis on the proper preparation for prayer and declared "that our heart and mind [must] be composed to a suitable frame."[14] Likewise those who engage in prayer should apply all their faculties and attention, "and not be distracted, as is commonly the case, with wandering thoughts."[15] He was also quite critical of those who "carelessly recite a form of prayer, as though they were discharging a task imposed on them by God."[16]

All prayers, in the mind of Calvin, should begin with a supplication for pardon and with a humble confession of guilt. In regard to the further content of prayer he maintained that the form or rule of prayer should be composed of six petitions, a form which he found in the Lord's Prayer as it is found in the Gospel of Matthew (Calvin insisted that what seems to be a seventh petition is really a part of the sixth).[17]

Such a requirement might seem to set forth a rather rigorous requirement for both public and private prayer, but this is not the case. He was by no means requiring a prayer book approach to God such as that which Cranmer had designed for the Church of England. He was quite willing to allow other forms of prayer for those situations which would require them. In fact, he showed a greater degree of flexibility than might be supposed. On the other hand, it is also true that his formula for prayer was a far cry from those prayers which are usually offered and at times, so casually offered, in both evangelical and liberal churches today.

---

[13]Ibid., III.XX.2.

[14]Ibid., III.XX.4.

[15]Ibid., III, XX.5.

[16]Ibid., III.XX.6.

[17]Ibid., III.XX.35.

In his discussion of proper worship, Calvin also treated rather briefly the use of music in the Church. Calling it an ancient custom, he cited the reference of St. Augustine to it and quoted it with approval to the effect that it was not until the time of Ambrose that the church at Milan adopted music for its services. He did admit, however, that music has a Biblical foundation and cited I Corinthians 14:15 and Colossians 3:16 in support of its use.

Calvin did place some limitations on its use, offered some guidelines if it were to be used, and said that "if singing be attempered to that gravity which becomes the presence of God and of angels, it adds a dignity and grace to sacred actions, and is very efficacious in exciting the mind to a true concern and ardour of devotion."[18] With this as a proper guide, he was willing to allow the Reformed Churches to give music a place in the worship service. It was for the inauguration of this kind of reverential music that Calvin called Louis Bourgeois to Geneva, specifically for the task of producing a Psalter suitable for Reformed worship.

It is quite evident that the kind of music which he envisaged for the church at Geneva was very different from the hymns and songs which are so prevalent today in the worship of evangelical churches and even in some which call themselves Reformed.

In spite of this fact, however, Calvin was intent upon creating a form of worship which would represent a sharp break with that of the Roman Church. In a rather surprising passage, which is seldom if ever quoted, Calvin revealed a kind of tolerance for its worship service. He was willing to admit that there remained some vestiges of the true church within the Church of Rome.

Nevertheless, as in former times, the Jews continued in possession of some peculiar privileges of the Church, so we refuse not to acknowledge, among the Papists of the present day, those vestiges of the Church which it has pleased the Lord should remain among

---

[18] *Ibid.*, III, XX, 32.

them after its removal. When God had once made his covenant with the Jews, it continued among them, rather because it was supported by its own stability in opposition to their impiety, than in consequence of their observance of it.[19]

This rather grudging admission was no doubt prompted by his realization that the Roman Church did hold to the creedal pronouncements of the first four ecumenical councils and therefore to the doctrines of the Trinity and the two natures in the Person of Jesus Christ as it had been formulated by the Council of Chalcedon in 451.

In concluding our study of Calvin's position on worship, it becomes quite apparent that not only in his theology, but also in his concept of what constitutes true Biblical worship, he held to what might well be called a "High Presbyterianism." This position cannot be equated with that of the Church of England on the one hand, but it is also quite different from the liberal and evangelical forms of worship of our day. He most certainly would frown on the kind of music so frequently heard today, the casual character of many religious services, and the growing custom of clapping for musical presentation, even though many of them are obviously planned to be entertaining rather than to be spiritually and religiously oriented. It can almost be said that Calvin would have sternly reproved a congregation if these activities had been carried on in its worship services. He was always conscious that we must worship a sovereign God and thus our worship services must always reflect this consciousness on the part of those who worship Him--that we are engaged in worshipping our Sovereign Creator and that the worship of the Church must always be in harmony with this overwhelmingly great Biblical mandate.

For this reason, Calvin was well aware of the need for giving practical guidance in suggesting an order of worship. It was no easy task to lead the people of Geneva away from traditional forms and persuade them to use a new one which would be in harmony with the new theology. Soon after he arrived in Geneva, he set out to reform not only the worship of the

---

[19] *Ibid.*, IV.II.11.

Church but the whole life of Geneva as well. Late in 1536 he and William Farel presented to the Council of Two Hundred their proposals and in January 1537 they were published as an Ordinance. This document provided for holding communion once a month, and called for congregational singing as an integral part of the worship service. For this, the metrical version of the Psalms was alone to be used. The Council also issued a series of orders, dealing with the prohibition of all images in the churches of Geneva and calling for the proper and strict observance of the Sabbath Day.

These reforms, as might have been expected, produced a severe reaction, and in 1537 Calvin and Farel were forced to leave Geneva. They went to Strassburg to stay with Martin Bucer. However, in 1541 they were invited to return to Geneva. Calvin returned, but Farel decided not to go.

His return was something of a personal triumph and vindication, for in this same year both councils accepted a new set of proposals which became the well-known Ecclesiastical Ordinance of 1541.

The document provided for four groups of officers for the churches of Geneva: the pastors who were to preach, to admonish the wayward and to administer the sacraments; the doctors or teachers who were to instruct the Christian community in sound doctrine; the elders who were to have the spiritual care and discipline of the congregation; and deacons who were to have the care for the poor and the sick.

The formula for public worship, a part of the Ecclesiastical Ordinance, was based on the order of worship which Calvin had introduced into the service of the church in Strassburg where he had been a pastor while in exile. It consisted of an opening exhortation to prayer, followed by the confession of faith, the singing of a Psalm and prayer for enlightenment, at the end of which the Pastor was to pronounce the absolution from sin. The high point of the service was a lengthy sermon, which was followed by the benediction.

Later John Knox adopted this form of worship for the emerging Presbyterian Church of Scotland. Calvin's form of worship called for the holding of catechetical class for the children at the close of the morning service. In the afternoon there was to be a second service with a second sermon. In addition to these services on the Sabbath Day there was to be preaching on Monday, Tuesday and Friday.

The Reformation of Worship After Calvin

Although the Gallican Confession was drafted in 1559, eighteen years after the publication of Calvin's Ecclesiastical Ordinance, it had comparatively little to say or add in positive terms as to how worship should be conducted.   Rather, its framers seemingly were content to issue a condemnation of the belief in Purgatory as an illusion and other Roman Catholic practices such as auricular confession, the sale and use of indulgences, "and all such things by which they hope to merit forgiveness and salvation."[20]

Striking a more general note, this confession also declared that "we reject all human inventions, and all laws which men may introduce under the pretense of serving God, by which they wish to bind consciences; and we receive only that which conduces to concord and holds all in obedience, from the greatest to the least."[21]

In regard to the nature of the sacraments, this creed declared that they are pledges and seals of God and that "their substance and truth is in Jesus Christ, and that of themselves they are only smoke and shadow."[22] In this vein it held that baptism is a pledge of our adoption, "for by it we are grafted into the body of Christ, so as to be washed and cleansed by his blood."[23] In accordance with the other Reformed creeds, it called for the baptim of children of believing parents.

In similar fashion it declared that the Lord's Supper is a witness of our union with Christ, and it "also feeds and nourishes us truly with his flesh

---

[20]Schaff, *Creeds of Christendom*, III, 373-74.

[21]*Ibid.*, 378.

[22]*Ibid.*, 379.

[23]*Ibid.*

and blood, so that we may be one in him, and that our life may be in common."[24]

It is difficult to understand why this confession had so little of a positive nature to say in regard to the proper mode of worship. But this same apparent satisfaction with a negative approach can also be found in the Belgic Confession. It was somewhat more explicit in its renunication and condemnation of false practices in worship, holding that

> though it is useful and beneficial, that those who are rulers of the Church institute and establish certain ordinances among themselves for maintaining the body of the Church, yet they ought studiously to take care that they do not depart from those things which Christ, our only master, hath instituted. And, therefore, we reject all human inventions, and all laws which man would introduce into the worship of God, thereby to bind and compel the conscience in any manner whatever.[25]

The Belgic Confession sought to safeguard the purity of worship and the celebration of the two sacraments, for it contains some very stringent, if not the most stringent, indictments of Roman Catholic worship to be found in any of the Reformed creeds:

> Therefore, we reject all mixtures and damnable inventions, which men have added unto and blended with the Sacraments, as profanations of them, and affirm that we ought to rest satisfied with the ordinance which Christ and his Apostles have taught us, and that we must speak of them in the same manner as they have spoken.[26]

---

[24] *Ibid.*, 380.

[25] *Ibid.*, 423.

[26] *Ibid.*, 431.

The Second Helvetic Confession of 1566, the longest of all the Reformed creeds, was in some respects more complete than the Belgic in its statements concerning the necessity and kind of worship which should take place in the churches. After setting forth the orthodox doctrine of the Trinity, it immediately used this Biblical truth as the foundation for a pointed rejection of all false and idolatrous worship, holding that since God is an invisible spirit and immense being he cannot be expressed by any art or human imagination.[27] It thus rejected not only the idols of the Gentiles but all representations of Christ as well.[28] This prohibition included images and "vain" pictures. The ground for this was the fact that it turned the eyes of the worshippers from the True God to vain representations.

This confession is unusual among those produced on the Continent in that it presented injunctions on the role of both public and private prayers. In the case of private prayer it declared that it was permissible to pray in whatever language the one engaging in it knew best. But in the public prayers in the worship service, the prayer must always be made in the language common to the country, in that language which would be understood by all the people.[29] Public prayers were to include petitions for magistrates, kings and all those holding office in the church as well as for the ministers.[30]

This confession also contained some injunctions on the use of music in the worship services, asserting that its use must be in moderation. This confession was again unusual in that it expressly rejected the use of Gregorian chants on the ground that they contained many absurdities and that their use had already been rejected not only by "our own Church" (the Reformed Church in Germany) but by many others as well.[31] The use of congregational singing was permitted, however, but apparently without much enthusiasm.

---

[27] Ibid., 241.

[28] Ibid., 242.

[29] Ibid., 296.

[30] Ibid., 297.

[31] Ibid., 242.

Reformed Worship in Presbyterianism

Turning now from the reformation of worship as it took place on the Continent we come to the role of John Knox and the Westminster Assembly for the final and most comprehensive statements concerning the reformation of worship. In 1556, while he was still in Geneva in close contact with Calvin and looking forward to his work in Scotland, Knox prepared his well-known Form of Prayer, which consisted of a confession of faith, an order of worship and a form of government. The nature of this document was well summarized in its introduction in which Knox declared that the doctrine, the worship and the discipline of the Church must always be in accord with the Word of God. In the Presbyterian Church in Scotland there was to be no room for custom, tradition, or philosophy.

The order of service which he prepared was quite simple. The service was to be opened with a confession of sins and this in turn was followed by the singing of a Psalm (and only Psalms were to be used), the prayer of invocation and the pastoral prayer. The service was to come to a close with the singing of another Psalm and the benediction.

Knox called for the observance of the Lord's Supper at least once a month and more often if the congregation should desire. But there is no indication that it should be observed every service.

When the Lord's Supper was served, the minister was to sit at the table on the same level as the congregation and the communion was to be celebrated in a simple but reverent manner.

In his directions for every aspect of the worship of the Church, Knox had in mind a Biblical simplicity without any use of humanly devised rituals. In his thinking, all forms of human innovations were nothing but forms of idolatry and as such could not be tolerated. When Knox returned to Scotland he was able to have this proposed worship adopted in his own church (St. Giles) and by the Church of Scotland.

The Westminster Assembly and Confession of Faith

It remained for the Westminster Assembly (1643-1649) to bring to its conclusion the thinking of the Calvinistic Churches of England, Ireland and Scotland as to the proper Biblical worship of God. In setting forth their confessional standards, they were very mindful of the work of their predecessors both on the continent of Europe and the British Isles. Their efforts to bring together into one confessional statement all the best efforts of their predecessors were not in vain. The great doctrinal affirmations of this assembly brought with them an inescapable and most appropriate standard for Christian worship. It could not have been otherwise, in view of the contents of this climactic statement of Reformed theology. The depths and insights of this confession underlie at every point its declarations concerning the necessity and nature of Biblical worship.

Although the decisions of this assembly to place the location of the necessity of worship in the light of nature was not a novelty, for there had been some references to it in some of the earlier creeds of the Reformation, the Westminster Divines gave to it its most thorough and truly Biblical statement:

> The light of nature showeth that there is a God, who hath lordship and sovereignty over all; is good, and doeth good unto all; and is therefore to be feared, loved, praised, called upon, trusted in, and served, with all the heart, and with all the soul, and with all the might. But the acceptable way of worshipping the true God is instituted by himself, and so limited by his own revealed will, that he may not be worshipped according to the imaginations and devices of men, or the suggestions of Satan, under any visible representation, or in any other way not prescribed in the Holy Scripture.[32]

---

[32]Westminster Confession of Faith, XXI.1.

This is a very clear statement in regard to two fundamental aspects of proper worship. The first is that all men by the light of nature can know that God exists and that He is to be worshipped. This necessity arises from the fact that God has placed His image in man and the resulting knowledge which man has of God is indestructable. It is given to man not only through creation, but because man bears this image in him.

The Confession speaks with equal force, however, to the fact that the natural man because of his sin is no longer capable of fulfilling the divinely imposed duty of worship. Thus the light of nature can no longer penetrate the darkness of the sin-ridden soul of man in this natural state nor be sufficient to demonstrate the necessity and nature of true worship.

For this reason the Confession provides in some detail just how men are to worship. The first prescription is that true worship must be rendered to God through the Father, Son and Holy Spirit and to Him alone.[33] This directive swept aside all Roman Catholic accretions to the Biblical norm and at the same time condemned Unitarian and other forms of worship which are not directed to the Triune God.

Perhaps one of the most beautiful sections in the whole Confession is that which defines the nature of Biblical prayer. It regards prayer as an integral part of the worship service. It declared that prayer with thanksgiving is a special part of religious worship and that it is acceptable to God if "it is made in the name of the Son, by the help of his Spirit, according to his will, with understanding, reverence, humility, fervency, faith, love, and perseverance; and, if vocal, in a known tongue."[34]

That this approach to God was no idle injunction is amply demonstrated by the prayers of both Calvin and Knox and their many colleagues in the Reformed Churches in which they ministered in both Europe and Scotland. These prayers stand in a sharp and melancholy contrast with those prayers which are all too often hurriedly and even light-heartedly offered in too many pulpits of the present day.

---

[33] *Ibid.*, XXI.2.
[34] *Ibid.*, XXI.3.

The Confession then went on to set forth the component parts of Biblical worship more fully than any other Reformed creed. All proper worship was to include "the reading of the Scriptures with godly fear; the sound preaching, and conscionable hearing of the word, in obedience unto God, with understanding, faith, and reverence; singing of psalms with grace in the heart; as also, the due administration and worthy receiving of the sacraments . . ."[35]

The Confession also recognized the legitimacy of occasional elements: "religious oaths and vows, solemn fastings, and thanksgivings upon special occasions, which are, in their several times and seasons, to be used in a holy and religious manner."[36]

One of the most important and unusual features of the Assembly's work, however, was the attention it paid to the proper observance of the Sabbath as necessary for the worship of the Church. Again it had recourse to the law of nature for the original institution of such a day, declaring that

> as it is the law of nature, that, in general, a due proportion of time be set apart for the worship of God; so, in His Word, by a positive, moral, and perpetual commandment, binding all men in all ages, he hath particularly appointed one day in seven, for a Sabbath, to be kept holy unto Him: which, from the beginning of the world to the resurrection of Christ, was the last day of the week; and, from the resurrection of Christ, was changed into the first day of the week, which, in Scripture, is called the Lord's Day, and is to be continued to the end of the world, as the Christian Sabbath.[37]

It should be noted that by the term "the law of nature" the Westminster Assembly was in no way referring to this law as that which was a basic part of the subsequent Deism or of the natural philosophy of the Middle Ages. Rather did it have in mind the law implanted in the heart

---

[35] *Ibid.*, XXI.5.

[36] *Ibid.*

[37] *Ibid.*, XXI.7.

and mind of man by God at creation and therefore an innate possession of man as part of his original nature.

The Westminster fathers in no way believed that the observance of the Sabbath was a temporary promulgation of the law for that particular period in the history of the Church or the race, as many would have us believe today. For them it was intended to be a permanent part of the divine legislation for the life of man on earth until Christ should come in the fullness of His power and glory.

Having laid down this basic premise as to the place of the Sabbath in the life of mankind in general and in the Church in particular, the Confession then presented a brief and yet thorough statement as to how this day should be spent.

It is to be kept holy unto the Lord and for this purpose Christians were to prepare their hearts for its proper observance. On this day they must not engage in their usual work or their usual conversation or manner of life, not even in their own thoughts. Christians are to refrain from their usual means of recreation and center their attention on the Word of God throughout the course of the day, while they are attending the worship services and at home.

This injunction is not merely negative as many would seem to think today. The Sabbath is not a day in which Christians are to do nothing, far from it. Their whole time is to be taken up in both public and private worship and individual Bible study. Provision was also made for those necessary works such as running a household and works of mercy.[38]

This high regard for the meaning and observance of this day has long been one of the chief characteristics of Presbyterianism. No other group has had such an important and prolonged impact not only upon the Church at large, but also upon those nations in which Presbyterianism became an authoritative voice and at times a dominant influence in their political life.

The Presbyterian insistence on a proper regard for the meaning of this day and proper way of observing it had given a tremendous moral and

---

[38] *Ibid.*, XXI.8.

spiritual strength to the Church and to this nation--until the advent of the flagrant disregard for it in recent decades. There can be little doubt that the increasing disregard for the Sabbath has helped to bring about the moral and ultimately political collapse of those governments which have allowed such a desecration to take place.

Summary

Because Calvinism gave the highest expression of Biblical truth yet set forth from the Scripture for the life of the Church, the various forms of worship adopted by the Reformed Churches have likewise reflected the strength of this doctrinal foundation. This development of creed and worship received its highest expression in the work of the Westminster Assembly. Its achievements stand as a sharp rebuke not only to modern liberals, but also to many evangelicals in the Church today who seek to free themselves from the Biblical modes of worship in favor of those new schemes which they feel are adapted to the needs of the present day and are somehow more able to capture the attention of those who have become the slavish victims of modern cultural life. This is particularly true as this culture is expressed in the music of the day. Against all these un-Biblical deviations the Westminster Assembly spoke with a Biblical authority and clarity which we must not ignore or neglect. We are the custodians of the work and achievments of the Reformation in all its aspects. We have an inheritance that is truly Biblical and we are its stewards. We dare not surrender any part of it.

18 - JOHN KNOX AND THE REFORMATION OF WORSHIP IN THE SCOTTISH REFORMATION

Kevin Reed

In the battle to reform Scotland, John Knox sent forth a call for purity of worship. Indeed, the struggle between true and false worship was the central conflict of the Scottish Reformation. Therefore, it is important to examine Knox's thought concerning the worship of God.

Basically, there are two predominant themes which emerge during Knox's struggle to establish proper worship in Scotland. The first theme concerns the basis for evaluating our worship; the second theme concerns the importance of true worship.

At the heart of Knox's arguments is an appeal to Deuteronomy 4 and 12. These portions of Scripture teach that it is unlawful to add to, or take away from, the worship which God has instituted in His Word. Consequently, all religious ceremonies and institutions must have direct Scriptural warrant, if they are to be admitted as valid expressions of worship. This concept has subsequently become known as the *regulative principle* of worship.

In addition to the regulative principle, the other reoccurring theme stresses the primacy of pure worship. Knox had many matters which were of deep concern to him; but it is fair to say that nothing took precedence over his concern for the pure worship of God. Knox's regard for worship took top priority in all his labors as a Reformer.

A survey of Knox's writings will demonstrate these two major themes. They are applied numerous times in a variety of settings. They are pervasive and controlling features in the entire theology of John Knox.

The Beginning of Knox's Ministry

From the outset of his public ministry, Knox based his Reformed outlook on the regulative principle. After Knox's first sermon, he and John Rough were called before a convention of Papal clerics to answer for certain doctrines which the Protestants had espoused. Among the doctrines in dispute were the Protestant claims that "the Pope is an Antichrist," and "the Mass is abominable idolatry." A key point of contention was the Reformer's position that "man may neither make nor devise a religion that is acceptable to God: but man is bound to observe and keep the religion that from God is received, without chopping or changing thereof."[1]

This last point hit at the central issue: the limits of Church power. The issue soon became the focal point of the discussion. The Subprior asked Knox, "Why may not the Kirk, for good causes, devise Ceremonies to decor the Sacraments, and others [of] God's services?"[2]

Knox replies, "Because the Kirk ought to do nothing but in faith, and ought not to go before; but is bound to follow the voice of the true Pastor." Later during the exchange, Knox adds:

> It is not enough that man invent a ceremony, and then give it a signification, according to his pleasure . . . . But if that anything proceed from faith, it must have the word of God for the assurance; for ye are not ignorant, 'That faith comes by hearing, and hearing by the word of God.' Now, if ye will prove that your ceremonies proceed from faith, and do please God, ye must prove God in expressed words has commanded them: Or else shall ye never prove, That they proceed from faith, nor yet that they please God; but that

---

[1] *John Knox's History of the Reformation in Scotland* (Ed. by William Croft Dickinson; New York: Philosophical Library, 1950), I, 87.

[2] *Ibid.*, I, 88.

they are sin, and do displease him, according to the words of the Apostle, 'Whatsoever is not of faith is sin.'[3]

When the Subprior then attempts to divert the discussion from the main issue, Knox returns to the Scriptural data. Says Knox,

> May we cast away what we please, and retain what we please? If it be well remembered, Moses, in the name of God, says to the people of Israel, 'All that the Lord thy God commands thee to do, that do thou to the Lord thy God: add nothing to it; diminish nothing from it.' By this rule think I that the Kirk of Christ will measure God's religion, and not by that which seems good in their own eyes.[4]

A Friar then sought to establish the validity of Papal ceremonies by alluding to I Corinthians 3:11-12, claiming that the ceremonies have withstood the refiner's fire, because they have endured. Knox seized the same text and used it to disarm his opponents. Knox proved from Scripture that the things which pass through the refiner's fire are those which are established by the written Word of God; and, further, the written Word actually militates against the ceremonies.

"God's word condemns your ceremonies: Therefore they do not abide the trial thereof," asserts Knox. He then provides a paraphrased reference to Deuteronomy 4, a passage which he would cite many times during his work as a Reformer.

> That God's word damns your ceremonies, it is evident; for the plain and straight commandment of God is, 'Not that thing which appears good in thy eyes, shalt thou do to the Lord thy God, but what the Lord thy God has commanded thee, that do thou: add

---

[3] *Ibid.*, I, 88-89.

[4] *Ibid.*, I, 89. *Cf.* Calvin, *Tracts & Treatises*, III, 262-63.

nothing to it; diminish nothing from it.' Now unless that ye are able to prove that God has commanded your ceremonies, this his former commandment will damn both you and them.[5]

Knox's understanding of worship is thereby founded upon a serious consideration of the abiding validity of the law of God. It also seeks to guard the prerogatives of Christ, as Head of the Church; the Church must operate on the basis of His Word for authority to sanction all activities.

This foundational understanding has many far-reaching ramifications. It limits the Church from assuming an innovative role in worship. It also places restrictions on what elements may be properly introduced into worship services. Thus, the principle regulates both the government and worship of the Church by requiring Biblical warrant for all ecclesiastical actions.

Battling Papal Idolatry

Over many years, Knox repeatedly appeals to the regulative principle as he speaks on topics in dispute. A proper understanding of worship is essential to the work of Reformation; therefore, it is readily apparent why Knox broaches the topic in so many situations. If a dispute arises over matters of worship, he must first establish the general rule, and then apply it to the dispute in question.

Of course, the central dispute of the Reformation comes from a repudiation of the teachings of the Roman Church. Knox does not waste words. He lashes out against the corruptions of worship fostered by Papal superstition. The entire Papal religion "is a confusion patched from time to time by the subtlety of Satan, and by the foolish brains of men." The Mass is an "idol and bastard service." The doctrine of transubstantiation is "the bird that the Devil hatched by Pope Nicholas, and since that time fostered

---

[5]Knox, *History*, I, 91. *Cf.* Calvin, *Tracts*, I, 128.

and nourished by all his children, priests, friars, monks, and others his conjured and sworn soldiers."[6]

In 1550, Knox published *A Vindication of the Doctrine that the Sacrifice of the Mass is Idolatry.*[7] As Knox unfolds his arguments against the Mass, he provides a more enlarged defense of the regulative principle.

At the beginning of his presentation, Knox states a syllogism which underlies his whole discussion: "All worshipping, honoring, or service invented by the brain of man in the religion of God, without his own express commandment, is idolatry. The Mass is invented by the brain of man, without any commandment of God. Therefore, it is idolatry."[8]

Of course, the conclusion of the syllogism is dependent upon the validity of the major premise, and that premise is a statement of the regulative principle of worship. Therefore, Knox devotes great energy to his proofs for the major premise.

Knox starts his proofs with a reference to Saul's unlawful sacrifice and disobedience, as recorded in I Samuel 13:8-14 and 15:10-35.

> Here is the ground of all his [Saul's] iniquity; and of this proceedeth the causes of his dejection from the kingdom, that he would honor God otherwise than was commanded by his express word. For he, being none of the tribe of Levi ([the tribe] appointed by God's commandment to make sacrifice), usurpeth that office not due to him, which was most high abomination before God, as by the punishment appeareth.
>
> . . . For no honoring knoweth God, nor will accept, without it have the express commmandment of his own Word to be done in all points. And no commandment was given unto the King to make or

---

[6]Knox, *History*, II, 48; *The Works of John Knox* (Ed. by David Laing; Edinburgh: James Thin, 1895), III, 278-79.

[7]Throughout his writings, Knox routinely states his position that the Mass is idolatry. For a few random samples, see *History*, I, 120, II, 18; *Works*, III, 344-45, VI, 170.

[8]Knox, *Works*, III, 34.

offer unto God any manner of sacrifice; which, because he took upon him to do, he and his posterity were deprived from all honors in Israel.[9]   When Saul sought to excuse his behavior, "neither availed his preeminence, the necessity wherein he stood, nor yet his good intent." Thus, we are to learn that none of these excuses will justify our actions if we presume to worship God in a manner not set forth in His Word. It is not valid to plead the dignity of our position, the dire circumstances we find ourselves in, or our ostensibly good motives. "To obey is better than sacrifice" (I Sam. 15:22).

Knox dwells on the fallacious attempt to plead good motives as an excuse for innovation in worship:

Disobedience to God's voice is not only when man doeth wickedly contrary to the precepts of God, but also when of good zeal, or good intent, as we commonly speak man doeth anything to the honor or service of God not commanded by the express Word of God, as in this matter plainly may be espied.[10]

In fact, says Knox, this innovative spirit is of the very essence of idolatry:

And that is principal idolatry when our own inventions we defend to be righteous in the sight of God, because we think them good, laudable, and pleasant. We may not think us so free nor so wise, that we may do unto God, and unto his honor, what we think expedient. No! The contrary is commanded by God, saying, "Unto my Word shall ye add nothing; nothing shall ye diminish therefrom, that ye might observe the precepts of your Lord God" [Deut. 4:2]. Which words are not to be understood of the Decalogue and Law

---

[9]*Ibid.*, III, 35-36.

[10]*Ibid.*, III, 36.

Moral only, but of statutes, rites, and ceremonies; for equal obedience of all his Laws requireth God.[11]

For collaborating testimony to his major premise, Knox cites the case of Nadab and Abihu (Lev. 10:1-3). These two men were punished instantly with death for offering strange fire before the Lord. This incident serves to illustrate that God is highly displeased when men add to His religion. He punishes "the inventor and doers thereof" in order to demonstrate His rejection of their "setting up something to honor God, whereof they had no express commandment."[12]

Knox rejects the contention that the Church has legitimate authority to institute new means to worship God. "It profiteth nothing to say the Kirk hath power to set up, devise, or invent honoring of God, as it thinketh most expedient for the glory of God. This is the continual cry of the Papists, 'The Kirk, the Kirk hath all power; it cannot err. . . .'"[13]

Knox remarks that he could prove the Roman Catholic religion is not the true Church, but he defers that point for the moment. He simply notes that the Church is bound by that rule of the law: "Not that thing which appeareth righteous in thine own eyes, that shall thou do, but what God hath commanded, that observe and keep."[14]

Further, Christ confirmed the same principle, when He said, "My sheep hear my voice, and a stranger they will not hear, but flee from him." To hear His voice means we understand and obey His words; "and to flee from a stranger, is to admit none other doctrine, worshipping, nor honoring God than hath proceeded forth of his own mouth."[15]

---

[11] *Ibid.*, III, 37. *Cf.* Calvin, *Tracts,* I, 128-29; III, 261.

[12] Knox, *Works,* III, 37-38. *Cf.* Calvin, *Tracts,* I, 133, 152-53.

[13] Knox, *Works,* III, 40.

[14] *Ibid.*, III, 40; *cf.* IV, 81.

[15] *Ibid.*, III, 40-41.

Knox derives further support for his argument from a consideration of the kingship of Christ. Since Christ is King, it is His prerogative alone to make laws for His people. No human authority shares in this kingly function. Instead, we must submit, without alteration, to the religious exercises established in His Word.[16]

Later, Knox cites Revelation 2:24, putting emphasis on the words of Christ, "I will put on you no other burden." He poses the question that, if Christ lays upon us no other burden than His revealed Word, at whose instigation do men presume to add to the worship of God?

> O God Eternal! hast thou laid none other burden upon our backs than Jesus Christ laid by his Word? Then who hath burdened us with all these ceremonies, prescribed fasting, compelled chastity, unlawful vows, invocation of saints, and with the idolatry of the Mass? The Devil, the Devil, brethren, invented all these burdens to depress imprudent men to perdition.[17]

With other citations and allusions to Scripture, Knox continues his principal theme: "all which is added to the religion of God, without his own express Word, is idolatry."[18]

Having established his major premise, Knox moves to the next point of his syllogism, to "prove the Mass to be the mere invention of man, set up without all commandment of God."[19]

Knox inveighs against the Papal notion that the Mass is a sacrifice for the sins of the living and the dead. He also explains how, over many centuries, various liturgical elements were progressively brought into the service of the Mass. These elements had no apostolic antiquity or Scriptural warrant. They were man-made additions to worship, which had found their

---

[16] *Ibid.*, III, 41-42.

[17] *Ibid.*, III, 42; cf. IV, 81. Cf. Calvin, *Tracts*, III, 275.

[18] Knox, *Works*, III, 42.

[19] *Ibid.*, III, 47.

way into the service, as it evolved over many years. Knox condemns the innovations of altars, special coverings for the altars, candles, clerical attire, service prayers, and ritual sayings.

Additionally, Knox speaks against the Romish practice of withholding the cup from the laity. He later criticizes the reception of the Lord's Supper in a kneeling posture. And he shows how the words of the Papal service distort the sacrament from its Scriptural institution.

In a manner of rebuke to the priests, Knox says,

> In the Papistical Mass, the congregation getteth nothing except the beholding of your jukings [duckings], noddings, crossings, turning, uplifting, which all are nothing but a diabolical profanation of Christ's supper. Now, juke, cross, and nod as ye list, they are but your own inventions.[20]

Having established his major and minor premises, Knox has easily proven his conclusion, that the Mass is idolatry. Nevertheless, he does not close his discussion yet. In order to underscore his conclusion, he proposes a second syllogism: "All honoring or service of God, whereunto is added a wicked opinion, is abomination. Unto the Mass is added a wicked opinion. Therefore, it is abomination."[21]

With citations from Isaiah 1, 55, 66, Amos 5, Jeremiah 2 and 7, and Hosea 7, Knox shows God's displeasure with sacrifices which are offered with a false idea concerning their function. Even God-given institutions, when they are perverted, may become a stumbling block. Such was the case in the Old Testament, when men wrongly sought to establish their own righteousness by the outward performance of ritual sacrifices. They had distorted the true meaning of those sacrifices, which were designed to point them to the redemption in Christ's atoning work.

---

[20] *Ibid.*, III, 67.

[21] *Ibid.*, III, 52. Similarly, *cf.* Calvin, *Tracts*, I, 167.

Likewise, the Papists completely pervert the meaning of the sacrament of the Lord's Supper. Knox reviews the common Papal opinion that the Mass is a sacrifice which procures the remission of sins. He refutes this opinion by proving Biblically "that remission of sins cometh only of the mere mercy of God, without all deserving of us, or of our work proceding of ourselves; as Isaiah writeth, saying, 'I am he which removeth iniquity, and that for my own sake.'" Yea, Christ has said, "It is finished." It is therefore blasphemous to seek remission of sins from any other supposed sacrifice. Thus, the Mass is "false and vain." Knox establishes this point with additional references to Scripture, and also deals with some Papal evasions which were often used to avoid the force of the argument.[22]

Toward his conclusion, Knox summarizes his attack on the Mass, based on the two syllogisms:

> Consider now, beloved brethren, what hath the fruits of the Mass been, even in her greatest purity. The Mass is nothing but the invention of man, set up without all authority of God's Word, for honoring of God; and therefore it is idolatry. Unto it is added a vain, false, deceivable, and most wicked opinion: that is, that by it is obtained remission of sins; and therefore it is abomination before God. It is contrary unto the Supper of Jesus Christ, and hath taken away both the right use and remembrance thereof, and therefore it is blasphemous to Christ's death.[23]

Knox never retreated from his view that Roman Catholic worship is idolatry. Although the Mass is the preemienent expression of this false worship, Knox does not isolate his comments to the Mass alone. Indeed, he

---

[22]Knox, *Works,* III, 54, 56.

[23]*Ibid.,* III, 69.

contends, "All the glistering ceremonies of the Papists are very dung, and abomination before God."[24]

The entire Romish system is corrupt precisely because it constructs its worship on a faulty foundation: traditions and inventions of human origination. By way of contrast, Knox always stresses the necessity of Scriptural warrant for worship which is acceptable to God:

> And the same we affirm of religion, which, if it be pleasing and acceptable unto God, must have his own commandment approbation for a warrant. Otherwise, it cannot be but odious in his presence, as a thing repugning to his express commandment, saying, "Not that thing which appears good in thy own eyes shall thou do to the Lord thy God, but what the Lord thy God has commanded thee, that do thou: add nothing to it, diminish nothing from it."
>
> By this precept of that eternal God, who is immutable, and that can command nothing but that which is just, are all people, realms, and nations (that will avow themselves to be the inheritance of the Lord) bound and obliged to measure their religion, not by the example of other realms, neither yet by their own good intention, or determination of men, but only by the expressed word of God. So that what therein is commanded, ought to be done by the people of God, what appearance or external show of holiness ever it has. And, therefore, have we most justly rejected the rabble of ceremonies which the Papists held for the chief exercise of their religion, as things having no better ground than the invention and consent of men.[25]

---

[24] *Ibid.*, III, 183, footnote 3; *cf.* IV, 158.

[25] *Ibid.*, VI, 488; *cf.* VI, 498.

Purging Protestant Worship

While Roman Catholics were addicted to their superstitions, they were not the only ones to whom Knox addressed admonitions concerning purity of worship. Several times during his life, Knox was also compelled to issue warnings against the Anglican order of worship.

During the reign of Edward, when Knox was preaching in England, Knox refused a living in a position as an English minister. Knox was called before the Privy Council to account for his behavior. Among the questions posed to Knox was, "If kneeling at the Lord's Table was not indifferent?"[26]

Of course, to kneel upon receiving the Lord's Supper smacks of Popery, as though the recipient is rendering reverence to the elements. In response to the inquiry of the Privy Council, Knox states, "That Christ's action in itself was most perfect, and Christ's action was done without kneeling; that kneeling was man's addition or imagination; that it was most sure to follow the example of Christ, whose action was done sitting and not kneeling."[27]

The Lords of the English Council engaged in a dispute with Knox over this matter. Finally, they concluded that Knox "was not called of any evil mind"; but "they were sorry to know him of a contrary mind to the common Order." Knox answered, "that he was more sorry that a common Order should be contrary to Christ's institution."[28]

The English Order again became the subject of conflict during Knox's pastorate among the English exiles in Frankfort. The congregation had been formed in the summer of 1554. Under its arrangements with the local magistrates, the congregation expressed the desire to call two or three ministers to carry out regular ministrations. Letters were also sent to other Englishmen who were living in Europe, urging them to join with these Protestants in Frankfort.

---

[26] *Ibid.*, III, 86.

[27] *Ibid.*, III, 87.

[28] *Ibid.*, III, 87.

Knox began his ministry in this congregation in the autumn of 1554. A dispute soon arose, when a faction within the Church insisted upon using the English Order in worship. Knox took his stand, saying he would not administer the communion according to the Anglican service. "There were things in it placed," he said, "only by warrant of man's authority, and no ground in God's Word for the same, and had also a long time very superstitiously in the Mass been wickedly abused." Knox said, if they would not allow him to administer the sacrament according to his conscience, he would limit his ministry to preaching, and another minister could administer the sacrament.[29]

The congregation was unable to resolve upon its order of worship, since there was no general consent. Knox, William Whittingham, and others wrote a letter to Calvin; the letter included a summary of the Anglican service, requesting Calvin's judgment of the English Order of worship. The letter contained a rather tame description of various elements in the liturgy. From this listing, the reader can gather what things were part of the dispute: the minister's surplice, appointed lessons, prescribed prayers and fasts, high feasts and holidays, reception of communion in a kneeling posture, allowance for private administration of the Lord's Supper, the use of the sign of the cross in baptism, godfathers making vows in the name of the child at the time of baptism, and the purification of women after childbirth.

The Frankfort congregation passed through two compromise settlements; neither was lasting. The second arrangement was disrupted by the appearance of some new exiles who came to the congregation. Led by Richard Cox, this faction publicly disrupted the Church, by reading the Anglican litany during a worship service, without the prior consent of the congregation.

Knox chided the disrupters, saying, "By the Word of God we must seek the warrant for the establishing of religion, and without that to thrust nothing into any Christian congregation." Knox continues with this rebuke:

---

[29] *Ibid.*, IV, 21.

. . . forasmuch as in the English Book were things both superstitious, unpure, and unperfect (which he offered to prove before all men), he would not consent that of that Church it should be received; and that in case men would go about to burden that free congregation therewith, so oft as he should come in that place (the text offering occasion) he would not fail to speak against it.[30]

Knox further affirmed his view that a slackness to reform religion was one reason why God's anger had been provoked against England.[31]

Cox, and his company, quarrelled and said, "their Church should have an English face." Knox's response was, "The Lord grant it to have the face of Christ's Church, which is the only matter that I sought, God is my record; and therefore I would have had it agreeable in outward rites and ceremonies with Christian Churches reformed."[32]

Through political maneuvering, the Coxian faction was able to gain the upper hand in Frankfort. They got rid of Knox by implicating him with treason before the civil authorities; they asserted that Knox espoused treasonous positions in his *Faithful Admonition to the Professor of God's Truth in England* (1554). Knox was thereafter pressured into leaving Frankfort, and so he returned to Geneva in 1555.

The episode in Frankfort shows Knox's application of the regulative principle to Protestants concerned with the issue of worship. Knox was unwilling to exempt professing Protestants from the same critique he earlier had addressed to Papists. All alike are enjoined to submit their practices to the regulative authority of God's Word.

The issue is not simply a dispute over a few outward ceremonies and forms of worship.[33] Rather, it is a battle between two radically different

---

[30] *Ibid.*, IV, 32-33.

[31] *Ibid.*, III, 33; cf. IV, 161.

[32] *Ibid.*, IV, 42; cf. *History*, I, 110.

[33] Cf. Knox, *Works*, VI, 83-84.

underlying conceptions of worship. One view contains the very seed of idolatry, because it allows men to fashion worship in a manner of their own choosing. The other view seeks jealously to preserve the purity of God's worship, by admitting only those practices established in the Scripture.

Therefore, Knox was compelled to stand firm against "all these dregs of Papistry" which were left in the English Order. They are "diabolical inventions" that he could "never counsel any man to use." In making such statements, Knox realized he would "be judged extreme and rigorous." Nevertheless, he was compelled to follow the rule of God.[34]

The precepts he cited again are from Deuteronomy 4 and 12, which seem ever-present in Knox's consideration of matters of worship. Based upon the commands of Deuteronomy, Knox draws forth a pointed application:

> Stronger reason have I none to give unto you, neither yet to assure my own conscience, when I dissent from the multitude, than is the precept of my God, thus commanding not Israel only, but the whole kirks of the Gentiles, to the end: "Not that thing which appeareth good in thy eyes shall thou do to the Lord thy God, but what the Lord thy God hath commanded thee, that do; add nothing to it, diminish nothing from it," etc. If this was commanded in these ceremonies which did prefigure Christ Jesus, what, think we, God doth require in these mysteries, which exhibit and declare Christ present?[35]

Although Knox was "dissenting from the multitude," he was not alone in his assessment of the Anglican ritual. The Frankfort Church received a letter from John Calvin, who expressed his judgment of the Frankfort dispute.

---

[34] *Ibid.*, IV, 11-12.

[35] *Ibid.*, VI, 83-84.

Calvin's letter begins with a rebuke to the congregation for becoming embroiled in such a quarrel over these matters. Calvin is grieved: "That some of you should be stirring up contentions about forms of prayers and ceremonies, as if you were at ease and in a session of tranquility, and thus throwing an obstacle in the way of your coalescing in one body of worshippers, this is really too unreasonable."

Calvin's appeal for unity, however, does not prompt him to evade the substance of the dispute. He makes it clear that he does not blame those who are unwillingly drawn into controversy, and seek to uphold a just cause. Calvin then offers his opinion of the English order of worship:

> In the Anglican liturgy, such as you describe it to me, I see that there are many silly things that might be tolerated. By this phrase I mean that it did not possess that purity which was to be desired. The faults, however, which could not straightway be corrected on the first day, if there lurked under them no manifest impiety, were to be endured for a time. Thus then it was lawful to begin from such rudiments, but still so that it might be proper for learned, grave, and virtuous ministers of Christ to proceed farther, and prune away unsightly excrescences, and aim at something purer. If undefiled religion had flourished up to this moment in England, there would have been a necessity for having many things corrected for the better, and many others lopped off. Now that, these first beginnings have been destroyed, a church is to be built up by you elsewhere, and you are at liberty to compose anew the form which will seem best adapted for the use and edification of that church, I really know not what those persons would be at, who take delight in the scum and dregs of Papistry.[36]

Elsewhere, Calvin later addressed Cox and his company:

---

[36] *Letters of John Calvin* (ed. by Jules Bonnet; 1858; rpt. New York: Lenox Hill Pub. & Dist. Co., 1972), III, 117-19; *cf.* Knox, *Works,* V, 515.

Verily no man well instructed, or of a sound judgment, will deny (as I think) that lights and crossings, or such like trifles, sprang or issued out of superstition. Whereupon I am persuaded that they which retain these ceremonies in a free choice, when they may otherwise do, they are over-greedy and desirous to drink of the dregs. Neither do I see to what purpose it is to burden the Church with triffling and unprofitable ceremonies--or, as I may term then with their proper name, hurtful and offensive ceremonies, when there is liberty to have a simple and pure order.[37]

Knox, the Regulative Principle, and the Work of Reformation

The regulative principle is not simply a club with which Knox beats his ecclesiastical adversaries. It forms the basis for his entire view of worship. Consequently, when Knox has the opportunity to engage in tasks of Reformation, the regulative principle also provides the foundation for building many public standards of Reformed worship.

After the fiasco in Frankfort, a number of Englishmen moved to Geneva, where an English-speaking congregation was formed. In November of 1556, Knox was elected as a minister in the congregation, joining with Christopher Goodman in the ministry of the Church. The English congregation in Geneva used an order of worship which had originally been drawn up by Knox, William Whittingham, Anthony Gilby, John Foxe, and Thomas Cole. In form, the order follows closely the Genevan Order of John Calvin. The Order of the English Congregation is characterized by great simplicity, and bears definite marks of Knox's influence.

In the Preface to the Genevan English Order, the reader is told:

---

[37] Cited in Knox, *Works*, IV, 59. Knox also speaks of the "unprofitable ceremonies" of the English liturgy, *History*, I, 110 and *Works*, IV, 43.

> We . . . present unto you . . . a form and order of a reformed
> church, limited within the compass of God's Word, which our
> Saviour hath left unto us as only sufficient to govern all our actions
> by; so that whatsoever is added to this Word by man's device, seem
> it never so good, holy, or beautiful, yet before God, which is jealous
> and cannot admit any companion or counsellor, it is evil, wicked,
> and abominable.[38]

Because of the disputes which had erupted over cermonies, the
Preface undertakes a discussion of them. This treatment begins:

> For as ceremonies grounded upon God's Word, and approved in
> the New Testament, are commendable (as the circumstance thereof
> doth support), so those that man hath invented, though he had
> never so good occasion thereunto, if they be once abused, import a
> necessity, hinder God's Word, or be drawn into a superstition,
> without respect ought to be abolished.[39]

The example of the breaking of the brazen serpent (II Ki. 18) is
noted; it demonstrates the necessity of destroying even a God-given
instrument, in a case where it was superstitiously used to foster idolatry.
How much more, then, ought we to take heed against man-made elements
which foster idolatry? Further, God commands that the remnants of false
worship should be utterly purged from among His people (Deut. 12 and 13;
II Ki. 18). Therefore, "take heed, that those things which the Papists and
other idolaters have invented, or else observe as invented by man, may not
enter Christ's Church."[40]

The Preface then relates how three Scriptural practices were
corrupted to become a source of superstition: foot-washing, the Lord's

----

[38] Knox, *Works*, IV, 160-61.

[39] *Ibid.*, IV, 162.

[40] *Ibid.*, IV, 162.

Supper, and circumcision. These three actions were perverted when men conceived and added wrong notions of their meaning.

Having observed the means by which superstition grows, the Genevan Order seeks to avoid these pitfalls. It includes only such elements of worship as may be established by God's Word. Hence, it focuses on the pure preaching of the Word, the sincere administration of the sacraments, prayers, and discipline.

The Preface does not dwell upon preaching, because there was no dispute over the propriety of preaching. It also omits any extensive discussion of the sacraments, since the Order itself adquately treats that topic.

The Preface does discuss the prayers of the Church. It addresses the question of whether prayers should given "in words only, or else with song joined thereunto." With citations of pertinent Scriptural passages (I Cor. 14, Eph. 5, Jam. 5), the Biblical warrant for singing is established. The Psalms are set forth for use in the Church; and we are pointed to "Moses, Hezekiah, Judith, Deborah, Mary, Zechariah, and others, who by songs and metre, rather than in their common speech and prose, gave thanks to God for such comfort as he sent them."[41]

After the Preface, the Book of Order contains a Confession of Faith, which is basically a brief exposition of the Apostles' Creed. The Confession is followed by a section on Church government, in which each main section provides numerous Biblical prooftexts in order to display the warrant for the practices adopted by the congregation.[42]

The Order contains a number of prayers and admonitions for worship, but an explanatory note makes it clear that ministers are not bound in a slavish adherence to the liturgy:

---

[41] *Ibid.*, IV, 164, 166.

[42] *Ibid.*, IV, 169-79.

It shall not be necessary for the Minister daily to repeat all these things before mentioned, but beginning with some manner of Confession, to proceed to the Sermon; which ended, he either useth the prayer for all Estates before mentioned, or else prayeth, as the Spirit of God shall move his heart, framing the same according to the time and matter which he hath intreated of.[43]

With this understanding of the liturgy, the Book of Order contains forms for Baptism, the Lord's Supper, a marriage service, Church discipline, and other ministerial directions. All of these forms are extremely simple, and exclude un-Scriptural ceremonial impositions; each section rests upon many proof-texts, which exhibit the warrant for their place in worship.

Within the services found in the Book of Order, there are several comments which underscore the regulative principle. "The Sacraments are not ordained of God to be used in private corners as charms or sorceries, but left to the Congregation, and necessarily annexed to God's Word as seals of the same." An explanation is included as to the manner in which the Lord's Supper is observed. The explanation concludes with this statement: "without his [Christ's] word and warrant, there is nothing in this holy action attempted."[44]

It is significant that the practice of fasting is mentioned at the end of a section of prayers. Fasting is appropriately observed in times of "plague, famine, pestilence, war, or such like, which be evident tokens of God's wrath." From Biblical examples, we may discern that we are "appointed by the Scriptures to give ourselves to mourning, fasting, and prayer, as the means to turn away God's heavy displeasure."[45]

This treatment of fasting demonstrates the use of a Scriptural example to establish Biblical warrant for a practice in worship. Knox

---

[43] *Ibid.*, IV, 186.

[44] *Ibid.*, IV, 186, 197.

[45] *Ibid.*, IV, 186.

acknowledges this aspect elsewhere in his writings. In some cases, a Scriptural example may function as equivalent to a direct command.

Knox repeatedly argues for simplicitly in the observance of the Lord's Supper, based upon the simplicity of Christ's example. The incident of Nadab and Abihu provides an argument drawn from example in support of the regulative principle, since the text does not contain a direct precept (Lev. 10:1-3).

Knox is careful to note that many examples are extraordinary. Thus, they do not always provide an abiding pattern to be followed. As an illustration, he cites the action of the Israelites in taking the possessions of the Egyptians as spoils when departing from Egypt. Such an example cannot be regulative, unless someone could prove a "like cause, and the like commandment that the Israelites had; and that because their fact repugned to this commandment of God, 'Thou shalt not steal.'"[46]

In a similar vein, Knox criticizes the Papal observance of Lent. The Papists have invented this seasonal observance by a misappropriation of Christ's forty day fast in the wilderness. Knox asserts that Christ's wilderness is *not* setting a pattern to follow in this regard, any more than His miracles provide examples for imitation. In the case of Christ's extraordinary and redemptive ministry, we must not seek an apelike imitation of His actions. In the Great Commission, "Christ Jesus requireth the observation of his precepts and commandments, and not of his actions, except in so far as he hath also comanded them." We cannot follow after Him in "the ministry of our redemption" or His "marvellous works."[47]

When, then, is it appropriate to use an example as warrant for our practice?

Where the example agrees with the law, as it were, the execution of God's judgments expressed in the same, I say that the example

<hr />

[46]Knox, *History*, II, 124-25.

[47]Knox, *Works*, IV, 99-100.

approved of God stands to us in place of a commandment. For, as God of his nature is constant, immutable, so can he not damn in the ages subsequent that which he has approved in his servant before us.[48]

The Scottish Reformation

When Knox was finally able to return to Scotland in 1559, it was to lead in the work of Reformation. First and foremost, the Reformation consisted of a purification of worship. This task was the preeminent work of the Scottish Reformer. He continually sought to cleanse the Church and the nation from the corruptions of false religion.

In his labors, Knox's greatest tool was his fearless preaching of the Word of God. In June 1559, Knox headed toward St. Andrews, planning to preach "for reformation to be made there." When the local Papal bishop heard about these plans, he took measures to stop Knox. The Bishop's design was simple: if Knox presented himself to preach at St. Andrews, Knox should be saluted with a dozen guns, "whereof the most part should light upon his nose."[49]

Fully aware of the "Bishop's good mind" toward him, Knox went ahead with his plans to preach, refusing to be intimidated in the slightest way. Instead, he took as his text selections from Matthew and John, wherein the Scripture describes Jesus' cleansing of the Temple. Knox drew parallels between the corruption in the Temple and the present corruption of Papistry. He noted Christ's actions to stress the responsiblity of reformation by "those to whom God giveth power and zeal thereto." Knox's message was so effective that "the magistrates, the Provist and Bailies, [as well] as the commonalty for the most part, within the town, did agree to remove all monuments of idolatry, which also they did with expedition."

---

[48]Knox, *History*, II, 125.

[49]*Ibid.*, I, 181.

During the process, the Papal priests remained stupefied, "even as dumb as their idols who were burnt in their presence."[50]

This was the pattern of Reformation which became widespread in Scotland. The Word of God was preached in boldness; the people were seriously impressed with their responsiblity to purify their worship and service unto the Lord; public manifestations of corruption were removed.

At first, the Reformation began within the Churches, and had the support of only a small number of persons among the nobility. In order to justify the actions of the Church, the Congregation wrote a letter to the nobility of Scotland, saying, "Whatsoever we have done, the same we have done at God's commandment, who plainly commands idolatry, and all monuments of the same to be destroyed and abolished."[51] Later, as the Reformation gained further momentum, a larger number from the nobility joined the Protestant cause.

In one letter, the Protestant Lords state their duty to "set forth the glory of God, maintain and defend the true preachers of his word; and according to the same, abolish and put away idolatry and false abuses, which may not stand within the said word of God."[52]

Scotland emerged from the struggle as the recipient of a thorough Reformation. Throughout the land, the Papal Mass was abolished, as well as other "monuments of idolatry." The monuments of idolatry included religious images, the ritual trimmings of the Papal ceremonies, ecclesiastical holidays, and other implements of superstition.

Knox describes the conquest of the land with great vigor. "The images were stolen away in all parts of the country; and in Edinburgh was that great idol called St. Giles, first drowned in the North Loch, [and] after burnt, which raised no small trouble in the town." Of course, the Papists did not take too kindly to these activities. "For the Friars rowping [croaking]

---

[50] *Ibid.*, I, 181-82; *Works*, VI, 25.

[51] Knox, *History*, I, 167.

[52] *Ibid.*, I, 194.

like ravens upon the Bishops, the Bishops ran upon the Queen, who to them was favorable enough, but that she thought it could not stand with her advantage to offend such a multitude as then took upon them the defence of the Evangel, and the name Protestants."[53]

Knox describes the reformation of St. Johnston: "the places of idolatry of Gray and Black Friars, and of the charterhouse monks, were made equal with the ground; all monuments of idolatry, that could be apprehended, consumed with fire; and priests commanded, under pain of death, to desist from their blasphemous Mass." An Abbey, twelve miles from St. Andrews, "was reformed, their altars overthrown, their idols, vestments of idolatry, and Mass books, were burnt in their own presence, and they commanded to cast away their monkish [habits]."[54]

In order to build up true religion, a new Confession of Faith (1560) was drawn up. It expounds upon the attributes and works of God, the sinful condition of mankind, the incarnation and redemptive work of Christ, the nature of salvation, sanctification, the Church, the Scriptures, the sacraments, and other vital topics. Of course, there was always the preaching of the Word to instruct the people in the true faith. Preaching is the primary task of the gospel minister, and it was the principal means used to promote pure worship.

Along with the Confession of Faith, a Book of Discipline was produced for use within the realm of Scotland. This book was written by Knox and several others. Although this book was not ratified by the civil authorities, it demonstrates the forward-looking vision of the proponents of the Scottish Reformation. It shows that their zeal to foster true religion could produce a systematic plan designed to maintain purity of worship and godly manners. The Book contains measures to promote true preaching, proper administration of the sacraments, and the removal of idolatry. It has programs to support Protestant ministers and ecclesiastical discipline, plus

---

[53] *Ibid.*, I, 125.

[54] Knox, *Works,* VI, 23, 26.

an extensive plan of Church government. To spread the knowledge of the truth, the Book calls for the establishment of schools and universities.[55]

Unlike the iconoclasts of the eighth century, the Reformers had something substantive to replace the corruptions of the past. The dead idols of Popery were replaced by the living Word of God, as true knowledge and pure worship began to flourish.

What was the foundation on which this extensive reform was built? The bedrock of the Scottish Reformation was the restoration of pure worship. And the tool which extensively built the structure of this restoration was the regulative principle.

In the Explication of the First Head of Doctrine, the Book of Discipline asserts the regulative authority of Scripture, and also adds some pointed applications:

> By preaching of the Evangel, we understand not only the Scriptures of the New Testament, but also of the Old; to wit, the Law, the Prophets, and Histories, in which Christ Jesus is no less contained in figure, than we have Him now expressed in verity. And, therefore, with the Apostle, we affirm that "All Scripture inspired of God is profitable to instruct, to reprove, and to exhort." In which Books of Old and New Testaments we affirm that all things necessary for the instruction of the Kirk, and to make the man of God perfect, are contained and sufficiently expressed.
>
> By the contrary Doctrine, we understand whatsoever men, by Laws, Councils, or Constitutions have imposed upon the consciences of men, without the expressed commandment of God's word: such as be vows of chastity, foreswearing of marriage, binding of men and women to several and disguised apparels, to the superstitious observation of fasting days, difference of meat for conscience sake, prayer for the dead; and keeping of holy days of certain Saints commanded by man, such as be all those that the Papists have

---

[55]Knox, *History*, I, 343; II, 280-325.

invented, as the Feasts (as they term them) of Apostles, Martyrs,
Virgins, of Christmas, Circumcision, Epiphany, Purification, and
other fond feasts of our Lady. Which things, because in God's
scriptures they neither have commandment nor assurance, we judge
them utterly to be abolished from this Realm; affirming further, that
the obstinate maintainers and teachers of such abominations ought
not to escape the punishment of the Civil Magistrate.[56]

With this concern for purity of worship, it is no wonder that the
Scottish Reformation was the most thorough among any of the Protestant
nations. Knox lauds this fact: "in how great purity God did establish
amongst us his true religion, as well in doctrine as in ceremonies!" Knox
extols God's work among the Scots.

For, as touching the doctrine taught by our ministers, and as
touching the administration of Sacraments used in our Churches, we
are bold to affirm that there is no realm this day upon the face of
the earth, that hath them in greater purity; yea (we must speak the
truth whomsoever we offend), there is none (no realm, we mean)

---

[56] *Ibid.*, II, 281. With the Scottish Reformation, there was a uniform rejection of all
ecclesiastical holidays (other than the Lord's Day). In Book V of *The History of the
Reformation in Scotland,* Knox's continuator writes: "in the keeping of some Festival days our
Church assented not, for only the Sabbath-day was kept in Scotland." (*History,* II, 90).

In one interesting episode, Beza wrote to Knox to seek Scottish approval of the
Second Helvetic Confession (1566). The General Assembly responded with a letter happily to
express their general approval. Nevertheless, the Scots could "scarcely refrain from mentioning,
with regard to what is written in the 24th chapter of the aforesaid Confession concerning 'the
festival of our Lord's nativity, circumcision, passion, resurrection, ascension, and sending of the
Holy Ghost upon his disciples,' that these festivals at the present time obtain no place among
us; for we dare not religiously celebrate any other feast-day than what the divine oracles have
prescribed." (Knox, *Works,* VI, 547-48. The letter to Beza is dated 4 September 1566, and is
signed by ministers from throughout Scotland, including Knox.)

In another place, Knox refers to "that day which men call Good Friday," thereby
indicating his disapproval of the significance attached to the day (*Works,* VI, 140).

that hath them in the like purity. For all others (how sincere that ever the doctrine be, that by some is taught), retain in their Churches, and the ministers thereof, some footsteps of Antichrist, and some dregs of papistry; but we (all praise to God alone) have nothing within our Churches that ever flowed from that Man of Sin.[57]

In these last comments, Knox points out an extremely important concept in the work of reformation. It is not simply a Reformed doctrinal statement that constitutes a Reformed Church. Rather, the litmus test is whether these Reformed principles are applied to achieve purity in worship. The corporate worship of a Church is the most truthful indicator of its spiritual condition.

One other Reformation document deserves attention as we explore Knox's presentation on worship. It is the Order of the General Fast, which was composed by Knox and John Craig at the direction of the General Assembly in 1565.

Unlike the Papists, the Reformed Church did not keep set days on the calendar for fasting. Rather, a fast would be called when circumstances made it appropriate. In other words, as the Church is directed by providence, a fast may be observed. This procedure mirrors Biblical *examples*, and thus illustrates how certain examples from the Bible may provide a regulative guide in worship.

When the Order of the General Fast was reprinted in 1574, a supplemental statement notes: "Our public fasting and humilation is not bound to man's command precisely, nor to old customs, as the Papists use their ceremonies; but as God visits us, so in that manner we seek him as he teacheth us and giveth us examples in his most holy Word. . . ."[58] Several

---

[57]Knox, *History*, II, 3.

[58]Knox, *Works*, VI, 428.

cases for a public fast are given: times of pestilence, famine, and general impiety.

Preserving the Reformation

In the closing years of his life, Knox fought many battles to guard against civil encroachments which threatened the purity of worship. After Mary Queen of Scots arrived in Scotland, to assume her rule in 1561, she sought many ways to undermine the Reformation. Mary was a Papist, yet she now ruled over a Protestant nation. Knox frequently exhorted the nobility to check the designs of the Queen. In this context, Knox made many statements relative to the maintenance of undefiled worship.

Soon after her return to Scotland, Mary reinstituted the Mass by having it observed privately in her chapel. This action caused a furor among the Protestant nobility. The question was posed, "Shall that idol be suffered again to take place within this realm?" Certain gentlemen adamantly cried, "The idolater priest should die the death," according to the Law of God.[59] Despite the uproar, tolerance won the day, and the Queen was allowed to observe the Mass.

Knox did not sit still in this situation. From the pulpit, he thundered against idolatry. He stated that one Mass "was more fearful to him than if ten thousand armed enemies were landed in any part of the realm, of purpose to suppress the whole religion." Knox's rationale was based upon the primacy of worship. "In our God there is strength to resist and confound multitudes," he said; "but when we join hands with idolatry, it is no doubt that both God's amicable presence and comfortable defence leaveth us, and what shall become of us?"[60]

During the ensuing controversy, Knox became engaged in many discussions on the removal of idolatry. Whose responsibility is it to take

---

[59]Knox, *History*, II, 8.

[60]*Ibid.*, II, 9.

direct action against idolatrous practices? How should various individuals respond to manifest corruption of religion?

The basic principle underlying Knox's position is that every man is responsible to suppress idolatry, according to his means and station in life.

> The punishment of such crimes as are idolatry, blasphemy, and others that touch the Majesty of God, doth not appertain to kings and chief rulers only, but also to the whole body of that people, and to every member of the same, according to the vocation of every man, and according to that possibility and occasion which God doth minister to revenge the injury done against his glory, what time that impiety is manifestly known.[61]

Over the course of his writings, Knox delineates the responsibilities of each class among the people.

The general population, those who hold no civil authority or ecclesiastical office, are not exempt from actively opposing idolatry. They have definite responsibilities, depending on their circumstances. In times of national apostasy and corruption, the private citizen must personally abstain from idolatry and participation in religious corruption. Godly examples are provided in the Bible to demonstrate this truth: notably, Daniel, Shadrach, Meshach, and Abed-Nego. Many New Testament admonitions also fit within this category (see I Cor. 10).[62]

When it is within the power of the general population to suppress idolatry, they must exert their energies to do so. Based upon Deuteronomy 12, 13, and 27, Knox illustrates that God holds the nation corporately responsible to keep the realm free from idolatry. A Reformed nation is one which has been brought out of spiritual bondage and is under obligations to keep God's Law. Therefore, it is the duty of "the people assembled together

---

[61] Knox, *Works,* IV, 498-99; *cf.* V, 516-17.

[62] *Ibid.,* III, 194, 325.

in one body of a Commonwealth, unto whom God has given sufficient force, not only to resist, but also to suppress all kind of open idolatry: and such a people yet again I affirm, are bound to keep their land clean and unpolluted."[63]

In Knox's *First Blast of the Trumpet*, he asserts the duty of magistrates to uphold *both* tables of the Law. Therefore, the King must (1) know the law; (2) punish vice, as it is manifest in violations of the second table of the Law; (3) punish *vice*, as it is manifest in violations of the first table of the Law--offenses "as openly impugn the glory of God, as idolatry, blasphemy, and manifest heresy, taught and obstinately maintained"; and (4) destroy monuments of idolatry.[64]

In his view of first table violations, Knox reveals a significant understanding of the nature of false religion. Religious deviation is not merely an academic matter. It is a form of *moral corruption* to adhere to false worship, or to advocate wrong opinions about God. How this principle needs to be reasserted today! People may readily see that adultery, murder, and lying are immoral. But how seldom do men perceive that false religion is *immoral* in God's sight--a seriously evil offense.

Since Knox advocates the punishment of idolaters, the question naturally follows, "What then? Shall we go and slay all idolaters?" Such is not the responsibility of the private citizen, says Knox. Rather, that is "the office of every civil magistrate within his realm."[65]

In Scotland, however, a unique situation existed with the tension between the Protestant nobility and a Queen who was a Papist. In order to keep the land undefiled, it was the duty of the nobility to restrain the wicked designs of the Queen.[66] Meanwhile, Knox sometimes spoke of God's extraordinary means of deliverance from oppressive and tyrannical idolaters.

---

[63] *Ibid.*, IV, 498-99; *History*, II, 120-22.

[64] Knox, *Works*, IV, 398-99; *cf.* IV, 83.

[65] *Ibid.*, III, 94; *cf.* IV, 490.

[66] *Ibid.*, IV, 497-98.

During Bloody Mary's reign in England, Knox had cried, "God, for his great mercy's sake, stir up some Phineas, Elijah, or Jehu, that the blood of abominable idolaters may pacify God's wrath, that it consume not the whole multitude."[67]

Thus, opposition to idolatry must come from various quarters. The average citizen must abstain from idolatry in all cases, and pressure those in authority to suppress public idolatry. Rulers should carry out God's Law within their jurisdictions; they must also restrain corrupting influences from higher authorities. The highest authorities should act as foster-fathers and nursing mothers to the Church (Is. 49:23), and take the lead in protecting the realm from influences which seek to corrupt the nation.

Of course, the chief defenders against idolatry must be preachers and other Church officers. According to a man's vocation, he must oppose the corruption of worship. The preacher's vocation is to strip the vestiges of idolatry from men's hearts. He must then exhort every man to perform his duty. If the preachers become negligent, it has a devasting effect upon the nations.

Incredible as it may seem, Knox confesses his remorse for shirking his responsibility when Mary reinstituted the Mass in Scotland. Knox chides himself for not being "more vehement and upright in the suppressing of that idol in the beginning."[68] Knox states his sin of omission:

> Albeit that I spake that which offende some . . ., yet did I not that which I might have done; for God had not only given unto me knowledge and tongue to make the impiety of that idol known unto this realm, but he had given unto me credit with many, who would

---

[67] *Ibid.*, III, 309; cf. 247.

[68] Knox, *History*, I, 13. In commenting on his lack of zeal, Knox writes: "Men delighting to swim betwixt two waters have often complaine upon my severity--fearing, as it seemed, that the same should trouble the quietness of brethren. But I do fear, that that which with men term lenity and dulceness [sweetness] do bring upon themselves and others more fearful destruction, than yet hath ensured the vehemency of any preacher within this realm" (*Works*, VI, 131).

have put into execution God's judgments, if I would only have consented thereto. But so careful was I of that common tranquility, and so loth was I to have offended those of whom I had conceived a good opinion, that in secret conference with earnest and zealous men, I travailed rather to mitigate, yea, to slaken, that fervency that God had kindled in others, than to animate or encourage them to put their hands to the Lord's work. Whereintill I unfeignedly acknowledge myself to have done most wickedly. . . . [69]

The tolerance shown toward the Queen's Mass led to a more brazen display of her idolaltry. The Queen began to travel amongst the nobility, massing all the way. Knox began to pray in public in the following manner: "Deliver us, O Lord, from the bondage of idolatry"; and "continue us in quietness and concord amongst ourselves, if thy good pleasure be, O Lord, for a season."

Knox was asked by some associates why he prayed for quietness only for a season, instead of entreating God to preserve quietness absolutely. Knox responded to those inquiries, "That he durst not pray but in faith; and faith in God's word assured him that constant quietness could not continue in that Realm where idolatry had been suppressed and then was permitted to be erected again."[70]

Conflict over these religious matters continued in Scotland until the Queen was deposed in 1567. Knox also passed from the scene shortly after, dying in 1572. He left behind a nation which would never be the same, as a result of his tireless reforming efforts.

The Legacy of John Knox

The legacy of John Knox was passed on to subsequent generations within Presbyterianism. Because of their firm resolve on the purity of

---

[69] Knox, *History*, II, 13.

[70] *Ibid.*, II, 85.

worship, the Scots were able to withstand several critical assaults upon the worship and government of the Church.

During the seventeenth century, tensions persisted in the Scottish Church because of attempts to impose an Anglican order upon the Scots. The Church of England had never been purged of many liturgical superstitions which were carried over from Roman Catholicism. When the Anglican rituals were obtruded on the Scottish Church, militant opposition arose among the Scots.

One spokesman for the Scottish cause was George Gillespie (1613-49). He wrote a definitive response to the advocates of the Anglican order. Gillespie was a premier theologian, and later served as a Scottish Commissioner to the Westminster Assembly. In 1637, Gillespie's book on the liturgical controversy was published: *A Dispute Against the English-Popish Ceremonies, Obtruded upon the Church of Scotland.*

Gillespie's work contains a four-fold assault upon the ceremonies in general. First, he argues against their necessity; second, he dispels notions that they are expedient; third, he demonstrates their unlawfulness; and fourth, he shows they are not indifferent. In each section, he draws applications of general principles to specific ceremonies which he finds objectionable. Specifically, he disputes the propriety of kneeling in the act of receiving the Lord's Supper, the use of the sign of the cross in Baptism, confirmation, the surplice, and ecclesiastical holidays.

During his discussion on the unlawfulness of the ceremonies, Gillispie cites Knox to demonstrate the regulative principle of worship. Gillespie notes Knox's dispute with the abbot of St. Andrews, and refers to Knox's appeal to Deuteronomy 4.[71]

Later, Gillespie mentions the import of the Second Commandment to the discussion. Says Gillespie, "The Christian Church hath no more liberty to add to the commandments of God than the Jewish Church had. For the second commandment is moral and perpetual, and forbiddeth to us as well as to them the additions and inventions of men in the worship of

---

[71] See the first three pages of this essay; Gillespie, Part III, 87-88.

God." Gillespie then quotes a passage from Knox, wherein Knox shows how God punishes all who alter or change His ceremonies and statutes. Knox illustrates the point with Saul, Uzziah, and Nadab and Abihu (I Sam. 13 and 15; II Chron. 26; Lev. 10). The quotation closes with Knox's reference to Deuteronomy.[72]

It is interesting to note how the same thoughts are brought together in the Westminster Standards. Of course, Gillespie served in the Assembly, where he played a prominent role. This fact only reinforces the impact of Knox's thought upon the Confessional Standards, since Gillespie consciously drew upon it.

The Confession gives close attention to the distinction between true and false worship. Article I of the twenty-first chapter states:

> . . . the acceptable way of worshipping the true God is instituted by himself, and so limited to his own revealed will, that he may not be worshipped according to the imaginations and devices of men, or the suggestions of Satan, under any visible representation, or any other way not prescribed in the holy Scripture.[73]

The proof-texts offered for this article include Deuteronomy 12:32; Matthew 15:9; Acts 17:25; Matthew 4:9-10; Exodus 20:4-6 (the Second Commandment); and Colossians 2:23.

Similarly, the Larger Catechism deals with purity of worship. Answer #108 lists among the "duties required in the second commandment" the need for "disapproving, detesting, opposing all false worship; and, according to each one's place and calling, removing it, and all monuments of idolatry." Among the proof-texts are Deuteronomy 7:5 and Isaiah 30:22.[74]

---

[72]Gillespie, Part III, 118. The reference to Knox is found in his "Letter to the Regent of Scotland."

[73]Consult any standard edition of the Westminster Confession and Catechism.

[74]*Cf.* Knox's views in his *First Blast of the Trumpet*, as discussed above.

Likewise, Answer #109 states that the "sins forbidden in the second commandment" include "using and any wise approving, any religious worship not instituted by God himself." It also forbids "all superstitious devices, corrupting the worship of God, adding to it, or taking from it, whether invented and taken up of ourselves, or received by tradition from others, though under the title of antiquity, custom, devotion, good intent, or any other pretence whatsoever." The proof-texts for these assertions are taken from I Kings 11:33; 12:33; Deuteronomy 12:30-32; Deuteronomy 4:2; Psalm 106:39; Matthew 15:9; I Samuel 13:11-12; 15:21; as well as others.

The conformity of the Confessional Standards with Knox's earlier expression on worship is striking. It as though Knox's thought formed the blueprint with which the builders constructed the Standards, using Knox's design and adding a few kindred thoughts to serve as embellishments for the finished structure.

Conclusions

The example of Knox stands as a sharp reprimand to Christians in the present day. It points to our need to think about worship. We need to contemplate the grounds of our religous activities. Many areas of contemporary worship need to come under the scrutiny of the Word of God.

The Church needs to reaffirm the regulative principle of worship. Nothing should be admitted into the worship of God, unless it possesses a clear Scriptural warrant. This principle is merely an extension of the *sola scriptura* perspective of Protestant theology, as applied to the realm of worship. Anything less is a violation of the demands of the living God, who says, "You shall not add to the word which I command you, nor take anything from it, that you may keep the commandments of the Lord your God which I command you." "Whatever I command you, be careful to observe it; you shall not add to it nor take away from it" (Deut. 4:2; 12:32).

It follows from this principle that the Church has some serious housecleaning to do. Protestant Churches are presently full of un-Scriptural devices which have corrupted the worship of God. The struggle between the Bride of Christ and Antichrist has never ceased; there are many Papal institutions which have sought entrance into Protestant Churches. Away with such baggage from Rome! For example cast out those graven images. Let's get specific: we should rid the Church of all graven images, including those 'pictures of Christ' which are found in the foyer and children's Sunday School literature. Further, we should have no "holy days" but the Lord's Day; that means that saints' days, Christmas, Easter, etc., must all be banished from the practice of those who would please God.

In addition to the corruptions of Rome, Protestants have added a few of their own over the past two or three centuries. For example, a neglect of the proper use of the sacraments has given rise to a number of 'false sacraments'--that is, to many practices which have come to serve as 'sealing ordinances,' but which have no warrant from the Word of God. The altar call constitutes such a false sacrament; it serves to confirm religious professions of faith, and it is used to provide assurance to the adherents of modern 'evangelicalism.' Its function is quite similar to the false sacraments of Roman Catholicism; and in each case, the false practices are reflective of Pelagian notions of salvation. May we work for the elimination of altar calls, and other manipulative techniques which have no Scriptural sanction.

Let us also purge out the many hymns of dubious origin, and those 'hokey' songs that help spread false doctrines.

These are merely suggestions of some places to begin. There are multitudes of other things which have inappropriately found a place in the Church. May we pledge ourselves, before God, to unceasing labor, until we have cleansed the temple of God from all the modern monuments of idolatry.

In this vein, the officers of the Church have a special duty to carry out the work of Reformation. We may not live to see idolatry entirely eradicated from our society; but it can be removed from within the walls of the Church. It is the province of Church officers to perform this task in all matters under their jurisdiction. Church officers: awaken to your responsibilities. One day you must render an account for how well you have discharged your responsibilities.

In addition to purging the Church of false worship, there is a need to promote elements of true worship which will glorify God and edify the people. The Westminster Confession mentions such elements: prayer, the reading of the Scriptures, sound preaching, singing of psalms, and the proper adminstration of the sacraments (see chapter XXI.5). In contemporary Churches, these things are often obscured: prayer meetings have turned into occasions for mere social gatherings; the reading of the Scriptures and the preaching are often performed in a sullen and drab manner; Scriptural songs, in praise of God, have virtually disappeared, in deference to flippant ditties which ooze with subjective effervescence; and the sacraments, when they are observed, are treated as a mere appendage to the 'regular' service. Further, the entire exercise exhibits a lack of reverence toward our Redeemer King. How tragic! The Church has spurned the precious ordinances of God.

It is time to rebuild the walls of Zion. Typically, a fascination with religious ceremonies is an indication of a decline in gospel preaching. Conversely, sound preaching is a powerful instrument in the cause of Reformation. Pastors need to confront their congregations with lively preaching; and Church members need to approach the services in a prepared and attentive manner. The Scriptures must be read with a recognition that they are the very oracles of God. Church members must come together to render adoration to the Lord, not simply to see what benefits they can extract from religious observances.

The sacraments need to be given their proper place in the worship of God. As visible signs and seals, they were given to aid our infirmities; hence, we cannot dispense with them. They should be observed regularly and reverently, and in a simple manner, according to their Scriptural design. We should seek no other outward ceremonial symbols to stir up our faith. The yearning for other outward rites and ceremonies is usually a sign of a defective view of the sacraments.

These elements are part of the ordinary worship of God. But what about the extraordinary? For example, when was the last time your church had a congregational fast to implore God's mercies upon His people and our nation? The desperate condition of both the Church and the nation would seem to provide an indication that such religious exercises are in order.

Finally, it is important to realize the primacy of pure worship.

On the individual level, there is nothing more important. Knox saw that human innovation in worship is the very seed of idolatry. He took it very seriously because idolatry "separateth man altogether from God."[75] A pastoral concern for the souls of men fueled Knox's opposition to corrupt worship.

In the modern pluralistic age, the Church has lost a sense of *the immorality of false worship*. False religious opinions and practices are not simply academic differences; they are a form of moral corruption which destroys the souls of men. This truth should provide the Church with a sense of urgency as it confronts men in their false worship.

The primacy of worship also has tremendous ramifications on the corporate level. Today in America, there are many cries for a 'new Reformation.' Yet, these calls often come from groups which have no conception of the priority of worship.

A new Reformation cannot be based upon an attempt to preserve a social structure or a cultural way of life. The Scottish Reformation was preeminently a struggle over worship. Certainly, it had social and political ramifications; and those who seek to divorce religion from social and political life are being naive. But, likewise, it is folly to seek to 'reform' America without a primary emphasis on worship.

Frequently, the new social reformers join hands with Papists, Pelagians, Mormons, and others, in an attempt to save our nation. Yet, God's blessings are to be found when His people seek refuge in Him--not when they can construct a coalition from among the various factions of religious idolaters in the land. To think otherwise is to miss the main point of the Scottish Reformation.

While Knox would share the abhorrence for the general lawlessness in our society, it is doubtful if he would approve of the selective emphases

---

[75] Knox, *Works*, V, 487.

of the modern social reformers. These contemporary cultural reformers wax eloquent in their denunciation of certain forms of lawlessness: homosexuality, adultery, government theft by taxation, and federal intrusions into family life. It is very popular to denounce these practices. Yet, our modern social critics are strangely silent when it comes to violators of the first table of God's law, such as idolaters (including Papists, Pelagians, Mormons, etc.) and Sabbath-breakers. Says Knox,

> But vain it is to crave reformation in manners, where the religion is corrupted. For like as a man cannot do the office of a man, except first he have a being or a life, so to work works pleasant in the sight of God the Father can no man do without the Spirit of the Lord Jesus, which doth not abide in the hearts of idolaters.[76]

In closing, let us hear the words of John Knox, who calls us to that preeminent concern for true worship:

> The matter is not of so small importance, as some suppose. The question is, whether God or man ought to be obeyed in matters of religion? In mouth, all do confess that God is only worthy of sovereignty. But after that many--by the instigation of the devil, and by the presumptuous arrogance of carnal wisdom, and worldly policy--have defaced God's holy ordinance, men fear not to follow what laws and common consent (mother to all mischief, and nurse most favorable to superstition) hath established and commanded. But thus continually I can do nothing but hold, and affirm all things polluted, yea, execrable and accursed, which God by his Word hath not sanctified in his religion. God grant you his Holy Spirit rightly to judge.[77]

---

[76] *Ibid.*, VI, 81.

[77] *Ibid.*, VI, 14.

19 - 'The Acceptable Way of Worshipping the True God'[1]: Recent Writings on Worship of Particular Interest to Reformed Christians

Thomas G. Reid, Jr.

The "information explosion" has not left the subject of worship unaffected. Reformed Christians face a mound of material published just since the mid-1970's. This essay will, therefore, only be able to highlight some of the literature in the field. Following an overview of general works on worship, historical studies will be reviewed, and then each of the elements of worship -- as recognized by the Westminster Confession of Faith -- will be discussed in turn.

General Works

Theological liberals have been busy during this period, with Abingdon Press seeming to lead the way. Three trends should be noted. First, the desire of liberals for "non-sexist" language in worship has provoked *An Inclusive Language Lectionary* (New York: National Council of Churches, 1982: *Readings for Year A*; 1984: *Readings for Year B*, and 1985: *Readings for Year C)*. Second, another kind of freedom is sought through liberation theology: Rafael Avila attempts to reformulate the Roman Catholic understanding of the Eucharist in terms of the class struggle (*Worship and Politics,* Maryknoll, NY: Orbis, 1981).

---

[1]Westminster Confession of Faith XXI. 1.

Third, to add some sparkle to dull worship, liturgical dance is being introduced. Perhaps the most definitive recent work is by John Gordon Davies: *Liturgical Dance: An Historical, Theological and Practical Handbook* (London: SCM, 1984). This kind of chic novelty has been effectively countered by Brian H. Edwards in *Shall We Dance?* (Welwyn: Evangelical Press, 1984), and John Marshall in "Dance and Drama in Worship and Evangelism: A Contemporary Problem" (*The Banner of Truth* n. 178, July 1978, pp. 19-29).

For an overview of worship in modern Pentecostal churches, turn to *Pentecostal Worship*, edited by Cecil B. Knight (Cleveland, TN: Pathway Press, 1974).[2]

Evangelicals have been busy writing too. General works in this tradition include (in chronological order): Paul W. Wohlgemuth, *Rethinking Church Music* (Chicago: Moody Press, 1973; revised edition, Carol Stream, IL: Hope, 1981); James L. Christensen, *Don't Waste Your Time in Worship* (Old Tappan, NJ: Revell, 1978)[3]; Kenneth W. Osbeck, *Singing with Understanding, including 101 Favorite Hymn Backgrounds* (Grand Rapids: Kregel, 1979); Donald P. Hustad, *Jubilate! Church Music in the Evangelical Tradition* (Carol Stream, IL: Hope, 1981)[4]; Derek Prime, *Created to Praise* (Downer's Grove, IL: Inter-Varsity Press, 1981); Ronald Allen and Gordon Borror, *Worship: Rediscovering the Missing Jewel* (Portland, OR: Multnomah Books, 1982); John MacArthur, *The Ultimate Priority: John MacArthur, Jr., on Worship* (Chicago: Moody Press, 1983); A.W. Tozer, *Whatever Happened to Worship?* (Camp Hill, PA: Christian Publications, 1985); Robert Berglund, *A Philosophy of Church Music* (Chicago: Moody Press, 1985); and Warren W. Wiersbe, *Real Worship: It Will Transform Your Life* (Nashville: Thomas Nelson, 1986).

---

[2]Reformed believers will be interested to read that "Recently, the singing of Psalms directly from the Bible has begun to enjoy a new acceptance and popularity among Pentecostal worshipers, particularly among the youth" (p. 68).

[3]Christensen avers: "Many Protestant services which I have attended have been little more than promotion rallies or soapbox stands for egocentric preachers and musicians" (p. 38).

[4]His principles rise no higher than this: "Church music should be approached as a functional art" (p. 4).

Ralph P. Martin, who earlier wrote a speculative work on *Worship in the Early Church* (Grand Rapids: Eerdmans, 1964; revised edition Grand Rapids: Eerdmans, 1974), considered more broadly *The Worship of God: Some Theological, Pastoral, and Practical Reflections* (Grand Rapids: Eerdmans, 1982). Martin's discussions of singing in worship builds on his earlier "New Testament songs" speculations (pp. 51-53).

Some evangelicals have had enough of vapid gospel ditties and clown preachers. Robert Webber of Wheaton College looks to the rediscovery of Liturgy (with a capital L) to lead the people of God out of the wilderness of free form worship, first in *Worship Old and New* (Grand Rapids: Zondervan, 1982), then by *Worship is a Verb* (Waco, TX: Word, 1985) and *In Heart and Home: A Woman's Workbook on Worship* (Grand Rapids: Zondervan, 1985), and still further by *Evangelicals on the Canterbury Trail: Why Evangelicals are Attracted to the Liturgical Church* (Waco, TX: Word, 1985). A good dose of the regulative principle of worship would have spared us all this non-solution. Thomas Howard, then of Gordon College, had a similar vision. First, *The Liturgy Explained* (Witton, CT: Morehouse-Barlow, 1981) came from his pen. Then Howard claimed that *Evangelical is Not Enough* (Nashville, TN: Nelson, 1984). Next, he converted to Roman Catholicism, a warning to those attracted by the worship of the Liturgical churches.

The award for "what-might-have-been" goes to *O Come Let Us Worship: Corporate Worship in the Evangelical Church* (Grand Rapids: Baker, 1980), by the late Robert G. Rayburn, President of Covenant Theological Seminary. Instead of penning a Reformed book on worship, he wrote "for all evangelicals" (p. 8). While what follows may have its high points, one wonders about a Presbyterian seminary professor who mistakenly writes that the Westminster Confession advocates singing hymns in worship when it speaks of "singing of psalms" (pp. 94-95), and can praise to the heavens Isaac Watts (p. 223), whose influence on Reformed worship has been catastrophic.

From the Reformed Baptist perspective comes Pastor Herbert Carson's *Hallelujah! Christian Worship* (Welwyn: Evangelical Press, 1980). He states that "the governing principle is still the same as in the Old

Testament, in that the Word of God is the standard by which every practice is to be assessed" (p. 21); the looseness of this basic premise is worked out to predictable results. The title of Robert Morey's *Worship Is All of Life* (Camp Hill, PA: Christian Publications, 1984), shows what he thinks: everything is worship. Which means that nothing is worship! Better but briefer are three articles by prominent Reformed Baptists. Geoffrey Thomas in "The Nature of True Worship" (*The Banner of Truth* n. 153, June 1976, pp. 1-3) gives ten pithy descriptions of worship. Erroll Hulse writes of the "Reformation of the Public Worship of God: A Plea for God-centered, Vertical, Structured Worship" (*Reformation Today* n. 70, Nov.-Dec. 1982, pp. 3-9). He observes that "the regulative principle liberates because it frees God's people from innovations" (p. 4), and that musical concerts, "films, videos, protracted testimonies, descriptions of experiences, slide shows, travelogues, narrations of missionary service, and biographies have their place, but not in worship" (pp. 7-8). The creative illustrations are particularly noteworthy. Daniel E. Wray argues eight reasons for "The Importance of Worship" in *The Banner of Truth* (n. 253, Oct. 1984, pp. 1-5).

Presbyterian Worship: Its Meaning and Method by Donald Macleod (Richmond, VA: John Knox, 1965; revised edition 1981) has little of note to offer. Hughes Oliphant Old writes more helpfully of *Worship that is Reformed according to Scripture* (Richmond, VA: John Knox, 1984), with an extensive bibliography. Still, "Reformed worship" is defined as worship "according to Scripture", which he hastens to add is not "Bible-thumping literalism" but using the Word as a general guide (p. 3). So it is not surprizing that Dr. Old judges exclusive psalmody as "extreme" (p. 55), although admitting that exclusive hymnody is as well!

Other attempts at discussing Reformed worship abound. David Peterson attempts to develop a New Testament theology of worship out of the Epistle to the Hebrews ("Towards a New Testament Theology of Worship", *Reformed Theological Review* 43:3, Sept.-Dec. 1984, pp. 65-73), concluding that "Hebrews does not apply the language of worship specifically to what goes on when Christians meet together" (p. 72). E. Glenn Hinson's "Reassessing the Puritan Heritage in Worship and Spirituality: A Search for a Method" (*Worship* 53:4, July 1979, pp. 318-326) eventually concludes that the Puritan's main concern was for heart worship, that their arguments for simple, spiritual worship were invalid, and that Reformed worship needs to be liturgicized. *Discovering the Fulness of Worship* by Paul E. Engle (Philadelphia: Great Commission Publications, 1978) discusses the worship of the Old and New Covenants, and then the history of Christian worship. It is surprizing that the Reformation is discussed without any mention of the Reformed confessions, catechisms, or directories for worship. Engle has also since produced a *Worship Planbook: A Manual for Worship Leaders* (Philadelphia: Great Commission Publications, 1981), which is very practical, but shows a love of liturgy and reviews four hymnals but no psalter.

An attempt to teach a Presbyterian congregation more about its heritage in worship was conducted by James L. Shull as a Doctor of Ministry project at Reformed Theological Seminary in Jackson, Mississippi: *Equipping Members of North Park Presbyterian Church for Biblical and Meaningful Worship through Education* (1985). A three month course attempted to teach "the Reformed distinctives of worship" (p. 2), but it is difficult to determine the content of this course, and the regulative principle, while mentioned (pp. 15-16), is thereafter dropped. Similarly, Peter Toon wants to help Anglicans in *Knowing God through the Liturgy* (Bramscote: Grove Books, 1975), a very practical guide. A general discussion that could have gone much farther is offered by William Edgar in his *In Spirit and in Truth: Ten Bible Studies on Worship* (Downers Grove, IL: Inter-Varsity Press, 1976). The same observation can be made of Edmund P. Clowney's article "The Worship God Wants" in *Moody Monthly* (79:1, Sept. 1978, pp. 49-50, 132-133). "We cannot turn back to imitate the rites of the Old Testament temple," he writes, "that would draw the people of God away from realities to the shadows" (p. 133). But is he willing to do without musical instruments and choir as well as sacrifice and vestment? Michael G. Smith is refreshingly direct -- and off-the-mark -- in his "The Reforming of Reformed Worship" (*New Horizons in the Orthodox Presbyterian Church*, 4:4, April 1983, pp. 13-15). Anglicans and Puritans were both right and wrong, "terribly" so (p. 14). Reformed Christians need to look back to practices before the Westminster Directory of Worship for help in improving their praise, Smith concludes. Similarly, in the same periodical, John M. Frame looks way beyond the Westminster formulation of worship in his discussion of "Music in Worship" (7:4, April 1986, pp. 1-2).

From the Dutch Reformed tradition comes G. Vandooren's *The Beauty of Reformed Liturgy* (Winnipeg, MN: Premier, 1980), reprinted from a series of articles in *The Clarion*. This work shows the usual Dutch concern with the order of worship above the content of worship, and seems unaware that the regulative principle of worship is in the Belgic Confession[5] as well as the Westminster. Vandooren does include a lengthy "intermezzo" on catechism preaching in the second worship service, which will be of special interest to those not familiar with this practice.

In "The Regulative Principle of Worship: A Reconsideration of Its Application" (*Covenanter Witness* 100:2, Feb. 1984, pp. 4-9), Dr. Edward A. Robson defends four theses in a fresh way: first, the R.P.W. (as he fondly terms it), is one principle among many; all are important. Second, the R.P.W. incorrectly applied becomes prohibitionism, which is the attitude that "condemns one evil in specific terms, but always misses or even practices the same type of evil in a different context" (p. 6). Third, the R.P.W. inconsistently applied allows us to fall into didactic and theological error. The errors of hymns in the *Trinity Hymnal* and the *Psalter Hymnal* -- of which he discusses only a few -- show this. Fourth, the R.P.W., correctly applied, is a source of praise to God and edification to man.

Equally stimulating is Lyndsey F. Blakston's *The Temple and Christian Worship* (Geelong: Hilltop Press, ca. 1974). Blakston argues this way: "1) The temple institution from beginning to end is inseparable from Jesus Christ. 2) When Christ came as the Messiah of God and the redeemer of his people a distinct Christian worship came alongside that of the temple, sometimes causing a conflict of ideas. 3) This worship is performed by a spiritual community, that is, one which the Spirit pervades and empowers. 4) As a result, the New Testament shows a spiritual community worshipping

---

[5]"We believe that these Holy Scriptures fully contain the will of God . . . The *whole manner of worship God required of us is written in them* . . ." Art. VII. "We reject human invention . . . where *man would introduce* into the worship of God." Art. XXXII. My emphasis.

without temple specialists, officers of the temple trained to perform special mediatorial tasks on behalf of others, but rather having new and distinct ministries of its own suitable to a community of Christians" (p. 6). Blakston draws the right conclusions from the right premises, and issues this particularly helpful reminder: "Too often it is assumed that the Lord's gifts are to be used in the church assembled for worship" (p. 39). Only those gifts that are designed for use in New Testament worship are for that work.

Also well worth consulting is an unpublished paper *My Praise Shall be of Thee: The Biblical Doctrine of Worship* by Donald Weilersbacher,[6] who begins by arguing the unique authority of Scripture, even for worship, then for the regulative principle of worship as such, before showing how exclusive psalmody and a cappella singing follow from this major premise. His argumentation concerning the function of instrumental music in Old Covenant worship is creative.

The simple, spiritual worship of the Free Church of Scotland is defended by Hector Cameron in the assemblage of articles published as *Hold Fast Your Confession* ("Purity of Worship"; Edinburgh: Knox Press, 1977, pp. 95-128). He sets out the regulative principle (p. 109f) before moving on to its application. "No divine commission and no divine gift seem ever to have been conferred in apostolic times, with the enlarging of the song praise repertoire of the Christian Church as its distinctive assignment" (p. 117). Such forcefulness trails off needlessly at the end (pp. 126-127). Another Free Churchman, Prof. Donald Macleod, discusses "Scripture and Worship" (*Presbyterian Banner*, March 1986, p. 8). The New Testament does not have a lot to say about worship practice, but all of it suggests sober, orderly worship quite different from pentecostal worship.[7]

The most significant publication on worship for Reformed Christians appeared at the beginning of the period under review: *The Biblical Doctrine of Worship* (Pittsburgh, PA: Reformed Presbyterian Church of

---

[6]3832 Loma Alta Drive, San Diego, CA 92115.

[7]He also writes that: "People who claim to be calling us back to primitive, apostolic Christianity are creating a new ecclesiastical office: choreographer. It does not occur to such men to ask, Is there divine authority for this?"

North America, 1974). Some of the chapters are of immense value; others are not. Unfortunately, some potential subjects of interest were not discussed.[8] The articles are generally in Biblical order, but Norman Shepherd's contribution, "The Biblical Basis for the Regulative Principle of Worship", really should have come first, for it is programmatic for what follows. He sees the regulative principle in the context of a Bible that is normative for doctrine *and life*, a conclusion that many Christians schizophrenically refuse to make. The bulk of the articles exegete various Biblical passages, but there are also careful historical accounts of the decline of Reformed worship in various Presbyterian and Reformed churches.[9] Two excellent contributions by G.I. Williamson--one defending exclusive psalmody and the other opposing musical instruments in worship--are models of apologies for these positions. The former has been published in pamphlet form (*The Singing of Psalms in the Worship of God*, Belfast, Northern Ireland: Covenanter Bookshop, ca. 1973), and the latter deserves to be. The volume lacks an index, but does include four lengthy appendices.[10]

Finally, various reference works must be mentioned. *The Hymn*, the magazine of the Hymn Society of America, *Reformed Liturgy and Music, Reformed Worship*, and the *Jahrbuch fur Liturgik und Hymnologie*, are all periodicals worth consulting for their lists of recent publications, theses, and

[8]They are listed in Appendix A, including Paul's view of worship, Calvin's understanding of worship, the Puritan development of worship, and the "hymns" of Luke 1 and 2.

[9]Several reprints appear in this symposium, including Williamson on exclusive psalmody, J.G. Vos' "Ashamed of the Tents of Shem", Frank D. Frazer's "Psalms and Hymns and Spiritual Songs", and William Young's "The Second Commandment".

[10]See above for the first. The second is a transcript of the open discussion at the Symposium, which is not as helpful as it might have been. The third, by Charles R. McBurney, lists New Testament references to the Psalms. The last, by McBurney and Edward Robson, is the most original. Called "Selected Doctrines of the Book of Psalms," this appendix gives Psalm selections from *The Book of Psalms for Singing* for each of the six major foci of Systematic Theology, organized into fairly original sub-headings. This type of organization is not only advantageous for the theology professor but for the pastor as well, "rightly dividing the word of Truth" in song as well as in word.

articles, as well as for their own contribution to our knowledge of worship, although they exhibit little understanding of distinctively Reformed worship. To locate psalters in library collections, two possible sources are: Louis Voigt and Ellen Jane L. Porter, *Hymnbook Collections of North America* (Springfield, OH: Hymn Society of America, ca. 1979), listing 179 sources, of which eleven specify psalters as a particular collection strength; and Phillip Sims and Scotty Gray, "Psalters of the Maurice Frost Collection at Southwestern Baptist Theological Seminary" (*The Hymn* 30:2, April 1979, pp. 89-92) detailing a significant holding of mostly English-language psalters. *The Westminster Dictionary of Worship* (Philadelphia: Westminster, 1979) covers "Reformed Worship" from a very liturgical slant (pp. 331-332), and discusses "Psalmody" only in terms of the early church. *The New Grove Dictionary of Music and Musicians* (London: Macmillan, 1980; 20 vols.) provides forty-five illustrated pages of information on "psalmody" and "psalms, metrical" by several well-known authorities on these subjects, with bibliographies.

Historical Works

Occasionally, a doctoral thesis rises above the merely academic and technical to deal in a provocative way with a familiar subject. Such is Hughes Oliphant Old's 1970 Neuchatel dissertation, published in 1975 as *The Patristic Roots of Reformed Worship* (Zurich: Theologischer Verlag). All subsequent historical writing on early Reformed worship will be either elaborations or denials of his thesis: the Reformers, caught in a battle with the Romanists, returned to what they considered the common heritage of all Christians, the Fathers of the Church, for their theory and practice of worship. Long quotations from the original sources permit the Reformers to express their own thoughts. Psalm-singing had as its primary function the praise of God (p. 253f). "This attitude of the Reformers was greatly encouraged by their knowledge of the literature of the ancient Church. Countless passages of the Fathers could be quoted which indicate that the ancient Church was accustomed to singing Psalms in praise to God" (p. 255).

Thus, the Reformers preferred the Psalms to man-made hymns, not for principial but pragmatic reasons (pp. 262-263). They also opposed instrumental music in worship, once again because of the patristic position (pp. 265f). Other sections of Old's book may be less controversial but are no less illuminating.

Four other works that look only at the worship of the early church are: *The Eucharist of the Early Christians* (by various authors; New York: Pueblo Pub. Co., 1978); Roger T. Beckwith, "The Daily and Weekly Worship of the Primitive Church in relation to Its Jewish Antecedents" (*Evangelical Quarterly* 56:2, April 1984, pp. 65-80; 56:3, July 1984, pp. 139-158); Johannes Quasten's *Music & Worship in Pagan & Christian Antiquity* (Washington, D.C.: National Association of Pastoral Musicians, 1983; from the 1973 German revision of the 1927 original); and Thomas K. Carroll and Thomas Halton, *Liturgical Practice in the Fathers* (Wilmington, DE: Michael Glazier, 1988). The first contains the efforts of ten authors to help the "faithful," trying to recover their spiritual roots in a technological age. Beckwith's work traces the Old Testament background of early Christian worship. Quasten begins with pagan worship and the mystery cults before considering Christian worship at great length, utilizing extensive notes, indices, and illustrations. This world-renowned patristic expert delineates the concept of singing without musical accompaniment in early Christian worship, which he believes was somewhat influenced by pagan antagonism to instruments (p. 72). Carroll and Halton's book demonstrates--although that is hardly their goal--how fast the early church declined from its apostolic purity, as they present texts and comments on the Lord's Day, the Paschal Night, and New Days and Weeks and Seasons.

To return to Reformation themes, Oliver C. Rupprecht writes "From Exalted Precept to Pattern of Excellence: Luther's Psalm Hymns" (*The Hymn* 33:2, Apr. 1982, pp. 89-93). These were really paraphrases, or, as Mr. Rupprect would put it, "modernizing" (p. 90). Nevertheless, "Luther's Psalm hymns do not represent an attempt to replace scriptural forms. They can never be a substitute for what is offered in the Bible" (p. 90).

The key problem with medieval Romanism identified by Luther was the sacrifice of the mass, according to John M. Barkley in "Pleading His Eternal

Sacrifice in the Reformed Liturgy" (*The Sacrifice of Praise: Studies on the Themes of Thanksgiving and Redemption in the Central Prayers of the Eucharistic and Baptismal Liturgies, In Honour of Arthur Hubert Couratin*, Roma: C.L.V.--Edizioni liturgiche, 1981, pp. 123-140). Barkley outlines the development of the Reformed understanding of the Lord's Supper before arguing his thesis that Reformed believers have always believed that Christ's sacrifice is present now in the Supper because His sacrifice is eternal as well as once-for-all. In the same collection, A. C. Honders makes some "Remarks on the Postcommunio in Some Reformed Liturgies" (pp. 143-157), recounting changes in the written prayer given after the Lord's Supper, including the distinctively Arminian ones used by the Remonstrants after the Synod of Dordt (pp. 155-156).

Hughes Oliphant Old has continued to write in the area of Reformed worship, including the essay, "Daily Prayer in the Reformed Church of Strasbourg, 1523-1530" (*Worship* 52:2, 1978, pp. 121-138). "The Reformers reaffirmed the basic insight of the daily office, that daily prayer is an essential service of the whole body of the Church" (p. 122). But instead of a mere form of entertainment offered by the priest, this daily prayer consisted of invocation, psalmody,[11] Scripture lessons, canticles (mostly New Testament but a few Old), the collect, and benediction. He concludes: "We need a new psalter for the contemporary American Church!" (p. 137)

John Calvin's understanding of worship has not been ignored. James M. Nichols established "The Intent of the Calvinist Liturgy" (*The Heritage of John Calvin*, Grand Rapids: Eerdmans, 1973, pp. 87-109). The title is a little misleading, as the article is really a discussion of the four major parts of worship according to Calvin: preaching, prayer (spoken and sung), Lord's Supper, and alms-giving. Calvin's liturgical principles receive adequate treatment here, with several entertaining asides. In *The Origins of Calvin's Theology of Music 1536-1543* (Philadelphia: American Philosophical Society, 1979), Charles Garside finds that the main features were set early

---

[11]"The Reformers did not blush at christianizing the Psalms" (p. 127).

on. For instance, by 1537, for Calvin, "the singing of Psalms was not an indifferent matter. To the contrary, it was essential for public worship" (p. 8). In the singing, Calvin rejected Luther's position that obviously secular music could be adapted to worship purposes (p. 19). "Calvin would have no specially trained choirs set apart from the rest of the congregation" (p. 27). Psalms and prayers of the New Testament were sung (p. 18), but by 1543 "Calvin proposes now that even outside the liturgy only the psalms be sung" (p. 24). Two appendices and a bibliography[12] anchor the work well. Ford Lewis Battles translated a short document from Calvin's pen in "The Form of Prayers and Songs of the Church 1542: Letter to the Reader" (*Calvin Theological Journal* 15:2, November 1980, pp. 160-165).[13]

Other Reformers have not been ignored. Martin Bucer's *Censura* and *De Ordinatione Legitima* have been printed in both English and Latin as *Martin Bucer and the Book of Common Prayer*, with an introduction by E. C. Whitaker (Great Wokering, England: Mayhew-McCrimmon, 1974). James M. Kittelson discusses "Martin Bucer and the Sacramentarian Controversy: The Origins of his Policy of Concord" (*Archiv für Reformationsgeschichte* 64, 1973, pp. 166-183), with Kittelson pointing to Erasmus as that source. A massive study by Benedictine Rene Bornert, *La reforme protestante du culte a Strasbourg au XVIe siecle (1523-1598): approche sociologique et interpretation theologique* (Leiden: Brill, 1981) maintains that the Vatican II revolution in Roman Catholicism parallels

---

[12]Although curiously some of the footnotes refer to titles not listed in the bibliography.

[13]Let the Reformer of Geneva speak across the centuries: "There are three things which our Lord has commanded us to observe in our spiritual assemblies. These are the preaching of the Word, public and solemn prayer and the administration of his sacraments" (p. 161). Prayer includes the singing of "Psalms, which are sung in the church in the presence of God and his angels" (p. 163). Because singing has such power over man, "We ought to be even more diligent to regulate it, to the end that it may be useful for us and not dangerous" (p. 164). "For when we have searched here and there, we will not find better songs nor ones more appropriate for this purpose than the Psalms of David, which the Holy Spirit has spoken to him and made. Therefore, when we sing them, we are certain that God has put the words in our mouth as if they themselves sang in us to exalt his glory" (p. 164). The whole world "should accustom itself . . . to sing these divine and heavenly songs with good King David" (p. 165).

developments in sixteenth century Strasbourg. Elfriede Jacobs writes of *Die Sakramentslehre Wilhelm Farels* (Zurich: Theologischer Verlag, 1978), a doctoral dissertation. Hughes Oliphant Old continues his basic thesis of *The Patristic Roots of Reformed Worship* by concentrating on Bullinger's sermon on baptism in the *Decades* of 1551: "Bullinger and the Scholastic Works on Baptism: A Study in the History of Christian Worship" (*Heinrich Bullinger, 1504-1575: Gesammelte Aufsatze zum 400. Todestag*, Zurich: Theologischer Verlag, 1975, vol. 1, pp. 191-207). At much greater length, Salvatore Corda writes *Veritas sacramenti: A Study in Vermigli's Doctrine of the Lord's Supper* (Zurich: Theologischer Verlag, 1975). Vermigli seems to have been influenced by his Italian background, but eventually became clearly indebted to Calvin, Bullinger, and Bucer. G. J. Cuming argues in "John Knox and the Book of Common Prayer: A Short Note" (*Liturgical Review* 10:2 Nov. 1980, pp. 80-81) that Knox's writings show that he was not as antagonistic to it as sometimes suggested. "L'influence de la pedagogie et de la musique humaniste sur le styl du choral lutherien et du psaume huguenot" receives an interdisciplinary study from Edith Weber in *Actes du colloque: L'amiral de Coligny et son temps* (Paris: Societe de l'histoire du protestantisme francais, 1974).

Additional works that begin in the Reformation period but cover Reformed worship up to the present day include *Prayers of the Eucharist: Early and Reformed Texts* (edited by R.C.D. Jasper and G.J. Cuming; New York: Oxford University Press, first edition 1975, second edition 1980). Twenty-six of the forty texts in this useful anthology are from the "early" period; all are briefly introduced and followed by a bibliography. Henri Capieu, Albert Grenier, and Albert Nicolas produced *Tous invites: la Cene du Seigneur celebree dans les Eglises de la Reforme* (Paris: Le Centurion, 1982), a collection of texts and studies from the Reformation to the present, but strangely lacking Article 26 of the Confession of La Rochelle. The history of worship in the Presbyterian Churches, particularly in the U.S.A., is recounted by Robert G. Rayburn in "Worship in the Reformed Church" (*Presbuterion: Covenant Seminary Review* 6:1 Spring 1980, pp. 17-32). Dr. Rayburn believes that "New School" Presbyterianism has shaped modern Presbyterian worship (p. 23). They "were mostly concerned for the evangelistic effectiveness of their services, so this became the principle criterion for their worship" (pp. 22-23). Dr. Rayburn argues for written prayers (p. 27), and maintains that " . . . the Lord's Supper is, in my opinion, the central act of Christian worship . . ." (p. 29). It should not surprize us then to read a few pages farther on: "It was English Puritanism, however, with its rebellion against the pressures of established religion, which carried the reforming of the church too far by applying its emphasis upon the Word of God so rigidly that a great barrenness was produced in the worship services of those who followed the Puritan theology. In their eagerness to eliminate everything that did not have what they considered specific scriptural authority they indiscriminately removed the legacies of centuries from their worship" (p. 32). What a very sad reflection on Dr. Rayburn! For, this position he denounces is that of the Westminster Confession of Faith and Catechisms, the epitome of English Puritanism (and Scottish Presbyterianism as well).

This leads us on to the Puritan period in Reformed worship, when the remaining Romanist influences were effectively removed from worship. Leslie A. Rawlinson considers "Worship in Liturgy and Form" in *Anglican and Puritan Thinking* (London: Westminster Conference, 1977, pp. 71-88), highlighting the history of the Puritan struggle against liturgists from the Elizabethan settlement of 1559 to the Act of Uniformity in 1662.[14] In the same book, Robert W. Oliver discusses "The Externals of Worship" (pp. 58-70), treating both buildings, which were cleared of "papist gear" in faithfulness to the Second Commandment during the reigns of Edward and Elizabeth (p. 60), and vestments, which "provoked the first serious divisions in the ranks of English Protestantism" (p. 64).[15] Another Westminster

---

[14]The contrast is well delineated: "with their characteristic reverence for antiquity and tradition, the Anglicans tended to idealize the worship of the early church Fathers and to model their worship upon it" (p. 73) while "the Puritans emphasized inwardness, simplicity, and sincerity, in all approaches to God" (p. 85).

[15]The "full black gown," which vestment-supporters cited as a precedent from Geneva and other continental centers, was not a vestment at all, but "was the usual dress of the academic and professional classes" in Switzerland (p. 65).

Conference record, *Spiritual Worship* (London: 1985), contains four historical studies from this period: Kenneth Brownell on "Worship and the Marian Exiles in Frankfurt" (pp. 1-16); Christopher Bennett on "Worship among the Puritans--the Regulative Principle" (pp. 17-32); Peter Lewis on "Preaching from Calvin to Bunyan" (pp. 33-50); and Alan Clifford on "Benjamin Keach and Non-conformist Hymnology" (pp. 69-93). In another Puritan alteration, the "daily office" of medieval Romanism gave way to family worship morning and evening, according to the indefagitable Hughes Olipant Old: "The Reformed Daily Office: A Puritan Perspective" (*Reformed Liturgy and Music* 12:4 1978, pp. 9-18). Old analyzes Matthew Henry's *Family Hymns* (1694) and *Directions for Beginning, Spending, and Closing Each Day with God* (1712), a collection of three sermons,[16] and concludes that "we should take care that this tradition be continued in our own generation" (p. 17).

The famous *Bay Psalm Book* has prompted some continued interest. Richard Gilmore Appel considered *The Music of the Bay Psalm Book* (9th ed., Brooklyn: Institute for Studies in American Music, 1975), providing a brief commentary and notes followed by selections from the *Bay Psalm Book*, with music in modern notation on the facing page. John Milton and others were greatly influenced by the *Bay Psalm Book*, according to Margaret P. Hannay, "'Psalms Done into Metre': The Common Psalms of John Milton and of the Bay Colony" (*Christianity and Literature* 32:3, Spring 1983, pp. 19-29). A new edition of Wilberforce Eames' *A List of Editions of the Bay Psalm Book or New England Version of the Psalms* was published in New York by Burt Franklin in 1973.

The Reformed love for the exclusive singing of Psalms in worship did not survive the eighteenth century. Despite attempts to improve the quality of singing, the lining-out of the Psalms hastened their demise,

---

[16]The former contains 95 selections from the Psalms, although Henry was not adverse to deleting the imprecatory verses from Psalm 139 (p. 13)! Old generalizes that "morning prayer was particularly marked by praise and petition for God's guidance, while evening prayer was characterized by thanksgiving for the mercies of the day, confession, and supplication of God's grace" (p. 17).

according to Timothy A. Smith ("Congregational Singing in Colonial New England: Problems addressed by the Singing School," *Journal of Church Music* 26:7, Sept. 1984, pp. 10-15, 46-48). Moreover, the Psalm versions were considered antiquated. Madeleine Forell Marshall and Janet Todd explain in *English Congregational Hymns in the Eighteenth Century* (Lexington, KY: University Press of Kentucky, 1982), that Watts and Wesley condemned the existing Psalters, but, to these authors, this "seems extreme. The psalters appear no more rigid or antique than they were impersonal or irrelevant. They are timeless expressions of the human situation in relationship to God" (p. 14). They go on to recount the rise of hymnody in Watts, Wesley, Newton, and Cowper. Isaac Watts receives a complimentary treatment from David G. Fountain in *Isaac Watts Remembered* (Worthing: Henry E. Walter, 1974) and from Paul E.G. Cook in "Isaac Watts: Father of English Hymnody" in *Living the Christian Life* (London: Westminster Conference, 1974, pp. 28-44). To wit: "The really *good* hymns are the *really* old hymns written by Isaac Watts" (Cook, p. 29; emphasis his), because of their grandeur, evangelicalism, objectivity, fervour, and catholicity. A more accurate portrayal comes from Robin A. Leaver in "Isaac Watts's Hermeneutical Principles and the Decline of English Metrical Psalmody" (*Churchman* 92:1, 1978, pp. 56-60; reprinted from *Arbeitsgemeinschaft fur Hymnologie Bulletin* 4, April 1977, pp. 54-59). "When Watts published his *Psalms* he also introduced a new hermeneutic which was to prove destructive of the concept and practice of Christians singing parts of the Old Testament" (p. 56); it was in fact a "dispensational theology" (p. 58). In sixteen recent hymnals, a "general pattern of reductionism and humanitarianism" (p. 135) has been found, according to "Changes in the Emphases of Evangelical Belief, 1970-1980: Evidence from the New Hymnody" (*The Churchman* 95:2, 1981, pp. 123-138) by Bill Hopkinson.

How unaccompanied singing (mostly of Psalms) developed in the centuries after the Reformation is the central concern of Nicholas Temperley in "The Old Way of Singing: Its Origin and Development" (*Journal of the American Musicological Society* 34:3, 1981, pp. 511-544). A reevaluation of accepted notions is being made, particularly in light of increasing contact with contemporary "old singing." John William Worst analyzes the music of what he calls "the first distinctively American musical idiom"[17] in his 1974 University of Michigan Ph.D. thesis, *New England Psalmody, 1760-1810: Analysis of an American Idiom*,[18] finding many common features among the 174 tunes considered.

Within the German Reformed Churches in the U.S.A., a liturgical revolution occurred in the mid-nineteenth century under the leadership of the famous Mercersburg theologians John W. Nevin and Philip Schaff. Jack Martin Maxwell believes that they were successful because they "established and demonstrated the imperative practical and theoretical relationship between theology and liturgy" (*Worship and Reformed Theology: The Liturgical Lessons of Mercersburg*. Pittsburgh, PA: Pickwick Press, 1976; p. 5). Nathan D. Mitchell in his 1978 Notre Dame Ph.D. thesis *Church, Eucharist, and Liturgical Reform at Mercersburg, 1843-1857*,[19] maintains that this coupling stems from the source of their theology: German liberalism (p. 5). Certainly the two were opposed to Calvin in some important particulars (*e.g.*, pp. 456f). On the other hand, Gregg Alan Mast sees the origin of Mercersburg's theology and liturgy of the Lord's Supper in the curious Catholic Apostolic Church or "Irvingites" (*The Eucharistic Service of the Catholic Apostolic Church and Its Influence on Reformed Liturgical Renewals of the 19th Century*, Ph.D. thesis, Drew University, 1985).[20] He also sees some lesser Irvingite influence in the worship of the Church of Scotland and the Dutch Reformed Church in America.

The Dutch Reformed tradition has produced its students as well. Marion Frances Vree wrote her University of Southern California D.M.A. thesis (1975) on *The Development of Netherlands Psalmody from 1565-1773 through the Study of the Bourgeouis Tune for Psalm 42*.[21] Her interesting

---

[17] Abstract, Dissertation Abstracts International, 35A, p. 4605.

[18] Available from University Microfilms International (UMI, 300 N. Zeeb Rd., Ann Arbor, MI 48106), order number 75-857.

[19] Available from UMI, order number 79-00135.

[20] Available from UMI, order number 85-15821.

[21] Available from UMI, order number 75-15592.

approach begins with DeHeere's 1565 versification of Psalm 42 into Dutch (the first one) and continues with the history and practice of psalmody, including some material on the use of organs. Three appendices list psalters, publishers/versifiers, and no fewer than 37 revisions of Psalm 42! Events in America during the second half of Vree's period of interest are dealt with by Alice P. Kenney in "Hudson Valley Dutch Psalmody" (*The Hymn* 25:1, Jan. 1974, pp. 15-26). The two most important factors in the decline of the almost exclusive psalmody of the Dutch Reformed churches were the pietistic/revivalistic movement in the 18th century and the perceived inadequacy of the existing psalter (p. 19). Why a new psalter could not have sufficed is never really considered. More modern developments in the Netherlands are recounted in *The Liturgical Movement in the Netherlands Reformed Church, 1911-1955, with Special Reference to the Anglican Dimension* (Utrecht: Interuniversitair Instituut voor Missiologie en Oecumenica, 1983) by Peter Staples, which makes much interesting material available in English that would otherwise be inaccessible to Anglophones.

The Christian Reformed Church in North America has attracted some attention, and concern, for its liturgical development. Bertus F. Polman's 1980 University of Minnesota Ph.D. thesis, *Music in the Christian Reformed Church: Its Relationship to Genevan Psalmody and Reformed Liturgy, 1834-1972*,[22] traces the roots and development of this church's sung praise. He concludes that hymns are increasingly replacing the Psalms, as does Rudolf Zuiderveld in "Ethnic Hymnody Series: Some Musical Traditions in Dutch Reformed Churches in America" (*The Hymn* 36:3, July 1985, pp. 23-25). "The structure of a typical Christian Reformed worship service is dialogic and uses song in congregational responses led by the ministers" (p. 23). But, ". . . the old rules requiring psalms as well as hymns are in retreat . . ." (p. 24). "Choirs, traditionally not important or even allowed in Calvinist church services in the Netherlands, have made great inroads into Dutch Reformed worship in America" (p. 25). "Other 'special music', such as the occasional soloist, is also destructive of the Reformed

---

[22]Available from UMI, order number 81-15028.

liturgical logic best preserved in the careful choice of responsive psalms and hymns by the minister" (p. 25). Virginia K. Folgers, a Christian Reformed organist, sounds a similar alarm in her brief description of "Hymnody in the Christian Reformed Church" (*The American Organist*, Jan. 1981, pp. 28-29).

The Protestant Reformed Churches of America have continued most of the old Dutch ways, judging from Herman Hanko's long series of articles in *The Standard Bearer* (in various issues from 60:7, Jan. 1, 1984 through 62:1, Oct. 1, 1985). There does seem to be some conception of a regulative principle of worship at work in these Churches, but the discussion is not set out along these lines. It is striking, however, to see Prof. Hanko come to sound conclusions via theological reflection and/or practical considerations.[23]   Confirming this impression of the Protestant Reformed Churches is Steven Key's "A Reformed Liturgy" (*Protestant Reformed Theological Journal* 19:2, April 1986, pp. 14-27).[24]

Studies in the History of Worship in Scotland (edited by Duncan B. Forrester and Douglas M. Murray, Edinburgh: T. & T. Clark, 1984) complains that "there can hardly be another aspect of Scottish history which has been so dominated by prejudices, sectarian bias, parochialism, and carefully nurtured myths as this" (p. vii). The various authors then go on to show their objectivity by positively presenting the decline in Scriptural worship in Scottish Reformed circles in chapters 5 and 6, flailing the

---

[23] Because of historical differences between the Scottish and Dutch Reformed traditions, the Dutch have tended to approach worship more pragmatically; such is reflected in this transplanted church.

[24] Key quotes Calvin's support of the regulative principle, then confuses the matter: "By the words 'expressly sanctioned' Calvin did not mean that only those elements specifically commanded by God were to be included in the liturgy. There is no explicit command, for example, to read the Ten Commandments or to pronounce the votum or to recite the Creed. But Calvin's point was this: every element of the liturgy must be permitted and approved and supported by the Scriptures" (p. 16). He believes that Ephesians 5:18-20 and Colossians 3:16 refer to the singing of the Book of Psalms (p. 19), and opposes the custom of singing the "Doxology" in Protestant Reformed Churches because it "is inconsistent with our insistence on exclusive psalmody" (p. 20). Finally, "various passages speak of giving as part of the worship service (Rom. 15:26; II Cor. 8:9; I Cor. 16:1-3)" (pp. 26-27).

Covenanters on pp. 57 and 60, writing of "those who struggled against *ignorant prejudice* for the introduction of an organ . . ." (p. 147),[25] pontificating that "we owe a great deal" to the Scoto-catholic movement which aped the Episcopalians in their churches (p. 149), and observing that "the smaller Presbyterian churches, and particularly the Free Church and the Free Presbyterians, have allowed their worship to ossify . . ." (p. 168). We need more real honesty here and less so-called "objectivity"! At least the volume includes an appreciative chapter on Scottish preaching by David H. C. Read.

One of the prejudices of the previous volume is drawn out by John M. Barkley in "Renaissance of Public Worship in the Church of Scotland, 1865-1905," in *Renaissance and Renewal in Christian History: Papers Read at the Fifteenth and Sixteenth Meetings of the Ecclesiastical History Society* (Oxford: Blackwell, 1977, pp. 339-350). Prof. Barkley waxes eloquent over the valiant efforts of the Church Service Society, founded in 1865, to engage in constant innovation until the nirvana of Liturgicalism pervaded the Church of Scotland. Further refinements have led to a plethora of productions from that church in recent years: *Prayers for Contemporary Worship* (1977), *Book of Common Order* (1979), *Prayers for Sunday Services: Companion Volume to the Book of Common Order (1980),* and *New Ways to Worship* (1980), all published by St. Andrew Press in Edinburgh. These have spawned a traditionalist response in the *Reformed Book of Common Order* (Edinburgh: The National Church Association of the Church of Scotland, 1977).

The Reformed Presbyterian Church of North America maintains a form of worship little changed from the seventeenth century, according to John Allen Delivuk in his S.T.M. thesis at Concordia Theological Seminary, St. Louis, 1982 (Pittsburgh: Reformed Presbyterian Theological Seminary, 1982): *The Doctrine and History of Worship in the Reformed Presbyterian Church of North America.* This work is comprehensive and careful, but does not quite give the "sense" of Reformed Presbyterian worship, nor does

---

[25]My emphasis.

it place that worship very clearly in its current historical context. Still, as a description of a Reformed church that still seeks to worship only as the Bible commands, this work is illuminating.

Prayer

Perhaps because it is less controversial, the place of prayer in worship -- the first of several elements mentioned in the Westminster Confession of Faith, Chapter XXI -- has provoked relatively little recent comment. Thomas F. Torrance does discuss "The Mind of Christ in Worship: The Problem of Apollinarianism in the Liturgy" in *Theology in Reconciliation: Essays toward Evangelical and Catholic Unity in East and West* (Grand Rapids: Eerdmans, 1976; London: Geoffrey Chapman, 1975; pp. 139-214). As one would expect this book-length article is careful, clear, solid. The title does not communicate the exact concern however: prayer offered through the mediation of Christ as opposed to that offered through the mediation of others.

Jean Calvin made regular use of the Lord's Prayer in worship, so Pierre Marcel's "Dites notre Pere, la priere selon Jean Calvin" (*La Revue Reformee* n. 140, Dec. 1984, pp. 156-209) rewards close scrutiny. While Marcel deals with all of Calvin's writings concerning the Lord's Prayer, a major concern of this article is the place of prayer in worship.[26] An English-language taste of Calvin's beliefs on prayer and samples of his written prayers are included in Ford Lewis Battles' *The Piety of John Calvin* (Grand Rapids: Baker, 1978), although Battles does not justify his arrangements of the prayers into verse form.

---

[26]The section on "les prieres chantees" (sung prayers) is a little vague (pp. 205-206), but otherwise this article is helpful.

Singing of Psalms

Many modern Reformed Christians do not realize that their forebears advocated the exclusive use of the Biblical Psalms in worship. However, some in other theological traditions are beginning to recognize what has been lost by the modern slide into exclusive hymnody. "There is evidence of renewed appreciation in our day for the practice of singing Old Testament Psalms, because it continues a tradition that confirms the continuity of our Judeo-Christian faith, and because of the unique, emotional experience it brings to the individual in corporate worship" (Donald P. Hustad, "The Psalms as Worship Expression: Personal and Congregational," *Review and Expositor* 81:3, Summer 1983, pp. 407-424).[27] Ronald Barclay Allen wrote *Praise! A Matter of Life and Breath* (Nashville: Thomas Nelson, 1980) "to bring the current excitement about praise to its *source book*, the Psalms" (p. 12), although paradoxically he believes that "a study of the Book of Psalms leads finally to a renewed commitment to our own hymnody" (p. 13). "There are encouraging signs of renewed interest in the Psalms," claims Grady Hardin (*The Leadership of Worship*, Nashville: Abingdon, 1980); "some ministers and music leaders are 'lining out' Psalms very much like they were sung in early American churches" (p. 38). Two articles in The *Alliance Witness* wax eloquent over the Psalms, which "lead us into the highest spiritual acts of worship: praise and prayer. A wise use of the Psalms will give a freshness to our prayers and add vitality to our devotions" (Gordon Chilvers, "Can We Use the Psalms Today?" 116:23, Nov. 11, 1981, pp. 9-10). "A hopeful sign is the increasing use of singable versions drawing upon the Psalms . . ." (J. Buchanan MacMillan, 119:3, Feb. 1, 1984, pp. 6-7, 22).

Erik Routley has penned an entire book showing the applicability of 93 of the Psalms in worship (*Exploring the Psalms*, Philadelphia: Westminster, 1975), unfortunately relating them to the "Church Year." For an historical outline of the Psalms' use in worship turn to Bruce H.

---

[27]Although he had earlier issued the gratuitous insult that "no one will argue that the Church did not need the new hymns of Watts and Wesley and their successors . . ." (p. 417).

Leafblad, "The Psalms in Christian Worship" (*Southwestern Journal of Theology* 27:1, Fall 1984, pp. 40-53).[28] More questionable is Kenneth M. Campbell's "The Role of Music in Worship" (*The Evangelical Quarterly* 52:1, 1980, pp. 43-46), which claims that in the Old Testament period "not only were the Psalms sung (or chanted) in worship, but the entire Scripture was" (p. 45). His proof? There are accents in the Hebrew text!

More believable is Hughes Oliphant Old's "The Psalms of Praise in the Worship of the New Testament Church" (*Interpretation* 39:1, Jan. 1985, pp. 20-33), which actually only deals with Psalms 93, 96-99. He maintains that in the hymns of the Revelation "in every case what we have is a Christian paraphrase. Does this mean the earliest Christians rewrote the Psalms for their worship? Probably not. They would no more have rewritten the canonical Psalms than they would have rewritten the canonical prophets. They no doubt continued to sing the canonical text of the Psalms just as they always had, but what they sang they understood in a specifically Christian way" (p. 32). To the Psalms they added their midrash-like hymns (p. 32). Similar to the latter speculation is Leonard Thompson's view in "Hymns in Early Christian Worship" (*Anglican Theological Review* 55:4, Oct. 1973, pp. 458-472): "In summary we may say that, although there is undeniable evidence that hymns were used in the worship of the earliest church, there is virtually no explicit citation of hymns in its literature" (p. 46). Then he goes pot-rocking[29] for "New Testament hymns," especially in Philippians 2 and Colossians 1. Anyone familiar with the vagaries of form criticism will not be surprized by all this.

---

[28] He highlights the Jewish inheritance ("By the time of Christ the Psalter occupied a secure position in Jewish worship," p. 41), the New Testament practice ("the Psalms were a familiar, stabilizing force in early Christian worship," p. 45), the medieval situation (as singing became the specialized work of a few, the variety of singing styles multiplied, p. 48), the reformation revitalization ("in every way the metrical Psalms were an immediate success . . .", p. 51), and finally, the twentieth century scene ("The use of the Psalms in Christian worship has been in gradual decline, by and large, in this century," p. 52).

[29] That is, looking under every "pot" and "rock" of Scripture to find what you have predetermined should be there.

Despite these continuing speculations that wedge man-made songs into worship, the use of Psalms is being advocated and planned with renewed vigor in some circles where their use has long languished. Paul Westermeyer surveys "Prospects of Psalmody in the American Church Today" in *The Hymn* (33:2, April 1982, pp. 74-79). Despite the ecumenicity of the Psalms, their singing in worship had all but disappeared before Gelineau's melodies were published in 1953. Yet, "in spite of these increases, there is as yet no psalmodic revival" (p. 75). Why? The Psalms "are for the mature". While "they cry out to be sung" (p. 76), prospects for them "are mixed," depending upon "those of us who are parish musicians" (p. 78). Techniques for professional church musicians are found in such writings as Kenneth E. Williams' article, "Ways to Sing Psalms" (*Reformed Liturgy and Music* 18:1, Winter 1984, pp. 12-16), which is clear but highly liturgical and whose lengthy, annotated bibliography completely ignores confessionally Reformed viewpoints, and Mark Bangert's "Wooing Worshippers with a Sung Psalter: Psalm Singing, in *The Lutheran Book of Worship"* (*The Hymn* 33:2, April 1982, pp. 94-101), which waxes ecstatic over chanting the Psalms, and the response of worshippers to this practice.

"There has been a growing awareness among Calvinists during the past few years that borrowing and substituting hymns from other sources has led to worship that is sometimes more 'deformed' than 'reformed'," Virginia Kickert Folgers maintains in "The Importance of Psalmody in the Reformed Tradition" (*The Hymn* 33:2, April 1982, pp. 79-83). She goes on to recount the history of Reformed psalmody (pp. 80-83), during which she points an accusing finger at the practice of "lining out" the Psalms, which "was generally ponderous and out of tune. This practice contributed to the decline in popularity of Psalm-singing" (p. 82).

Because some Reformed people continue to call for the exclusive use of Psalms in the worship of God--the viewpoint of the Westminster Confession, Chapter 21--strong attacks on it have been spawned from various quarters. Vern S. Poythress contributed to this effort: "Ezra 3, Union with Christ, and Exclusive Psalmody" in *The Westminster Theological Journal* (37, 1974, pp. 74-94, 218-235). Here is a good example of modern

"Biblical theology" run rampant, engaging in speculation and pot-rocking.[30]

Exclusive Psalmody must be having an impact in Reformed Baptist circles, for that irrepressible writer Robert Morey has lambasted it, first in a periodical article ("Exclusive Psalmody," *Baptist Reformation Review* 4:4, Winter 1976, pp. 41-56), then in a pamphlet, *An Examination of Exclusive Psalmody* (Shermansdale, PA: New Life Ministries, 1980), a reproduction of the article.[31] It is hard to take seriously someone who would write, "when we turn to the New Testament, we find that there are a number of Christian hymns quoted by the apostles" (p. 48), or argue that exclusive psalmody really wasn't the practice of the Reformed or Presbyterian churches (p. 53),[32] or that the Christian Reformed Church sang "some uninspired hymns as well as Psalms" (p. 53), for they only sang "songs" from Scripture--or does Morey believe such were uninspired? Such factual errors are grievous enough, but the tone of his attack is unbecoming any Christian, especially a minister of the gospel. And certainly a position once so widely held among Baptists deserves a more respectful treatment than it receives here.

The same phenomenon has apparently surfaced in the United Kingdom, where W.J. Seaton of the Reformed Baptist Church in Inverness, Scotland, devoted part of the June/July 1983 issue of his church's magazine, *The Wicket Gate*, to attack exclusive psalmody. "W.T." replied in an article in *The Free Presbyterian Magazine* (89:2, Feb. 1984, pp. 55-59): "Psalm-Singing in the Public Worship of God".[33]

---

[30] A world-renowned New Testament scholar commented to this writer at the time: "No one would be convinced by that article"--but I was, to the view Dr. Poythress was attacking!

[31] Apparently the first effort failed to stem the tide!

[32] So why did we need Isaac Watts?

[33] One highlight will suffice to give a flavor of the interchange. Mr. Seaton wrote: "undoubtedly you can sing *about* Christ in the psalms--in type, and in shadow, and in picture; but you cannot sing *of* Christ in the psalms . . ." (his emphasis). W.T. immediately and properly rejoins: "It is passing strange how people (yes, religious people) will stretch their vain imagination to justify an end which is in contradiction to the mind of God, without considering the implication . . . there is more of Christ in every Psalm written by Him before He came to the world, than in any hymn written by mere men after He came" (p. 58).

Supporters of exclusive psalmody have not merely waited to fend off attacks on their belief. In *The Book of Books: Essays on the Scriptures in Honor of Johannes G. Vos* (Nutley, N.J.: Presbyterian and Reformed, 1978, pp. 73-88, "Biblical Worship: the Place of the Psalms"), Duncan Lowe has given an insightful accounting not only of the Biblical requirement of exclusive psalmody, but of two subjects not often addressed in defending it: *why* God requires only Psalms in worship (which he sees rooted in the unique inspiration of the Bible and the union of the believer with Christ), and *how* music (or, as he terms it, "melody") is distinguishable from other aspects of the Church's worship. John W. Keddie crams a lot into his small pamphlet *Why Psalms Only?* (Edinburgh; Scottish Reformed Fellowship, 1978), considering the textual and historical evidence, making some accurate conclusions, and finishing off with a mine of footnotes. Bruce C. Stewart gives an equally brief and solid defense in *Psalm-Singing Revisited: The Case for Exclusive Psalmody* (Pittsburgh, PA: Reformed Presbyterian Board of Education and Publication, ca. 1981). More substantive is Rowland Ward's *Psalm-Singing in Scripture and History: A Study in History and Doctrine* (Ulverstone, Tasmania: The author, 1979; "revised and enlarged edition": Melbourne: The author, 1985). Always careful not to overreach in his generalizations, his treatment winsomely argues for a rediscovery of exclusive psalmody for Scriptural, historical, and doctrinal reasons. And a worthwhile reprint appeared in *The Free Presbyterian Magazine* (89:6, June 1984, pp. 186-189) consisting of Hugh Martin's speech to the General Assembly of the Free Church of Scotland on June 3, 1872. Densely argued in the style of the age and warmly experimental in the best Scottish tradition, Martin's address stresses the positive features of the Psalms,[34] including these strong but true

---

[34]"First of all, then, on behalf of human hymns, it has been said, 'We live now under a better and brighter dispensation than that of the Old Testament, therefore the inspired Psalms of David, and other Psalms in Holy Scripture, are insufficient.' But the question is not whether the dispensation under which we now live is better and brighter than that which preceded it; but whether, under this better and brighter dispensation, there is any security for better and brighter hymns than the Psalms of David, and whether there is a promise given to any man, or any body of men, of a richer unction of the Spirit--and not a richer unction only, but a specifically

words: "The Psalms are the grand Catholic hymnal and the singing of them provides for Christian union and for perfect catholicity" (p. 189). Hymnody divides, psalmody unites!

The most substantive defence of exclusive psalmody appears in *The Songs of Zion* by Michael Bushell (Pittsburgh: Crown and Covenant, 1980), originally a Westminster Theological Seminary research paper. Bushell begins with the regulative principle, then deals with the testimony of Scripture. The heart of the work argues for the sufficiency and propriety of the Psalms in Christian worship, evidenced by the large and often exclusive place they have held in Christian worship since the early church. Extensive notes and an eleven page bibliography are provided--but no index! Bushell is careful, ready to disagree with the "authorities," and unanswerable, but observes that "the strongest argument for Exclusive Psalmody is the one that inevitably wells up from within when a sincere Christian begins to sing the Psalms with grace in his heart" (p. v).

Psalmody continues in the British Isles, according to a surprized Terry E. Miller ("Oral Tradition Psalmody Surviving in England and Scotland" *The Hymn* 35:1, Jan. 1984, pp. 15-22). He believes that the Westminster Directory for Worship was the first formal recognition of lining out a song (p. 16), a practice now limited in the British Isles to Gaelic Scotland (p. 16). He describes accurately and not unsympathetically that "the precentor's behavior, like that of every one else, is self-effacing and impersonal" (p. 17). He is amazed that all the tunes are common meter (C.M.), and that most are non-Gaelic in origin (pp. 18-19). The tunes are simple, but "ornamentation is part of the style" (p. 20). This type of singing is similar but distinct from current Old Regular Baptist hymnody in the

---

inspiring action of the Spirit--for the purpose of composing hymns for the public worship of God in the Church than was given to him, of whom it is written, that in his blessed swan song he spoke as follows:--'David, the son of Jesse, said, and the man who was raised up on high, the anointed of the God of Jacob, and the sweet Psalmist of Israel, said, The Spirit of the Lord spoke by me, and His Word was in my tongue.' Is there any modern hymnologist in circumstances to say that? Dr. Adam must tell us who he is, before his argument from the greater brightness of the New Testament dispensation is of any worth, otherwise it is an argument not only on behalf of hymns, but against the Book of Psalms."

U.S.A. (p. 20).   Miller provides some informative "figures" and a discography for those interested in hearing this Psalmody for themselves.[35]

A more tendentious goal controls John Locker Clugston's *Making and Marring the Scottish Psalter* (Sydney: Reformer Print, 1974): the 1650 Scottish Psalter must always remain the church's songbook, a sort of *Textus receptus*, permitting no interference or change. His ten arguments against all post-1650 Psalters on pages 45-47 are unconvincing; most of them could have been levelled against the Psalter he is devoted to defending when it was first introduced!

The quality of the psalters available seems to be increasing. The Reformed Presbyterian ("Covenanter") Church of North America published *The Book of Psalms for Singing* (Pittsburgh, 1973), which has since gone through five reprintings.[36]   Over 400 tunes make this Psalter rich and challenging, and several non-metered settings of various Psalms spice the wordings.[37] The Reformed Presbyterians have also produced a selection of 39 new versions of the Psalms in *Sing a New Song: Selections from the Book of Psalms for Singing* (Pittsburgh: Board of Education and Publication, 1973).   This relatively inexpensive selection book would serve well to introduce a congregation to the Psalms. Another selection book, a more substantial offering of 162 Psalm portions, was published in 1987: *Praise Him: Psalm Selections for Singing.* A supplementary collection of Psalm

---

[35] Nicholas Temperley responds to Dr. Miller's article in *The Hymn* (35:3, July 1984, pp. 170-172).

[36] The second and succeeding printings include a topical index that was sorely lacking in the original edition. The many printing errors of the first edition have been corrected in subsequent printings as well.

[37] Particularly the doxologies of Psalms 41, 72, and so forth. The Psalms appear in good-sized print, numbered according to the Psalms (Psalm 8A, 8B, etc.) rather than the page numbers, as in preceding Reformed Presbyterian Psalters. Two striking features of the versions are the extensive use made of modern language (42% of the total), including addressing God with the familiar "You," and the numerous examples of unrhythmed verse, which are rarely noticeable but is more accurate. Several chants are included, but always with an alternative tune.

versions, *Psalm Selections: Psalter Supplement No. 1*, appeared the following year, designed to provide a wider variation in music.

The Reformed Presbyterian Church in Ireland has produced a more traditional psalter. *The Psalms in Metre: Scottish Metrical Version with Tunes, Supplement, and Additional Versions* (London: Oxford University Press, 1979) consists of three parts: the 1650 Psalter, an earlier supplement, and new versions, mostly culled from the 1950 RPCNA *Book of Psalms in Metre* (the newer version having been considered a wee bit too modern). This split-leaf psalter is attractively produced and significantly expands the number of versions available to its users.[38] The Free Church of Scotland also republished its traditional psalter, with most of the changes found in the harmonization, as *The Scottish Psalmody* (General Assembly of the Free Church of Scotland, 1977). The Free Presbyterian Church of Scotland Publications Committee printed a *Concordance on the Psalms in Metre* (Inverness: John G. Eccles, 1979), which is highly useful for those familiar with the traditional metrical Psalms.

Fred R. Anderson produced 52 selections of Psalms in inclusive language as *Singing Psalms of Joy and Praise* (Philadelphia: Westminster Press, 1986). First developed at the Pine Street Presbyterian Church in Harrisburg, Pennsylvania, they all can be sung to familiar hymn tunes. Similar is *A Psalm Sampler* by the same publisher (1986), with 22 Psalms, Hymns of Light, and the "songs" of Zechariah, Mary, and Simeon, with a wide range of musical styles and faithfulness to the original words. A *Liturgical Psalter for the Christian Year* (Minneapolis: Augsburg, 1976) by Massey H. Shepherd sets out the Psalms, minus the imprecatory ones, mostly for use with the Eucharist. Shepherd added *The Psalms in Christian Worship: A Practical Guide* (Minneapolis: Augsburg, 1976) to encourage their use in liturgy. Ford Lewis Battles arranges some of Calvin's translations of the Psalms into meter in his *The Piety of John Calvin* (Grand

---

[38]However, the original plates were used for earlier sections of both the music and the words, so some tune references are incorrect (for instance, at Psalm 43, tune Invocation is 295 not 221).

Rapids: Baker, 1978), but his introduction to them is marred by unfounded speculations.

The Reformed practice of Psalmody is making something of a comeback in the French-speaking world, too. Francois Gonin rejoices in recent progress in "Vers une restauration du Psautier francais" (*La Revue Reformee* n. 188, Juin 1979, pp. 96-100), pointing particularly to the reprint of the first fifty Psalms of Marot and Beza: *Psaumes 1 a 50: Version poetique de Clement Marot et Theodore de Beze en francais moderne avec les melodies du 16eme siecle* (Lausanne: Editions Pierre Viret, 1978), with the rest to follow later. The characteristics of Marot and Beza's original work are listed as: faithfulness to the text, all the Psalms, popular language, and variety (p. [iii]).[39] Gonin also notes that the number of Psalms in the two most recent Protestant hymnals in French has significantly increased: *Psaumes, cantiques et textes pour le culte: a l'usage des Eglises reformees suisses de langue francaise* (Lausanne: Fondation d'edition des Eglises protestantes romandes, 1976), with 71 Psalms in four-part harmony, and *Nos coeurs te chantent: recueil a l'usage des Eglises de la Federation protestante de France* (Strasbourg: Editions Oberlin, 1979), with 75 Psalms for unison singing.

Similar tendencies were at work in *Psalm Praise* (London: Falcon, 1973), consisting of original, copyrighted material in a distinctively modern idiom. One hundred fifty selections, most Psalm paraphrases, but some Biblical paraphrases, are offered.[40]

---

[39]The restoration involves all of the first 50 Psalms, not just the popular ones, and seeks to get even closer to the originals (p. [iii-iv]). Four introductory extracts (two by Marot, one each by Calvin and Beza), notes about the original poetical version, a concordance with the New Testament, and index (if only of one page!), add to the usefulness of the volume. Each Psalm has one tune and an introduction, and is sung to one unison melody.

[40]Most of the songs have chords printed for guitar accompaniment; one verse only is printed between the lines of music, with the other stanzas straggling along at the rear. The producers write in the Introduction: "We hope that the use of Psalm Praise will often lead people back to the original Psalms in the Scriptures with fresh understanding and joy."

Erik Routley's valedictory to a distinguished career, *Rejoice in the Lord* (Grand Rapids: Eerdmans, 1985) offers a very wide choice of songs, with many Psalms included. Unfortunately, it does not seem that the same can be said of the rest of recent hymnals in the English language.

Of related interest to Reformed Christians is the question of instrumental music in worship. "Musical Instruments in Old Testament Worship" is adequately covered by Bryant Wood in *Bible and Spade* (10:2, Spring 1981, pp. 33-41). All the passages he covers are associated with the temple or its constituent parts. A distinctly dispensational hermeneutic characterizes several major attacks on instrumental music in Christian worship coming from the Churches of Christ tradition. Everett Ferguson considers the New Testament, church history, and Christian doctrine before concluding his *A Capella Music in the Public Worship of the Church* (Abilene, TX: Biblical Research Press, 1972; revised edition sometime before 1984) with an appeal for no instruments. He observes: "Instrumental music can express feelings and emotions. Vocal music can express the will and intellect. The latter is better suited for the communion of spirit with Spirit" (p. 88). It is striking that he does not deal with the Old Testament; it is irrelevant in his scheme. James D. Bales' *Instrumental Music and New Testament Worship* (Searcy, Ark. (?): n.p., 1973) takes considerably more time to make the same case, and also produces much more heat in the process. While committed to a regulative principle of worship (p. 10), its implementation is limited to what the New Testament alone advocates. Finally, Foy Esco Wallace has published reprints of materials by M.C. Kurfees, Adam Clarke, Don H. Morris, Moses E. Lurd, and John L. Girardeau (the last requires "some necessary sifting in a few places," p. ix), with some original material of a controversial and historical nature, in *The Instrumental Music Question, consisting of Material by the Author in Public Discussion Refuting the Arguments for the Use of Mechanical Instruments of Music in the Worship* (Fort Worth, TX: F.E. Wallace, Jr. Publications, 1980).[41]

---

[41]The reprint of Girardeau's work is from Wallace's personal copy, and includes his underlining and marginal comments.

John L. Girardeau's classic work against *Instrumental Music in the Public Worship of the Church* has also been reprinted by New Covenant Publication Society (Havertown, PA: 1983).[42]   Rowland S. Ward of the Presbyterian Church of Eastern Australia advocates a similar position in *Instrumental Music in Scripture and History: A Study in History and Doctrine* (East St. Kilda: The author, 1982).   Like his work on Psalm-singing, this presentation lacks a bit of thunder, but does at least produce more light than heat.   "It is difficult to find a reputable writer in the pre-Reformation church who favours or allows the use of instrumental music in the public worship of God" (p. 10).   As a matter of fact, "the Council of Trent (1545-1563) considered banning instrumental music but in the end, did not do so" (p. 14).   Mostly historical in approach, the thesis could be more tightly argued and better expressed.

Preaching in Worship

One of the few recent publications to consider preaching more as an integral part of worship than on its own is Erik Routley's thoughtful, posthumous *Preachers and Musicians and All Who Celebrate the Mysteries* (Princeton, NJ: Prestige Publications, 1986).   But his main interests, not surprizingly, lie elsewhere.   Historical studies dealing with preaching *in worship* are equally rare; one finds some materials in Prof. Hanko's series of articles and in Jack Delivuk's thesis (both mentioned above), and in Carl Eugene Zylstra's *God-centered Preaching in a Human-centered Age: The Developing Crisis confronting a Conservative Calvinist Theology of Preaching in the Christian Reformed Church, 1935-1975* (Ph.D. thesis,

---

[42]Dr. J.G. Vos was once asked what supporters of musical instruments in worship had to say about this work. He replied that they had not answered Girardeau, but simply ignored him.

Princeton University, 1983)[43] and in Richard Stoll Armstrong's *The Pastor-Evangelist in Worship* (Philadelphia: Westminster, 1986). But the relation of preaching to the concept of worship and to the other elements of worship remains a relatively unfallowed field.

The Lord's Supper

Several historical studies highlight the development of Reformed thought concerning the Supper in worship. John D. Nicholls writes of "Union with Christ: John Calvin on the Lord's Supper" in *Union and Communion* (London: The Westminster Conference, 1979, pp. 35-54), first dealing with Calvin's theology,[44] then his practice. In the same collection of addresses, Hywel W. Roberts looks at later developments ("'The Cup of Blessing': Puritan and Separatist Sacramental Discourses," pp. 55-71). The two groups had a common theology of the Supper, but disagreed on admission to and administration of the sacrament (p. 55). The Puritans usually observed the Supper on a monthly basis (p. 56). The ensuing discussion of many different leaders in both camps is fascinating (pp. 57-69). Bryan D. Spinks considers the same subject at greater length but with less sympathy in *From the Lord and "the Best Reformed Churches": A Study of the Eucharistic Liturgy in the English Puritan and Separatist Traditions, 1550-1633* (Roma: C.L.V. - Edizioni Liturgiche, 1984). Two helpful appendices contain Calvin's *La forme des prieres* (1550), and John a Lasco's *Forma ac ratio* (1555). Spinks continues his narrative in *Freedom or Order? The Eucharistic Liturgy in English Congregationalism, 1645-1980* (Pittsburgh: Pickwick Publications, 1984), although one wonders about the twelve year period he skipped between them (1633-1645)! For a French view

---

[43] Available from UMI, order number 83-20295.

[44] Summarized as: it shows our union with Christ; it needs the decisive role of the Holy Spirit; the weakness of our faith is the reason for it; and it is a means of grace (pp. 36f).

consult Alain Martin's "Quelques notes sur la Parole et les Sacrements dans la pensee reformee" (*La Revue Reformee* n. 113, 1978, pp. 1-7).

Summary

The explosion of writing on worship continues, and many other items could have been cited. But much food for thought has been published, encouraging Reformed Christians to question whether they have Biblical warrant for all of their current practices of worship in the presence of God.

APPENDIX A – ABOUT THE AUTHORS

Almost two decades of missionary service in Cyprus mark the career of **E. CLARK COPELAND**. After his overseas ministry, Dr. Copeland held a joint pastorate at the Old Bethel and Bethel congregations of the Reformed Presbyterian Church of North America in Sparta, Illinois. The RPCNA Synod elected him as Professor of Biblical Languages and Literature, a post he held from 1962 until his retirement in 1989. Since retirement, he has lectured extensively, including at the Reformed Presbyterian Theological Hall in Belfast, Northern Ireland. Dr. Copeland is a graduate of Sterling College (A.B.), the Reformed Presbyterian Theological Seminary, and Concordia Theological Seminary (S.T.M. and Th.D.) in St. Louis. He also did graduate work at the University of Pittsburgh and Pittsburgh-Xenia Theological Seminary. Geneva College honored him with the D.D. degree in 1962.

A member of the Presbytery of the American Presbyterian Church since 1979, **LOUIS F. DEBOER** is editor of the American Presbyterian Press. In that capacity, he oversaw the republication of several significant historical works, including Charles Hodge's *The Constitutional History of the Presbyterian Church in the United States of America*. He authored *The New Phariseeism: A Study in the Logical Implications of the Theology of British-Israelism And A Defense of Paul's Gospel* and *Hymns, Heretics, and History*. Pastor DeBoer holds a degree in Mechanical Engineering from the University of Toronto.

Born in Africa the son of missionary parents of the Free Presbyterian Church of Scotland, **J. CAMERON FRASER** graduated from University of Edinburgh (B.A.), Westminster Theological Seminary (M.Div. and Th.M.) and Trinity Evangelical Divinity School (D.Min.). He served from 1978 to 1980 as managing editor of the *Presbyterian Guardian* magazine, and from 1992 to 1994 as editor of *Coast to Coast*, a publication which served the Canadian constituency of the Presbyterian Church in America (PCA). He was ordained in 1985 as organizing pastor of a PCA congregation in Sechelt, British Columbia, and presently pastors First Christian Reformed Church, Lethbridge, Alberta.

A native of Iowa, **HERMAN HANKO** represents the second of three generations of ministers in the Protestant Reformed Churches (PRC): his father was a pastor and two of his eight children are in the pastorate. He graduated from Calvin College (B.A.), the Theological Seminary of the Protestant Reformed Churches (B.D.), and Calvin Theological Seminary (Th.M.). Ordained in 1955, he served two churches.   In 1965, he became Professor of Church History and New Testament Studies at his denomination's seminary. He retired from the Seminary in 2000, but still teaches a course from time to time.   However, even though officially retired, he has remained active in ministry, speaking frequently both in this country and overseas.   He has written *We and Our Children: The Reformed Doctrine of Infant Baptism*; *The Mysteries of the Kingdom* (an explanation of the parables); *God's Everlasting Covenant of Grace*; *For Thy Truth's Sake* (a doctrinal history of the PRC written for the 75th anniversary); and *Portraits of Faithful Saints* (a series of short biographies of fifty-two influential people in the history of the New Testament church); and has been a frequent contributor to the *Protestant Reformed Theological Journal* and *The Standard Bearer*. He also edited and contributed to *Ready to Give an Answer* (a book in question and answer form on the doctrines involved in the controversies of 1924 and 1953 in the PRC) and *The Virtuous Woman* (a collection of essays on Scripture's teaching concerning the role of women in the church, the home and society); and edited and wrote a preface to *Sin and Grace* (a critique of Abraham Kuyper's view of common grace by Rev. H. Hoeksema). A book on prayer, *When Ye Pray. . .*, is slated to be published in summer 2006.

KERRY W. "PETE" HURST graduated from King College (B.A.) and Reformed Theological Seminary (M.Div.).   He pastored the Coeburn, Mary Martin Memorial, and Mt. Olivet Presbyterian Churches in Coeburn, Virginia; Westminster Presbyterian Church, Kingsport, Tennessee; and Faith Presbyterian Church, Birmingham, Alabama; and is presently pastor of Calvary Reformed Presbyterian Church, Hampton, Virginia. He taught for over twenty years as an adjunct faculty member of St. Leo College.

Born in Mississippi, **R. SHERMAN ISBELL** graduated from Edinburgh University (M.A.), the Free Church of Scotland College, and Westminster Theological Seminary (Th.M.), and did graduate work at Bern University. He serves as minister of the Westminster Presbyterian Church, near Washington, D.C.   He is Clerk of Presbytery for the North American presbytery of the Free Church of Scotland (Continuing), and an editor of the presbytery's periodical, *The Master's Trumpet*.   He has also contributed articles to the *Banner of Truth* magazine, *The Ordained Servant*, and the *Dictionary of Scottish Church History and Theology*.

Born in Lumberton, North Carolina, **DOUGLAS F. KELLY** graduated from the University of North Carolina (B.A.), Union Theological Seminary in Virginia (M.Div.), and Edinburgh University (Ph.D.).   After serving as assistant pastor at First Presbyterian Church, Raeford, North Carolina, and as pastor of First Presbyterian Church, Dillon, South Carolina, he became a professor at Reformed Theological Seminary in Jackson, Mississippi. He presently serves at the RTS campus in Charlotte, North Carolina. Among his published works are *If God Already Knows, Why Pray?*; *Preachers with Power: Four Stalwarts of the South*; *The Emergence of Liberty in the Modern World*; *Creation and Change: Genesis 1.1-2.4 in the Light of Changing Scientific Paradigms*; and *Carolina Scots: An Historical and Genealogical Study of Over 100 Years of Emigration* (co-written with his wife, Caroline Switzer Kelly). He was a co-author of *Westminster Confession of Faith: A New Edition* and *The Westminster Shorter Catechism in Modern English* and a contributor to *Southern Reformed Theology: Reformed Theology in America*. Dr. Kelly also translated John Calvin's sermons on II Samuel from French into English. He is a teaching elder in the Presbyterian Church in America.

HENRY KRABBENDAM graduated from the Theologische Hoogeschool, Kampen (B.A. and M.Div.) in his native Holland, and from Westminster Theological Seminary (Th.M. and Th.D.). He was ordained in the Canadian Reformed Church in 1960, later served the Orthodox Presbyterian Church in Sunnyvale, California, and helped to start an OPC congregation in Hixson, Tennessee. Since 1973 he has taught at Covenant College, and has also taught apologetics and ethics at Greenville Presbyterian Theological Seminary. Dr. Krabbendam has ministered extensively throughout the world, especially in Uganda. He has written *Sovereignty and Responsibility* and *The Epistle of James*; and contributed to *Inerrancy*; *Challenges to Inerrancy* . . . ; *Hermeneutics, Inerrancy and the Bible* . . . ; *The Preacher and Preaching* . . .; and *The Agony of Deceit*.

DAVID C. LACHMAN graduated from Houghton College (B.A.), the University of Pennsylvania (M.A.), Westminster Theological Seminary (B.D. and Th.M.), and the University of St. Andrews (Ph.D.). His dissertation on The Marrow Controversy was published by Rutherford House in Scotland. He served as one of the general editors of the *Dictionary of Scottish Church History and Theology*, to which he contributed many articles; he has also written articles for other publications, including the *New Dictionary of National Biography*, and has written introductions to a number of books, including George Gillespie's *Aaron's Rod Blossoming* and Thomas Murphy's *Pastoral Theology*. He was editor of the *Presbyterian Advocate* magazine. An antiquarian theological bookseller, Dr. Lachman has also lectured in church history at Westminster Theological

Seminary. As a ruling elder in the Presbyterian Church in America, he served as moderator and parliamentarian of the Philadelphia Presbytery, as well as on various committees and commissions.

The late **JOHN MURRAY** grew up in the Free Presbyterian Church of Scotland. Following military service in the British Army in World War I, he graduated from Glasgow University (M.A.), Princeton Theological Seminary (Th.B. and Th.M.), and New College, Edinburgh (Th.M.). He taught for one year at Princeton, and in 1930 he began teaching at Westminster Theological Seminary—a career that would last until his retirement in 1967. He was also actively involved in organizing congregations for the Orthodox Presbyterian Church in New England. Professor Murray's published works include *Christian Baptism, Divorce, Covenant of Grace, Principles of Conduct, Imputation of Adam's Sin, Calvin on Scripture and Divine Sovereignty, Atonement, Pattern of the Lord's Day, Epistle to the Romans,* and *Redemption, Accomplished and Applied.* Four volumes of his collected writings have been published posthumously.

KEVIN REED is the founder of Presbyterian Heritage Publications, which has reprinted many classic books and treatises which advocate traditional Presbyterian worship and polity. Among these are some by Samuel Miller, the second professor at Princeton Theological Seminary. Mr. Reid has written a couple of booklets: *The Canterbury Tales* (a warning against Anglo-Catholic worship being promoted in certain "Reformed" circles) and *Christmas: An Historical Survey Regarding Its Origins and Opposition to It.* He has also edited and introduced various of his publications.

THOMAS G. REID, JR., graduated from Westmont College (B.A.) and Westminster Theological Seminary (M.Div.). Interest in reviving the Reformation in the land of Jean Calvin led him to study at the Reformed Seminary at Aix-en-Provence, France, from which he earned a Th.M. degree. He was ordained by the Reformed Presbyterian Church of Ireland and was librarian at the Theological Hall in Belfast besides pastoring in the Republic of Ireland. Following completion of the M.L.S. degree at the University of Pittsburgh, he became library director at Reformed Theological Seminary, Jackson, Mississippi. He also pastored the Reformed Presbyterian Church of North America congregation in Quinter, Kansas; and served as stated supply for the Free Church of Scotland in Edmonton, Alberta, Canada. Since 1996, he has been librarian at the Reformed Presbyterian Theological Seminary in Pittsburgh; he also serves as registrar.

After graduating from Belhaven College (B.A.) and Columbia Theological Seminary (B.D.), **A. MICHAEL SCHNEIDER III** pastored the Williamston (South Carolina) Presbyterian Church; Jackson Street Presbyterian Church, Alexandria, Louisiana; and St. Paul Presbyterian Church, Jackson, Mississippi. Since 1986, he has been pastor of Trinity Presbyterian Church, Valparaiso, Florida.

The late **C. GREGG SINGER** graduated from Haverford College (A.B.) and the University of Pennsylvania (A.M. and Ph.D.). In 1986 the Atlanta School of Biblical Studies awarded him the honorary D.D. degree. Dr. Singer was the chairman of the history departments of several colleges. Among the places at which he taught were Wheaton College, Salem College, the University of Pennsylvania, Belhaven College, Montreat-Anderson College, Catawba College, Furman University, and Atlanta School of Biblical Studies. At the time of his death, he was an active member of the faculty of Greenville (S.C.) Presbyterian Theological Seminary. After having been a ruling elder in the Presbyterian Church in the United States and the Associate Reformed Presbyterian Church, he was ordained as a teaching elder in 1987 in the Presbyterian Church in America. One of the leaders of Concerned Presbyterians, Inc., an organization that helped spark the formation of the Presbyterian Church in America in 1973, Dr. Singer was no stranger to ecclesiastical and intellectual controversy. Among his published works are *From Rationalism to Irrationality*, *A Theological Interpretation of American History*, *John Calvin: His Roots and Fruits*, *Arnold Toynbee: A Critical Study*, *A Christian Introduction to History and Philosophy*, *The Church and the Sword*, *South Carolina in the Confederation, 1781-1789*, and *The Unholy Alliance* (a critique of the National Council of Churches).

The first ministerial candidate of the Presbyterian Church in America, **FRANK J. SMITH** is a graduate of Covenant College (B.A.), Westminster Theological Seminary (M.Div. and Th.M.), and City University of New York (M.Phil. and Ph.D.). In 2005, the Methodist Episcopal Church USA, in conjunction with the National Clergy Council, awarded him a D.D. degree (honoris causae). His book, *The History of the Presbyterian Church in America: The Silver Anniversary Edition*, is an expanded version of an earlier volume. He assisted his father in establishing a church in Westchester County, New York, and in 1986 became senior pastor of that congregation, Affirmation Presbyterian Church. He later pastored the Coeburn (Va.) Presbyterian Church. Presently he is pastor of the Covenant Reformed Presbyterian Church (CRPC) congregation in Sheboygan, Wisconsin. Articles of his have appeared in a variety of publications, including the *Westminster Theological Journal* and *Contra Mundum*. He has co-authored articles for *The Confessional Presbyterian*: "Reframing Presbyterian Worship: A Critical Survey of the Worship Views of John M. Frame and R. J. Gore" (with Dr. David C. Lachman); and a two-part series on "The Regulative Principle of Worship: Sixty Years in Reformed Literature" (with Chris Coldwell); and has contributed several articles for the forthcoming *Encyclopedia of American Science*. He edited *Tales from the City: Real Stories of Urban Christian Ministry*, a book about the work of the Synod of the City in Atlanta. He was the founding editor of Presbyterian International News Service and its publications, *Presbyterian & Reformed News* (1995-2004) and *Presbyterian Heritage* magazine (2005-present).

WILLIAM YOUNG is a graduate of Columbia University (B.A.), Westminster Theological Seminary (Th.B. and Th.M.), Union Theological Seminary in New York (Th.D.), and Oxford University (M.Litt.). After ordination by the Orthodox Presbyterian Church in 1942, he was stated supply at the Bloor East Presbyterian Church (unaffiliated) in Toronto, Canada, from 1944 to 1946. Dr. Young was Assistant Professor of Philosophy at Butler University and Professor of Philosophy and Psychology at Belhaven College before his appointment as Professor of Philosophy at the University of Rhode Island in 1960. He is currently pastor of the Presbyterian Reformed Church in East Greenwich, Rhode Island. A co-translator of Herman Dooyeweerd's *New Critique of Theoretical Thought, Vol. I*, he wrote *The Development of Protestant Philosophy in Dutch Calvinistic Thought*; *Toward a Reformed Philosophy*; *Foundations in Theory*; and Hegel's *Dialectical Method*.

APPENDIX B
REPORT OF THE COMMITTEE ON SONG IN WORSHIP PRESENTED TO THE THIRTEENTH AND FOURTEENTH GENERAL ASSEMBLIES OF THE ORTHODOX PRESBYTERIAN CHURCH

A. The teaching of the Subordinate Standards respecting the Regulative Principle of Worship.

There is a principle clearly expressed in our subordinate Standards which has frequently been called the *regulative* principle of worship. There is an appropriateness in the word "regulative," because it is the principle that deals with the question: in what way or ways are we to worship God? What are the elements which constitute the true and acceptable worship of God? How may we know that the way in which we worship God is acceptable to Him?

To be quite concrete and historical, there are at least two well-defined answers to this question in Christian churches. One of these is that of the Romish Church, followed in principle by Lutherans and Episcopalians, namely, that it is proper to worship God in ways not forbidden in the Word. In contrast with this there is another answer, namely, that God may be worshipped only in ways instituted, prescribed or commanded in the Word. The contrast is patent--the one says: what is not forbidden is permitted, the other says: what is not prescribed is forbidden.

It is in relation to this question that the regulative principle is to be understood. It will surely be conceded that it has a right to such a denomination. The following examination of our Standards will show that a regulative principle is clearly enunciated and that it is precisely formulated in answer to the questions stated above.

I. The first statement in our subordinate Standards bearing upon this question is that in the Confession of Faith, Chapter I, Section vi, namely, "there are some circumstances concerning the worship of God, and government of the Church, common to human actions and societies, which are to be ordered by the light of nature and Christian prudence, according to the general rules of the Word, which are always to be observed."

With respect to this statement it should be noted that it is one of two acknowledgements made with reference to the doctrine that, "The whole counsel of God concerning all things necessary for His own glory, man's salvation, faith, and life, is either expressly set down in Scripture, or by good and necessary consequence may be deduced from Scripture: unto which nothing at any time is to be added, whether by new revelations of the Spirit or traditions of men." We are now interested simply in the import of the above acknowledgement with respect to worship as it bears upon the doctrine of the sufficiency of Scripture just quoted. The teaching of this section as applied to worship would run as follows:

"The whole counsel of God concerning all things necessary" for the worship of God "is either expressly set down in Scripture, or by good and necessary consequence may be deduced from Scripture" except that "there are some circumstances concerning the worship of God, . . . common to human actions and societies, which are to be ordered by the light of nature and Christian prudence, according to the general rules of the Word, which are always to be observed." We may now proceed to analyze this statement.

     1. The exception stated applies only to *circumstances* of worship. It cannot apply to any substantial part or element of the worship. It cannot apply to anything that enters into the worship itself but only to certain conditions under which the worship is given or conducted.

     2. The exception stated applies only to *some* circumstances. The effect of this restriction is to allow that there may be circumstances of worship that are either expressly set down in Scripture or by good and necessary consequence may be deduced from Scripture.

     3. The exception stated applies only to some circumstances common to *human actions and societies.* They are therefore circumstances that are not peculiar to worship. Such are, for example, the circumstances of time and place. They may also include order and length of service, for since human societies are mentioned it is natural for us to think of the meetings of such societies in this connection. The obvious meaning of this section of the Confession is that all that does not fall into the category of "some circumstances, . . . common to human actions and societies" must conform to what is "expressly set down in Scripture, or by good and necessary consequence may be deduced from Scripture," in other words, the authority of Scripture is necessary for the whole content of worship--that for which we have Scripture authority is that which is expressly set down in Scripture or by good and necessary consequence may be deduced from it and *vice versa.*

II. The next statement in our subordinate Standards bearing upon the question is that in the Confession, Chapter XX, Section ii: "God alone is Lord of the conscience, and hath left it free from the doctrines and commandments of men, which are in anything contrary to His Word; or beside it, if matters of faith or worship." This does not, of course, expressly state the principle regulative of worship, but it does teach something closely companionate with it. In matters of worship, as well as of faith, the conscience is free not only from what is contrary to the Word but also from what is beside it. That is to say, in the matter of worship the conscience is not bound by anything unless it is taught or enjoined in the Word, either by express statement or by good and necessary consequence. What is outwith the deliverances of the Word has no authority for the conscience. The law for the conscience in worship is that which is authorized by Scripture.

     This section does not reflect on the question whether the Christian is free to worship God in ways not taught in Scripture or not authorized by Scripture. It would have been outside the purpose and scope of this section to introduce this question. However, it must be noted carefully that this section does not say or imply that the Christian is free to worship in ways that are beside the teaching of Scripture. What the section says is that the conscience is free *from* all that is beside the Word in matters of worship; it does not say that the conscience is free to use what is beside the Word.

This section, however, does say emphatically that to include in worship anything that is beside the Word, *out of conscience*, is to betray true liberty of conscience. For the section proceeds: "So that, to believe such doctrines, or to obey such commands, out of conscience, is to betray true liberty of conscience." The only worship that can be rendered *out of conscience*, then, is the worship authorized by Scripture, that is to say, worship not beside the Word but worship authorized in the Word.

It should be observed, furthermore, that, in matters that are beside the Word, worship and faith are put on the same level. It is pertinent to ask if, in the teaching of the Confession, we are conceded the liberty of incorporating into our *faith* anything that is beside the Word? It would appear that we are not. If so, are we not justified in presuming, to say the least, that the Confession meant the same principle to apply to worship, even in the terms of this section?

III. In Chapter XXI, Section i, of the Confession the principle regulative of worship is expressly and unequivocally formulated. It says: "But the acceptable way of worshipping the true God is instituted by Himself, and so limited by His own revealed will, that He may not be worshipped according to the imaginations and devices of men, or the suggestions of Satan, under any visible representation, or any other way not prescribed in the holy Scripture."

The following points may be made regarding this section.

1. It enunciates a principle that applies to *all* worship of God, a principle *regulative* of all worship. This principle is that God may be worshipped only in a way or in ways prescribed, instituted, or revealed in the Word.

2. That the regulative principle of worship enunciated in the Confession is that God may be worshipped only in a way prescribed in His Word is quite obvious from the following considerations:

(a) The Confession says, "the acceptable way of worshipping the true God is instituted by Himself." If "instituted," it must be positively ordained and not left to human invention or imagination.

(b) The acceptable way is "limited by His own revealed will." True worship, therefore, is exercised within the limits of what God has revealed to be acceptable. Obviously, if we worship God in a manner or way which Scripture does not determine our worship cannot be within these limits, and is therefore, in terms of the Confession, unacceptable.

(c) The Confession is negative and exclusive as well as positive--God "may not be worshipped according to the imaginations and devices of men, or the suggestions of Satan, under any visible representation, or any other way not prescribed in the holy Scripture." This defines the extent of the limitation mentioned in the preceding clause, or it may be regarded as a consequence flowing from the said limitation. It is so limited that the succeeding are excluded.

A word must be said about the construction of this latter part of the section. At the end we have the alternatives "under any visible representation" and "any other way not prescribed in the holy Scripture." The immediately preceding part of the sentence, namely, "may not be worshipped according to the imaginations and devices of men, or the suggestions of Satan," applies to both. So the construction is to the effect that God "may not be worshipped according to the imaginations and devices of men, or the suggestions of Satan, under any visible representation, or any other way not prescribed in the holy Scripture." By the former negation human imagination or device and Satanic suggestions are to be given no quarter in exercising their ingenuity in the direction of visualizing the worship of God. The Confession apparently felt the need of making special mention of this corruption. By the latter negation there is the most unequivocal statement that every way not prescribed in the holy Scripture is excluded, and this means that any particular element of worship that is not able to plead divine prescription in the Scripture is forbidden. To state it more positively, God may be worshipped only in the manner prescribed in the holy Scripture.

IV. The Larger Catechism, Questions 108 and 109, and the Shorter Catechism, Questions 50 and 51, clearly enunciate the same principle as we have already found in the Confession. It is stated both positively and negatively in both Catechisms. We shall see that it is most important to note the principle of exclusion as well as that of inclusion.

In Question 108 the Larger Catechism says: "The duties required in the second commandment are, the receiving, observing, and keeping pure and entire, all such religious worship and ordinances as God hath instituted in his word" and the Shorter Catechism, Question 50, says: "The second commandment requireth the receiving, observing, and keeping pure and entire, all such religious worship and ordinances as God hath appointed in his word." It might be argued that this positive statement, though it makes mandatory the worship of God instituted in His Word, yet does not rigidly exclude the propriety of worshipping God in ways not instituted in the Word. It is here that the effect of the principle of exclusion, formulated in Question 109 and 51 of the respective Catechisms, becomes apparent. The Larger Catechism, Question 109, reads: "The sins forbidden in the second commandment are, all devising, counselling, commanding, using, or any wise approving, any religious worship not instituted by God himself," and the Shorter Catechism, Question 51: "The second commandment forbiddeth the worshipping of God by images, or any other way not appointed in his word."

Any further observation seems unnecessary other than to say that the worship authorized and enjoined is that instituted or appointed in the Word and that *any religious worship* or *any way* of worshipping God not appointed in the Word would be characterized in the language of Question 108 of the Larger Catechism as "false worship" and therefore to be disapproved, detested and opposed, and according to each one's place and calling, removed.

V. It remains to deal with "The Directory for the Public Worship of God," adopted by the Sixth General Assembly of The Orthodox Presbyterian Church.

There is an obvious distinction between the Confession, Larger and Shorter Catechisms on the one hand, and the Standards of Government, Discipline and Worship, on the other. The former are accorded a higher place in the constitution than the latter, inasmuch as the former are expressly mentioned in the formulae of subscription, whereas the latter are not thus mentioned, even though the approval of the government and discipline of the Church is required in some of the formulae.

It should observed that the "Directory" is "The Directory for the Public Worship of God" and is more limited in its scope than the statements from the Confession and Catechisms dealt with already.

The relevant sections of the "Directory" may, however, be discussed briefly.

In Chapter II, Section 1, the "Directory" says: "Since the holy Scriptures are the only infallible rule of faith and practice, the principles of public worship must be derived from the Bible, and from no other source." In the succeeding sections some of these principles are formulated. The principle regulative of worship, found in the Confession and Catechisms, is not formulated, and there is no unequivocal statement affirming or denying it.

There are some remarks, however, that may be made.

1. Chapter II, Section 1, quoted above, says, "the principles of public worship must be derived from the Bible, and from no other source." Since the principle regulative of worship applies to public worship and since such a principle is enunciated in the Confession and Catechisms, this must be one of the principles the "Directory" says must be derived from the Bible, and from no other source. This means that, according to the "Directory," the regulative principle must be that taught in the Word of God. What this teaching is the "Directory" itself does not say.

2. In Chapter II, Section 7, the Directory says, "The Lord Jesus Christ has prescribed no fixed forms for public worship but, in the interest of life and power in worship, has given his church a large measure of liberty in this matter. It must not be forgotten, however, that there is true liberty only the rules of God's Word are observed and the Spirit of the Lord is, that all things must be done decently and in order, and that God's people should serve him with reverence and in the beauty of holiness." It is possible that the phrase, "a large measure of liberty," might be appealed to as expressing a different principle from that already dealt with as taught in the Confession and Catechisms. Furthermore, it is possible that it may have been intended in this way by the framers of the "Directory." With respect to any such contention or intention two things must be said.

(a) The phrase "a large measure of liberty" refers to "forms for public worship." It is entirely reasonable to assume that "forms" refer to something different from that which comes within the scope of the regulative principle enunciated in the Confession and Catechisms. Surely this section should be interpreted as referring to the kind of fixed liturgical forms to which the framers of the Westminster Standards were consistently opposed. It can at least be said that the regulative principle of the Confession and Catechisms is not in the least inconsistent with such denial of fixed forms as is expressed in this section.

(b) The large measure of liberty must be exercised, according to this section, within "the rules of God's Word." It is not, therefore, unrestricted liberty, and so, if the regulative principle be a principle of God's Word. the liberty must exercised within, and compatibly with, that principle or rule.

(c) Even supposing that the phrase, "a large measure of liberty," was intended to express a different principle from that enunciated in the Confession and Catechisms, the occurrence of this phrase could not have the effect of abrogating the plain and unequivocal statements of the other Standards.

B. The Teaching of our Subordinate Standards Respecting the Songs that may be Sung in the Public Worship of God.

So far as we have been able to find, the only place where there is express reference in the Confession of Faith and Catechisms to the materials of songs to be used in the worship of God is in Chapter XXI, Section v of the Confession. This chapter deals with "Religious Worship and the Sabbath Day." Its teaching is not limited to public worship, though it includes public worship. As found already in the other study, this chapter enunciates in Section i the regulative principle of all worship. In Section ii as well as in the first part of Section i some other principles of worship are formulated. In Sections iii, iv and v, the parts of worship are enumerated. It is in connection with these that "singing of psalms with grace in the heart" is stated to be one part of "the ordinary religious worship of God." It is coordinated with "prayer, with thanksgiving," "the reading of the Scriptures with godly fear," "the sound preaching and conscionable hearing of the Word," and "the due administration and worthy receiving of the sacraments instituted by Christ." The ordinary religious worship of God is distinguished from the worship rendered upon "special occasions" such as "religious oaths, vows, solemn fastings, and thanksgivings."

So far as the Confession is concerned, then, singing is one part of the ordinary religious worship of God. By obvious implication it is part of the ordinary public worship of God. The material to be used in such singing is "psalms." In other words, in that part of worship that consists in singing, it is the "singing of psalms" that defines that in which it consists, not simply singing, not simply singing of God's praises, and not simply singing with grace in the heart, but "singing of psalms." The song-part of worship is the "singing of psalms." Hence the Confession does not provide for the use of any materials of song other than "psalms" in the worship of God.

The proof texts given in the Westminster Confession are Colossians 3:16; Ephesians 5:19; James 5:13. The proof texts given in the Confession of the Presbyterian Church in the U. S. A. are these three with Acts 16:25 added.

"The Directory for the Public Worship of God" of The Orthodox Presbyterian Church deals with this question in Chapter III which bears the heading, "Of the Usual Parts of Public Worship." Section 6 deals with "congregational singing." It is implied that it is a part of public worship, coordinate with the other parts mentioned in other sections. In this section there occurs the following: "Since the metrical versions of the Psalms are based upon the Word of God, they ought to be used frequently in public worship. Great care must be taken that all the materials of song are in perfect accord with the teaching of holy Scripture."

There can be no doubt but "the Psalms" mentioned in "the Directory" are the book of Psalms. With respect to such it is said that the metrical versions, being based upon the Word of God, should be used frequently in public worship. The context makes it plain that what is meant is that they are to be used frequently as the materials of congregational singing. A few observations regarding this statement of the Directory are in order.

1. The metrical versions are not called the Word of God. Rather are they said to be based upon it.

2. These metrical versions, "the Directory" says, ought to be used "frequently." It does not say expressly that the "congregational singing" *consists* in the singing of these metrical versions of the Psalms. The omission of any such identification, together with the use of the word, "frequently," might be said to concede the propriety, so far as the Directory is concerned, of singing materials other than the metrical versions of the Psalms. This interpretation could plead support from the sentence that follows, namely, "Great care must be taken that all the materials of song are in perfect accord with the teaching of holy Scripture." It could be argued that the phrase "all the materials of song" makes allowance for materials other than the metrical versions of the Psalms and that the latter are only part of the materials of song. Further support for this interpretation might be drawn from the phrase, "in perfect accord with the teaching of holy Scripture." It would hardly seem necessary to issue this warning with respect to the metrical versions of the Psalms since these Psalms are the Word of God and the metrical versions are directly based upon it.

3. It should be noted, however, that this section of the Directory does not expressly endorse the use in congregational singing of any other materials than what is called "the metrical versions of the Psalms" but would seem to allow for them.

4. In Chapter IV, C., Section 3, "The Directory for the Public Worship of God" says, "A psalm or hymn should then be sung, and the congregation dismissed with the following or some other benediction." This has to do with the conclusion of the communion service.

Since in the language of Scripture the words "psalm" and "hymn" may be used synonymously it cannot be affirmed dogmatically that this statement endorses the use of sacred songs other than psalms in the public worship of God.

However, even though in the language of Scripture the word "hymn" may be used with reference to a psalm, yet in this statement the word "hymn" probably has to be taken as referring to a sacred song that is not a psalm. Here therefore the Directory may provide for the singing of sacred songs other than psalms in the public worship of God. In this place the provision is restricted to the conclusion of the communion service. But since the conclusion of the communion service is as integral a part of the public worship of God as any other part, it can be said that, on this interpretation, "the Directory" does here in principle make provision for, and states the propriety of, the singing of materials other than psalms in the public worship of God.

C. The Teaching of the Word of God Concerning the Regulative Principle of Worship.

The Scriptures are the authoritative and sufficient rule for us in all of faith and practice. In worship we are bound to observe the principles, regulations, and ordinances which they enjoin upon us--and those principles, regulations, and ordinances alone; what they do not prescribe we are not to observe. The Second Commandment (Ex. 20:4-6; Deut. 5:8-10) emphatically enunciates this principle. This commandment is rightly interpreted in the Larger Catechism, Q. 108, as requiring among other duties "the receiving, observing, and keeping pure and entire, all such religious worship and ordinances as God hath established in his word . . . ." It is also rightly held, in the Larger Catechism, Q. 109, to forbid, along with other sins, "all devising, counselling, condoning, using, and any wise approving, any religious worship not instituted by God himself . . . all superstitious devices, corrupting the worship of God, adding to it, or taking from it, whether invented and taken up of ourselves, or received by tradition from others, though under the title of antiquity, custom, devotion, good intent, or any other pretense whatsoever." Of relevance to worship is Moses' commandment: "Ye shall not add unto the word which I command you, neither shall ye diminish *ought* from it, that ye may keep the commandments of the Lord your God which I command you" (Deut. 4:2; see also Deut. 12:32). Obviously relevant is our Lord's condemnation of the Pharisees (Mark 7:5-8). See also Colossians 2:20-23.

God who is a most pure Spirit and absolute Sovereign is the sole object of worship. Nothing that has not come from Him as its source is fit to be returned to Him as its end. Autonomous human reason and will, sense, emotion and imagination are not competent to originate acts or methods of worship. God as the supreme Law-giver claims for Himself the prerogative of appointing the ordinances of His worship. How then can it be anything other than presumption in a subject of this absolute Sovereign to offer as worship anything which He has not prescribed? That God allows worship that He has not prescribed is contrary to the Scripture. The attitude of God to the worshipper is expressed in such a passage as: "When ye come before me, who hath required this at your hand?" (Is. 1:12), and the religious attitude of the worshipper who is keenly conscious of God's sovereignty is expressed in such a passage as: "Wherewith shall I come before the Lord, and bow myself before the high God?" (Micah 6:6). The connection between the spirituality and sovereignty of God is also evident in the Second Commandment. The express prohibition of image-worship in this commandment is seen to rest upon the fact that false worship consists in the invention of modes of worshipping God inconsistent with His spirituality. "Making to oneself" is opposed to the regulative principle as it expresses the divine sovereignty, and likenesses of sensible things are opposed to the pure spirituality of the Deity. Proper regard for God's prerogative of sovereignty in worship is the supreme safeguard against the adulterations of the spirituality of worship; disregard of God's prerogative of sovereignty in worship definitely tends toward the adulteration of the spirituality of worship.

The necessity of observing this principle is accentuated by the fallen state of man. The total corruption and deceitfulness of the unregenerate human heart disqualify men from judging as to what may be admitted into the content of worship. The necessity of external revelation as an unerring and sufficient guide for worship is evident. The repeated admonitions of Scripture is both Testaments (Deut. 4:9, 15, 23; 12:13, 19, 30; Num. 15:39, 40; I Cor. 11:17, 20, 28, 29) show the vanity and folly of looking to the consciousness even of the regenerate man for the rule or source of the content of worship.

Many direct and specific commandments regarding worship are given to us in the Bible. But it is not only by express commands that the Bible gives warrant for certain practices of worship and renders them obligatory. What is to be derived by good and necessary consequence from the express statements of Scripture is to be regarded as taught, sanctioned, or warranted by Scripture. We have, for example, no express command to baptize infants, but we believe that we have divine warrant and authorization for the practice. To refuse to baptize infants is a serious violation of divine ordinance. Authorization may also be given in Scripture by approved example. If God has authorized a certain element of worship by some other method than that of express command, it is still a revelation to us of what is acceptable to Him.

Although it is true that the Scripture teaches that God is to be worshipped only in ways prescribed, instituted, revealed, or commanded in His Word, it is also true that the Scripture does not prescribe every circumstance concerning worship. This applies both to the Old Testament and the New; but in the New, because of the greater liberty bestowed by the outpouring of the Holy Spirit at Pentecost, fewer circumstances of worship are prescribed than in the Old. It is to be remarked, for example, that no precise time is set in the Scripture for such an important matter as the baptizing of infants, although circumcision was administered in the Old Testament period on the eighth day after birth, according to specific command.

It is further to be observed that the Word of God makes provision for the exercise of a measure of liberty as regards the content of worship. Here too, there is a difference of degree between Israel of the old dispensation, which was under the law, and the New Testament Church, which is delivered from the law. Nevertheless in both dispensations the Scripture grants to the people of God a measure of liberty in the content of worship. An obvious example is afforded by prayer. Although the Bible gives us much instruction and direction in the matter of prayer, indeed even though the whole Word of God is of use to direct us in prayer and even though our Lord gave us a special rule of direction in prayer, we are not required to use any set form of words exclusively and invariably in our prayers. We are not limited in our prayers, for example, to the words of the prayer of Hannah, to the words of the prayers of David, as given in the Book of Psalms, or to the words of any other prayer given in the Scriptures--even to the words of the special rule which our Lord has provided for us. Prayer has been ordained by Scripture to reflect not only God's revelation in the Old Testament, but also in the New Testament period, in relation to the developing particular circumstances in the lives of God's people in all ages. This freedom in relation to prayer is not regarded by the Scripture as incompatible with the regulative principle which the Second Commandment and other declarations of Scripture establish for our worship.

It may be asked whether the freedom granted in prayer is granted also in song. It is true that the freedom is clearly or expressly granted in the case of prayer. Will not the regulative principle for worship taught by Scripture require us to take such freedom in the case only of those forms or elements of worship for which the Scripture specifically authorizes such freedom? It might possibly be maintained in answer to this question that if the Scripture makes it clear that freedom is permissible in connection with one element of worship--and to no prejudice of the regulative principle--it is a warrantable inference that freedom of the same sort is permissible in connection with other elements of worship, *if the Scripture does not clearly and specifically prohibit our taking that freedom in connection with those other elements*. But even if this position is not taken, it might well be maintained that in the absence of any specific statement in the Bible to the contrary, the freedom granted in the case of prayer is certainly to be regarded as obtaining also in the case of songs used in worship, even if no statement can be found in Scripture expressly granting it in the case of songs. The resemblance in content between prayers and songs might be maintained to be so close and important as to lead us to infer that the liberty granted in the case of prayer is quite legitimately to be taken in the case of song. If the Scripture itself calls psalms prayers, may we not regard it as reasonable to think that the freedom of content granted in the one case is to be taken in the other also and not to be denied because of certain external or secondary points of difference. More will be said about this matter later in this report.

D. The Scriptural Teaching Concerning the Songs That May Be Sung in Worship

1. The Old Testament

The first recorded instance in the Old Testament of the use of song in the public worship of God is the song of praise and thanksgiving sung by Moses and the children of Israel after the deliverance from Egypt (Ex. 15:1ff). If singing was employed in public worship during the pre-Moosaic period or in connection with the service of the tabernacle, there is no record of the fact.

It was David who laid the foundations for musical service at the sanctuary of the Lord. David was the first good king of the theocracy, and his task consisted largely in building up and making secure the foundations of that theocracy. He instructed the Levites to appoint their brethren as singers, i.e., those who were to sing songs which could be accompanied on a musical instrument (I Chron. 15:16). These were to sing with uplifted voice and joyfully. The singers were divided into three companies according to the type of instrument which they played. Some musicians were to sound with cymbals of brass, some were to employ psalteries on Alamoth (I Chron. 15:20), whereas others were to play harps on the Sheminith (v. 21) and Chenaniah was leader in song (*massa'*). The musical terms herein employed may refer to different types of tunes, although this is by no means certain. Some of the terms are used as headings of the Psalms. Thus "Alamoth" occurs in the heading of Psalm 46, and "Sheminith" in the headings of Psalms 6 and 12, and these terms may refer to these specific Psalms. None of the Psalms bears the heading *massa'*, and if any compositions did bear this heading these compositions are now lost. David further had constructed musical instruments (*kelim*) for the purpose of praise (I Chron. 23:5), and certain men were separated for the purpose of prophesying upon harps and other musical instruments (I Chron. 25:1ff). In all, four thousand singers were employed, and of these, 288 were skilled (I Chron. 23:5 with 25:1-7).

During the reign of Solomon this service was continued and probably developed (*cf.* I Ki. 10:12, II Chron. 7:6, 9:11). The same was true of the revivals under Jehoiada, Hezekiah and Josiah (II Chron. 23:18, 20:20ff, 35:15).

When the foundations of the Second Temple were laid, the musical service was in accord with the command of David (Ezra 3:10). At the dedication of the walls of Jerusalem the musical instruments employed were those of David the man of God (Neh. 12:36).

While these arrangements for musical service in the sanctuary were explicit as to the number of singers and the variety of instruments used in accompaniment, little is given us as to the content of song. The words *Alamoth* and *Sheminith*, as already mentioned, may possibly refer to specific Psalms. Nehemiah 12:46 mentions the songs which were in use at the time of David and Asaph as being "songs of praise and of thanksgiving unto God." The word for "praise" occurs in the titles of some Psalms, but the word "thanksgiving" does not. We know definitely from I Chronicles 16 that the content of some of our present Psalms was used in worship. In this chapter it is recorded that a service of worship was held in the tabernacle on the removal of the ark of the covenant to Jerusalem, and that a psalm was given by David to Asaph and his brethren wherewith to thank the Lord. This psalm, as sung on that occasion, is recorded in vs. 8-36. But this psalm is also reporduced in various parts of the book of Psalms: Psalm 105:1-15, Psalm 96:1-13, probably Psalm 106:1, 47, and perhaps Psalm 72:18. It is obvious from other psalms that they were intended for use in the public worship of God; see Psalms 95:2, 27:6, and 100:4. Another reference which clearly gives an indication as to the content of song is II Chronicles 29:30, where Hezekiah expressly commanded the use of the words of David and Asaph the seer for a certain occasion of worship. Embraced in this description may be those Psalms of David and of Asaph which are now preserved in the Scriptures. However, for another special occasion Hezekiah did not make use of the psalms already in existence but composed a new psalm suitable to the circumstances, which is not included in our present Psalter; and provided for its use in the house of the Lord (Is. 38:10-20).

There is not to be found in the Old Testament any explicit command which would require the Israelites to employ the entire Psalter which is preserved, and only the Psalter, as the exclusive manual of praise in worship. Neither does it appear that the Talmud, which is the main source of information concerning worship during the inter-testamental period, makes any reference to the entire Psalter as the exclusive manual of praise, although it does require the use of certain Psalms on set occasions. Thus after the completion of the canon, or after the Psalter had become fixed as containing the present 150 Psalms, there is no evidence, or at least no remaining evidence, that the entire Psalter was used as the exclusive book of praise in worship. This lack of evidence obtains not only with reference to the inter-testamental period but also to the time of Christ.

2. The New Testament

The teaching of the New Testament concerning the content of the songs that are to be sung in the worship of God very largely depends on the usage of the words *psalm, hymn,* and *song.* Although in classical Greek *song* is the generic word for song, *hymn* signifies a song of praise, and *psalm* appears in the *Rhesus,* of the time of Euripides, for love song, yet these words as used in the New Testament clearly mean songs of praise to God. More exactly the decisive question is whether they refer in the New Testament only to the Old Testament Psalms.

The word *psalm* is used in I Corinthians 14:26, where Paul says, "How is it then, brethren? when ye come together, every one of you hath a psalm, hath a doctrine, hath a revelation, hath an interpretation. Let all things be done unto edifying." The particular question confronting us here is the exact nature of the songs that were sung. Were they Old Testament Psalms, or charismatic psalms, or impromptu songs uninspired in their content? The impression given by the entire context is that the songs were charismatic. From the beginning of Chapter 12 to the end of Chapter 14 the special gifts of the Spirit are under consideration. Even the excellence and necessity of love as set forth in Chapter 13, is shown as the best way to obtain and use these gifts. The Corinthian Christians were especially zealous of the Spiritual gifts (14:12). It is to be assumed that all men and perhaps the women mistakenly also (v. 34) endeavored to obtain them. Perhaps some who thought they had these gifts really did not, and as a consequence their utterances were unedifying; but because of the difficulty of separating the true gift of tongues, for example, from a kind of empty babbling, it was hard to keep order in the meetings. Whether or not there were counterfeit charisms, there was evidently too much emphasis on the gift of tongues at Corinth, for Paul urges the superiority of the gift of prophecy (vv. 1-25). It would be strange to find a sudden transition in v. 26 to that which is not charismatic. "Every one of you hath a psalm, hath a doctrine, hath a revelation, hath a tongue, hath an interpretation." This is a list of some of the special gifts of the Spirit. As the last four are charismatic, it is to be presumed that the psalm also is charismatic. Since the Holy Spirit blessed the infant Church with apostles, prophets, teachers, miracles, healings, helps, governments, and tongues (12:28) in order to establish it in sound doctrine, and thus provided so fully for its organization and worship, we might expect that special provision was made also for song.

Three arguments, however, may be employed to the effect that *psalmos* in v. 26 means a Psalm of the Old Testament. The first is that the Psalms may have been the actual content of charismatic song. But then there is no reason why the songs should have been given in a special manner by the Spirit. Second, the use of the Greek word. But in this context there seems ample justification to translate it as "song," or to regard it as designating song similar in certain respects to the Psalms. Third, the use of the word *echei,* each *hath* a psalm, might suggest a song already composed and at hand rather than the special inspiration of the moment. But *echei* is used also in the case of the other four gifts: viz., doctrine, revelation, tongue, and interpretation. We conclude then that the Greek word *psalmos* in the New Testament appears to have a generic sense wider than that of Old Testament Psalm.

The word *to hymn* occurs in Matthew 26:30 and Mark 14:26, with probable although not certain reference to certain Old Testament Psalms. As for the word *song*, the book of Revelation refers to the singing of new *songs* which are not quotations of Old Testament Psalms but which praise God in terms characteristic of the new dispensation (Rev. 5:9-10, 7:10; cf. also 14:3 and 15:3).

In Ephesians 5:19 and Colossians 3:16 Paul enjoins the use of psalms, hymns and spiritual songs. The phrase "psalms, hymns and songs" is not known to have been a technical designation of the Old Testament Psalms as a body. Moreover, the word *psalms* alone, or the word *hymns*, or *songs*, cannot be clearly demonstrated to mean specifically the 150 Psalms of the Old Testament. It is possible that each of these terms may refer to such Psalms, since each is used in the LXX in the titles of the Psalms. However, the usage in the LXX merely shows the possibility that in the New Testament the words may refer to the Old Testament Psalms; a possibility which is not denied. On the other hand they could refer to New Testament productions as well. Indeed, the word *psalm* is used in I Corinthians 14:26 to mean a charismatic song, or a song given in the early church as a special gift of the Spirit. The word *song* also is not confined in New Testament usage to the meaning Old Testament Psalm. In Ephesians 5:19 and Colossians 3:16, therefore, we cannot be sure whether Paul had in mind the use of Old Testament Psalms alone, or New Testament productions alone, or both.

Moreover in Colossians 3:16 there is a presumption against the exclusion of New Testament songs from the songs there mentioned. Paul says, "Let the word of Christ dwell in you richly, in all wisdom teaching and admonishing one another in psalms and hymns and spiritual songs . . . ." To the Colossians, who had lately been brought from darkness into light through the gospel message, the phrase "the word of Christ" would probably mean the gospel message about Christ. And, as the word of Christ dwells in them richly, psalms, hymns and spiritual songs will flow forth in consequence; these songs will reflect the content of the word of Christ; and by means of these songs believers are urged to teach and admonish one another in all wisdom. Thus at least some of these songs would be newly composed, either extemporaneously or as the result of some thought. It is well to consider in this connection that music in the time of the early church was rudimentary in comparison with the highly developed music of modern times. Authorities seem to be in general agreement that early Christian music was without harmony or elaborate melody, and consisted mainly in chanting. "The old Hebrew music was played thoroughly in unison. . . . In the place of harmony, rhythm plays a leading part, even at the expense of melody. . . . The singing was mainly a sort of rhythmic declamation." (*The New Schaff-Herzog Encyclopedia*, article "Sacred Music"). While the writer quoted speaks of the music of the Old Testament, it may be inferred that vocal music had changed little by New Testament times. The early Christians with their background in the synagogue, probably chanted their songs. Moreover the ancient Greeks presumably attained as high a development of music as the Hebrews, but even they adhered to the simplest melodies.

Evidence of this is found in the fact that although they had a rude system of writing down music by using the letters of the alphabet to indicate degrees of the scale, between 200 and 500 A.D. this system dropped out of use and was lost; so that even Boethius (480-525), who in many ways was the connecting link between the wisdom of the ancient world and that of the middle ages, knew of no means of writing music. (See *Grove's Dictionary of Music and Musicians*, article "Notation"). If the Greek notation died out it may be inferred that their music was of so undeveloped and impromptu a nature as not to be worth preserving. The early Christians could not have known this Greek method of notation or they, in a developing and expanding movement, would have preserved it if *their* music had been elaborate enough to keep. But it was not until about 680 that a new system of notation, by accents, was devised to preserve the melodies of the Christian Church. In all this there seems a good argument that the early Christians had very simple music and probably chanted. And it is suggested that the mode of rendering the Biblical lyrics in the early Church was as follows: "They were recited by a single person, while the congregation, or, as representing it, the choir, simply responded at the end of each verse with a short refrain." (*Hastings Encyclopedia of Religion and Ethics*, article "Hymns, Greek Christian," by Baumstark). "The Psalms were chanted, antiphonally or as a solo with a limited congregational refrain" (*Idem.*, article "Music, Christian," by Westerby). Chanting may be defined as monotonic recitation with cadences, with occasional rise or fall in pitch. Since there was no repetition of a specific melody, there was no need or desire for rhymed metric stanzas. Instead, simple lyrical utterance, freely chanted, was the custom of the time. These circumstances show how relatively simple was the composition of songs at the time of the early Church, and go far to explain how Paul could urge the Colossians to compose songs, either extemporaneously or after some meditation, for the general use of the Christian community. Such songs, flowing forth out of the rich indwelling store of gospel truth, would have that truth as their content. Thus while the Old Testament Psalms were probably used by the New Testament Church they were not exclusively used and they were not commanded in the New Testament to be the specific and exclusive manual of praise.

According to the Westminster Standards we may not incorporate into the worship of God any element which is neither expressly set down in Scripture nor by good and necessary consequence to be deduced from Scripture. The New Testament definitely provides for the element of song in public worship in I Corinthians 14:15 and 26, and probably also in Acts 4:23-31. However, the content of song is not expressly limited in the New Testament, and accordingly we deduce it from the New Testament by good and necessary consequence.

In this respect song is like prayer, which although expressly given as a part of worship is not confined in Scripture to a set form of words. Indeed there is a very close connection between song and prayer. In Psalm 72:20, Psalms in the preceding subdivision are characterized as "prayers": "the prayers of David the son of Jesse are ended." Paul and Silas in prison engaged in both song and prayer at the same time, by one act: "praying, they were singing hymns" (Acts 16:25). There is also good reason to believe that the prayer of the early church in Acts 4:24-31 was chanted. The majority of commentators say that the prayer was spoken aloud by Peter alone and silently assented to by the rest. Thus they explain "they lifted up their voice to God with one accord." To be sure, the words "with one accord" may mean no more than they joined silently and unanimously in the prayer. But the words "they lifted up [their] voice" are hard to reconcile with the interpretation that the voice of Peter only was heard. In Acts 14:11 and 22:22 many voices are meant by the words, "lifted up their voices." If Peter only had spoken, he would presumably have been mentioned as the speaker. The impression given by the Greek is that all joined aloud in the utterance. Perhaps, as has been conjectured, the second Psalm, or the part of it given here, was sung by all; and then Peter alone prayed aloud. But this is contrary to the apparent unity of the whole utterance as a prayer. Ellicott suggests that this whole phrase ("they lifted up their voice with one accord") "seems to imply an intonation, or chant, different from that of common speech. The joint utterance described may be conceived of as the result either (1) of a direct inspiration, suggesting the same words to all who were present; (2) of the people following St. Peter, clause by clause; (3) of the hymn being already familiar to the disciples. On the whole, (2) seems the most probable, the special fitness of the hymn for the occasion being against (3), and (1) involving a miracle of so startling a nature that we can hardly take it for granted without a more definite statement." In support of Ellicott's view may be urged the fact already mentioned, that the early Christians most probably chanted their songs of praise, thus enabling them to improvise their songs to suit the occasion. To be sure, much of the prayer is not poetry; but even prose may be chanted. Moreover it was suggested in the discussion of chanting earlier in this report that songs may have been chanted as a solo with a limited congregational refrain. Thus if Peter, or another leader of the Church, chanted the words given here, the rest may have joined in by the repetition of certain words according to the probable custom of the synagogue, thus explaining "they lifted up their voice."

In studying the New Testament teaching concerning the content of songs, a problem of terminology arises. In our investigation we prefer to use the distinction "psalms" and "hymns" rather than "inspired" and "uninspired" song. Argument based upon the latter distinction sometimes fails to take due account of the fact that the New Testament deals with conditions in the early church which have not been continued and which cannot be our present norm. Any singing by the apostles could be considered "inspired"; and charismatic song, also "inspired," was then prevalent. But the apostles had no successors and the charismata have ceased. To adopt the distinction "inspired" and "uninspired" may thus introduce the fallacy of arguing from the temporary practice of the early church to our permanent duty. It is better to use a distinction which can be employed without this confusion in a statement of the permanent requirements of Scripture for the Christian church. "Psalms" may be used to specify the 150 Psalms of the Old Testament, "hymns" to specify other songs of praise which may or may not be confined to the very words of Scripture.

Moreover, argument based on the distinction between "inspired" and "uninspired" song may fail to take into consideration all the Biblical evidence. Thus to describe all Biblical songs as "inspired" is not a full description for the purpose of argument; it does not lead to the

conclusion that we should sing only "inspired" songs. For certain inspired songs in the New
Testament may also exemplify the very principles that sanction our use of at least some songs
which are not confined to the very words of Scripture, and which are thus "uninspired." Such
a principle is the principle to be discussed below, i.e., that our song should embrace the whole
extent of God's revelation in Scripture.

The New Testament clearly represents itself not only as a fulfillment of the Old
Testament but also as a fuller and more particular revelation. Thus the Old Testament Psalms,
inasmuch as they are a part of the Old Testament, are admittedly an incomplete revelation.
Their expression of praise as to God's glory in creation and providence, and his covenant mercy
and faithfulness to his people, for example, are enduringly suited for the use of God's people in
both dispensations. Nevertheless in certain other respects, as they concern the great events of
the gospel and the gospel teachings that are recorded in the New Testament, they represent only
a preliminary stage in the growth of Biblical revelation. On the other hand there is in the New
Testament an expansion of song in adjustment to the wider limits of revelation. New songs were
used in praise, songs fitted for the new dispensation, and not confined to the words of the Old
Testament. Such was the hymn of Mary, recorded in Luke 1:46-55, and known as "the
magnificat." Although based upon the song of Hannah in I Samuel 2:1-10 and in conformity
to Old Testament teaching, it is not merely a verbal repetition. The songs of Zacharias (Luke
1:67-69) and Simeon (Luke 2:29-32) introduce New Testament elements; Zacharias expressly
refers to John, while Simeon, having looked on the infant Jesus, says, "for mine eyes have seen
thy salvation." Thus at the first dawning of the new dispensation the content of song expanded
as revelation recommenced. There is a probability that in Acts 4:23-31 the early church
continued the expansion of song in a chanted prayer shortly after the Day of Pentecost, that is,
at another particularly significant point in the gradual change from the old economy to the new:
"for of a truth in this city against thy holy child Jesus, whom thou hast anointed, both Herod
and Pontius Pilate, with the Gentiles and the people of Israel were gathered together, for to do
whatsoever thy hand and thy counsel determined before to be done. And now, Lord, behold
their threatenings . . . ."   A further example of a song containing New Testament elements
may occur in I Timothy 3:16. "And confessedly great is the mystery of godliness:

> Who was manifested in flesh,
> Was justified in spirit,
> Was seen by angels,
> Was preached in nations,
> Was believed in [the] world,
> Was received up in glory."

This literal translation is given by Lenski and is quoted here to show that the Greek in this verse
actually does present the appearance of poetry. The Greek read aloud is striking in its
"rhythmical movement and the parallelism of the six balanced clauses" (Plummer). Lock, in *The*

International Critical Commentary, suggests that "this represents two stanzas of three lines each, which balance each other, contrasting the Incarnate Lord with the Ascended Lord." Olshausen quotes Mack to the effect that "the short unconnected sentences in which the words are similarly arranged, and the number of syllables almost equal, while the ideas are antithetically related, are so suitable to religious hymns that we find all these characteristics in a series of later hymns used by the Greek and Latin Church." Besides the four commentators already mentioned, Meyer, Ellicott, Scott, Falconer, de Wette, van Oosterzee, and A. T. Robertson consider this passage a hymn or a fragment of a hymn. Westcott and Hort, Nestle, and the American Standard Version print it as poetry. The short lines would be especially well adapted to chanted music. Lock cites three reasons why it is at least a quotation: the rhythmical form, the use of words not found elsewhere in Paul ("manifested," "believed," "received"), and the statement of ideas which go beyond the requirements of the text. Another reason is "confessedly," in the clause introductory to the six balanced lines, implying that these words were a customary and familiar embodiment of gospel truth. Thus while there cannot be dogmatic certainty there is at least strong assurance that the best of all suggested interpretations is that which regards this passage as a hymn of praise, customarily employed in early Christian worship. If so, it is again an example of song, the materials of which are derived explicitly from the New Testament revelation.

Conclusions

Although it does not appear that God has expressly commanded the New Testament Church to sing the Psalms, yet it may be asserted without any hesitation on the ground of good and necessary consequence, that the frequent use of the Psalms by the New Testament Church is highly pleasing to Him. The Psalms were divinely inspired for the very purpose of praise. They are theocentric in character, and worship is theocentric in its very essence. By the use of the Psalms in public worship the New Testament Church also gives expression to the essential unity of the body of Christ in both dispensations. To be sure, in scattered passages, the writers of the Psalms undertake vows in terms of the observance of the ceremonial law, which observance has now been abrogated. But, without pronouncing judgment on the propriety of singing such passages, we may assert that unquestionably the content of the Psalms, by and large, is highly appropriate for the worship of God's covenant people today. It is also fitting, and honorable to God's Word, that the Psalms be available for song in versions that are not only as faithful as possible to the inspired text, but also expressed in language of beauty and clarity. In such versions the Psalms "ought to be used frequntly in public worship," as our Directory for Worship provides.

Our worship of God is nothing else than our response to divine revelation. That is the very essence of Christian worship. How clear it is that New Testament worship must be in response not only to God's revelation in the Old Testament but also to His fuller revelation in the New Testament! The saints in the New Testament worshipped God thus--and in particular did they worship Him thus in song. They did not confine themselves in praise to a preliminary stage of revelation but adjusted the content of their songs to the full limit of completed revelation. We should do likewise.

Again it may be said that true worship is our response to divine revelation under the controlling influence of the Holy Spirit. Where the Spirit of the Lord is, there is liberty. Most assuredly, where the Spirit of the Lord is, there is no license. True liberty is always liberty under law. Therefore we may worship only in ways prescribed by the Word of God. But God's Word warrants the exercise of liberty in the content of prayer. Both by implication and by the approved examples of the New Testament saints it also warrants the exercise of liberty with regard to the content of song. The content of song, then, like the content of our prayer, need not be restricted to the very words of Scripture, although it must be assuredly Scriptural in teaching.

TOPICAL INDEX

396

402

SCRIPTURE INDEX

Printed in the United States
55790LVS00007B/22-39

9 780977 344222